The PEARL

The PEARL

A FAILED SLAVE ESCAPE ON THE POTOMAC

Josephine F. Pacheco

THE UNIVERSITY OF NORTH CAROLINA PRESS

Chapel Hill and London

Set in Monotype Bulmer, Engravers Bold, and Kunstler Medium
by Tseng Information Systems, Inc.

Manufactured in the United States of America

The paper in this book meets the guidelines for permanence and
durability of the Committee on Production Guidelines for Book
Longevity of the Council on Library Resources.

Library of Congress Cataloging-in-Publication Data

Pacheco, Josephine F.

The Pearl / a failed slave escape on the Potomac / by Josephine F.
Pacheco.

   p. cm.

Includes bibliographical references and index.

ISBN 0-8078-2918-8 (cloth : alk. paper)

1. Fugitive slaves—Washington Region—History—19th century.
2. Antislavery movements—Washington Region—History—19th
century. 3. Pearl (Schooner) I. Title.

E445.D6P33 2005

973.7'115—dc22   2004013917

09 08 07 06 05 5 4 3 2 1

In memory of

HALLIE BEAZLEY FENNELL

and

ROBERT HENRY FENNELL

CONTENTS

ILLUSTRATIONS

ACKNOWLEDGMENTS

I am grateful to the many people who provided assistance and encouragement when I was writing this book about runaway slaves.

Ralph Pacheco demonstrated skill and patience in keeping a computer functioning, editing chapters, and correcting errors. Anita Pacheco, Ginny Mark, and Peter Pacheco were editors of great skill and unbelievable patience. I am very grateful to them.

Mona Dearborn read the *Alexandria Gazette* and provided valuable items about slave trading. Ruth Kerns, Linda Ruggles, and Mary Martha Thomas read much of the manuscript and offered especially useful suggestions. Thomas Carr rendered valuable service as a researcher. Dr. Marion B. W. Holmes provided an important quotation from her grandmother's remembrance of Frederick Douglass. Mr. and Mrs. Paul Johnson gave me the opportunity to meet members of the Edmondson family, who spell their name with one *d*. Mrs. Lonise Robinson shared her knowledge of Asbury Church and generously provided me with a copy of the history of that historic institution. Muriel Parry, a true fount of wisdom, helped with information about matters nautical. Catherine M. Hanchett was very helpful in answering questions. I am grateful to the people in New Bedford, Massachusetts, who remain interested in Daniel Drayton.

William Creech and Robert Ellis provided valuable assistance in searching the records of the National Archives. Jeffrey Malick of the Clerk's Office of Montgomery County, Maryland, went to a great deal of trouble to provide important information about land holdings in the county. Several people did research on my behalf in several libraries and archives: Barbara Steadman, Susan Moutoux, Kevin Smead, Steve Saltzgiver, and Larry Hunter. I am grateful to them for their hard work. I also wish to thank Abby Gilbert for searching records in the federal government, especially the Treasury Department.

I owe a debt of gratitude to many librarians and archivists; through their skill and knowledge they open up treasures for researchers that otherwise would never be available. I am grateful to the Lovely Lane Methodist Museum in Baltimore, Maryland; the Oberlin College Archives in Oberlin, Ohio; the Massachusetts Historical Society in Boston; the Library of Virginia in Richmond; Houghton Library at Harvard University in Cambridge, Massachusetts; the Moorland-Spingarn Research Center at Howard University in Washington, D.C.; Alderman Library at the University of Virginia in Charlottesville; and the New Hampshire Historical Society in Concord.

The greatest pleasure in doing research is to work in the Library of Congress, certainly the finest research library in the world. It is not said often enough that the research librarians at the Library of Congress are the best of their profession. I am more deeply indebted to them than I could ever say. I have been helped immeasurably by librarians in the Periodicals Division, especially by Georgia Higley; the Prints and Photographs Division; the Manuscript Division; the Rare Book and Special Collections Division; the Geography and Map Division; the Law Library, especially by the late David Rabasca; and the Local History and Genealogy Reading Room, especially by Virginia Wood. My greatest debt is to the wonderful people in the Humanities and Social Sciences Division, who have fought the battle of the stacks, pointed me in the right direction to find material, saved me from many errors, preserved the old card catalog and the notations of generations of librarians, and provided a shelf for books currently in use (bless Bruce Martin!). Over the years they never made me feel that I was a burden, and I am blessed to have known them. I am grateful to every member of the division, but the book could not have been written without the assistance of Marilyn Parr and Thomas Mann, who pointed out errors, suggested sources, provided encouragement, and in every way served as models of what a research librarian should be. Gratitude is not an adequate response to the help they have given me, but that they have in abundance.

The PEARL

INTRODUCTION

In the spring of 1848 watermen Daniel Drayton and Edward Sayres undertook to lead one of the largest slave escape attempts in the United States. The two men planned to use a schooner, the *Pearl*, to carry seventy-six runaway slaves from Washington, D.C., to freedom in Pennsylvania and points north. They went down the Potomac River and expected to sail up the Chesapeake Bay, but stormy weather frustrated their project. When they anchored to wait for the storm to abate, their pursuers overtook them and returned Drayton, Sayres, and the fugitives to Washington. The two seamen ended up in jail and most of the runaways in the hands of slave dealers, awaiting sale to owners in the Deep South.

In the pages that follow, the events surrounding the thwarted flight will lead to an examination of slavery and the slave trade in the District of Columbia, the religious and political climate in the United States in the middle of the nineteenth century, and the sentiments and actions of antislavery and proslavery activists. The attempted escape is revealing about Americans both black and white, slave and free, powerful and powerless; it was significant in the story of American slavery and antislavery.

Slaves ran away wherever slavery existed. Owners knew that losing a slave because of flight was a hazard of slavery. According to a former bondman, "The white folks down south don't seem to sleep much, nights. They are watching for runaways." A fugitive from Maryland declared that "no power in this world will arrest the exodus of the slaves from the South." He called fleeing from bondage "the divinely ordered method for the effectual destruction of American slavery."[1]

Although they could not prevent flight, slave masters let their human property know that terrible punishment awaited them if they were caught or even if they returned of their own volition. Decisions about the punishment of runaways were left to their owners; the government did not interfere because punishment was a private matter between a master and his property. Governments stepped in if there were indications that someone had enticed a bondman or woman to flee, for that was a very serious offense, as this account will show.[2]

In the years following the American Revolution, northern states either ended slavery or made plans to do so; southern states did not. The men that met in Philadelphia in 1787 to write our Constitution accepted both the reality of human bondage and the accompanying reality of slave flight. Consequently, Article 4, Section 2, paragraph 3 of the United States Constitution provided that a person "held to service or labor in one state," on fleeing to another, "shall be delivered up on claim of the party to whom such service or labor may be due."

In 1793, not long after the new government began to function, Congress enacted a law giving legal effect to that constitutional provision. It dealt with both fugitives from justice and fugitives from enslavement. Sections 3 and 4 of the law provided that a slave owner, or "his agent or attorney," could seize the fugitive, take him before a judge of the federal court or "any magistrate of a county, city or town corporate, wherein such seizure or arrest shall be made," and provide testimony of ownership. If the evidence satisfied the judge or magistrate, he would issue a "certificate" that gave the owner the right to return the slave to the place from which he had fled. Anybody interfering with such a process was liable for the very large fine of $500. At least one historian has claimed that the law was not enforced, that nonslaveholders encouraged and protected runaways.[3] Whether or not the law was enforced, it did not and could not stop bondmen and bondwomen from seeking freedom.

Slaves ran away for a short time or for life. They ran *away* from something or somebody, or they ran *toward* something or somebody. They ran away because they feared they would be sold. They ran away from a beating or other punishment, and they ran toward family members from whom they were separated. They ran away to get some rest because they had been worked to exhaustion or to find food because they were always hungry. They ran away on the spur of the moment or after careful planning. They ran away because they could no longer endure the burden of bondage: they had to be free. As one bondwoman, Hannah Craft, put it, "The soul, the immortal soul must ever long and yearn for a thousand things inseperable [*sic*] to liberty."[4]

Sometimes when slaves fled, they knew where they were going; more often they had no idea of what lay beyond the limited span of their own experience. The willingness of slaves to set out into a strange and hostile world without guidance or a map or a friend is convincing proof of their desire for freedom, regardless of the potential obstacles.

Whatever the reason for flight, runaways usually stayed within the South, as extraordinary recent research makes clear.[5] In states where human bondage was legal, sending runaways back to their owners was not a serious problem. In the North, where there was growing opposition to slavery, the 1793 law proved inadequate. The Fugitive Slave Act of 1850, which is discussed in chapter 8, was an attempt to correct the flaws in the earlier statute.

Runaways living in southern towns or cities were not without resources, taking refuge with friends or relatives. By the 1830s many slaves, having been hired out by their owners, were allowed to find their own housing and live "on their own." Even though such housing might be no better than a hovel, it gave those hired-out slaves a considerable measure of independence and possible sanctuary for runaways. Over the years urban slaves had been able to keep the backyard of an owner's house as a more or less private preserve, off limits to masters and mistresses. A fugitive might take refuge there with a friend or relative, but only for a short time, since owners or policemen could invade the preserve whenever they wanted. In southern cities there were increasing numbers of *free* blacks who might take in a fugitive in a gesture of mercy; it was a very dangerous thing for them to do, perhaps leading to their own enslavement.[6] Country slaves reaching a city might take advantage of such precarious havens if they knew someone willing to help. Sometimes runaways successfully passed themselves off as free and found employment with home owners anxious for household help.[7]

When country or village slaves ran away, they took refuge in a nearby forest, cave, or swamp. For example, Isaac D. Williams, fleeing from

Fredericksburg, a Virginia town south of Washington, hid in the woods because he did not know the direction of freedom.[8] Slave narratives repeatedly reported a sense of loss and disorientation; and though runaways received assistance from fellow slaves,[9] they also feared betrayal. "Many of the slaves themselves were treacherous to each other, and while giving the Judas kiss would betray those they professed to love," wrote one bondman.[10]

In some areas of the South slaves established more or less permanent colonies of runaways, especially where there were inaccessible swamps and deep woods, such as "the Santee swamps, the Great Dismal Swamp, and the Appalachians." These communities, whether large or small, were well known to both blacks and whites, and they represented enough of a threat that southern legislatures took action against them.[11]

As long as there were large numbers of Native Americans in the South, slaves could flee to them for protection. Though some Native Americans enslaved fugitives, they were seen by blacks, rightly or wrongly, as offering a good alternative to white bondage. Slave owners, understandably wary of Native Americans as a threat to their labor force, demanded government assistance in retrieving runaways. Agreeing that the recovery of slaves was a valid reason for military action, the United States launched an attack against the Seminoles in Florida. A member of Congress claimed that the Seminole War cost $40 million to regain 500 fugitives, "making *each slave* cost the nation about *eighty thousand dollars*."[12] This demonstrated the lengths to which the government would go in its attempt to undermine slaves' search for freedom.

Because the perpetuation of slavery depended to a great extent on involvement by the entire citizenry and not merely government officials, any white person could stop any black person and demand proof of freedom and of permission to travel. Southern states established patrols, much hated by slaves, to catch runaways.[13] When the city of Washington established an auxiliary night patrol, its members looked for fugitives and searched out possible hiding places.

The runaways most likely to reach free soil lived in the Upper South — in Maryland, Virginia, and the District of Columbia. In spite of the best efforts of slave owners and the governments of those two states and the District, slaves slipped away, sometimes successfully reaching Pennsylvania or crossing the Ohio River to freedom. Members of

Congress from Maryland and Virginia were especially outraged at the loss of their constituents' property; as congressional debates would show, they feared that flight endangered the very institution of human bondage.

✳

Slavery in the District of Columbia depended on the unique nature of the nation's capital: it is the only geographic unit solely under the control of the Congress of the United States. According to Article 1, Section 8, paragraph 17, the Constitution gave Congress the right to "exercise exclusive legislation in all cases whatsoever" over the district that was to be created as "the seat of the Government of the United States." When the donation of adjacent portions of Virginia and Maryland led to the establishment of the District on the banks of the Potomac River, the states gave up all right to those areas. Within the ten-mile-square District, congressional control was absolute, as mandated by the Constitution.

But when Congress first moved to the District, members were too busy setting up the government of the United States to serve at the same time as a city government. So they provided that the laws of Maryland should continue to apply to the portion of the District ceded by Maryland, and Virginia laws to the portion ceded by that state.[14] Since slavery was legal in Maryland and Virginia, Congress's action ensured that the institution would continue in the new capital of the United States. Slavery was important to the economy of the towns of Alexandria in Virginia and Georgetown in Maryland, and the surrounding rural areas, all of which became the District of Columbia. The action of Congress in continuing the states' laws in the District gave legal force to human bondage.

The new government had confronted the issue of slavery even before the move to Washington, for the first Congress under the Constitution of 1787 received petitions against slavery and the slave trade. Moving the capital to slave territory brought protests, Benjamin Rush of Pennsylvania warning of a city on the banks of the Potomac "where Negro slaves will be your servants by day, mosquitoes your sentinels by night, and bilious fevers your companions every summer and fall, and pleurisies every spring." John Dickinson, also of Pennsylvania, questioned "the wisdom of locating the seat of government of a republic in that part of its territory in which slavery thrived."[15]

There was continuing tension over the institution of human bondage in the nation's capital. William Chambers, an Englishman visiting in Washington, lamented its presence because it meant that slavery existed in a federal enclave, "making federal authority responsible for the institution [slavery] which American writers never cease to represent as belonging exclusively to the states in their individual capacity." He went on, "If anyone up till this time imagined slavery was independent of national administration, his faith, we think, must have received a considerable shock." As Henry Wilson would write after the Civil War, "The fact that the District of Columbia was placed under the special jurisdiction of Congress . . . committed the nation to the existence and maintenance of slavery, giving it a prestige . . . it never could have gained as a State institution."[16]

Even before the government's actual removal to the District, slavery had become integral to the development of the city of Washington. By 1794 as many as forty-six slaves were working on the construction of public buildings, and that same year the commissioners responsible for the new capitol decided to "hire one hundred slaves, paying their owners sixty dollars a year in wages." Slave owners in the area were delighted to rent out their workers; it was better than using them for unprofitable farming.[17]

As early as 1794 a slave was sold in Washington,[18] foreshadowing the centrality of the slave trade in the economy of the nation's capital. No one had anticipated such a role for the District of Columbia; George Washington and many other Virginians had envisioned a commercially important city, but not with slaves as a major product. Nevertheless, by 1802 dealing in slaves had become sufficiently significant that there were complaints against the trade.

That the protests were ineffective is easy to demonstrate, for by 1834 the Alexandria firm of Franklin and Armfield was reported to have sold, during that year, 1,000 slaves. District slave dealer William Williams boasted in 1850 that he had made $30,000 in a few months. The development of a slave trading center was the result of several events coming together, though the termination of the foreign slave trade in 1808 was of primary significance. When the demand for workers could no longer be legally met with labor from abroad, the only recourse was to further develop the domestic slave-trading market.[19]

In the Constitutional Convention of 1787 disagreements over the foreign slave trade led to a compromise that was set forth in Article 1,

Section 9, paragraph 1. It provided that the foreign slave trade could not be ended for twenty years, and during that time any tax that was levied could not exceed $10 per head. In other words, Congress could not tax the foreign slave trade out of existence during the twenty years that slave owners were building up their stock. In spite of growing tension over slavery in the first half of the nineteenth century, Congress voted to end the foreign slave trade in 1807, the law to take effect on January 1, 1808.[20] Although the foreign trade probably continued illegally, the result of the 1807 law was an increase in the importance of the domestic slave trade; transporting slaves from one American location to another, whether by sea or by land, was domestic trade and therefore exempt from the 1807 law.

This commerce coincided with the expansion of agriculture in the region bordering the Mississippi River, which had been acquired in the Louisiana Purchase of 1803. The removal, several decades later, of Native Americans to land west of the Mississippi River increased the acreage available for farming. As agriculture requiring large amounts of manual labor—notably the production of cotton and sugar—spread throughout the Mississippi South, the demand for slaves was so great that it seemed limitless. At about the time this was happening, slave owners in Virginia and Maryland were increasingly aware that they had surplus bondmen and bondwomen, both because of natural population increase and a gradual change in farming from labor-intensive tobacco cultivation to the production of wheat, for which fewer workers were needed. Much of the farmland in those two states suffered from worn-out soil. Nothing seemed more appropriate than to establish a slave trade from the Upper South to the Lower South, transferring property from an area with a surplus to one with a shortage. It was good commercial practice, and it did not seem to bother the traders that the property consisted of human beings. In this profitable business, of increasing importance during the first half of the nineteenth century, Washington and Alexandria played a central role.

At the same time that economic factors were increasing the attractiveness of a domestic slave trade, geography was concentrating much of it in Washington, Alexandria, and Baltimore. The District, which included Alexandria until 1846 (when it was part of the retrocession to Virginia), was easily accessible to those wanting to sell or to buy slaves, and its location on the Potomac River facilitated their shipment south. In the early part of the century, the trade was usually with South

"*United States Slave Trade. 1830.*" *(Courtesy of the Library of Congress)*

Carolina or Georgia (the common name for a slave dealer's quarters was "Georgia Pen"), but by the 1840s New Orleans became the most important center in the Lower South for buying and selling. Slaves transported by water left Washington or Alexandria, sailed down the Potomac River, into the Chesapeake Bay, and then south on the Atlantic Ocean. After the railroad reached Washington, it was easy to transfer slaves to Baltimore, and from there slave ships sailed straight down the bay.

As an alternative to shipment by water, dealers organized slaves into coffles (from the Arabic word for "caravans") that traveled overland to a more southerly destination, the slaves walking, the traders riding. By the 1840s coffles frequently went southwest to Memphis and Natchez, where the slaves were either sold or shipped down the Mississippi to New Orleans. The advantage of an overland route was that a slaver could buy and sell along the way; the disadvantage was that the property arrived in worse shape than when shipped by water. Whatever the means of transportation, slavery and the slave trade became essential aspects of the District's economy.

Or so it increasingly appeared to Washingtonians. Early in the century there were two antislavery societies in the District, the Washington Anti-Slavery Society and the Benevolent Society of Alexandria. Residents signed petitions asking Congress to end slavery in the nation's capital, and Alexandrians rescued blacks from the hands of slave dealers.[21] By the end of the 1830s, however, a change had occurred, for a memorial to the Senate and the House of Representatives, signed by 220 men living in the District, asked that slavery be continued; ending it would "have an injurious influence on the peace and tranquillity of the community."[22] Some of the signers of the petition had slaves that would flee on the *Pearl.* Prejudice against antislavery activities became oppressive in towns as southern in sentiment as Washington, Georgetown, and Alexandria;[23] District residents appeared to accept the permanent existence of slavery.

The trend was in the opposite direction in parts of the North and West (today the Middle West), where an awakening to the horrors of slavery resulted in agitation for its termination in the District. Slavery, it is important to remember, was a state institution, protected by state laws and existing only where states established and guarded the complicated web of relationships at the heart of the reality of human bondage. Defenders of slavery insisted on the centrality of state control, and for the most part opponents of slavery reluctantly agreed. In 1833 the Declaration of the Anti-Slavery Convention recognized that Congress had no right to interfere with slavery in the states, but it maintained "that Congress has a right, and is solemnly bound, to suppress the domestic slave trade between the several States, and to abolish slavery in those portions of our territory which the Constitution has placed under its exclusive jurisdiction."[24]

Even so vehement an opponent of slavery as Congressman Joshua Giddings of Ohio admitted that, as much as he would have liked to, he could not propose action against human bondage in the states where it already existed. But the District of Columbia was different. The states had no authority over the federal enclave, and when Virginia and Maryland gave the land to create the District, Congress assumed control. Therefore, when people in the North and West began to agitate for an end to the institution, they agreed to concentrate on that ten-mile-square district.

In the 1830s thousands of petitions bearing hundreds of thousands of signatures poured into Congress, urging that it do what it had the power to do: end slavery and the slave trade in the nation's capital. A visitor to Washington saw huge piles of the petitions stacked in the corridors of the Capitol. "The late Dr. C. H. Van Tyne used to tell his classes at the University of Michigan how, when he was making his *Guide to the Archives* [published in 1904], he found a caretaker in the Capitol keeping his stove hot with bundles of antislavery petitions.

There were so many of them, the caretaker said, that those he used would never be missed."[25] The campaign assuredly gave emancipationists a sense of purpose, for they were striking at a slavery stronghold.

Politicians were understandably wary of fervor that might upset the status quo, the system that had made possible their election and reelection. Even northern congressmen who did not approve of slavery were unhappy with the flood of petitions but presented them to Congress because the right of petition was enshrined in the Bill of Rights. Caleb Cushing of Massachusetts put on record antislavery petitions from his constituents; and though he disagreed with the sentiments expressed, he defended with some eloquence a citizen's right to appeal to Congress.[26] As southern congressmen, day after day, heard requests that Congress end slavery and the slave trade in the District, they panicked. Such public discussion of their peculiar institution was unbearable, and eventually they were able to place a gag on all such petitions by requiring that they be automatically tabled without being read.

From the viewpoint of antislavery activists, this action proved that southerners, caring only about protecting the institution of human bondage, were willing to trample on the Constitution and the Bill of Rights. The fight to end the gag in the House of Representatives made a hero of John Quincy Adams, who, after serving as president of the United States, was elected to the House. There he became an eloquent defender of free speech and the right of petition. From 1836 to 1844 Adams sought to terminate the gag on antislavery petitions, and he was ultimately successful; but in the process he endured verbal attacks, an attempt to censure him in the House, and death threats from various parts of the country. He was warned that he would be lynched if he continued "to vindicate abolition" and that "your damned guts will be cut out in the dark." Some claimed that Adams wanted to see slavery maintained in the District because of its value for antislavery agitation.[27]

Because of the more or less general agreement that slavery was a state institution and therefore untouchable under the federal system of the United States, its existence in the District of Columbia became the center of an increasingly serious conflict and a symbol for those attacking and those defending slavery. One side of the argument held that since Congress had the power to end slavery there, it must do so; the other side maintained that Congress had the duty to protect the property of Americans. Northerners could point to the Constitution's grant of congressional control and insist that it was justification for action. Some northern members of Congress, even when deploring the petitions, insisted that Congress had unlimited authority over the District. Daniel Webster, speaking in the Senate in 1838, said that the words of the Constitution were "clear and plain." There was "no limitation, condition, or qualification whatever" in the cession by Virginia and Maryland to create the District. Indeed, said the senator from Massachusetts, the government would not have accepted the cession had it contained qualifications.[28]

Southern members of Congress had difficulty bypassing the Constitution, but they hoped that an 1836 committee, chaired by Henry Pinckney of South Carolina, would find a legal basis for the permanent protection of District slavery. It did not happen. In spite of an unusually lengthy report, the committee could only conclude that "Congress *ought not to interfere*, in any way, with slavery in the District of Columbia" because "it would be a violation of the public faith, unwise, impolitic, and dangerous to the Union."[29] Even a committee headed by a South Carolinian could not find a *legal* basis for denying congressional control over slavery in the nation's capital.

The report infuriated South Carolinians, and especially Senator John C. Calhoun; an "Address to the Electors of the Charleston District" distorted the committee findings by claiming that Pinckney had agreed that "Congress has authority to abolish slavery in the District of Columbia." Consequently, Pinckney lost the next election and did not return to the House. He had been correct in failing to find in the Constitution a legal basis for the protection of slavery in the District, but politically it was disastrous. A South Carolina governor went so far as to demand that northern state legislatures "make antislavery agitation a capital offense."[30]

Southerners fell back on the argument that Virginia and Maryland would never have ceded portions of their states had they thought the institution would be in peril. A Maryland history claimed that because slavery in that state predated the establishment of the District of Columbia, it was protected from action by Congress. The Virginia legislature took the threat to District slavery sufficiently seriously that in 1836 it proposed an amendment to the United States Constitution: "The powers of Congress shall not be so construed as to authorize the passage of any law for the emancipation of slaves in the District of

Columbia, without the consent of the individual proprietors thereof, unless by the sanction of the Legislatures of Virginia and Maryland, and under such conditions as they shall by law prescribe."[31] Congress, however, took no action.

A Philadelphia pamphleteer claimed that the South would never give up slavery in the District. "They [southerners] look upon this district in the light of a frontier post adjoining an enemy's territory, the yielding of which would open an avenue for their admission into the whole country." Furthermore, "the continual agitation of the question must be a source of exceeding irritation and apprehension." Indeed, Senator Calhoun referred to the District as the "'outworks' of the South to the enemy";[32] to yield that ten-mile square would be the beginning of the end of slavery.

The antislavery movement that began in the 1830s arose from the realization that slavery in the southern states was not going to die out naturally. Early in the nineteenth century, all states north of Delaware had provided for either immediate or gradual emancipation. It was hoped that southern states would do likewise, but it did not happen. Instead, the South claimed to find slavery more and more essential, and by the 1830s opponents of slavery realized that overt action was necessary. A religious revival known as the Second Great Awakening reinforced this conviction by emphasizing that human bondage was a sin and not merely a source of labor.

Antislavery enthusiasts differed on both strategy and tactics. Some thought the Constitution was proslavery; others saw the Constitution as a document that could be used to end slavery. Some believed that abolitionists should refuse to vote or have any connection with political parties because they were hopelessly corrupt. Others trusted that some politicians would support antislavery positions, and from time to time they worked with like-minded Whigs and Democrats. A variation on this political perception was the belief in the efficacy of an antislavery political party, which led to the formation of the Liberty Party, the Free Soil Party, and finally the Republican Party. Those deploring political involvement found it impossible to cooperate with those trying to form an antislavery party.

Southerners and their northern allies called all opponents of slavery "abolitionists," a term that many antislavery enthusiasts rejected, believing that it applied only to followers of William Lloyd Garrison. Bostonian Samuel Gridley Howe, for example, denied that he was an abolitionist, even though he worked very hard to end slavery.[33] Garrison's adherents were in essence "immediatists," urging opponents of slavery to withdraw from the political process, even though it meant leaving an open field to proslavery forces. In response to such a charge, one Garrisonian claimed that "honesty & truth are more important than even freeing slaves."[34]

Others could be called "gradualists," a term that applied to a wide range of activists, from politicians and lawyers such as Salmon P. Chase of Ohio to businessmen such as Lewis Tappan of New York. "Emancipationist" was a broad term that could be applied to all Americans willing to speak out in opposition to slavery, and it is probably true that even among antislavery enthusiasts the terms were used interchangeably.[35]

Slave owners, not comprehending the extent of disunion among their opponents, lumped them all together, perceiving them as a force operating in unison to destroy their livelihood and their way of life. In fact, those wanting to end slavery may well have been less united than southerners. They were a quarrelsome lot: If they could not agree on what to call themselves, there was little chance they could agree on how to end the curse of slavery.

Antislavery supporters disagreed not only over how best to end slavery but also on major issues, such as the rights of women within the movement. But they were never content to agree to disagree. As historian Joan Hedrick has written: "Full of visionaries, anarchists, antisabbatarians, millennialists, malcontents, and free-lovers, the antislavery movement reserved its most venomous attacks for fellow reformers whose ideological purity was suspect."[36] If opponents of human bondage were motivated by Christian beliefs, they showed little Christian charity toward men and women holding different views of how to bring about an end to the great sin of slavery.

Antislavery activists were clearly carrying on the Protestant tradition of churches splitting and splitting again, arguing over points of doctrine that an outsider might have deemed insignificant. The insistence on doctrinal purity was a great weakness of the antislavery movement, for it guaranteed that the people involved did not speak with one voice or act in unity. Hence the argument over who were true abolitionists. This factionalism had an impact on the role that the *Pearl* would play. For example, Gamaliel Bailey (see chapter 3) would not encourage slaves to flee, but Wendell Phillips, a leader of the Garrison wing of antislavery, "urged slaves to run away or to rebel" and asserted that "no slave proves his manhood, except those who rise and at least try to cut their masters' throat."[37] Even though much of what Phillips said or wrote can be discounted as rhetoric, it is understandable that he and his friends, having such a mind-set, despised Bailey and his supporters for living in Washington and hoping for a nonviolent end to slavery.

The *Pearl* brought these disagreements to the fore. What was the correct way to approach Drayton and Sayres? Who would pay their legal fees? Should any available funds be used to ransom the fugitives? Some opponents of slavery believed it wrong to buy the freedom of slaves,[38] for any money paid to slave owners or dealers would be used to buy more stock. Factionalism, surfacing in the events surrounding the *Pearl*, made it impossible to develop a unified strategy, not only with regard to Drayton, Sayres, and the fugitives, but also concerning the larger issue of ending slavery and the slave trade in the District of Columbia. Unity, however, might have made no difference in the long run because of the intransigence of the South.

SLAVERY *in the* NATION'S CAPITAL

Many Americans envision slavery as inseparable from plantations, not aware that the institution was also important in cities in the South, from Baltimore and Washington down to Mobile and New Orleans. According to David Goldfield, "Slavery and slave holding were as characteristic of the city as [they were] of the countryside, and perhaps even more so." Urban slavery was different from its rural counterpart, just as city life for nonslaves was different; people—black, white, slave, and free—adapted to their environment. "Slavery, far from being an albatross to urban progress, grew more valuable to city dwellers as secession approached."[1]

This chapter provides an examination of human bondage in the nation's capital, how slaves worked and lived and how they interacted with whites and other blacks, both slave and free. While "the web of slave interrelationships" was significant on a large plantation,[2] the same was true in an urban setting. The *Pearl* demonstrated that bondmen and bondwomen in the District used whatever devices were available to them to build a sense of community.

A very large number of slaves had known of the planned escape—not only the seventy-six that boarded the *Pearl* but also their families and friends. Yet no hint of the plan reached the ears of their owners. What their masters and mistresses described as cunning, slaves saw as the psychological mechanism needed to develop and maintain autonomy within the harsh regime of bondage. The story of American slavery is, to a very great extent, the ongoing conflict between the owners who wanted to erase initiative and a sense of self within their human property and the owned who used every possible means to protect and enlarge those same characteristics. Slavery, in spite of numerous instances to the contrary, was built on intimidation, exploitation, and violence. The story of the *Pearl* is extraordinary because it demonstrates concretely not only the extremity and complexity of any concerted effort to oppose slavery but also the swiftness and strength of the forces committed to maintaining it.

Slaves in the nation's capital had access to information about public events that was not available to those living anywhere else in the South. They knew that Congress debated slavery (at least when a gag was not in effect), that there were members of both Houses opposed to the institution, and that many visitors to the city loathed human bondage. Although bondmen and bondwomen did not need an invitation to run away, they knew that there would be a greater chance of success if they could count on sympathy and assistance. When they fled on their own, acting as individuals without much knowledge, they felt a great sense of loss and bewilderment, as James Pennington did when he ran away from his Maryland owner.[3] Washington slaves seem to have known whom to approach for help; they had some idea of the geographic distance to freedom; and they had a realistic view of the perils awaiting a fugitive.

Slaves thirsted for information, which they exchanged at every opportunity, and they were well aware of the importance of Congress's actions. During the congressional debates on the admission of Missouri to the Union as a slave or free state (1819–20), the galleries were "crowded with colored persons, almost to the exclusion of whites." Writing from Washington, a spectator said that though they understood "much less than half" of the debates, they knew it was "a question of servitude or freedom" and thought that they themselves would be affected. According to the observer, "When the slaves of the Southerners, now here [in Washington], return home with mutilated and exaggerated accounts of what they have heard, I fear that many deluded creatures will fall sacrifice to their misapprehension of the question."[4] Not only slaves residing permanently in Washington but also slaves brought to the capital as servants to members of Congress learned to listen for news of "servitude or freedom."

Washington slaves never lacked for occasions to share news; indeed, mobility was the characteristic of urban slavery that first attracted the attention of visitors. Whereas plantation owners might emphasize keeping workers close to home, slavery in a city was most viable, from an economic standpoint, when people in bondage could move freely, running errands, delivering goods, accompanying children to school, shopping for food and household supplies. Close supervision in all such activities was impossible, and slaves traveled around Washington with amazing ease.

Some errands provided slaves with natural gathering places. In the 1830s water in Washington was only available from wells, one on each square. Every morning slaves waited their turn to fill buckets for their households; a woman could carry three pails, one in each hand and one on her head.[5] Imagine the beauty of her posture! And the news and gossip she could exchange while she waited!

Male and female slaves filled the markets. An account of Richmond in 1853 could just as well apply to Washington: "Now go down to the markets, . . . and you will hear the voices of hundreds, wrangling, chaffering, buying and selling, till you would imagine yourself in Babel, but for the reason that the tongues are almost all of one kind, those of colored people."[6] They engaged in both buying and selling; indeed, one visitor observed that "negroes are the chief sellers." While Josiah Henson, who claimed to be the model for Uncle Tom in *Uncle Tom's Cabin*, lived in Montgomery County, Maryland, adjacent to the District, he regularly sold farm produce in the markets of Washington. It was there that he met a white man who talked freely about the evils of slavery and about his refusal, as a Christian, to own or even to hire a slave.[7] Frederick Law Olmsted, who viewed Washington with a jaundiced eye, felt contempt for both animals and people when he went to the market. He found "the most miserable, dwarfish, ugly, lean kine that I ever saw." The horses were as bad as the cattle, and, he added, "the human stock (negroes) is, if possible, worse than either."[8]

Many owners allowed their slaves to plant foodstuffs on their own, and early in its history the District held a market on Sundays. It was the only time slaves could bring their produce to be sold. The practice was discontinued both because it seemed to violate the holiness of the Sabbath and because of claims of troublemakers in the market.

Slave owners in the Virginia counties adjacent to Washington claimed that slaves "would steal various commodities from their owners and sell them to free Negroes or whites from the District who were passing through as itinerant peddlers."[9] Men and women in bondage made a place for themselves, either honestly or dishonestly, in the commerce of the Washington area.

Antebellum Washington hotel owners always employed slaves; a British traveler in the 1830s found seventy or eighty slaves working in Gadsby's Hotel. In addition to being the main labor force in hotels, slaves were sent by hotel owners to attract to their establishments visitors alighting from coaches, boats, or the train (after the railroad arrived in the city). Travelers always commented on the omnipresence and competence of slave coachmen and hack drivers. They were so knowledgeable that there was no need to give them directions, for they knew everybody and where everybody lived.[10]

Although African Americans were frequently members of the crews of coastal vessels, they were not expected to captain them. Before Daniel Drayton sailed from Washington with his shipload of runaways, he checked on other vessels anchored near the *Pearl*, hoping to avoid trouble. Anchored close by was a "small vessel" in which "her crew were all black." On speaking to the skipper, who apparently was African American, Drayton received assurance that he had nothing to fear, that the crew would be away from the waterfront and that he, the captain, "should go below and to sleep, so as neither to hear nor to see anything."[11]

Slaves were very valuable property. According to an advertisement in the *Sun* of Baltimore, the reward for the return of an apprentice was six and a half cents; for a runaway slave, $200. A Richmond dealer listed among his expenses "25" for "Arresting runaway." Nevertheless, as agriculture in the Upper South declined or changed its character, demand for farm labor decreased. Owners found it increasingly difficult to make a profit employing their slaves on farms and plantations. They had three choices: (1) they could migrate to the newly opened territory along the Mississippi River or in Texas, carrying their slaves with them; (2) they could sell off their surplus property to willing dealers and make trading in slaves a profitable business; or (3) they could rent their unneeded slaves in places such as the District. Some southerners followed the first alternative; one traveler encountered whole families, children, in-laws, and many slaves, on the move from the Old South to the New South. Historian James Oakes has shown the importance of the westward and southern movement of slave owners who hoped for a fresh start in a new region. Family migration probably accounted for about 30 percent of slaves traveling from the Upper to the Lower South. The third alternative, slave rental, appealed to Virginians and Marylanders who did not want to leave the area but needed additional income.[12]

The practice of hiring out unneeded slaves demonstrated the flexibility of the institution: it survived in areas where it should have died out because it was otherwise unprofitable. An owner, while retaining title to a slave, rented out the bondman or bondwoman and received payment for the enslaved person's labor. By deriving a profit from property they could not directly use, owners managed to perpetuate the institution of human bondage.

In the neighboring Virginia county of Fairfax, owners unable to find gainful employment at home for increasing numbers of the enslaved could sell them or, while retaining title, rent them out for a profit. Virginians did both, and though the District was the closest and most convenient place for renting, historians of the county have found evidence of the hiring out of Fairfax slaves as far south as Mississippi.[13]

Hiring out took two forms. The master could negotiate a contract whereby a worker would be leased for a designated period in return for a set amount of money and other terms such as housing and food. For the fifteen years before the Civil War the average annual hire for an unskilled male slave was $85 to $175. Alternatively, the slave himself carried on negotiations with an employer and arranged the amount he paid his owner. In either case the slave was outside the direct control of his master, and in many instances he could find his own housing, often with free blacks and working-class whites. Historian Ira Berlin sees hiring out as so popular that by 1850 "few slaves in the Upper South escaped being hired at one time or another, and some lived apart from their owners for most of their lives." According to another estimate, by the late 1840s one out of six slave households was "living out," often without any white supervision.[14] By providing profit through rental, these semifree bondmen made it possible for their owners to continue to hold property they might otherwise have lost; thus they helped the institution of slavery to survive. But their ability to live on their own made a mockery of claims that presumably childlike slaves required close direction in order to survive. The frequent use of middlemen and the introduction of contracts significantly altered master-slave relationships.

For the most part, hired slaves ignored the District's strict regulations about where they could live; in other words, they were not enforced. The same was true in Richmond, 100 miles to the south, where, in spite of the mayor's best efforts, he was unable to separate free blacks from slaves and to limit the mobility of hired slaves.[15]

Frederick Law Olmsted thought that most of the slaves in the District were brought into the city to work for people who had rented them. E. S. Abdy, an Englishman, said that his waiter at Gadsby's in Washington was the property of someone living in Alexandria; the same was true for many of the hotel staff. Gadsby rented out his own slaves when business was slow in his hotel; at least one Washingtonian found that they made excellent house servants. Tavern keepers also hired slaves, paying a monthly fee to the owners and providing food for the workers but not clothing; that was the responsibility of the slaves. No wonder they were shabbily dressed.

Rented slaves provided much of the labor during the construction of a canal on the Potomac River. One contractor reported hiring "a gang of sixty or seventy slaves, paying for each at the rate of seventy-five dollars a year." He claimed that he fed them well, never flogged them, and in return received good work; the men, it seems, were reluctant to return to their owners. The contractor believed that most slaves were "half-starved" and that if they stole, it was because they were always hungry.[16]

Many of those aboard the *Pearl* had been rented out. All of the children of Daniel Bell were sent out to work as soon as they were old enough and provided their owner, Mrs. Armstead, with almost her only income. Six members of the Edmondson family who fled aboard the *Pearl* were hired in the city, though born and raised in Maryland. After the capture of the *Pearl*, there was a delay in handing over some of the fugitives to their owners because they did not live near the jail.

The Washington Navy Yard was a favorite place to rent out slaves, especially skilled artisans. Visitors such as Emmeline Stuart Wortley reported seeing "coloured people acting as artisans" and "making chains, anchors, &c., for the United States navy." Charles Ball, hired out to the Navy Yard, was made ship's cook on a frigate, where he enjoyed plenty of food and money and wore clothes given him by the ship's officers. On Sunday afternoons he was free to wander through the city, where he saw other slaves walking around.[17] Historian Herbert Aptheker claimed that southerners worried about the reliability of the army and the navy in case of servile revolt. That is probably why Abel P. Upshur, secretary of the navy, said in 1842 that there were no slaves in the navy; he was mistaken.[18]

Slaves performed such menial tasks as cleaning the Capitol, but they also worked on public projects. Opponents of slavery lamented that "a great portion of the labor on the different public works in this city is performed by slaves" whom the owners had rented out.[19]

Bondmen laboring in hotels had access to visitors from the North and from Europe, where they learned what was going on in the rest of the country and discovered that the world was full of people who deplored slavery, even if they could not take positive steps to end it. Visitors, especially foreign visitors, enjoyed engaging in conversation with hotel workers, and they commented on the ease and clarity with which the supposedly benighted slaves discussed their lives and problems.

Adam Hodgson, an Englishman, expressed surprise, in his 1823 book, at "the ease, cheerfulness, and intelligence of the *domestic* slaves." (He had not conversed with plantation workers.) "Their manners, and their mode of expressing themselves, have generally been decidedly superior to those of many of the lower classes in England." Hodgson reported on a lengthy conversation with the man who made the fire in his hotel room. The firemaker, delighted to converse, "leaned his arm on the chimney-piece with considerable ease," and discussed with insight the pluses and minuses of a free black's life. The slave, who claimed that he would be free in three months, liked the idea of freedom but realistically wondered if he would be better off, since he probably would continue in the same occupation. It was true that he would be able to change masters "if he had a bad one," but when free he "must starve if he was idle."[20] So astute a man had carefully examined the institution of slavery and approached freedom well aware of its risks. He also had to have seen that the Englishman did not approve of human bondage, opening up for the bondman a perception of a wider world.

"A Black Servant." From Eyre Crowe's With Thackeray in America (1893). The British writer William Makepeace Thackeray went on lecture tours in the United States during the early 1850s. (Courtesy of the Library of Congress)

Frederick Law Olmsted, detesting his hotel, his room, and the service, was particularly indignant over the lack of a fire on a December day. Three Irish lads disappeared when he asked them for help; the fire finally got started when an elderly black man came to his rescue, not willingly, however, for he complained all the time he was working that he was too old to be exploited. Olmsted observed that the slave firemaker was "more indifferent to forms of subserviency than the Irish lads" who refused to make his fire.[21] Because their occupations often kept them in the streets and in the public eye, blacks drew the attention of newcomers, who found them "exceedingly conspicuous" and had the impression that they filled the streets. One man found District houses "smart and tasteful" and in the city itself "nothing incongruous" except "the number of negroes of both sexes, principally slaves." Another was amazed at the "swarms of negroes in the streets," though he thought many of them were free. In reality the District did not have an especially large black population, either slave or free. In 1840 there were 4,694 slaves and 8,461 free blacks in a total population of 43,712.

This included Georgetown and Alexandria; the latter was a part of the land returned to Virginia's jurisdiction in 1846.[22] Visitors would not have been able to discern the difference between enslaved and free men and women, for they were, for the most part, shabbily dressed.

Travelers, in spite of their obvious fascination with slaves, showed an amazing lack of insight into their behavior. They could not believe that enslaved people could laugh and sing—and, above all, make a joke at the expense of the traveler. Indeed, the visitors' obtuseness gives us insight into how men and women coped with their enslavement. Slaves, unloading sacks of flour from a boat that had come from Alexandria to Washington, tossed the bags from one to another, in what an observer called a spirit of "rollicking fun," doing anything "to raise a laugh."[23] A traveler staying in Gadsby's Hotel encountered "the inevitable devil-may-care, lazy, laughing carelessness of the darkies," who provided "assiduous considerations and attentions," standing behind his chair as he ate: "You are as helpless under their tyranny as a two-year-old baby." Never realizing that they were making fun of him, the traveler called them "idle laughing creatures" who did not act like slaves. They were "gleesome as kittens, especially when off to a fight or a fire."[24]

Visitors had difficulty comprehending the humor of slaves. An Englishman reported walking umbrella-less down Pennsylvania Avenue in "a heavy shower of rain" and encountering "two tall youths of colour, in very ragged attire, walking rather importantly arm in arm along, under an umbrella almost as ragged as themselves." As the Englishman passed, they raised their "all but brimless hats" to him and making sure he could hear them, engaged in the following exchange: "I say, Sam; I wonder how it is that all gennlemen [sic] does not use umbrellas," to which his friend replied, "I doesn't know, Tom, but s'pose they can't all afford it." And yet in the very next paragraph the traveler could declare that American blacks, though witty and amusing, were "extremely simple-minded."

The same visitor, after witnessing an exciting incident in which a slave stopped a pair of runaway horses, wrote: "However simple the negroes may be in a variety of ways, they are at least not deficient in courage; for the stopping of a pair of terrified runaway horses is a feat that none but the most courageous would attempt."[25] How could he continue to emphasize the simplicity of slaves after experiencing the sharp humor of the pair in the rain, whose irony was directed no less at themselves than at the Englishman? And surely the man who stopped the runaways knew very well the danger he was in: this was not the decision of a simple man.

Another visitor saw more deeply into the attitudes of Washington blacks: "Notwithstanding the weight with which oppression bears upon them, and the cruelties to which they are subjected, the negroes in America exhibit a light-heartedness which is surprising." He realized, however, what many did not, that their "playfulness of disposition" was a mask to fool the white world.[26]

Writing from Washington in 1835, Ethan Andrews commented on the difficulty of discovering the truth about slaves' lives, for they did not trust any white man. He reported many conversations in which slaves would insist that they had good masters, plenty of food, and easy work. A slave would deny wanting to leave his master and even insist that he did not want to be free: "O no, massa, me no want to be free, have good massa, take care of me when I sick, never 'buse nigger; no, me no want to be free." The slave knew very well the danger of showing discontent. Nevertheless, when Andrews visited the Alexandria slave trading establishment of Franklin and Armfield and was told of the happiness of the inmates, one young man, "of an interesting and intelligent countenance," shook his head whenever the "keeper" looked away. He "seemed desirous of having me understand, that he did not feel any such happiness as was described, and that he dissented from the representation made of his condition." Although Andrews was not able to talk to him, the young slave had found a means of communication so that the visitor understood the reality of enslavement.[27] When visitors to the District observed and commented on the self-confidence of the slaves, their skill in conversation, and their clear-sighted view of their condition, they acknowledged the slaves' sense of their own worth.

Such was the public face of slavery in the District; much less is known about slaves as private persons. In city life they moved about with great freedom during the daylight hours, but owners tried to keep them close to home after dark. Slaves and free blacks were subject to an evening curfew. When the bell of the Perseverance Fire Company, at Eighth Street and Pennsylvania Avenue, was rung at ten o'clock, all blacks, both slave and free, had to be off the streets of Washington. People assisting slaves to flee had to be careful to have the runaways safely hidden before the ten o'clock bell rang.[28]

Urban slaves lived in owners' attics or in backyards, where they could be supervised and where they would be on call when needed. In testimony during Daniel Drayton's trial, W. H. Upperman, owner of three of the fugitives, said that he had heard his "woman" come downstairs and go out to the backyard. Slaves sought to keep the backyards private and even dared to hide runaways there, hoping that masters would not intrude. When the body servants of two members of Congress, Robert Toombs and Alexander Stephens, decided to flee, they hid out in the backyard of Walter Jones, a leading citizen of the District, who would certainly not have wanted to be the protector of runaways. Slaves belonging to Congressman William F. Colcock of South Carolina ran away and found a hiding place with Washington bondmen. On their recapture after two or three months, Colcock sent them off to safety (from his point of view) in South Carolina, aware that he had to protect his property from contact with Washington slaves.[29]

Housing for slaves "living out," as for most free blacks, was wretched, though no worse than for those dwelling near their employers. Hotel guests were unnerved to discover that workers had no place to sleep; they simply lay down on the floor of a corridor, without blanket or mattress, wearing the same clothes day after day, having no laundry or bathing facilities. Just before the Civil War, Charles Lyell, the great geologist, reported that he found Washington hotels somewhat cleaner than on an earlier visit; the hallways were now unencumbered with sleeping slaves.[30]

The majority of District slaves were domestic workers—cooks, laundry women, housekeepers—and thus males were not as much in demand; by 1860 two-thirds of the slaves in Washington were female. District slavery was "synonymous with the employment of black female domestics."[31] The absence of males reinforced the legal view that slavery descended through the mother; as a slave child grew up, the mother was the parent more likely to be present. Even when a husband was in the city, he was not regarded as having authority over his offspring. Across the Potomac River in Virginia, female slaves had to depend on themselves or their owners, for "husbands never provided the sole or most significant means of financial support for their wives and children." It was a female who went from door to door in the District "with a subscription to 'buy her freedom'" or that of her child.[32]

African Americans in the District longed for educational opportunities. As early as 1829 members of the American Colonization Society formed an African Education Society of the United States in Washington, with the express purpose of educating slaves "placed at the society's disposal by their masters on the condition of their emigrating to Africa." They drew up elaborate plans that came to nothing; the African Education Society did not materialize. Charles T. Torrey reported in 1842 that there were eight schools with "colored" instructors and about 500 children enrolled; by 1855 that number had increased to 800. Since slave children were set to work at an early age, the 500 must have been free. In 1849 the "colored population of the District" formed an educational union that included, according to the *Sun* of Baltimore, eight schools, 600 scholars, and seventy teachers.[33]

A representative of the Anglican Church's Society for the Propagation of the Gospel in Foreign Parts attended a Sunday school in the District where 320 black and "coloured" children received oral instruction in the Bible, in reading and in spelling. He found the children anxious to learn, attentive, and making an "intelligent appearance," seeming brighter than "juvenile rustics in Wiltshire," back home in England. It is not clear whether the young students were slave or free. In 1848 a Scottish clergyman visited an Episcopal school in Alexandria, taught by a young Englishman attending "the Episcopal College in the neighbourhood" (the Virginia Seminary), who lamented that the church vestry had forbidden him to teach the black children of the town how to read.[34]

District blacks found companionship and emotional release in their religious experiences. The Washington directory for 1846 listed four "colored" churches: two Methodist, one Presbyterian, and one Baptist.[35] Visitors could not agree on the denominations to which blacks belonged, one claiming they were either Methodists or Baptists, another that they were Baptists or Roman Catholics. A visitor, while attending an Episcopal church, saw "richly dressed" women whom he called Creoles; their elegant clothing was rare enough to warrant comment. Their "bronze but beautifully regular countenances, formed a strong contrast to the pink complexions of their fair, white sisters."[36] Observers claimed that among District blacks there were 500 Roman Catholics and a few Episcopalians, but members of some of those churches had to endure segregated seating—in the case of Catholics, in "side galleries."

A Protestant clergyman, after lamenting a segregated Presbyterian church in Baltimore, was chagrined to observe that the Roman Catholic cathedral was the only church in the city where "black and coloured people . . . intermingled with the whites."[37]

Blacks, both slave and free, found diverse opportunities for worship. They attended white churches, which in some instances assisted African Americans in building chapels for separate worship, and they held religious services in their homes and in rooms above stores. African Americans, both free and enslaved, regarded separate churches as a small but important step toward autonomy, for supervisory committees of whites seem to have paid little attention to them. In 1841 District blacks formed their own Presbyterian church, complaining that "the colored members of the Presbyterian and other evangelical churches in good standing do not enjoy, in our white churches, [equal] privileges."[38]

Religion in the District was especially important because it brought together free blacks and slaves in common worship. According to historian David Goldfield, "The interaction [of the free and the enslaved] was greatest in the cities of the Upper South, where skin color, their own recent life as slaves, small numbers, and a harsh prejudice against free blacks combined to push the free into close association with the enslaved."[39]

When Charles T. Torrey arrived in Washington, anxious to find ways to free slaves, he attended a Methodist church where all the members were black; enjoying "the communion of saints," he resolved to attend only black churches while in Washington. Some members of the congregation were slave, others free, "and, when one of the poor women . . . spoke of the 'persecution' she endured, with sobs, I felt my heart filled with new energy to make war upon that hateful institution that so crushes the disciples of the Lord to the earth."[40]

Another visitor to a Methodist church commented on the "pious prayers" and "sensible, cheerful singing of the poor negroes." Fredrika Bremer observed the members of a Methodist church to be very well dressed but compassionate for those in trouble. When the preacher announced that one of their number was about to be sold south and separated from his wife and child, the congregation took up an offering to purchase his freedom so that he could remain in Washington. "A pewter plate was set upon a stool in the church, and one silver piece after another rang joyfully upon it."[41]

Methodism in the District had a bad reputation among slave owners. A runaway living in Canada remembered that his owner had forbidden him to attend a Methodist church, even though he was a member: "You shan't go to that church—they'll put the devil in you," meaning that "they would put me up to running off." [42] John Thompson, a Maryland slave, rejoiced in Methodism, for it was "preached in a manner so plain" that anyone could comprehend it. It "spread from plantation to plantation," where most of the slaves were converted, to the consternation of their owners, who broke up the slaves' religious services. Methodism, according to Thompson, "brought glad tidings to the poor bondman; it bound up the broken-hearted; it opened the prison doors to them that were bound and let the captive go free." Thompson, of course, used that last phrase metaphorically, but the owners feared that their property would interpret it literally. On the other hand, "colored people connected with Methodist churches" in Washington were "seldom or never brought before the criminal courts for misconduct," according to a Washington judge. [43]

One traveler in Washington gave a detailed account of a Baptist service she attended in a "large whitewashed apartment" over a grocer's warehouse. The room was about half filled, the preacher was already well launched in his sermon when she arrived, and she listened with some amazement as he "explained the Gospel means of salvation with great clearness, and really with admirably chosen words." "The discourse was at least equal to the sermons of many of our dissenting ministers, and appeared to come from the lips of an educated gentleman, although with a black skin." She praised the congregational singing: "The men's voices were very loud, but they all sang true, and with great spirit and energy." Since they had no musical instruments or hymn books, they sang either from memory or from the preacher's lining out the words. The visitor was less enthusiastic about the second part of the service, in which members of the congregation responded to another sermon with "twistings and contortions of the body, shakings of the head, lookings upward, lookings downward, and louder words of exclamation and approbation." Nor was she happy with the testifying that followed, for she thought that some of the worshipers became hysterical. [44]

Although I have felt it scarcely possible to describe the scene without a certain mixture of the ludicrous, no feeling of irreverence crossed my mind at the time. On the contrary, my sympathies were greatly drawn out towards those our poor fellow-creatures; and there was something most instructive in the sight of them there assembled to enjoy those highest blessings—blessings of which no man could rob them. Religion seemed to be to them not a mere sentiment or feeling, but a real tangible possession; and one could read, in their appreciation of it, a lesson to one's own heart of its power to lift man above all earthly sorrow, privation, and degradation into an upper world, as it were, even here below, of "joy and peace in believing."[45]

Although it was a long established legal principle that conversion to Christianity did not affect the status of a slave, it was nevertheless true that antislavery agitators found it especially obnoxious to witness the sale of Christians. For example, Joshua Giddings, speaking in Congress in 1843, lamented the sale of "Presbyterians, Baptists, Methodists, and Episcopalians." He thought that traders wanted to know the slave's religious denomination; a good Christian should make a more docile slave.[46] Church membership played an important role in northerners' perception of the institution, for they saw all too clearly that a brotherhood of Christians could not coexist with human bondage.

Religious enthusiasm reached its peak during outdoor summer camp meetings, attended by black and white, slave and free. In 1849 Methodists held a revival five miles outside Washington; it was primarily for African Americans, but whites also participated. A visiting Anglican clergyman regarded camp meetings (he did not specify the color of the participants) as "remarkable spectacles of enthusiasm," with shouts of "Glory" and "Amen" and prolonged hymn singing. "The assembled thousands become wonderfully excited; . . . they scream, jump, roar, clap their hands, and even fall into swoons, convulsions, and death-like trances."[47]

Slave owners looked on these gatherings with suspicion, especially because free men and women mingled with the enslaved. Maryland restricted free blacks' attendance at camp meetings, requiring that a white clergyman either be the preacher or give written permission for African Americans to attend when a black man led the service. An observer sympathetic to African Americans noted that when a revival was taking place, the slaves neglected their duties and became "troublesome and unmanageable." In despair over camp meetings, a Virginian observed that "it was the greatest misfortune that could happen . . . to have a nigger turn Christian."[48]

Although they had few sources of recreation, blacks did go to the theater, where they sat in a balcony set aside for them. But in 1838, when "The Gladiator" was performed in Washington, management denied them admittance because the play was about Spartacus and a Roman slave revolt. Dangerous ideas! African Americans in the District loved to hold balls, which must have been fairly grand, for they were not cheap to attend: in one case, a dollar for a couple and fifty cents for a single person. Those holding "an assembly or ball in their homes had . . . to state [the] number of guests expected and the hour at which it would end" and were subject to the enormous fine of $10 if they did not have a permit from the mayor.[49]

African Americans in the District belonged to fraternal organizations; they organized a lodge of Masons as early as 1826 and of Odd Fellows in 1846. It may be safe to assume that membership was limited to free blacks, but the boundaries between slave and free were not always clear. Blacks formed aid societies, helped in the purchase of cemetery plots, and provided relief for families in distress because of the death of the head of a family.[50]

In the District, whether slaves lived with their owners or temporary masters, whether they lived in housing they found for themselves, whether they were contented or dissatisfied, whether they were church members or not, there was one great fear always hanging over them: they might be sold to a trader and sent south. A register of African Americans in Mt. Zion United Methodist Church in Georgetown carries notations such as: "lost," "sold to Georgia trader," "sold to the South," "sold and gone," "sold." Slave owners were aware of the power of a threat of sale. When President James Monroe ordered a whipping for "a worthless scoundrel," he added, "Tell him that you are authorized to sell him to the New Orleans Purchasers, and that you will do it, for the next offense."[51]

If they were free blacks, they were liable to kidnapping or sale after false arrest. In 1843 William Jones petitioned Congress from the Washington jail, claiming that though he was free, he had been thrown into prison and advertised for sale.[52] Slaves might be sold to settle an estate, to pay off a debt, to redeem a bankruptcy, or merely for light and transient reasons. Washington was a major slave market, where traders were always hungry for prime stock, and there was an apparently insatiable demand for fresh merchandise. Horace Mann claimed that Washington had become "the Congo of America." "Virginia and Maryland are to the slave trade what the interior of Africa once was. ... [T]his District is the great Government barracoon, whence coffles are driven across the country to Alabama or Texas, as slave ships once bore their dreadful cargoes of agony and woe across the Atlantic." John R. Spears, in his 1900 study of the slave trade, called Alexandria "the Omaha of the human cattle trade"; he was writing at a time when Omaha was a meatpacking center.[53]

Joshua Giddings, the untiring opponent of slavery, deplored the skill of District traders: "I doubt whether any slave-market in Africa was ever attended by more expert dealers in human chattels, than was the market of this city [Washington]." He maintained that the "ulterior and important design" of annexing Texas to the Union was "to enhance the price of human flesh in our slave-breeding States, by opening up a slave-market" there. Once Texas had been annexed, "the price of human flesh in this district" would rise.[54]

As early as 1790 Virginia and Maryland were slave-exporting states, and though additional states sold their surplus, those two states continued to export slaves down to the Civil War. In 1855 John Gorham Palfrey quoted the *Virginia Examiner*: "Negroes have become the only reliable staple of the tobacco-growing sections of Virginia." George Lewis, a Scots clergyman, wrote of Virginia planters who "are finding slave breeding profitable."[55]

What historian Herbert Gutman called "one of the great forced migrations in world history" occurred between 1830 and 1860, when "about 575,000 enslaved blacks were shipped from the Upper to the Lower South." Gutman's number includes both people sold on the slave market and those accompanying slaveowning families that removed to the Lower South; Michael Tadman claims that after 1820 trade relocated more slaves than did family migration. Bruce Levine, extending the time span, estimates about two million people were involved in the interstate slave trade between 1790 and 1860.[56] The nation's capital played a major role in that transfer. In 1836 the *Virginia Times*, in an obvious exaggeration, estimated that 40,000 slaves were exported from Virginia in the previous year; many of those passed through the slave marts of the District. According to Tadman, "For slave children living in the Upper South in 1820, the cumulative chance of being 'sold South' by 1860 might have been something like 30 percent."[57]

A slave auction took place in Washington even before the federal government moved to the new city, and one historian of the District, Bob Arnebeck, claimed that as early as 1801 it had become "a central point for the trade in slaves." The following year an Alexandria grand jury protested "the practice of persons coming from distant parts of the United States into this District for the purpose of purchasing slaves, where they exhibit to our view a scene of wretchedness and human degradation, disgraceful to our characters as citizens of a free government." Citizen petitions and grand jury protests against the slave trade continued through the 1820s, all to no effect.[58]

In the face of an unsympathetic Congress, nothing was likely to happen. An 1829 committee of the House of Representatives, responding to Congress's instructions to look into the slave trade in Washington, refused to suggest changes. In fact, according to the committee's report, shipping slaves to the Deep South meant that their situation was "considerably mitigated by being transported to a more genial and beautiful clime." It was true that families might be separated, but since they were property, that was unavoidable: "It should be some consolation to those whose feelings are interested in their behalf, to know that their condition is more frequently bettered, and their minds happier by the exchange."[59]

Slaves were better informed. They knew that life on a cotton or sugar plantation was much worse than life in Washington. Giddings maintained that a slave working in cotton fields would survive for seven years, on a sugar plantation for only five. One visitor observed that the very name New Orleans struck "terror into the slave and free Negroes of the Middle States,"[60] who did not want to view separation of families as inevitable just because they were in bondage. Enslaved Washingtonians did not need reminders of the trade, for they were always before them. In spite of claims to the contrary, coffles regularly passed down Pennsylvania Avenue and other main streets. If they were headed for Baltimore, slaves in chains waited for the train at the foot of Capitol Hill; if destined for Alexandria, they usually walked over the Potomac bridge; if headed for the Deep South, they waited for a slave ship or set out westward through Virginia to walk to slave marts on the Mississippi River. In every instance they were visible to all in Washington willing to look. The slave Charles Ball "frequently saw large numbers of people of my colour chained together in long trains, and driven off towards the south." Even the quiet of a Sunday was broken by the passage of slaves in chains.[61]

Slave coffles going by the Capitol demonstrated the reality of the slave trade for members of Congress. Congressman John Van Dyke of New Jersey deplored the "droves of miserable half-naked negroes, bound together," which he saw "driven along the streets like cattle or swine." Joshua Giddings told the House of Representatives: "I have witnessed the chained coffle as they passed by the very walls of the building in which we are now sitting; where the star-spangled banner which floats over us, threw its shadow in bitter irony upon those victims of your barbarous law."[62]

The pattern was generally the same: women, babies, and small children rode in wagons, while the men were chained together in pairs, sometimes with shackles on their ankles. A long chain attached the male slaves to the coffle, and a driver on horseback preceded and followed the group. The noise of the chains and the cries of the enslaved must have heralded their passage, though the cries diminished as the drivers, armed with whips, threatened those openly lamenting their misfortune. Samuel Walter Chilton of Richmond remembered, years later, seeing large groups of slaves chained together: "setch a cryin' an' screamin.'"[63]

Many people in the District were involved in the slave trade. The most famous company was Franklin and Armfield in Alexandria, which in 1829 made a profit of $33,000. The Yellow House, owned by William Williams and located more or less across from the original Smithsonian Institution building (the Castle), was especially famous. James H. Birch operated out of the United States Hotel, located on Pennsylvania Avenue at Third Street; in other words, just down the hill from the Capitol. James Gannon's establishment was on Seventh Street, whence he tried to stab Captain Daniel Drayton. But listing the major dealers does not begin to explain the reach of slave selling in the District. Auctioneers such as R. W. Dyer and A. Green sold slaves along with furniture and other merchandise.[64]

Hotels and taverns played a crucial role in the District's trade in human beings. On arriving in Washington, Alexandria, or Baltimore, a man interested in dealing in slaves would register at a hotel and put notices in local newspapers that he was ready to buy or sell. Local slavers, when starting out in the business, advertised that customers, either buying or selling, could find them at a certain tavern. Three District taverns were especially popular for trading: McCandless's at Wisconsin Avenue and M Street in Georgetown, Lafayette on F Street between Thirteenth and Fourteenth streets, and Lloyd's at the corner of Seventh and Pennsylvania Avenue. There was a slave pen in Decatur House on Lafayette Square across from the White House. "In 1819, when Miller's Tavern at Thirteenth and F Streets was on fire, a bystander, William Gardiner, refused to join the customary bucket brigade and loudly denounced the place as a slave prison." That was probably where Jesse Torrey found a woman imprisoned in a garret on F Street awaiting sale to the South. He reported that "some of the rooms in a tavern devoted chiefly to that use [holding slaves], are occasionally so crowded, that the occupants hardly have sufficient space to extend themselves upon the floor to sleep."[65] In Baltimore Hope H. Slatter began by advertising that those interested in dealing with him could leave messages at a local tavern.

Southerners visited Washington on a regular basis to buy up stock for their own use or to sell to their neighbors, carrying as much as $50,000 to invest in human property. In this way they could undercut the prices charged by regular dealers; in 1840 a Tennessee man informed a relative in Washington that "Negroes sell very high here." Southerners on a personal shopping trip could buy exactly the slaves they wanted, whether, for example, there was need for a field hand, a carpenter, a cooper, or a lady's maid. A North Carolina man who had come to Washington "for the purpose of buying slaves" did not mention the total price he had paid for his new possessions, but the trip itself would cost $2 per head. An Arkansas planter, after spending three months in Richmond, left for home with "at least 12 adult slaves and fifteen children." By 1835 Virginia had become "a nursery for slaves": "'He is gone to Virginia to buy Negroes' . . . is as often applied to a temporarily absent [southern] planter, as 'he is gone to Boston to buy goods,' to a New England country merchant."[66]

Hotels provided holding cells in their basements where patrons could safely leave their merchandise prior to starting south. It was an effective business practice, and the owners were anxious to be of service to their customers. Or Washington owners could "commit their slaves for safe keeping to the public gaols"; in 1828 ninety-five slaves in

"Human Flesh at Auction." (Courtesy of the Library of Congress)

the District jail were held there to make sure they were "safe," though it is not clear exactly what "safe" meant.[67]

A red flag was the sign of a slave auction; an 1834 statement was surely symbolic: "The red sign of the auctioneer is stuck up under the flag which waves from the towers of the Capitol."[68] As an Englishman wrote: "While the orators in Congress are rounding periods about liberty in one part of the city, proclaiming, *alto voce*, that all men are equal and that 'resistance to tyrants is obedience to God,' the auctioneer is exposing human flesh to sale in another!" When Abraham Lincoln was a member of the House of Representatives, he noted that from the windows of the Capitol one could see "a sort of Negro-livery stable, where droves of Negroes were collected, temporarily kept, and finally taken to Southern market."[69]

The itinerant trader, the "roving speculator," was at the heart of the slave business, "chatting at the country stores and taverns, loitering, treating and asking questions at the barrooms, looking in at the county jails to see the latest arrivals, cordially greeting the slaveholding farmer, . . . as if specially concerned about his welfare." Local governments cooperated by providing jail cells to hold purchases until agents were ready to transport them to Alexandria, Washington, or some other trading center. Once they were in the District, they had to pay only thirty-four cents per day to lodge the slaves in the Washington jail, described as "an old and loathsome building." A visitor saw small stone cells filled with blacks, five or six to a space hardly large enough for one.[70]

Potential slavers served what amounted to an apprenticeship to major dealers. Joseph Bruin, an important figure in this story, was an employee of George Kephart, who had taken over the quarters of Franklin and Armfield in Alexandria. Bruin operated in the Virginia counties not too far from the District, buying up likely slaves and paying cash for them. Indeed, George Kephart sued Joseph Bruin for money advanced to buy slaves in rural Virginia.[71]

Ready money must have been especially welcome to Virginia farmers caught up in the agricultural decline that attracted the notice of every visitor to the area. *DeBow's Review* of New Orleans reported that Virginia had "ten thousand abandoned farms." A correspondent for the *Boston Whig* sketched a bleak picture: "half-cultivated lands around Washington, . . . the utter lack of ingenuity and enterprise, the rudeness and poverty that seems [*sic*] to be stamped upon animate and inanimate objects," a farming population "inert, degraded, [and] ignorant." A traveler on his way from Baltimore to Washington knew at once that he was in a slave state: "We saw only a few starved and ragged negroes driving bullock-wagons laden with firewood, and exhausted tobacco-fields, . . . and there was an air of gloom and desolation over the landscape."[72]

Even though the number of free blacks in the District increased during the antebellum period, their lives were hard, as the hotel worker expecting to be free admitted to his questioner, Alan Hodgson. Free blacks competed with other poor people—slaves and immigrant whites, especially the Irish—when they sought employment. Those who had struggled to buy their freedom all too often found survival as free men and women very difficult. When troublemakers threatened an antislavery newspaper in 1848, they loudly proclaimed that men with Irish names would not be sympathetic to blacks; they knew that immigrants and African Americans competed for jobs. On the other hand, Irish jurymen reportedly were reluctant to convict Daniel Drayton when he went on trial for larceny. By 1850 there were 178 black property owners in Washington, but the average value of a holding was only $611, as contrasted with New Orleans, where the average value of free black real estate ownership was $3,623. On the eve of the Civil War, the number of real property owners in the District had increased to 414, but the value of all real and personal property owned by blacks was only 1.4 percent of total District property value.[73]

The most serious problem was the constant peril of enslavement, for any free person of dark skin had to be able to prove at any moment that he or she was free. Otherwise he was lodged in the jail, from which, if no one presented proof that he was free, he would be sold south in order to pay his jail fees. A free black arriving in Washington from the North, unaware of such a law, could find himself in jail and then be sold into slavery. Willam Jay, the son of the first chief justice of the Supreme Court, became an active supporter of emancipation when he learned that a New York neighbor was about to be sold as a slave because he had arrived in Washington without proof of his freedom.[74] In 1828 the District jail held seventy-eight men and women charged with running away. Of that number, eleven went free, one was sold to pay jail fees, and sixty-six were "delivered to their masters."[75]

In 1861, when the Civil War was under way, congressmen learned that there were in the District jail "some sixty persons . . . imprisoned solely because they were suspected of being runaways, and had been allowed no opportunity to prove the contrary." Henry Wilson, a senator from Massachusetts, wrote: "There grew up a race of official and unofficial man-hunters, greedy, active, dexterous; ever ready, by falsehood, trickery, and violence, to clutch the black man who carried not with him his title to freedom."[76] It was Wilson who introduced the bill finally ending slavery in the District of Columbia.

Kidnapping free blacks was common. As early as 1817 Jesse Torrey reported his involvement in securing the release of free blacks who had been kidnapped in Delaware and Pennsylvania and brought to Washington for sale. Torrey wrote about a woman, imprisoned in the garret of a tavern on F Street, who flung herself from a third-floor window rather than face shipment to the South. She did not die but broke her back and both arms, instead. Torrey's account became the most quoted proof of the inhumanity of slavery, but in the horror over the incident, writers overlooked the point that Torrey explicitly made: the frequency of kidnapping of free men and women. Though the injured woman might have been legally enslaved, others in the garret were free; and kidnappers willingly used violence to acquire African Americans, slave or free, to sell to the South.[77]

Solomon Northup of Saratoga Springs, New York, became a famous example of kidnapping in the District. In 1841, invited to join a circus, he went to Washington, where he was drugged; and when he woke up, he was in chains. James H. Burch had abducted him, and when Northup complained, saying that he was free, the dealer beat him. Northup and forty-eight others were shipped to New Orleans, where they went on the slave market.[78]

From Northup we get a precise description of a Washington slave pen: a room about twelve feet square, with one small, barred window and an outside shutter. The room had a bench and a stove, but no bed, no blanket, or "any other things whatever." A brick wall ten or twelve feet high surrounded a backyard that held a structure akin to a cattle shed. "It was like a farmer's barnyard in most respects, save it was so constructed that the outside world could never see the human cattle that were herded there."[79]

When the New England Anti-Slavery Society undertook to document the kidnapping of free blacks, it had no difficulty finding evidence. "By a conspiracy of one or two needy and profligate men with a domestic slave trader, any free colored man in *any* state, may be, and a very considerable number annually are kidnapped *according to law!*" If a freeman had his freedom paper torn up and thrown away, he was vulnerable to sale and transport far from home. "A free colored man deprived of his free papers, can entertain very little hope of vindicating his freedom." According to the New England Anti-Slavery Society, several thousand free Americans were held in bondage.[80] A month after the *Pearl* disaster, men from Alexandria seized a free black man working at the United States Hotel, while members of Congress watched and Congressman Thomas H. Bayly of Virginia encouraged the kidnappers to hold on to their prey. A District visitor reported a free black man employed at the navy yard had been kidnapped with his family in the dead of night and sold to Georgia. The man had managed to escape, but his family was forever lost.[81]

When the price of cotton and the death rate from cholera were high, free blacks were in particular peril of kidnapping. Ethan Allen Andrews, writing from Baltimore in 1835, warned of the danger: "The present high price of negroes is presenting a great temptation to unprincipled men to attempt to sell such as are free." In 1844 five or six men broke down the door of John Wilkinson's house in Georgetown, grabbed his fourteen-year-old son, and carried him off to be sold into slavery. Wilkinson had no recourse. Lavinia Bell, interviewed in Canada in 1861, said that while still an infant she had been abducted from Washington, along with thirty or forty others, and sold in Texas. J. W. Lindsay, a blacksmith and a free black, had been kidnapped in Washington while still a child and taken to Tennessee. "If kidnapped at an early age, a free black child might grow up a slave never knowing that he or she had been born free."[82]

Slaves, tricked into running away, were captured and sold. Indeed, fugitives taking refuge in the District found Washington very dangerous. Christopher Nichols, fleeing from Stafford County, Virginia, south of the District, ended up in the jail in Alexandria, where "the traders came from Washington to examine us." Henry Banks, another Virginia slave, fled to Washington, where he encountered a ship captain who promised to take him to Boston and freedom. Instead, he was turned over to his former master and sold to a trader. Both Nichols and Banks ran away again and finally reached safety in Canada.[83]

Slaves could work for many years in order to buy their freedom. When slaves had almost finished paying the agreed-upon sums, they were especially in peril, for unscrupulous masters might sell the slaves and pocket the payments. This happened in Mrs. Spriggs's boardinghouse (located where the Jefferson Building of the Library of Congress sits today) when Joshua Giddings was living there. Among the rented slaves working for Mrs. Spriggs was a man who had already paid $240 of an agreed-upon freedom price of $300. But his owner sold him to a slaver, and though Giddings went to his rescue, the bondman was already aboard a ship in Alexandria on his way to a southern market.[84]

The slave trade, nourished by distressed farmers, unscrupulous traders, and cooperative government officials, and protected by both law and custom, was an integral part of the life of the nation's capital. When Solomon Northup wrote, "The voices of patriotic representatives boasting of freedom and equality, and the rattling of the poor slave's chains, almost commingled," he was not exaggerating.[85] There is no doubt that slavery and the slave trade aroused tremendous anger in the hearts of some northerners in Washington, but what really amazes anyone looking back on slavery is how many people accepted it as an inevitable part of American life. For example, in the 1840s, Alexandria, while still a part of the District of Columbia, was a town in deep depression, and yet Virginians were anxious for its return to the state because of the value of a thriving trade in slaves. In 1846 Congress, without serious debate, agreed to the retrocession, apparently giving little thought to its consequences. Alexandria blacks were most seriously affected, for though life under District laws had not been easy, they regarded the transfer to Virginia as intolerable. Gerrit Smith reported that Alexandrians were begging northern emancipationists to help "forty or fifty colored families move to a free state."[86]

The domestic slave trade was very well organized. The season for shipping from the Upper South was October to May; the trade in New Orleans began in November, when the weather was cooler and the threat of disease was less. By 1835 Franklin and Armfield was sending off a ship about every two weeks; in addition, the company also dispatched slaves overland. When Franklin and Armfield retired from slave trading in 1836, they sold two of their ships to William Williams and one to George Kephart, the latter being the slaver who took over their establishment in Alexandria. A Louisiana legislator said in 1831 that slaves reaching the Deep South from the more northerly slave states, "principally from . . . Maryland and Virginia," had an annual value of $2.5 million. Indeed, the domestic trade assumed such importance that it "led to a falling off in the illicit introduction of Negroes after 1825." W. E. B. Du Bois believed that "vested interests opposed smuggling Africans into the South because it would tend to decrease the value of the domestic product."[87]

A ship used in the slave trade had the hold divided in half: "the after hold will carry about eighty women, and the other about one hundred men." Platforms ran the length of the hold, "about five or six feet deep," where the slaves lay "as closely as they can be stowed away."[88] A committee for the New England Anti-Slavery Society observed that Congress had made laws about how much space had to be preserved for passengers on foreign voyages. How much more necessary were laws regulating how many slaves could be carried on a slave ship. "No one has yet told the secrets of an *American coasting slaver*." The 1807 law ending the foreign slave trade required manifests that listed each slave boarding a ship engaged in the domestic trade, but there was "absolutely no limit specified as to the number to be carried, nor was there any provision for the safety, let alone the health and comfort, of the slaves."[89]

When slave ships, battered by storms, sought refuge in a British port or were wrecked near a British island, the local government set the enslaved men and women free, and Joshua Giddings rejoiced.

William Jay reported such actions occurring several times in the 1830s, to the fury of not only the slave dealers but also the American government, which sought compensation from London. Nine of the slaves aboard an 1831 wreck (the brig *Comet*) were the property of Mrs. Ignatius Mudd; later, slaves belonging to her were to seek freedom on the *Pearl*.[90] Such misadventures at sea may have made overland coffles more appealing to owners and dealers.

Of all the aspects of slavery none infuriated opponents of the institution as much as witnessing a slave coffle wending its way south and west. A visitor from Great Britain exclaimed: "I had never seen so revolting a sight before! Black men in fetters, torn from the lands where they were born, from the ties they had formed . . . and driven by white men, with liberty and equality in their mouths, to a distant and unhealthy country, to perish in the sugar-mills of Louisiana." According to one estimate, a coffle required fifty days to reach New Orleans from Maryland, and whether the slaves traveled by land or by water, the cost was about the same.[91]

An eyewitness reported that a "drove" of fifty or sixty bondmen and bondwomen moving west through Virginia was allowed to spend the night inside a tavern because of particularly bad weather; they usually slept outside on the ground. Supper was potatoes and corn meal "in a trough two and a half feet long," and the "half-famished" slaves grabbed handfuls of the filthy "mess" that was not even good enough or clean enough to feed pigs. They slept on the floor, and when they moved on the next day, "the mud was so thick on the floor . . . that it was necessary to take a shovel . . . and clear it out." Lorenzo Ivy of southwestern Virginia remembered slave coffles "reachin' as far as you kin see," and there were claims (surely exaggerated) of coffles of a thousand slaves. Benjamin Lundy, a pioneer opponent of slavery, first encountered the trade in Wheeling, Virginia (now West Virginia), on the Ohio River: "Wheeling was a great thoroughfare for the traffickers in human flesh," as they loaded their merchandise on river boats.[92]

Although the slave trade with Memphis and Natchez was important, the major destination in the Lower South was New Orleans. In 1848 the average price of all slaves in the South was $133, whereas a prime field hand in a New Orleans market brought $830. The Louisiana city was the greatest slave-trading center in the country, with at least twenty-five slave depots within a half mile of the St. Charles Hotel, itself a popular location for auctions. It is estimated that in the 1840s more than 200 and probably as many as 300 men were engaged in the business in New Orleans, some of whom became "conspicuously wealthy." Profits were high, perhaps as high as 21 percent. Dealers in the Upper South usually had partners in New Orleans to supervise the exhibition and sale of their merchandise, as was the case with Joseph Bruin, who advertised the convenience of his New Orleans depot: "Omnibuses running on Royal and Chartres streets all pass my house."[93]

"I believe," wrote an Englishman, "New Orleans to be as vile a place as any under the sun; a perfect Ghetto . . . the rendezvous of all nations." True, it was a wealthy city, but since its wealth was purchased "by the blood and tears of thousands of slaves," he was "filled with disgust toward the whites." Another visitor found slavery in New Orleans lacking "those milder modifications which serve to dress and decorate . . . this ugly fiend." Hundreds of slaves, "exposed in the public bazaars for sale," made it possible for buyers to examine them "with as much care, and precisely in the same manner, as we examine horses."[94]

Visitors were welcome to attend daily auctions, where "the poor object of traffic is mounted on a table; intending purchasers examine his points, and put questions as to his age, health, &c." The auctioneer "dilates on his value, enumerates his accomplishments, and when the hammer at length falls, protests, in the usual phrase, that poor Sambo has been absolutely thrown away." With a woman up for sale, the auctioneer "usually puts his audience in good humour by a few indecent jokes."[95] The auctions in New Orleans did not differ except in size from those being held all over the South, but the great number of slaves and of auction houses overwhelmed visitors.

Newspapers reported the arrival in the city of shipments of "field hands" that planters were urged to examine. Virginia slaves were the most prized; a traveler reported that "most of those whom I asked from whence they came, were Virginians or South Carolinians, raised for sale."[96] In actuality there was a wide variety among the people put up for auction: "Amongst them were to be seen old and young, male and female, and each of them in succession stood forward and heard themselves described in relation to their capability for the various employments they were fitted to pursue, as well as in relation to their individual character." A visitor was surprised that the slaves "tried to show off to the best advantage, and to enjoy a spirited bidding," which he found "humiliating." That visitor did not understand that the men, women, and children on the auction block would be punished if they did not "show off to the best advantage." The traveler thought that the auctioneer was careful to guarantee both freedom from "personal blemishes" and "possession of skill, ability, and character." Although "fancy girls," a New Orleans specialty, would bring very high prices, field hands that would be dispatched to cotton and sugar plantations were the most valuable slaves. Consequently, prices fluctuated over time, reflecting not only supply and demand but also the state of the cotton and sugar markets.[97]

Washington slavery was not bondage at its worst; but it was still bondage, and many slaves clearly felt an overwhelming desire for freedom. As they did throughout the South, African Americans adjusted to the reality of their situation, renting themselves out in order to earn a little money, seeking to hold their families together against impossible odds, finding consolation and companionship in religion and church membership, and ameliorating the harshness of personal bondage in every way they could. They found pleasure in small things such as making a game of hard work or laughing at inept and unaware visitors, and they ran away if escape seemed possible. Success was more likely if assistance was available, but there were few reliable guides to help them along the way. In the late 1830s and early 1840s there were at least two free blacks in the District of Columbia willing to help runaways. Leonard Andrew Grimes, born free in Leesburg, Virginia, in 1815, moved to Washington as a young man, where he found employment as a hackney coach driver. Appalled at the plight of District slaves, he began to use his hack to help those desperate to escape bondage. He attracted the notice of suspicious Washingtonians, who, following his horse and buggy into Virginia, arrested Grimes and put him on trial. Found guilty of transporting runaways, he served two years in prison in Richmond, and though he returned to the District at the end of his term, he clearly could not continue to help fugitives. After a religious conversion and baptism in the Baptist Church, he moved to Massachusetts early in the 1840s; in 1848 he became founding pastor of Boston's Twelfth Baptist Church (often called the "fugitive slave church") and an important leader of the African American community.[98]

In spite of the obvious danger, Thomas Smallwood took up where Grimes had left off. Smallwood, a Maryland slave, was rented to the Washington Navy Yard. Eventually he worked out his freedom, learned to read and write, and decided to devote himself to helping slaves escape. There was no shortage of applicants, and, as he wrote later, they "crowded upon me by scores." Although Smallwood never said how many he helped, he rejoiced that he was able to transport to freedom all whom he agreed to assist—except for seven, "who through their own indiscretion and the treachery of others" were captured.[99] When Charles T. Torrey arrived in Washington in December 1841, he found Smallwood's escape route already functioning.[100]

Torrey, a graduate of Yale College and a Congregational clergyman, resigned his pastorate in a Rhode Island church in order to "engage in the anti-slavery struggle." He became editor of the *Patriot*, an Albany, New York, paper, and Washington correspondent for several other papers and so saw firsthand the reality of District slavery.[101] Having had experience assisting fugitives while belonging to the Boston Vigilance Committee, Torrey resolved to help in any way he could. Smallwood learned of the New Englander's interest through Mrs. Smallwood, who did laundry for Torrey's landlady. Convinced of Torrey's sincerity, he allowed him to join his team, which then consisted of Smallwood and his wife Elizabeth, another free black named Jacob Gibbs, Torrey, and Torrey's landlady, Mrs. Frances Padgett, who kept a boardinghouse on Thirteenth Street in the District.[102]

Their usual pattern was to collect fugitives, who arrived one, two, or three at a time, and hide them until there were a considerable number, or until the time seemed auspicious. In the 1930s former slaves remembered "churches whose basements served as layovers, and out-of-the-way Georgetown homes that were specially marked for the fugitive."[103] Smallwood's goal was to get the fugitives into Pennsylvania, a journey that he claimed required three nights of hard walking. He had found safe places along the way that made it possible for fugitives to reach freedom. When women and children were in the group, Smallwood and Torrey would have to hire a team of horses and either a wagon or carriage, for which they paid exorbitant rates because of the peril of the enterprise. The source of the money to pay teamsters and the owners of the safe houses is not known, but it is fair to speculate that Torrey was valuable to Smallwood and others like him because he knew how to raise money in the North among antislavery sympathizers. Smallwood lamented the ignorance and suspicion of the slaves and even the treachery on the part of some.[104]

Smallwood's employer, on learning of the enterprise from a free black, conspired with two police officers, who threatened arrest. Smallwood, knowing that they wanted a bribe, gave them $30, all that he had, and fled the city, leaving behind money that was owed him and all his household possessions. Foolhardily returning to Washington and collecting another group of runaways, Smallwood was seen by John H. Goddard, head of the Night Watch, who arrested the fugitives and returned them to their owners. Smallwood escaped once again, but the man whose livery stable held his horses was arrested and charged with aiding runaways; his lawyer was David A. Hall, who will reappear in this story.[105] Smallwood eventually reached Canada.

His colleague was not so fortunate. After the excitement over Smallwood, it seemed expedient for Torrey to suspend his efforts on behalf of runaways. The Reverend Daniel Payne, pastor of Bethel African Methodist Episcopal Church, warned Torrey not to come to Baltimore, but he paid no attention and was captured in Maryland while trying to help slaves escape. When charged with helping slaves to flee, he appealed to his friends to send him money to buy food and to pay for a witness at his trial in Baltimore; according to one historian, abolitionists "helped to raise thousands of dollars for his legal defense."[106]

Found guilty in 1844 of assisting slaves to run away, Torrey received a sentence of six years in prison. The Maryland judge was willing to free him if he would promise not to help any more enslaved people gain freedom, but that he would not do, even though he knew he was dying of tuberculosis. "It is better to die in prison with the peace of God in our breasts, than to live in freedom with a polluted conscience." He claimed that he had helped nearly 400 slaves to freedom, and blacks demonstrated their gratitude by raising money to lessen the hardship of his years in prison. Death came in 1846; he had what his pastor described as a "triumphant death-bed," which was very important in the culture of nineteenth-century America.[107]

His funeral in Boston was equally triumphant, attended by thousands, including many African Americans, and all agreed that he was a martyr to the cause of antislavery. Bostonian Theodore Parker placed him "high in my list of martyrs." A New Hampshire newspaperman wrote: "Torrey, to be sure, is murdered—but what of that? Who cares? He has been killed by slavery." Many people cared. Torrey's widow and children received almost $3,000 from those who had supported his endeavors. African Americans held meetings in his honor and planned a large monument that never became a reality because of the cost. They visited his grave in Mount Auburn Cemetery in Cambridge, Massachusetts, where his tomb bore the figure of a slave bound in chains and a poem with the last line: "And the slave shall be a man."[108]

⁂

Smallwood and Torrey demonstrated the possibility of arranging the flight of slaves from the nation's capital, but organizing a large-scale escape involving many slaves was almost impossible, for detection seemed inevitable. Owners watched for signs of discontent, groups of slaves were forbidden to come together without the presence of a white person, and informers were not unknown among the enslaved. Consequently, defenders of slavery found the *Pearl* occurrence especially distressing, for nothing had leaked out, no slave owner had had even a hint of the plan, and no informer had whispered a word to any owner. How could a complicated plot of this magnitude develop and almost succeed? What did this do to southern claims that slaves—childlike by nature—needed close supervision in order to accomplish any task? What of frequent assertions of slaves' inability to function without their masters, or the claim that slaves were contented in their bondage?

The obvious answer for slave owners was the existence in the North of a vast conspiracy, "a well organized system . . . for the purpose of abducting our slaves," wrote the *Charleston Mercury*. "The recent outrage at Washington" was "but the forerunner of many similar ones"[109] that would destroy the southern economy and turn loose on the South a horde of angry, vengeful slaves. Southerners in the nineteenth century did not see the contradiction of happy slaves becoming angry once they were free. It was because of the steadfast belief in a conspiracy that Drayton and Edward Sayres escaped lynching; presumably, the two men could provide names that would make possible the revelation of exactly what dastardly deeds abolitionists were planning. To southerners and their sympathizers, any opponent of slavery was dangerous and had to be punished. That justified an attack on the *National Era*, an antislavery paper edited by Gamaliel Bailey. Slave owners never comprehended that antislavery enthusiasts, far from constituting a coherent movement, held widely differing views on how to achieve emancipation.

⁂

To maintain order in the nation's capital, Congress in 1803 had authorized the hiring of police constables, who by the 1840s numbered thirteen.[110] Alarmed by noisy protests against President John Tyler that may have included a rock being thrown at him on the White House grounds, Congress decided in 1842 to augment the constabulary with an Auxiliary Guard and Night Watch of fifteen men, one half patrolling from nine until midnight, the other half from midnight until four. The captain was John H. Goddard, a native of Rhode Island who had gone into the grocery business in the District.[111] Goddard had confronted Smallwood, and Goddard's force would be in action in 1848 and 1850. Washington's government consisted of a mayor (in 1848 William W. Seaton), a board of aldermen, and a "common council." A criminal court met three times a year and a circuit court (of appeals) twice a year. At the time of the *Pearl* escape attempt, T. Hartley Crawford presided over the criminal court, at a salary of $2,000 a year. The district attorney, Philip Barton Key (son of Francis Scott Key, who wrote "The Star Spangled Banner"), received no salary but was dependent on court fees.[112] Antislavery papers would claim that he augmented the charges against Drayton and Sayres because he received $10 for each one.

Slavery in the District had been a source of deep antagonism for almost two decades when the *Pearl* arrived in Washington in the spring of 1848. Probably a majority of Washingtonians were anxious to silence any opposition to human bondage, believing that it should be the great unmentionable. A much smaller number were equally anxious to do anything possible to end the infamous institution. Those two views clashed in highly visible fashion when slaves fled aboard the schooner. So who planned the escape? What was the source of funds? Sayres did not know, and Drayton never told. He went to his death without revealing any information about the origin of the plan of escape, but it is possible to piece together some elements of the projected flight.

The Escape Attempt

Daniel Bell was a slave in the Washington Navy Yard. His owner, who lived in Maryland, found it profitable to rent him to the United States government, and for twenty years Bell labored in the smith's shop, engaged in the casting and molding of iron. People described him as "robust, worthy, [and] industrious." Bell's wife, Mary Bell, was also a slave, owned by the family of Robert and Susannah Armstead.[1] It was not uncommon for a husband and a wife to have different owners, as was the case with the Bells. In the American system of slavery, the status of the mother determined that of her children; therefore, all of the Bells' offspring were the property of the Armsteads. Even if their father had been free, his situation would have been irrelevant to the enslaved condition of his offspring from a slave woman.

Robert Armstead assured Mary Bell that his will provided for her freedom on his death and her children's freedom as each of them reached the age of twenty-five. On hearing this, Bell's master became enraged, fearing that news of Mary's good fortune would cause his own slave, Daniel, to seek freedom. Consequently, he arranged to sell Bell to a trader, who entered Bell's shop at the Navy Yard, knocked him down, put him in irons, and carried him off to a slave pen on Seventh Street.[2]

Bell's friends, hearing of his sale, cast about for help

and turned to a colonel stationed in Washington, who agreed to buy him, giving him a chance to work out his freedom, the price being $1,000. According to abolitionist accounts, Bell set to work and had almost paid off the entire amount when the colonel, after being transferred, died in Florida. Only then did Bell learn that the army officer "had mortgaged Bell to his sister-in-law for a thousand dollars." His new owner insisted that Bell pay her the entire amount; in other words, he would have to start over again. In the United States, property in slaves could be used as security, like other property.

Daniel Bell, understandably, gave up, for he could never hope to save so much money. However, a friend intervened and persuaded the new owner to reduce the size of his debt. According to one account, this friend was Thomas Blagden, a Washington lumber merchant and a trustee of the District's schools.[3] By 1847 Bell finally received his freedom papers, though they cost him $1,630 in all, not counting his many years of hard work.[4] Slaves, working on their own, in addition to their regular labors, raised large sums of money to buy their freedom. Sometimes slave owners sold their slaves just before the final installment of the freedom price was finally paid, pocketing both the freedom price and the sale price.[5] In Bell's case, there seems to have been no ill intent on the part of the colonel who had mortgaged him, though the result had been disastrous.

Mary Bell's road to freedom was even more perilous. According to Emancipation and Manumission Records, Robert Armstead had actually freed Mary Bell and prospectively freed her children in September 1835. As it turned out, the circumstances of the emancipation differed from Armstead's verbal assurances. Mary Bell was freed for $1, and her children would be free on the following schedule: Andrew, aged sixteen, when he was forty; Mary E. Bell, eight, when she was thirty; Caroline, six, when she was thirty; George W., four, when he was thirty-five; Daniel, two, when he reached thirty-five; and Harriet, three months, when she was thirty. In his statement of manumission, Armstead wrote: "And they the said slaves being able to work and gain a sufficient livelihood & maintenance, I do declare to be free when they shall have arrived at the respective ages aforesaid manumitted and discharged from all manner of servitude or service to me my executor or administrators forever." George Naylor, a justice of the peace, acknowledged the deed of manumission on September 14, 1835.[6] Mrs. Bell, believing that she was free and that her children would eventually be emancipated, began to hire out herself and her offspring and keep their wages.[7] On Robert Armstead's death in 1838, an inventory revealed the total value of his estate as $1,299.25, but of that amount $1,225 was in slaves:

Negro Boy Andrew aged about 13 years value $375
Negro Girl Mary aged about 11 years value $200
Negro Girl Caroline aged about 9 years value $250
Negro Boy George aged about 7 years value $200
Negro Boy Daniel aged about 5 years value $100
Negro Girl Harriet aged about 3 years value $100.

The inventory did not include the mother: "Negro Woman Mary about 40 years not Produced."[8]

Susannah Armstead, Robert's widow, supported the family by renting out the older slaves. In 1839, as executrix of her husband's estate, she reported that she had earned $101.50 by hiring out Andrew at $2 per month, Mary Ellen at $1.50 a month and then at $2 a month, and Caroline at $1.50 per month. They provided income that she needed to support her children and pay their school fees.[9] This contradicts Mary Bell's claim that she and her children kept the money they earned for their own use; her pay is not mentioned, but the children's wages were important for the Armsteads.

When Susannah Armstead contested her husband's will, in preparation for dividing the slaves among her children, Mary Bell resolved to sue.[10] In October 1847 the "verdict was for the defendant," and though there was a motion for a new trial and Mrs. Bell had a good lawyer,[11] the future was not bright.

As the Bells' case dragged on, they grew desperate. Taking into account "the law's delay" and the claimant's "pertinacity," they concluded that flight was the only choice, for Mrs. Armstead might "seize them unawares, and sell them to some trader." Or if she won her case and settled her husband's estate, Susannah Armstead would almost surely split up the Bell family and ship some of its members to the Deep South. Daniel Bell, concluding that this was more than he could endure, looked for a way to send to the North his wife, nine children, and two grandchildren.[12]

By the 1840s, although there was almost no open opposition to slavery in Washington, a few people had not given up hope of redeeming the nation's capital from the curse of human bondage. Daniel Bell, learning the identity of a man he believed was sympathetic to his cause, asked for help in freeing twelve members of his family. But no one could raise the large sum needed either to liberate them or to spirit them out of Washington. At some point, however, the Washington contact wrote to a friend in Philadelphia and suggested that all of the family members could flee aboard a ship brought to Washington for that purpose.

Slaves were well aware that ships sailing north offered a convenient and relatively safe route to freedom. When Moses Roper, for example, fled from slavery in Georgia, his goal was to reach Savannah, where he was sure he could find passage aboard a ship sailing north. William Grimes secreted himself among the cotton bales aboard a ship bound for New York. Abolitionists in New England frequently reported assisting fugitives leaving vessels that had just arrived from the South. When Benjamin Drew interviewed fugitives in Canada, he found that a considerable number had escaped from a seaport.[13]

A Virginian living on the shores of the Chesapeake Bay warned the governor in 1832 that swift action by the state was needed to halt the flight of slaves, or there would soon be none left in the area, to "the impoverishment and ruin of the people." Citizens of Richmond, meeting in 1835 to decide how to counteract "attempts . . . to interfere with the slave property of the South," resolved that Virginians should avoid using steamboats whose captains had "knowingly" transported "persons or papers of an incendiary character."[14]

Transporting the Bell family to the North via ship was a practical undertaking, subject only to the expense involved. But the emancipationist in Washington increased the danger many times over when he decided to assist not just one family, the Bells, but many families and individuals to seek freedom aboard the same vessel, guaranteeing a general alarm among slave owners and sympathizers. His friend in Philadelphia, setting out to locate a ship and a ship's captain to transport the Bells to a free state, did not know what the Washingtonian was planning. If he had been aware of the enlarged and much more dangerous project, would he have refused to participate? Did he hire a ship under false pretenses? The Philadelphian may well have been ignorant of the Washingtonian's plans and did not intend to deceive when, in the winter of 1848, he approached an unemployed ship cap-

Daniel Drayton. From Personal
Memoir of Daniel Drayton, for
Four Years and Four Months a
Prisoner (for Charity's Sake) in
Washington Jail *(1855)*.
*(Courtesy of the Library of
Congress)*

tain and offered him $100 to transport the Bell family from Washington
to freedom. The impecunious waterman was Daniel Drayton, and he
and a large number of slaves undertook a venture for freedom.

Daniel Drayton was born in New Jersey in 1802. He had little education, saying later that he could sign his name and "read with no great
fluency." Although apprenticed to "a cotton and woollen factory" and
then to a shoemaker, he was drawn to the sea and became a waterman, sailing for the most part in the Chesapeake and Delaware Bays
but occasionally going as far south as Savannah and as far north as St.
John's, Newfoundland. As a seaman and ship captain he had only bad
luck. His ships foundered, his cargo rotted, and sometimes he had to
sell even sound cargo at a loss. After years of struggle he had nothing to
show for his perils and hard work, and 1848 found him in Philadelphia,
depressed and destitute, with his family in want.[15]

Drayton came to feel a great longing to be a Christian, but he sought
in vain for the powerful conversion experience that he believed essential for salvation. Eventually he attended a camp meeting at Cape May,
New Jersey, where he struggled mightily, and finally felt, he said, "my

whole soul to be filled with joy and peace." After he was convinced that he had indeed been saved, he decided to become a Methodist, the denomination of his mother, but, according to his memoir, he soon became disillusioned because of the refusal of the church to condemn the institution of slavery.[16] The author of Drayton's memoir was Richard Hildreth, who belonged to a group of abolitionists that regularly attacked the Methodist Church. It is impossible to tell whether this statement of disillusionment represented Drayton's view or Hildreth's.

As Drayton had sailed the great bays, the Chesapeake and the Delaware, he had seen firsthand the horrors of slavery and had been besieged by slaves begging to be transported to freedom. In 1847 he helped a Washington woman and six children escape to the North, and in Philadelphia they spread the word of his brave action.[17]

In February 1848, when Drayton was down on his luck, a stranger approached the waterman with a proposal that he return to Washington and bring off some slaves "who expected daily and hourly to be sold." Having no ship of his own, Drayton canvassed the watermen of the Philadelphia area, but they turned him down "on account of the danger." He believed, however, that they approved of his project and, he said, "seemed to wish me success." One day he encountered Edward Sayres, who was sailing a "small bay-craft," the *Pearl*, a schooner of 150 tons burden, leased from Caleb Aaronson in Bordentown, New Jersey.[18] Sayres planned to transport coal from Pennsylvania to points north; but, having found no cargo, he was feeling as unlucky as Drayton, who offered him $100 to sail to the District and back.

Sayres understood the enormous risk in transporting runaways, but, according to Drayton, the money was appealing, "considerably more than the vessel could earn in any ordinary trip of the like duration." Sayres later claimed that $100 was a disappointing offer; however, having no other employment, he reluctantly accepted it but did not inform the owner that he was putting his schooner at risk. Drayton and Sayres agreed that while Drayton as supercargo would have control of who came aboard, Sayres would make all other decisions with regard to the vessel. This would have serious consequences for the success of the undertaking.[19]

Drayton acknowledged that both he and Sayres had agreed to the dangerous journey because they were going through hard times and needed the money. Nevertheless, when Drayton later recounted his adventures, he insisted that his motivation was not merely monetary; he was also spurred by his "sympathy for the enslaved" and his "desire to do something to further the cause of universal liberty."[20]

The third member of the crew, Chester English, was "cook and sailor," and he was excited at the prospect of going to Washington. Although Sayres knew that the goal of the voyage was to rescue slaves, he never met the person or persons planning the expedition, which later proved fortunate. English, believing that they were sailing south in order to take on a load of timber, knew nothing of Drayton's plans.[21]

Someone—and Drayton never said who—gave him enough money to pay Sayres and English and to purchase supplies for the voyage. They set off for the nation's capital on April 1, traveling down the Delaware River, through the Chesapeake and Delaware Canal, and down the Chesapeake Bay to the mouth of the Potomac River. Sayres, unfamiliar with the Potomac, allowed Drayton to take the wheel as they sailed up the river to Washington.[22] Drayton decided to stop at Machudock, Virginia, and take on a load of wood as an excuse for the trip and to help pay expenses. The *Pearl* arrived in the District on April 13, 1848, docking at the foot of Seventh Street.[23]

If Drayton had had any concerns about how the Bells would know of his arrival, they were soon dissipated, for blacks in Washington knew the purpose of his voyage and had been awaiting his arrival. Drayton's mission was a well-kept secret throughout the black community. In his memoir Drayton or his amanuensis was careful to state that prior to the sailing of the *Pearl*, "I neither saw nor had any direct communication with any of those who were to be my passengers." But he did see one person in Washington, almost surely the originator of the plan, who told him that in addition to the Bells there would be "quite a number of others" hoping to escape. Drayton replied that he "did not stand about the number; that all who were on board before eleven o'clock I should take."[24]

He busied himself trying to sell his load of wood, not an easy matter, since it was of poor quality; but when he finally succeeded, he used the money to replenish supplies for the return voyage, especially ship biscuit. Drayton knew there would be more than twelve passengers, but in his memoir he implied that he had little notion of the many mouths he would have to feed.[25]

After unloading the wood, Drayton and Sayres moved the *Pearl* down the river to a "lonely place, called White-house Wharf, where the high banks of the river" afforded protection from curious passersby. Between the river and the city there was "a wide extent of open field," and shortly after dark on April 15, a Saturday, slaves began to slip silently across the fields and on to the schooner. Only that day had Drayton let English into part of the secret, when he told him to allow access to any blacks seeking to come aboard.[26]

In his narrative Drayton did not explain how the fugitives knew when to arrive at the *Pearl*, but the word must have spread quickly once the schooner was declared open to all comers. Drayton never revealed the name of the person with whom he spoke when he reached the District, though Washingtonians suspected it was Joshua R. Giddings, the most outspoken opponent of slavery in the House of Representatives. But Giddings claimed to have learned of the escape only on the evening it occurred and not before, when he "pronounced the plan ill-advised, and stated his apprehension of a recapture." The congressman, in spite of his intense desire to see an end to slavery, was reluctant to provide support for or encouragement to group escape attempts, anticipating the danger to the slaves. He had, for example, denied involvement in Charles Torrey's efforts to assist runaways, as recounted in the previous chapter, but according to family tradition the congressman reserved a room for fugitives in his home in Ohio.[27]

Since the Washington wharves were not extensive, the fugitives would not have had difficulty finding the schooner, even if it was anchored in a remote location. Drayton would later claim that he did not know how many slaves came aboard, although he admitted that he had been in the vicinity of the *Pearl* all that Saturday evening. It is true that he had been occupied watching for possible trouble and so had not kept an eye on those going aboard. The correspondent of the *New York Herald*, in reporting the story, made a singularly unpleasant joke: "The Pearl came to the city a few days ago, openly, with a load of wood; and departed, clandestinely, with a cargo of wool."[28]

At about ten o'clock that Saturday evening Drayton, Sayres, and English made ready to sail, but there was a dead calm, and the *Pearl* was sailing against the tide. How could a man who had basically lived on the waters of the Chesapeake and Delaware Bays not know that the Potomac was a tidal river up to the falls above Washington? How was it that an experienced waterman did not take the elementary precaution of checking the tides? It was to prove a disastrous error, for time would be Drayton's and the fugitives' worst enemy. The *Pearl* lay becalmed until daylight, when, with a breeze springing up, they set off down the Potomac to freedom.[29]

The plan, based on geography, was to sail down the river to the Chesapeake, then up the bay to freedom. It was a daring and seemingly foolproof scheme, except that the planner had not taken into account the vagaries of the weather.

As the *Pearl* sailed down the river, Drayton went below and found the fugitives "thickly stowed." He distributed the bread he had bought the day before "and knocked down the bulkhead between the hold and the cabin, in order that they might get into the cabin to cook."[30]

By the time the *Pearl* had reached the mouth of the river, the wind had risen to such force that Sayres, as captain of the schooner, declared it impossible to sail up the Chesapeake Bay. Drayton suggested sailing south to the mouth of the bay, then heading north in the Atlantic Ocean to reach a free state. The *Pearl* would never survive in the open sea, said Sayres, and his colleague was forced to yield, since, according to their agreement, Sayres had the final say with regard to the schooner itself. So they anchored at the mouth of the Potomac in Cornfield Harbor under Point Lookout, Maryland, "a shelter usually sought by bay craft encountering contrary winds" and a "favorite anchoring and poker-playing site for numerous schooners passing up and down the Bay." All aboard knew the danger of pursuit; but since the weather had made further progress impossible, everyone lay down and went to sleep.[31]

Drayton, awakened at about two o'clock on Monday morning, heard "the noise of a steamer blowing off steam" and knew that all was lost. The fugitives wanted to fight, but since there were no weapons on board, resistance was useless. They heard the sound of men's feet on the schooner's deck; then someone lifted the hatch and cried out, "Niggers, by G–d!" In the hold of the *Pearl* they heard cheers from the decks of both schooner and steamer and the banging of musket butts.[32] If only Drayton or Sayres had checked the tide tables or the storm had not made it impossible to sail north on the Chesapeake Bay!

English, the cook, heard someone call, "You d'd son of a bitch come out," and when he did, he saw the posse armed with swords, pistols, and muskets. One man had "a spring dirk knife in his hand" with which he struck at Drayton — but missed. The man with the knife "sd he wd like to have his hands into his guts a little while."[33]

Drayton expected to be lynched. He soon learned that some of the men on the steamer were slave owners and that they would not hesitate to exact vengeance. This did not happen. What probably saved Drayton then and later was the determination of Washingtonians to discover the man or men behind the escape. Who paid for hiring the *Pearl* and its crew? Who paid for supplies for the journey? Not a poor waterman, that was certain. Drayton stayed alive because he could provide information about the machinations of antislavery enthusiasts in the North and maybe even in the nation's capital.

The fugitives, for their part, must have known that sale to the South was a probability. When they decided to go on board the *Pearl*, they knew that, if captured, they ran the risk of being sold away from family and friends, for an owner was likely to send a runaway to market before he or she could try again. In those terrifying moments as the posse banged around on deck, the slaves knew that for them life would be worse, not better, that the gamble for freedom had failed.

And aboard the steamer? A great sense of triumph. The members of the posse had been able to prevent the loss of valuable property and in the process provide a warning to all District slaves that flight meant failure. Perhaps most important of all: they could gain information about an infamous antislavery conspiracy.

※

There is no clear account of what happened in Washington on that April Sunday morning, but slave owners must have felt intense anger when they realized that their slaves had fled. Breakfasts were not ready, babies were not dressed, horses and chickens were going hungry; nobody was performing the morning tasks expected of urban slaves. Some of the owners set out to look for their slaves. W. H. Upperman, for example, realizing that Priscilla had run away with her two children, believed that she had gone north into Maryland, where she had relatives. So he set out in pursuit, going as far north as Frederick before deciding she must be in Baltimore; it was only on reaching there that he learned about the Potomac River escape route.[34]

It must have taken some time before slaveholding Washingtonians realized that *many* slaves had left. As they rushed about the city trying to discover what had happened, they were undoubtedly appalled to learn the apparent extent of the escape. Surely they uttered threats against the ungrateful wretches who had left them in the lurch. It may be that the members of the posse discovered the exact number of runaways only when they captured the *Pearl*. The rumors that reached the *Liberator* in Boston provide some idea of the confusion in Washington: there were sixty slaves, no fifty; they had gone to the bay, to Pennsylvania, to Delaware.[35]

By church-time on Sunday the report ran throughout Washington that "a large number of slaves" had fled, though no one guessed as many as seventy-six. They had fled from "highly respectable families," perhaps absconding with silver spoons and "other valuables." Writing in the *Mississippi Free Trader*, an opponent of slavery envisioned the scene in the District: "What noise and confusion, what wrath and cursing, what fear and trembling! Masters and mistresses, in rage and despair, crying out that they had been robbed and ruined—robbed of their hewers of wood and drawers of water—robbed of the bones and muscles of their human beasts of burden, by the sweat of whose brows, and the toil of whose limbs they had lived in laziness."[36]

When the approximate extent of the loss had become apparent, a posse planned to pursue the runaways. Had the searchers gone north into Maryland, the *Pearl* would have been safe. Once the storm in the bay moderated, Drayton and Sayres would have been able to carry out their plan. But, sealing the fate of the fugitives, the posse went down the river aboard a steamboat, the *Salem*, the property of the Georgetown Steamship Company. The principal owner was Francis Dodge Jr. of "the first family" of Georgetown; three Dodge slaves were on the *Pearl*.[37]

How did the slave owners discover that the *Pearl* had transported their property down the Potomac River? Like other aspects of this story, the explanation is not clear. The *New York Herald* reported immediately after the recapture that the owners tortured a timid slave until he revealed the plan, or alternatively that slaves unable to join the fugitives had angrily told what they knew. The *Liberator* lamented that it was "hard for a slave to escape from this city [Washington] in this day of railroads and telegraphs."[38]

In 1853, five years after these events occurred, Harriet Beecher Stowe published *A Key to "Uncle Tom's Cabin"*, her response to southern claims that *Uncle Tom's Cabin* painted a false picture of slavery. According to Stowe, "more than a hundred" horsemen gathered to pursue the District runaways, when "a colored man, by the name of Judson Diggs, betrayed the whole plot." Angry because one of the fugitives had not paid him twenty-five cents for transporting her baggage to the wharf, he directed the posse down the river and away from

Maryland. According to Stowe, "two hundred armed men" boarded a steamer to go down the Potomac. The "more than a hundred horsemen" and "two hundred armed men" are impossible, since the approximate number of men pursuing the *Pearl* is known. Stowe's information may have come from members of the Edmondson family who were in Washington that Sunday morning and must have been aware of what was happening, since some of the Edmondsons were aboard the schooner.[39]

In 1855 Daniel Drayton's *Memoir* claimed that "a colored hackman" had "thought it a fine opportunity to feather his nest by playing cat's-paw to the slave-holders," telling all that he knew. The drayman had learned of the flight when he had transported to the *Pearl* "two passengers who had been in hiding for some weeks previous, and who could not safely walk down, lest they might be met and recognized."[40] Drayton's memoir did not name the drayman, but in 1916, in the first volume of the *Journal of Negro History*, John H. Paynter, a member of the Edmondson family, claimed that the traitor was Judson Diggs (or Digges), who had not been paid for hauling to the wharf the belongings of one of the runaways. According to Paynter, the posse had actually started north when the drayman told them they were going the wrong way. The horsemen turned back and made arrangements to sail down the river in pursuit. According to Paynter, Diggs lived on into the 1860s, "despised and avoided," though his only punishment was to receive a beating from "a party of young men," who then tossed him into a creek.[41]

In 1930 Paynter published a novel about the *Pearl*, in which he again named Diggs as a traitor but explained the hackman's action as based on unrequited passion, not greed. In this fictional account, Diggs had fallen in love with one of the runaways; when she spurned him, he avenged himself on the young woman and her family by betraying the fugitives.[42]

Who was this man? In a District chancery court action, Judson Digges (note the different spelling) appears as a hard-working slave, longing for freedom. While still in bondage, he had gained such a reputation for honesty that he was able to buy a house and lot, with the understanding that he could pay for the property in installments. By 1845 he had gained his freedom. Three years later, in 1848, believing that he had been cheated, Digges sued James Carrico, the builder of his house. His attorney was Caleb Cushing, who would be attorney general of the United States from 1853 to 1857. The Circuit Court of the District of Columbia, sitting in chancery, found against Digges and required him to pay Carrico's costs.[43] In the court record, Digges appears as a man striving to better himself, struggling first to gain his freedom and then to protect his hard-won property. Did he feel justified in taking any action, even betraying the slaves of Washington, in order to improve his hard life?

On the other hand, perhaps Judson Digges was innocent, and his reputation should not have suffered through the years. Maybe there was someone in Washington who had a fairly clear idea of what the slaves were planning to do. If such a person existed, his information was not sufficiently accurate to prevent the departure of the *Pearl*. But he might have known that the flight was by water, not by land. It is possible that the posse did not start north, that some people in the District knew at once the direction of the flight. An 1849 legal action adds another element to the story.

The owners of the runaways rejoiced to recover their property, and they paid salvage to Francis Dodge Jr. for the use of the *Salem*, which pursued the fugitives. The Georgetown merchant in turn used that money to compensate those who had participated in the chase. The first and largest single payment of $100 went to John Adams, with the notation that it was "for important secret services and intelligence . . . which contributed largely to the success" of the recapture of the fugitives.[44] What "secret services and intelligence"? Did Adams have prior knowledge of the plan before the *Pearl* sailed down the Potomac? Did he know what the schooner would do? What else would justify so large a payment and so laudatory a statement? Did Dodge have his steamboat ready that Sunday morning?

But if John Adams knew about the plan, why did he not prevent the departure of the *Pearl*? Or did his contribution lie in determining the means and direction of the slaves' flight, once they were missed? Since the person that organized the escape was not arrested, Adams seems to have lacked detailed foreknowledge of the plot. Was Digges the source of Adams's information? Perhaps that was why members of the African American community in Washington believed in his guilt. A man named John Adams was a grocer in Washington, and in 1852–53 someone bearing that name was involved in a case concerning a disputed sale of a slave woman and her child; but there is no way of knowing whether he was Dodge's informer.[45]

In any case, whether or not Georgetown residents had foreknowledge of the planned escape, the posse climbed aboard the *Salem* to pursue the runaways down the river. By Sunday evening the entire city knew of the means of escape, and a telegram warned authorities in Baltimore to dispatch a steamer to intercept the schooner.[46]

According to Drayton, who had ample time to observe during the sad return to the District, the posse consisted of thirty-five men "armed to the teeth with guns, pistols, bowie-knives, &c., and well provided with brandy and other liquors."[47] The *New York Herald* reported thirty men with "two field pieces," an obvious exaggeration. A few days later the paper's Washington correspondent assured his readers that, contrary to popular report, there had been no artillery on board the *Salem*, only "a few old muskets and revolvers." According to the trial testimony of one of the pursuers, they were not heavily armed: ten or twelve muskets, a carbine, and a fowling piece.[48]

As they sailed down the Potomac in pursuit of the runaways, the posse aboard the *Salem* hailed every craft they met and learned that two vessels had seen the *Pearl*. When the steamer reached the entrance to the Chesapeake Bay and had not encountered the fugitives, they decided to abandon the search after first checking Cornfield Harbor. There they spotted their quarry, blew the whistle, and went aboard the schooner, where they found their property.

Family tradition had Richard Edmondson, a slave whose family is important in the story of the *Pearl*, attempting to avoid bloodshed by shouting to the posse that all the slaves were on board. His shout had the opposite effect, for he seems to have frightened the pursuers, who gave his brother Samuel a blow to the head as soon as he appeared on deck. There might have been more violence if Drayton had not protested. "But for this timely interference, there is but little doubt that some of these people would have been cruelly if not fatally injured."[49] There was little probability that the fugitives would be murdered, for they were valuable property, which everyone aboard the *Salem* knew very well.

As they made ready for the return trip, the members of the posse tied the hands of Drayton, Sayres, and English and transferred them to the steamer, while the fugitives, under close guard, remained aboard the *Pearl*. The *Salem* had to stop for wood, for it was, after all, a steamer, and then, with the *Pearl* in tow, they sailed back up the Potomac toward Washington.

Some of the pursuers aboard the *Salem* wanted to lynch the three men, and at least one threatened Drayton, but wiser heads prevailed; the leaders were aware that only Drayton could tell them who had planned the whole affair. It is worth repeating that throughout this story a continuing theme is the anxiety on the part of District authorities to determine whether "persons of note" in the antislavery movement had financed Drayton and the *Pearl*. Drayton was relieved that he had not revealed any secrets to Sayres and English, for they immediately told everything they knew, none of which could be helpful to anyone seeking evidence of a conspiracy. English burst into tears, insisting that he knew nothing of the plan: Drayton had deceived him, claiming that they would be taking a group of blacks on a pleasure ride down the river. The posse untied English's hands but not those of the other two men.[50]

As they sailed up the river, the Washingtonians set two men, one of them a police officer, to work on Drayton in order to persuade him that it was to his advantage to reveal names and plans. If he would do so, his interrogators assured him, the owners of the slaves would let him go or sign a petition for a pardon. Drayton must have been sorely tempted, for he was terrified that he might have to suffer life imprisonment or even be torn apart by an angry mob. When he considered the hostile attitude of some of his captors, the latter seemed a likely outcome. So he told them everything he could about his life, his family, and his "past misfortunes," while insisting that he had had "no connection with the persons called abolitionists." He admitted that he had previously refused requests to transport slaves and that he was being paid for the *Pearl* venture, but he would give no names.[51] Indeed, he never did.

When they passed Alexandria, they found a large crowd waiting for news, which cheered mightily when they saw Drayton, Sayres, and English on the deck of the *Salem* and the fugitives on the deck of the *Pearl*—everybody exhibited in full view of the Alexandrians. The *Salem* did not stop, however, for the members of the posse were anxious to display their prizes in the nation's capital. They must have felt disappointed when they arrived, for there was no welcoming throng. The steamboat wharf, where they docked, was between Eleventh and Twelfth streets, but by the time all the people had been brought ashore and lined up in marching order, a crowd had begun to gather. They set out on Seventh Street, heading for the jail and perhaps for the Capitol;

Drayton and Sayres, tied together with a guard on each side, headed the procession. Next came all seventy-six fugitives.[52]

As they marched up Seventh Street, the crowd grew much larger. When they passed James Gannon's slave pen, the trader rushed out with a knife and tried to stab Drayton, shouting that he would give three Negroes "for one thrust at this d——d scoundrel." According to one account, Gannon succeeded in slicing off a piece of Drayton's ear, and there was a later claim that Drayton's ear was dripping blood; but since Drayton himself never mentioned any such injury, he probably escaped unharmed.[53]

By this time the crowd had grown threatening. There were cries of "Lynch them! lynch them! the d—n villains." There were "taunts and jeers at every step." According to another account, people were shouting, "Drag him out!" "Knock his d——d brains out" "Shoot him! shoot the hell hound!" "Lay hold of him!" "Hang the d——villain." Whatever the precise wording of the curses, which "would have made even devils tremble,"[54] the intent was clear: Drayton and Sayres should be lynched.

One of the bystanders is supposed to have said to fugitive Emily Edmondson, "Aren't you ashamed to run away and make all this trouble for everybody?" She replied, "No sir, we are not and if we had to go through it again, we'd do the same thing." Some of the women were crying as they walked along, holding babies or leading young children. Their guards ordered them to "*hush* their snivelling," and "to make their order more imposing, [the guards] would raise their cudgels over their heads as if about to strike."[55] Members of the crowd vowed vengeance not only on the perpetrators of the flight but also on "every friend of liberty," especially Congressman Joshua Giddings. According to the congressman, the troublemakers were "half-grown boys, loafers, and drunken rowdies, attended by ruffian-looking strangers in various parts of the city."[56]

Drayton was not the only one apprehensive of a lynching; his guards knew that he was in danger. If Washingtonians were ever to discover who planned the escape attempt, Drayton had to be kept alive. So his captors commandeered a hackney coach, pushed Drayton and Sayres into it, and set off for the jail. Drayton believed that the plan had been to exhibit the entire group on the grounds of the Capitol, but keeping him alive was more important than receiving the praise of proslavery members of Congress.

Yet if the members of the posse expected to escape the mob, they were mistaken, for the troublemakers followed the coach to the jail and milled about, shouting threats and demanding lynchings. There were blacks in the crowd who, "with tears rolling down many cheeks," watched "in anguish" as they saw their friends and relatives hurried off to jail. "One gray headed old woman in particular, wrung her hands and cried, 'Oh, my son, my son.'"[57] Drayton and Sayres were lodged in the jail, and the slaves in the jail yard, though some were later placed in jail cells where the slave traders could examine them at their leisure.[58]

As for English, the posse had let him go free, being convinced of his innocence, but he had wandered around Washington, not knowing where to go, and eventually ended up in the jail. Drayton, exasperated, said later, "It was a pity he lacked the enterprise to take care of himself when set at liberty, as it cost him four months' imprisonment and his friends some money." The three Philadelphians had to sleep on a stone floor with only a thin blanket under them. The cell had "neither chair, table, stool, or any individual piece of furniture of any kind, except a night-bucket, and a water-can."[59] There is no record of the fugitives, held in the prison yard, having blankets or water-cans or any other comforts.

In the meantime, a resident of Virginia, having received word of the flight, urged the governor to demand the extradition of the three men because two of the runaway slaves belonged to Virginians. He needed to act quickly, for if bail became available, the guilty men might escape punishment. In response, the governor asked for the prisoners, but nothing came of it; Washingtonians looked forward to trying them in the nation's capital.[60]

Newspapers notified the slave owners in the District that they should claim their property on Wednesday, April 19. That same day two justices of the peace, Hampton C. Williams and John H. Goddard, "held a court within the jail," probably deciding that because of the unrest in the city it was not safe to transfer them to the court. Former Ohio congressman Edward Stowe Hamlin secured David Hall as counsel for Drayton, Sayres, and English (who had been rearrested), and the two men went to the jail to confer with the prisoners. In spite of threats from slave owners or slave traders, the lawyers held their ground until the time of the hearing. Philip Barton Key, the district attorney, appeared on behalf of the United States, and the jail provided him with a chair, a table, and pen and ink. Hamlin and Hall had to stand and were denied the use of a table for note taking. District officials would not show common courtesy even to a former congressman if he expressed sympathy for runaway slaves.[61]

The justices of the peace charged Drayton, Sayres, and English with stealing slaves and fixed bail at $1,000 per slave per person: $76,000 for each of the three men. The slaves were present as proof of the crime. An eyewitness reported: "There were a large number of them who had infant children in their arms, whose color and features did not fail to proclaim their paternity. Some of them appeared cast down, others reckless. . . . One woman . . . being asked how she could leave so good a home, replied, 'I wanted liberty, wouldn't you, sir?' The name of another being called, she replied, 'Here I am, sir; once free, again a slave.' — Another . . . turned to the prisoners, shook them by the hand, exclaiming, 'God bless you, sirs, you did all you could; it is not your fault that we are not free.'"[62]

The families of the fugitives arrived at the jail, but, not being allowed inside, they stood at the gate, calling to their relatives. There were tears and lamentations both inside and out.[63] Mothers, fathers, brothers, and sisters were making frantic efforts to raise money to buy the freedom of individual slaves or to persuade a person of goodwill to purchase a fugitive in order to keep him or her in Washington. With a very different purpose in mind, traders were arriving from Alexandria, Baltimore, and perhaps from farther afield, for they knew that prize slaves would be on the market. The escape attempt had been an utter failure; the slaves were in a much worse situation than before; and the three watermen faced, at best, life in prison. John Gorham Palfrey, a member of the House of Representatives from Massachusetts, hoped that the April events would "enlighten our people at the North," and Frederick Douglass thought that they might lead to a "speedy overthrow of slavery, or a dissolution of our unhallowed Union." But any claim of positive results sounded hollow.[64]

A man named William L. Chaplin wrote from Washington that the escape attempt was "the grandest event for the cause of Antislavery" that had occurred in many years: "It is working great good here [in the District] & elsewhere. If our Abolitionists will take hold, we can drive slavery out of this District at once!" While others were sunk in gloom, he was singularly reluctant to admit that the project had been a disaster. His enthusiasm is not surprising, in view of the fact that it was Chaplin who had been the instigator of the escape, as he told his patron Gerrit Smith.[65] Chaplin was the one who had conceived the plan of using a ship to achieve freedom for a very large number of District slaves. His was the name that everyone in authority in the nation's capital sought to discover.

According to William Chaplin's own statement, he planned the escape, having found that slaves, desperately anxious to escape from the District, needed assistance in their flight. The effort of two earlier slave smugglers had come to an end: ex-slave Thomas Smallwood had fled to Canada, Charles Torrey had died in a Maryland prison, and for a while no one took their place. While Torrey was imprisoned in Maryland, a number of his friends raised money to pay counsel to secure his release. Among those most active in this endeavor were William L. Chaplin and Charles Dexter Cleveland.[66] When the governor of Maryland refused to pardon Torrey, and it was plain that the prisoner was dying, his friends came to say farewell and to promise that they would carry on his antislavery work. None meant it more sincerely than Chaplin, a Massachusetts lawyer, son of a Congregational clergyman, and grandson of a hero of the battle of Bunker Hill. He became an agent for the American Anti-Slavery Society and the New York State Anti-Slavery Society and eventually editor of the *Albany Patriot*, the paper for which Torrey had written.[67]

Chaplin was a close associate of Gerrit Smith, a wealthy New Yorker who was more than liberal in his assistance to antislavery causes; and when Chaplin decided to move to Washington, Smith provided financial support. On his arrival in the nation's capital, Chaplin probably formed an alliance with Jacob Bigelow, who in 1845 was a congressional reporter and later became a claims representative. His nephew would later assert that Bigelow was "general manager of the Underground Railway from Washington to Philadelphia."[68]

Chaplin concluded that there were people in the District illegally enslaved, and he began to institute "suits for freedom," using funds provided by "philanthropical friends of liberty." One of those suits may have been Mary Bell's, for she had somehow found enough money to retain two lawyers, Joseph Bradley, a leader of the District bar, and James M. Carlisle, an up-and-coming young attorney.[69] Who else in the District except Chaplin had money for "suits for freedom"? When Mary Bell's court action against Susannah Armstead seemed destined to fail, and the Bells decided the only alternative was flight, they naturally turned to Chaplin for advice and assistance.

Other Washington slaves learned of Chaplin and "resorted to him, by day and by night, for assistance and advice," to such an extent that he felt overwhelmed, as he reported to Gerrit Smith.[70] Although no case seemed more desperate than the Bells', the accumulation of pleas for help led Chaplin to plan a major blow against slavery in Washington, a much larger escape attempt than anyone else had tried and larger than he was willing to reveal.

When he wrote to an antislavery sympathizer in Philadelphia, asking for a ship to transport the Bell family, he did not admit what he had in mind. Had he done so, he would have scared off anybody interested in helping desperate slaves, for transporting to freedom a large number of Washington slaves was extremely dangerous. Whereas Smallwood and Torrey had done slave escapes by retail, Chaplin planned a flight by wholesale: he would send all of his supplicants off to freedom at one time.

In March 1848 Chaplin reported to his patron Gerrit Smith: "The number of persons here, who are anxious to emigrate, is increasing on my hands daily. I believe there are not less than 75 now importunate for a passage." Chaplin cited examples of the desperate need for escape. Three sisters sold by Francis Dodge, the major owner of the *Salem*, escaped from a slave trader and for the moment were safely in hiding, but they had to leave the District or else face recapture. Dolley Madison's slave Hellen (also called Ellen) Stewart was safely in hiding, waiting for a means of escape, and Chaplin was much interested in "five brothers & two sisters," members of the Edmondson family. (It was Richard Edmondson who tried to prevent bloodshed when the *Salem* finally overtook the *Pearl*.) Chaplin told his patron that he was "every day expecting the arrival of a vessel from Philadelphia on purpose to take off 50 or more," and while the *Pearl* was sailing down the Potomac, carrying the load of fugitives, Chaplin shared with friends the news of his great undertaking, finding relief in confiding in fellow emancipationists.[71]

So Chaplin originated the plan of flight by ship and may have brought Drayton and Sayres to Washington under false pretenses. It must have been Chaplin to whom Drayton spoke on arrival at the foot of Seventh Street in the District. There Chaplin asked the waterman if he would transport additional Washingtonians seeking freedom, not just the Bell family. Drayton agreed, but it is not clear that he expected the schooner to be *filled* with fugitives.

To whom in Philadelphia did Chaplin write, asking for a ship? The solution to that part of the puzzle is not as clear, but it may have been Charles Dexter Cleveland, schoolmaster, author, and dedicated opponent of slavery. He had come to know Chaplin through their mutual concern for Charles Torrey when the latter was in prison; both had sought Torrey's freedom through every possible avenue.[72] Chaplin knew that Cleveland shared his devotion to antislavery, and it was therefore logical for him to ask the Philadelphian to find a ship to liberate a family threatened with sale to the Deep South. It is likely that Chaplin did not reveal his large-scale plans to Cleveland, so as not to scare him off from engaging a ship to free the Washington slaves.

With many ties to the antislavery community in Philadelphia, Cleveland had probably already heard that the previous year a ship captain named Daniel Drayton had brought to safety a District slave woman and her children. Nothing was more natural than for Cleveland to seek him out and offer to pay for a voyage to Washington to transport another family to freedom. Because he was destitute, the waterman agreed.

Cleveland, along with his friend Salmon P. Chase of Ohio, was one of the founders of the Liberty Party and insisted that slavery was illegal in the nation's capital: "The constitution gives no power to Congress to establish slavery. . . . The act of Congress, therefore, that was framed to introduce slavery into the District of Columbia, was a plain, open, total violation of the constitution."[73] Cleveland's antislavery views were not popular in Philadelphia; they even caused him to lose a leadership position in the Philadelphia Bible Society.

Born in Massachusetts and educated at Dartmouth College, Cleveland taught at Dickinson College and the University of the City of New York before opening a girls' school in Philadelphia, where his aim was "enlarging the sphere of female education, and giving it a more vigorous tone." According to his son, his skill as a teacher was so great that "for twenty-five years, all the odium that his activity in the Anti-Slavery cause drew upon him did not for a moment abate the public confidence accorded to his professional power."[74] Cleveland was well known in antislavery circles. When Jacob Bigelow was trying to prove that he could be trusted to assist fugitives, he claimed that he was "known to Prof. C. D. Cleveland." Antislavery visitors from England called on him, and he was present when the box containing Henry Box Brown was opened. (Brown, a slave in Richmond, had himself boxed up and shipped to freedom in Philadelphia, a famous act of liberation.)[75]

Why Cleveland? It had to be a Philadelphian, since Drayton was in that city when a stranger approached him. It had to be someone with ties to the black community in order to have knowledge of Drayton's previous assistance to a Washington slave family. It had to be a person with some money at his disposal, though not a great deal. And it had to be someone who cared deeply about Drayton and his ill-fated expedition; only Cleveland manifested such an abiding concern. While the members of the crew of the *Pearl* were imprisoned, Cleveland alone among Philadelphians worked frantically to raise money for them, even printing, at his own expense, appeals for assistance. He was the only one who regularly gave money to Mrs. Drayton to relieve the family's destitution. For example, in the winter of 1849 he sent her a ton of coal and paid her rent. He urged New Yorkers to show more zeal on Drayton's behalf and provided money for Mrs. Drayton to go to Washington to see if she could help secure her husband's freedom.[76]

In 1849, when Daniel Drayton's future was very bleak, Cleveland concluded that he would take one last step to help the waterman. He gave permission to the ship captain "to state publicly all the knowledge that I [Cleveland] had of the expedition of the Pearl, & how much I had aided him." In other words, he was willing to forgo his anonymity and run the risk of imprisonment if it would help Drayton gain his freedom.[77]

Thus it seems that the chain of events leading to the disaster of the *Pearl* was set in motion by William Chaplin in Washington, moved ahead by Charles Cleveland in Philadelphia, and carried out by watermen Drayton and Sayres. Ever since 1848, writers, hampered by the participants' silence, have sought to explain how it came about. In general they have underestimated both the difficulty of the undertaking and the extent of the financing and planning required. The *Pearl* escape attempt was not a minor project but a major blow against slavery in the nation's capital. Had it succeeded, it would have sent shock waves throughout the country, proving to northerners and southerners alike the vulnerability of the slave system. Even its failure had great import for slavery in the nation's capital, as southerners clearly recognized.

Harriet Beecher Stowe set the pattern for explaining the origin of the attempted flight. She claimed that a Washington celebration of the French Revolution in 1848 had inspired the slaves to seek freedom; but when she wrote *A Key to "Uncle Tom's Cabin"*, she probably did not know about Chaplin's role in the escape attempt.[78] John Paynter, a descendant of the Edmondsons, wrote two accounts of the *Pearl*. The first, as has been noted, was printed in volume one of the *Journal of Negro History*, and was clearly a historical narrative. The second account was fiction, which Paynter clearly labeled "A Novel," indicating that he did not intend it to be read as serious history. In that fictional account, *The Fugitives of the* Pearl, Paynter followed Stowe in attributing importance to stirring oratories about liberty.[79] He explained the arrival of the *Pearl* by stating that Paul Jennings, who was Daniel Webster's coachman, met Drayton in Baltimore and arranged for the *Pearl* to come to the Potomac River. One should never ignore a family's oral tradition, and Jennings may well have been involved; he could have seen Drayton when the waterman visited Washington either late in February or early in March 1848. But Jennings was unlikely to have had enough money to hire a ship and a crew. Drayton himself said that a person he would not name approached him *in Philadelphia* and offered money to finance the voyage.[80]

Contrary to Stowe's and Paynter's suppositions, the arrival of the *Pearl* in Washington in the spring of 1848 was the result of extensive planning and considerable expense. Locating a ship for such a dangerous undertaking was not easy, for ship captains did not want to put their vessels in peril. Drayton, Sayres, and the cook Chester English had to be paid and money found to purchase supplies. Long before congressmen and senators, in April 1848, celebrated a revolution in France, Chaplin had been working on the problem of getting more than seventy slaves out of the District and into a free state. He had corresponded with his friend Charles Cleveland in Philadelphia and with Gerrit Smith in New York, all the while probably urging patience on the bondmen and bondwomen who told him how desperate they were to flee. Slaves did not need speeches to demonstrate the value of freedom; they knew it from lifelong experience. As a defender of Drayton wrote about the fugitives, "The love of liberty burned within their souls."[81]

CHAPTER THREE

MEN *of* EXTRAORDINARY COURAGE

Newspapers played an integral role in American life in the nineteenth century, such that when any group wanted to present a point of view to the public, it brought a new paper into existence. The men and women opposing slavery held widely differing views of the institution and how to end it. For that reason the first half of the nineteenth century saw the birth of a number of antislavery newspapers, each one offering its own approach to the problem of terminating human bondage in the United States.

The people editing and writing for antislavery papers chose the work because of a deep commitment to the cause. Charles Torrey had been a clergyman, William Chaplin was a lawyer, and Gamaliel Bailey, whom we will now consider, was a physician. They felt drawn to writing for newspapers in hopes of reaching a wide audience and persuading their readers of the correctness of their particular solution to the intractable problem of slavery.

Torrey and Chaplin belonged to the antislavery group that was largely dependent on the support of Gerrit Smith of upstate New York. Gamaliel Bailey would find his surest assistance in New York City, the home of Lewis Tappan, a wealthy merchant. The editors' dependence on patrons derived from the inability of antislavery papers to make a profit, though Bailey would eventually break that pattern with the paper that he established in Washington, the *National Era*.

With the advantage of hindsight, it is possible to see that the southern position regarding slavery was hardening; southerners were becoming increasingly defensive and determined to avoid any breach in the line dividing free states from slave. Thus for southerners the District held symbolic importance: ending slavery in the nation's capital, it was believed, would lead to its collapse in the rest of the country. Given the firmness of the southern attitude, why would anybody believe that an antislavery newspaper could serve a useful purpose in the nation's capital? Yet some evidently did. Gamaliel Bailey and his friends wanted to be sure that their view of slavery and the way to end it had a voice in Washington; to achieve that goal they would venture money, reputation, and even their lives. Both Bailey and his newspaper, the *National Era*, which proved to be highly successful, would become the focus of mob action in the wake of the *Pearl*'s capture.

For those anxious to see an antislavery paper in Washington, the proper approach to the South was reasoned argument, not harsh confrontation, vitriolic name-calling, or the incitement of slaves to flight or rebellion. According to Bailey, "The effect of . . . efforts . . . to run off slaves from the border States . . . is to precipitate them into the hopeless and cruel bondage of the sugar plantations of the South."[1] Therefore, Bailey and his paper would never encourage the escape of District slaves. But Washingtonians—or certainly some Washingtonians—did not believe him and welcomed an excuse to put an end to the irritating presence of an antislavery paper in the city. They could not or would not see the differences in the spectrum of northern opinions on how to deal with the southern institution. By 1848 southerners had convinced themselves that there was only one antislavery voice, that of William Lloyd Garrison and the *Liberator*.

The Garrisonian wing of the antislavery movement roundly condemned the United States, the Constitution, and the democratic process, urging that abolitionists should neither vote nor hold office. By contrast, the group to which Gamaliel Bailey belonged claimed the Constitution as the very means whereby human bondage could be ended. Bailey stated his position with clarity. He wanted "the peaceful abolition of slavery . . . by the voluntary action of the masters, or the power of a Constitutional Legislation, the slaves being at once permitted to choose their own homes." Members of the American and Foreign Anti-Slavery Society, with headquarters in New York City, and members of the Liberty Party, the first antislavery political party, had not given up on either political action or persuasion, many of them believing that they had a Christian duty to show southern slave owners the error of their ways.[2]

Gamaliel Bailey would yield to no one in his hatred of slavery, but he came to Washington determined to avoid violence, having learned firsthand the heavy price that it exacted. While living in Cincinnati, Ohio, in the 1830s, he had seen friends beaten almost to the point of death for their antislavery views and had himself endured threats of violence because he openly opposed slavery. In 1836, soon after going to work for the *Philanthropist*, an antislavery paper in Cincinnati, Bailey twice witnessed the destruction of its press, which happened again in 1841.[3] Since he plainly knew the perils of working on an antislavery paper in a border city (Cincinnati was probably as pro-southern as Washington), Bailey showed exceptional courage in taking on such a task in the nation's capital.

With the generous support of Lewis Tappan and other loyal backers, including Salmon P. Chase, a leader of the Liberty Party in Ohio, Bailey moved to Washington in 1846 and began work establishing his newspaper. He arranged for the press to be housed on Seventh Street between D and E streets, adjacent to the *National Intelligencer* and near the United States Patent Office — at that time one of the few imposing buildings in Washington. Eventually the Patent Office would fill the entire area from F Street to G and from Seventh to Ninth; but when Bailey arrived in the city, only the section facing F Street had been completed. (The National Portrait Gallery now occupies the F Street side of the building. The G Street side of the Patent Office, now the home of the National Museum of American Art, had not been constructed in 1848.) Visitors admired the Patent Office, but in general they found the rest of the city appallingly shabby.[4]

Bailey settled his family nearby, at the corner of Eighth and E streets, next door to Mayor William Seaton. With the prominent location of both his press and his home, the editor demonstrated his determination to assume an important place in the life of the city. Before long he was giving "brilliant" parties, though the Baileys had initially found it difficult to establish themselves socially — Mrs. Bailey claiming that she received only one caller during their first six months on E Street.[5]

When in January 1847 Bailey launched the *National Era*, it became the third paper then being published in the District; the others were the *National Intelligencer*, edited by Joseph Gales and Mayor Seaton and somewhat middle of the road with regard to slavery, and the *Daily Union*, edited by Thomas Ritchie and vehemently pro-southern. An excellent editor, blessed with a good-quality press, Bailey produced a lively, attractive paper. According to Russel B. Nye, "Bailey's *National Era*, perhaps the best of the group [of antislavery papers] by journalistic standards, was especially competent in its treatment of political and economic questions, while its literary department . . . was probably the best of any newspaper of the decade." [6]

Bailey was a trailblazer in the decisions he made about the *Era*, for he solicited poetry, essays, and fiction to enliven its pages. He deserves a prominent place in American literary history: by inviting Harriet Beecher Stowe to contribute to his paper, he helped to sponsor the creation of *Uncle Tom's Cabin*. He sent Stowe a check for $100 to encourage her to write for the *Era*. What she envisioned as "three or four numbers" became weekly installments running in the paper from June 5, 1851, until April 1, 1852. Bailey sent additional money as her story gained popularity and attracted subscribers to the paper. [7]

From the beginning, Bailey's approach to Washingtonians was conciliatory, for though he never departed from his antislavery position, he sought friendship with the other newspapermen in the city and with members of Congress. "Not only did he avoid harsh language, address slave holders as reasonable beings, and disavow federal action to abolish slavery in the South, he did not immediately make an issue of abolition in the District of Columbia. Instead he concentrated on finding a legal way of ending the slave trade in the capital." The editor of the *National Era* would not encourage a scheme such as Chaplin's.

Anybody paying attention to Bailey's life, however, would have noted that his home had become a center for those few members of Congress working to end human bondage. [8] Proslavery inhabitants of the city saw no reason to trust him; and when the *Pearl* fugitives returned from their ill-fated escape attempt, some people exploited the incident as an opportunity to be rid of the *Era*.

As recounted in the previous chapter, a mob threatened Daniel Drayton and Edward Sayres when the posse marched the captives up Seventh Street toward the center of town. Congressman Joshua Giddings believed that slave dealers were leading the crowd, and the at-

Joshua R. Giddings. (Courtesy of the Library of Congress)

tempt of a slaver to murder Drayton lends validity to his view. Even
after Drayton and Sayres were inside the jail, the mob tried to enter
the yard and lynch the prisoners. The crowd, which Giddings claimed
included members of the House of Representatives, milled around all
afternoon, cursing Drayton and Sayres, proclaiming "vengeance upon
every friend of liberty," and threatening violence against the antislavery
congressman. Friends sent notes to warn Giddings that he should take
the threat seriously, for the rioters were shouting out the address of his
boardinghouse on Capitol Hill. Although it was an open secret that

Giddings "fed and sheltered fugitives," it was his unending defense of freedom that infuriated proslavery forces in the District. The *Charleston Courier*, after reporting that the congressman had been "threatened and derided," added, "as he well deserved to be."[9]

Proslavery mobs in the North were active during the 1830s and 1840s; Leonard Richards, a historian of anti-abolition mobs, counted 115 incidents in the 1830s and sixty-four in the subsequent decade. Richards pointed out that "many city magistrates sympathized with the mobs—either entirely or partially—as long as the rioters confined their activities to destroying the property of abolitionists and Negroes." Their complacency was reinforced by the shortage of policemen and the fact that calling out the National Guard was "cumbersome."[10] Washington had been the scene of such an outbreak in 1835, the Snow riot, in which blacks suffered extensive damage to their property, and the mayor had had to call for military protection against the mob. Fortunately there had been no loss of life.[11] African Americans, having seen what a Washington mob could do, must have been concerned in 1848 that the crowd's fury would turn against them, but the mob ultimately found a different target: the *National Era*.

By late in the afternoon of April 18, 1848, even the most determined troublemakers had to admit that they were not going to get into the jail, but they were having too much fun to go home. Urban unrest had entertainment value; it provided a welcome break in the monotony of having uninteresting jobs in a city that offered few opportunities for recreation. According to Richards, although members of the power structure supported proslavery riots, they themselves did not throw the rocks or carry the torches to set fires; the town's bully boys did that. It is likely that many of the men and boys milling around the Washington jail that April afternoon had never even read the *Era*, and no one knows who shouted, "Let's get the *Era!*" Giddings thought it was slavers. Whoever it was, the troublemakers responded enthusiastically to the instigator and set off for F Street. Drayton claimed that members of the posse that captured the *Pearl* had said that "the abolition press must be stopped." Indiana congressman William W. Wick said that Bailey chose the District of Columbia for his paper "on purpose to be mobbed, and demolished, so as to excite sympathy, and force abolition principles . . . upon the people of the northern States."[12]

Although Washington was called the city of magnificent distances, in 1848 the populated part of the city was small. Moving from Seventh

Street, where they tried to lynch Drayton and Sayres, to Pennsylvania Avenue, where they caused the prisoners to take refuge in a hackney coach, to the jail at Fourth and G streets, and then to the newspaper office on Seventh, the members of the mob needed to spend relatively little time or energy. And if "drunken rowdies" stopped off at bars to refresh themselves, it made for an exciting and not too strenuous day and night. During the presidency of Andrew Jackson, the nation's capital was estimated to have one drinking establishment for every ninety inhabitants,[13] and there is no reason to believe that any had since closed for lack of customers.

When it reached the office of the *Era*, the mob, encountering no resistance, began to throw stones at the building. They broke windows and blinds and may have smashed a door before John H. Goddard, captain of the Auxiliary Guard and the Night Watch, arrived with members of his small force. He said that the leaders were "worthless slave-traders," and former Ohio congressman Edward Stowe Hamlin, now the editor of the Cleveland *Daily True Democrat*, claimed that "one of the owners of the slave-pen of the district was there, urging the mob on to violence." A Treasury Department clerk, leading the attack, "fortunately received a wound on the head" from a stone thrown by one of the troublemakers. A member of Congress heard that the marines were being held in readiness in case of serious trouble, but in fact the military was not put on alert. A heavy April shower discouraged further action, and reports of a fire elsewhere in the city provided an alternative diversion. By midnight the troublemakers had dispersed, but not before agreeing to meet the next night.[14]

Threats and violence could not intimidate Congressman Giddings; they probably stimulated him to more active attempts to avert the crisis. Early the following morning—Wednesday, the nineteenth—he decided to go to the jail, assure the prisoners of his sympathy, and promise them legal assistance. He hoped for the companionship of John Parker Hale, an antislavery senator from New Hampshire, but when Hale was not available, Giddings moved on to the office of the *National Era* to confer with editor Bailey. There he saw "the broken window-blinds and windows" that resulted from the previous night's attack.[15]

On hearing that Giddings was on his way to the jail, the editor urged him not to expose himself to unnecessary danger. Undeterred by Bailey's plea and by visual evidence of the mob's violence, Giddings pressed on and found a colleague in Edward Stowe Hamlin, and together they walked to the jail.[16]

The mob, numbering thirty or forty, was there before them. Although Giddings identified himself as a member of the House of Representatives, the jailer was reluctant to admit the two men. Was it because of Giddings's antislavery reputation or the threatening gestures of the troublemakers? The jailer finally let Giddings and Hamlin into the jail yard, which was crowded with the fugitives, slave traders, hangers-on, and curiosity seekers; the two men had to push their way through. According to Giddings, the crowd at the jail was made up "principally of slave-dealers, from Baltimore, Richmond, Alexandria, Annapolis," and Washington, who had come to purchase the fugitives. "Like the offensive buzzards gathering around disgusting carrion, these cormorants had gathered around the slave-breeders, who claimed to own the children and mothers confined in that slave-market." It was, said Giddings, "this mass of moral putridity which constituted the mob at the prison."[17]

Once inside the jail, the congressman and the former congressman passed through a gate, which the jailer locked after they entered; they went up a flight of stairs and then through a second gate, also locked behind them. Although the jailer had let them into the jail, he would not permit them to enter the prisoners' cells; they had to talk to Drayton and Sayres through the grating in the doors.

After identifying himself, Congressman Giddings assured the prisoners that they would not suffer a lynching and that they would have a regular trial with their legal rights protected. Hamlin himself offered to serve as their counsel, since Giddings would be busy in Congress. The prisoners "had been in great distress, not knowing their fate; and on hearing the voice of friendship and kindness, they were melted to tears."[18] In spite of the kind words, the prisoners could not have been reassured when the mob interrupted their conversation. Having gained access to the inner stairway of the jail by getting possession of the key, the troublemakers bounded up the stairs and demanded that Giddings leave at once or "his life would be in danger."[19]

The congressman would not be intimidated and refused to leave the jail until he had completed his conversation. After a loud argument between the jailer and the intruders, the custodian finally persuaded the crowd to retreat down the stairs, but he warned the congressman and the former congressman that he could not guarantee their safety.

Again assuring the prisoners of their concern, Giddings and Hamlin descended the stairs. There they found themselves in the middle of a "dense and highly enraged" crowd, "uttering profane imprecations" against Giddings and "all abolitionists." A way opened, however, and they left the jail without suffering any physical harm; Giddings went on to Capitol Hill, where he found his friends understandably worried.[20]

The slavers and their supporters appeared to be in control of Washington. The jailer could not guarantee the safety of a member of Congress even inside the jail, and the editor of a Washington paper knew that threats against him were not idle: broken windows were only a prelude to promised attacks on subsequent nights. Giddings and Hamlin, true to their word, retained a lawyer for the prisoners, and soon David A. Hall arrived at the jail. He and Hamlin, he told the men, would appear as their counsel "at the examination at one o'clock." Hall, born in Vermont and proud of his Yankee background, moved to Washington to study and then to practice law, where he was notably successful. His reputation was that of being a "strong anti-slavery man," willing to assist the slave smugglers Torrey and Smallwood but unwilling to "affiliate with the abolitionists."[21]

Philip Barton Key, the district attorney for Washington, arriving at the jail at the same time as Hall, warned him that he had better leave at once, since "the people outside were furious, and he ran the risk of his life." Had they come to the point, asked Hall, where a lawyer could not safely consult with his client? He did not leave. Meanwhile, the owners of the slaves began to arrive to claim their property.[22] Two justices of the peace came to the jail and held court there, with Hall as counsel for the defendants. Each man was recommitted to jail, on a charge of stealing slaves, with bail so excessive that freedom was impossible. Now it looked as if the prisoners would either spend the rest of their lives in jail or be murdered by a mob.

Gamaliel Bailey was also vulnerable. He knew that he, his newspaper, and his family were in danger. The previous night (the eighteenth), the crowd had dispersed after agreeing to reconvene the following night. The mayor of Washington, William Seaton, and Walter Lenox, the president of the board of aldermen, became increasingly alarmed at the prospect of greater violence and asked Bailey to issue a statement denying any connection with the *Pearl*. Having agreed to do so, he was unable to accompany Giddings to the jail on the morning of the nineteenth because he was composing a public disclaimer.[23]

Addressing the letter "To the Citizens of Washington," Bailey reminded his readers that when he began publication in 1847, he had stated that he would never advocate violence, and he assured them that he had not changed his stance. He had stayed away from "invective and denunciation," appealing rather to "the reason, the conscience, the patriotism and sense of honor of the slaveholders." Bailey believed that it was hardly necessary for him to affirm that he had nothing to do with the escape attempt, but he wanted to inform Washingtonians unfamiliar with his point of view that he would never "take part in any movement which would involve the necessity of strategy or trickery of any kind."

Bailey was convinced that slavery could be ended through the use of persuasion, the Constitution, and the law. Nevertheless, he wrote, "if illegal violence be inflicted upon me for writing and printing freely about slavery, or any other subject which it may suit an American citizen to discuss, then will I suffer cheerfully, in the confident hope that when passion and prejudice shall have been dispelled, justice will be done to my character." Bailey's statement appeared as a flyer to be circulated throughout the city and as a column in the *Intelligencer*, but it had no effect, either because it did not reach many people or because the troublemakers were not interested in a defense of any antislavery point of view. Giddings believed that the *Daily Union*, the District's proslavery, pro-southern newspaper, encouraged the mob.[24]

As night fell on April 19, an "immense crowd" began to gather outside the *Era* building but soon moved on to the Patent Office, where "a massive Doric portico" with "a broad and lofty flight of steps" offered a convenient platform for anyone wishing to harangue the throng. The assemblage completely blocked F Street. So far as Bailey could tell, there were "multitudes of boys, and many strangers from adjoining counties in Maryland and Virginia, who knew nothing of the paper save from vague report." The *New York Herald* claimed that the crowd was made up of young men and boys out for a "frolic," and the *Charleston Courier* was pleased to declare that they were engaging in "a respectable soiree." Others had more serious matters in mind, and Congressman John Gorham Palfrey believed that the night of April 19 was a dangerous time.[25]

Estimates of the number of people on F Street that night vary from 1,500 to 3,000 or 4,000. As the throng grew, city leaders mounted the wings of the Patent Office steps and began to speak. President Walter Lenox of the board of aldermen led off, reminding the crowd that he was a native of the District and that he thought it better to use law than force. Someone in the crowd called out, "It's too late!" No, said Lenox, it was not too late to preserve their reputation as good citizens. But the crowd shouted, "Down with the *Era*!" Well, said Lenox, if they destroyed the newspaper buildings, the city would have to pay damages. "Damn the expense!" shouted one man in the crowd.[26]

The crowd began to call for E. B. Robinson, a printer and a popular figure in the city; his remarks were much more pleasing to the mob than Lenox's had been. "The feelings of the public [have] been outraged," "an insult [has] been offered to the community," the *Era* should have been declared a nuisance and forced to leave town. The crowd became increasingly noisy and excited, shouting repeatedly, "Down with the *Era*!" Robinson declared that "these moderate scoundrels are the worst kind of scoundrels," and the crowd thought that very funny. Robinson would give Bailey only until the following day to leave town, and he ended his speech with the inflammatory statement: "If the law will not protect us, we must take the remedy into our own hands." More cries of "Down with the *Era*!"

This was a crowd very fond of speeches, threatening violence but enjoying the oratory, such as it was. Had they come out for a night's entertainment? Was the mob's bark worse than its bite? Instead of rushing down Seventh Street to set fire to the *Era*'s office and press, they called for Daniel Ratcliffe, a Washington lawyer, whose office was nearby at Eighth and E streets.[27] He mounted the steps of the Patent Office and proposed delay: they should all go home, come back on Friday, and in the meantime "deliberate." The crowd responded with shouts of "Tear down the office now!" and "It's too late!" Ratcliffe then asked if they would do the deed in the dark of night, to which someone called out, "The moon is shining." They were in a much better humor than when attacking the jail; perhaps the influence of the hard-core troublemakers had been diluted by people less involved in the issue of slavery.

But no matter how good humored they might have been, they were intent on destruction. Ratcliffe, known for his southern sympathies,[28] agreed that Washingtonians had reason to feel "aggrieved," for, said the lawyer, "if the mad schemes of deluded people are persevered in, our houses may be given to the flames." At which the crowd shouted, "Apply the flames to the *Era*." There was a temporary diversion when shouts went up of "Let Baker out! Release Baker!"—referring to a drunk who had been arrested earlier in the day in front of the *Era*. Ignoring that, Ratcliffe continued to urge that everybody go home.

Finally the moderate leaders of the city persuaded the crowd that the proper way to handle the matter was to choose a committee to wait on Bailey at his home about a block away and issue an ultimatum. Ratcliffe read off possible names, a list that obviously had been prepared well beforehand. Some names the crowd approved, others they rejected; when the name Boyle was read, someone shouted, "That's good, he's an Irishman, and hates Negroes." In the 1840s Irish immigrants, moving into American cities in large numbers, competed with African Americans, both slave and free, for low-wage jobs. "A deadly hatred resulted which constantly manifested itself in quarreling and fighting between the two groups." With Ratcliffe leading the way, the committee, five from each ward plus Georgetown and Tenleytown, (outlying parts of the District), walked over to Bailey's house, where the editor came out to meet them. Bailey's friends and neighbors were sufficiently alarmed that they rushed to his house and carried his children next door to Mayor Seaton's.[29]

A bystander named John Smith claimed that he took full notes of the encounter "without the knowledge of any of the parties,"[30] providing a transcript of the remarkable encounter. Ratcliffe, assuming the role of spokesman, told the editor about the session on F Street, which was surely unnecessary, for Bailey could easily hear the noise from his house. According to the lawyer, there was dangerous excitement in the city because of the attacks on Washington property (he was referring to the slaves), and the citizens had decided that since Bailey's press represented a threat to the community, it had to go. "We have therefore waited upon you," said Ratcliffe, "for the purpose of inquiring whether you are prepared to remove your press by ten o'clock to-morrow morning, and we beseech you, as you value the peace of this District, to accede to our request." As he was speaking, there were loud shouts from the Patent Office.

Bailey replied equally courteously that he was sure they meant no harm to him, but they were demanding from him "the surrender of a great constitutional right." How could they ask this of him? Ratcliffe, who after all was a lawyer, admitted the truth of Bailey's statement, but he insisted that it was the newspaperman's duty as a good citizen to take his press and leave town.

A committee member who had been a leader of the posse that pursued the *Pearl* seconded the lawyer's appeal, saying that he primarily wanted to avoid violence: "The prisoners were in my hands, but I would not allow my men to inflict any punishment on them." According to him, the only way to prevent violence now was to report to the waiting crowd that Bailey would leave town.

Bailey responded by asking if there were any on the committee who would, by acceding to the demands of a mob, give up their rights as American citizens. Oh yes, they knew it would be a great sacrifice, but it would ease the tension in the city. Bailey too wanted peace; he had taken no steps to protect either his home or his office, and now all he could do was "appeal to the good sense and intelligence of the community." He stood on his rights as an American citizen, expecting the law to protect him. Ratcliffe, aware that he had to report back to the noisy crowd at the Patent Office, insisted that Bailey give him a direct answer: Would he remove his press from Washington the next day? No, he would not, though he would offer no resistance: "The press is there—it is undefended—you can do as you think proper."

Still another committee member warned the editor that if trouble followed, he would be responsible. This shifting of blame onto Bailey went on for some time, with members of the committee insisting that whatever happened would be his fault. The entire community was against Bailey, said one man, while another reminded him that once a mob started destroying property, nobody could tell where they would stop. Ratcliffe summed up by advising Bailey to agree to leave the city: "The people think that your press endangers their property and their lives, and they have appointed us to tell you so and ask you to remove it tomorrow. If you say that you will do so, they will retire satisfied. If you refuse they say they will tear it [the press] down."

In the course of this strange committee meeting, Bailey's eighty-year-old father came to the door and began remonstrating with the people in the front of the house. The younger Bailey urged his father not to be angry, for they were only doing what the crowd had required them to do. Then he turned back to the committee and gave his last word: "I cannot surrender my right. Were I to die for it, I cannot surrender my rights! Tell those who sent you hither that my press and my house are undefended—they must do as they see proper. I maintain my rights and make no resistance!"[31] Ratcliffe and his committee returned to the Patent Office, where the mob had been waiting more or less quietly. It is difficult to gauge the mood of the F Street crowd, for while they seemed intent on destroying the newspaper, they had been easily diverted by the proposal to form a committee. And yet nobody seems to have had any inclination to go home. Pete Hutchins, a drunken former bailiff, mounted the steps of the Patent Office and addressed the crowd, though his voice was so thick and husky that no one could understand what he said. At one point he declared that he "would break somebody's head, if they didn't stop pulling his coat tail," at which the crowd began to yell, "Down with Hutchins" and "You're a damn fool," and pushed him off the steps. One of the boys in the crowd grabbed his hat; he shook his stick at the youngsters, who began to race around, while the men chatted among themselves.[32]

In some ways it appeared to be a relatively good-natured crowd — after all, the *New York Herald* called it a frolic. Yet its purpose was the destruction of the *Era*, and it generated an atmosphere of menace. In front of the newspaper office, a member of the mob approached the correspondent of the *Boston Whig* and demanded to know whether he was an abolitionist. When the journalist answered that he was, the man declared, "We intend to hang every d——d one of you." The *Whig* correspondent responded by raising his cane, but a bystander intervened and urged him to leave before there was trouble, for the crowd had "marked" him. But he did not leave and was able to stay until midnight without further trouble.[33]

At the same location Congressman John I. Slingerland of New York remarked to a friend that he was opposed to the action of the mob. A bystander, overhearing, demanded to know whether the congressman was an abolitionist. "I am," said Slingerland, "and what are you going to do about it?" Slingerland started to pull off his coat to get ready for combat and then, raising his hickory cane, exclaimed, "If you wish to save your skull, you'd better move out of my way." Slingerland's friend intervened, warning him that other members of the mob were eyeing him, but the New York congressman refused to be intimidated. He stayed to watch the proceedings of the entire evening. He wished that there had been a Napoleon there to give the mob "a lesson with grape and cannister!" On the other hand, Senator James D. Westcott of Florida, also present at the "large assemblage" on F Street, said that he had heard indignation expressed but no threats of violence.[34]

After the committee's meeting with Bailey, Ratcliffe once again climbed up on the wing of the steps of the Patent Office and reported to the waiting crowd that Bailey had been very respectful but had talked of "constitutional rights," at which there were hisses. But cheers rang out when the lawyer said that he had told the editor that it was too late for that. On hearing that Bailey would promise nothing, the mob rushed toward the office of the *Era*, shouting, "Down with the *Era!*" and "Get the office!" They paused when they saw that Captain Goddard of the Night Watch and fewer than a dozen officers had positioned themselves in front of the building. Although voices cried out, "Fire it!" and "Down with it!" and there were sounds of glass breaking, Goddard stood firm and warned that it would be worse than when the British took Washington if the mob tried to burn the *Era*. "The mob swayed to and fro, and shouted wildly and fiercely," but Goddard and his few men refused to move.

The members of the Night Watch were supposed to wear gray uniforms with brass buttons bearing the letters AG for Auxiliary Guard, and their gray caps were decorated with the same letters. They would have looked impressive in their attractive uniforms. But in fact the watch probably had no uniforms in 1848, for Congress did not appropriate money for them until ten years later. The bully boys hesitated to rush the watch, whose weapons were lethal. The members of the guard did not carry guns but were armed with "spontoons," clubs two feet long and an inch and a quarter thick, with an iron spear attached to the end, reputedly of a design carried by sergeants in the British army.[35]

District Attorney Philip Barton Key came on the scene at this moment of confrontation. Mounting a horse trough in front of the building, he tried to speak, but the crowd was so noisy and excited that he could not make himself heard. Eventually, according to the *New-York Tribune*, they calmed down enough to hear him attack "the lawless spirit" of the mob in an attempt to shame them into giving up; apparently some "skulked off ashamed." The correspondent of the *Richmond Enquirer* claimed that Key then "pledged himself to see the nuisance [the *National Era*] removed from this city."

There were still many people in the street, and speeches continued, including a government clerk making "coarse and vulgar" remarks. But he was not brave enough to face Captain Goddard and called on his followers to wait until the next night. He would meet them at the same place at five o'clock the following evening and lead them against the enemy. Now, he said, he was off for home, and hundreds followed him. In a few minutes the street was empty, and quiet descended on the city.[36]

It is impossible to avoid the conclusion that nobody really cared if some antislavery supporters got roughed up or even that newspaper-man Bailey might be driven out of town, as long as it could be done without setting the city on fire. But it became clear to thoughtful Washingtonians that, if and when the attack began, others besides antislavery enthusiasts might get hurt. Alderman Lenox and Captain Goddard issued a handbill to be widely circulated, calling for peace and quiet in the city.[37]

The Washington leadership too was taking seriously the threat to the *Era*. On Thursday morning, April 20, Elisha Whittlesey, a former congressman from Ohio, and Cave Johnson, the postmaster general, called on President James K. Polk in order to report "great excitement" in the city. The two men told Polk that a serious riot probably would occur that night and asked him to use the power of his office to prevent trouble. In his diary Polk made plain where his sympathies lay: "The outrage committed by stealing or seducing the slaves from their owners, and the attempt of abolitionists to defend the White men who had perpetrated it, had produced the excitement & the threatened violence on the abolition press."

Polk was prepared to cooperate with the city authorities to maintain peace and quiet. He called together the members of his cabinet and told them "to issue an order to the Clerks & other employees in their respective Departments not to engage in the unlawful or riotous proceeding which was anticipated." He then met with Deputy Marshal William R. Woodward,[38] Captain Goddard (who must have been exhausted by this time), Walter Lenox of the board of aldermen, and six members of the city council. In their presence President Polk told Marshal Woodward that though he should "aid the City authorities in suppressing any outbreak such as was apprehended," the president cautioned him "to avoid violence or the shedding of blood, unless in self-defence & the discharge of his lawful duties." Polk believed it unnecessary to call out the militia or the army, and he claimed that the city fathers agreed with him.[39]

By April 20 some of the steam had gone out of the demonstrators. Perhaps they were tired; perhaps the slave traders had looked over the merchandise and bought what they wanted; perhaps more sensible Washingtonians found the increasing police power intimidating. In any case, on the evening of the twentieth the crowd understandably "showed no symptoms of a disposition to violence" when they confronted "seventy-five to a hundred" peace officers posted around the *Era*. It is hard to know where all the officers came from, since in 1846 there were only thirteen police constables in the city. Captain Goddard must have deputized many citizens in order to make up so large a force. A considerable number of Treasury clerks were out on F Street "to act as conservators of law and order" and to have a good time. They had cheered when Secretary Robert J. Walker, at the instigation of the president, had asked for their help.[40]

A correspondent of the *New York Herald* objected bitterly to President Polk's use of government employees to keep order in the city. "What right had the President to dictate a line of conduct to those in the employ of the departments? Is he commander-in-chief of the clerks, as well as of the army and navy?" He wondered if this showed Polk's "lust for power."[41] More likely it showed the president's recognition of the weakness of the peace keeping forces in the District.

It turned out, however, that the crowd was not as peaceable as it appeared, for after the police and the clerks had gone home, about 200 men, having settled on a strategy earlier in the day, slipped quietly down to E Street and called Bailey to come out. When the editor appeared, the crowd's designated speaker told him that they had come to tar and feather him before destroying his press. Agreeing to hear Bailey's defense prior to setting to work, the crowd listened politely and some men even applauded the editor. The leader, infuriated, turned on them and shouted, "What have you to say? you don't own any niggers." This resulted in a "disputation." Lawyer Ratcliffe happening by, he urged the men to adjourn, which they did, leaving a quiet street.

It appears that social and economic stress played a role in the mob's action in the District. On the previous night the rioters had been loud in commenting on the apparently well-known conflict over employment between African Americans and Irish immigrants. Now a "disputation" had taken place over who had a right to express an opinion on matters related to slavery. Their leader, seeming to lose control of his followers, angrily indicated that only those owning slaves had a right to speak out on the matter. Rioting released tension: not only did it provide a welcome break in monotony; it also gave powerless men an opportunity to assert themselves. Maybe some of the crowd confronting Bailey decided they were on the wrong side, that supporting slave owners was not in their interest, for the leader's remark "was resented."[42] In any event, the city's leaders decided that the time had come to put an end to the trouble before it got out of hand.

The unrest had finally come to a halt, and there were many in the District who congratulated themselves for the restoration of order. How well they had handled the disturbance, how cooperative President Polk had been, how brave Captain Goddard and the guard had proven themselves! The board of aldermen and the common council adopted a resolution thanking President Polk for "his prompt and efficient co-operation with the authorities of this Corporation in maintaining the peace of our city." Even emancipationist Lewis Tappan, Bailey's chief supporter, noted President Polk's concern with containing the riot and rejoiced that "freedom of the press" had been "most signally sustained at Washington."[43] It was possible to claim that there had not really been a riot because nobody had been seriously hurt, and the city had gone about the important business of selling runaways and indicting the captain and crew of the *Pearl*, unaffected by troublemakers.

The *New York Herald* praised Captain Goddard and his men for their handling of the crowd, "that hydra-headed monster, which, under the pretext of public indignation, so often finds occasion for the exercise of its vulgar and lawless propensities." The police had shown energy in responding to "an irresponsible mob," though the paper made plain its lack of sympathy for Drayton and Sayres, suggesting that the two watermen had planned to carry the fugitives off to Brazil for sale. The *Herald* also congratulated the slaveholding and property-holding citizens of the District for the way they had acted "under the exasperation which this bold invasion of the slave stealers awakened." On the other hand, a Washingtonian chastised himself for cowardice: "We good citizens, held ourselves ready to be walked over by the mob, for three successive nights, if they chose to do it."[44]

Congressman Slingerland believed that a gang of "ruffians" was meeting in a local hotel, planning further trouble. The *Liberator* in Boston reported that "the jail is constantly watched by men who have nothing to do with it, but who are determined that none of the prisoners shall ever go acquitted." The *Emancipator*, also in Boston, refused to praise the chief executive.[45]

Even though the *Sun* of Baltimore had proslavery sympathies, it did not regard mob action as lightly as did the *New York Herald*. How dare those troublemakers appoint a committee to tell Bailey he had to leave Washington! By what authority did they assume the right to run the city? It was, in the *Sun*'s view, a dangerous precedent to allow an "illegal assemblage" to call on an American citizen "to vacate the premises he occupies, abandon his business, and go forth [out] of the city, an outcast of the people." The *Sun* called it unjust, unpardonable, and inexcusable to permit such an action in the nation's capital.[46] But the Baltimore paper was barely heard amid the rejoicing that a moment of crisis had been so quickly resolved.

Within the District, the *Intelligencer* wrote that thanks to "the firmness of the order-loving People of Washington, the few irresponsible evil spirits who would have cast a stigma on the well-established character of our law-abiding community have been indignantly rebuked and frowned down." A Washingtonian reproached the Baltimore paper for criticizing his city: "Property and life are better protected here [in the District] than anywhere; and in no city in the country would Congress be as safe as in this."[47]

In summing up the April events, editor Bailey, having survived the crisis, emphasized that Washington was the capital of the entire nation. If anarchy ruled, the disgrace would extend throughout the country. "If it were once ascertained that the Freedom of the Press could not exist here, the whole nation would be implicated in the violation of the great Constitutional guaranty of this Freedom."

Bailey was happy to reprint editorials from around the country, including even southern newspapers, commending Washingtonians for avoiding serious violence and preserving press freedom. But the *Charleston Mercury* warned that the *National Era* used its "moderate tone" to calm the community, while Bailey, busily hatching "mischief," was, in fact, "in the position of a foreign enemy, creeping about under disguises, and demanding for malice and treachery the protection due to honesty and good faith."[48]

Bailey's difficulties in those stressful April days revealed the factionalism in antislavery ranks. Gerrit Smith, William Chaplin's patron, wrote to Lewis Tappan, Bailey's chief supporter, attacking Bailey for "*cowardly and heartless disclaimers and utterances* at the time of the sad failure of the Pearl enterprise." William Lloyd Garrison was equally unsympathetic. According to the *Liberator*, the District editor showed too much "prudence" in assuring Washingtonians that he would not publish anything too "excitingly" antislavery. In Garrison's eyes, Bailey was "muzzling" the *Era* and failing in loyalty to liberty of the press. But then, as Lewis Tappan said, "Dr. Bailey is never ultra." [49]

The *National Anti-Slavery Standard*, published in New York, launched a bitter attack on editor Bailey, praising Congressman Giddings for defending Drayton and Sayres and contrasting his bravery with Bailey's actions: "We appreciate entirely the difficulty of a man who is confronted by a mob; we understand the delicacy of his position, and how much depends on his moderation and calmness; but it seems to us, if Dr. Bailey had ventured to show some sympathy for these poor creatures, and had defended their inalienable right to run away from Slavery, at the same time that he published his apologetic card to the citizens of Washington, nobody would have blamed him." Bailey should be ashamed that a Washington mob found him deserving of no worse punishment than "the smashing of a few panes of glass, and shouting, for two or three nights, 'down with the Era!' without putting it down." According to the *Standard*, "these are times when not to be thought worthy of some degree of persecution, is a proof of the highest degree of moral cowardice." [50]

A week later the *Standard* poked fun at Bailey, saying how surprising it was that a Washington mob would even suspect him "of so manly an impulse as a participation in that flight [of slaves] would imply." If the *Era* were a true antislavery paper, it "could not exist there [in Washington] for a week." The *Standard* probably was not aware that William Lloyd Garrison had made serious efforts to establish an antislavery paper in the District of Columbia, turning to Boston only when he could not find funding for his Washington plans. [51] Much of the country expressed satisfaction at the avoidance of more serious trouble; the only antislavery voices that deplored Bailey's actions were far from Washington.

Southerners and southern sympathizers liked to refer to discussions about slavery as "delicate." The *Daily Union*, Washington's proslavery newspaper, attacked Giddings and his friends for "incessant and impertinent intermeddling with the most delicate question in our social relations." [52] What did this mean? The treatment of slaves was never itself "delicate," the institution having been built on power and profitability, where delicacy of any kind was irrelevant. It was only southern ears and eyes that were delicate, disinclined to listen to accounts of the reality of the southern institution. Proslavery Washingtonians hated and feared Bailey's paper not because it incited violence, for it never did, but because it wrote about slavery as it was and showed southerners the necessity of ending human bondage.

Many members of Congress and pro-southern Washingtonians were probably delighted to see troublemakers running around the city, throwing rocks and bricks, making a lot of noise, even threatening antislavery members of Congress and the antislavery newspaper. The *New-York Tribune*'s Washington correspondent reported that "the more sober opinion of the community here is this: that the spirit of illegal violence . . . has been fed and stimulated by the speeches . . . of Southern Members of Congress," one congressman publicly declaring that the mob would have been justified in hanging Drayton and Sayres "without examination and without trial."[53] Those members of Congress did not want a full-scale riot, however, for that would attract too much attention and maybe imperil southern control of the city, which remained unchanged. A grand jury in the District refused to indict any of the troublemakers.[54]

In the end there was no major physical damage, though if Gamaliel Bailey and Joshua Giddings had not been men of extraordinary courage, the *Era*'s press might have been destroyed and a member of Congress beaten up. Riots have a way of getting out of hand. In this instance the city grew quiet after a few days, the *Era* would not be threatened again until 1850, and it appeared that slavery and the slave trade in the District could continue as before.

The CHAPLAIN *and the* SLAVER

On the evening of April 21, 1848, John I. Slingerland, the member of Congress from near Albany, New York, who was present at the Patent Office on the first night of the near-rioting, was walking past the railroad station at the foot of Capitol Hill in Washington. He happened to see a crowd of blacks standing around the train. They were in great distress, weeping and lamenting their sad fate, and the congressman soon learned that fifty slaves, most of them *Pearl* fugitives, were being put on the cars bound for Baltimore, where they would be shipped off to the Deep South. (It required less than two hours by train to go from Washington to Baltimore.) If Slingerland had ever had any doubts about the cruelty of slavery, they came to an end as he watched between 100 and 200 relatives and friends bidding farewell to those they knew they would never see again. Hope H. Slatter, a Baltimore slave trader, was directing guards "with large canes in their hands" as they loaded their cargo on the cars and prevented relatives from approaching. One man, perhaps Daniel Bell, begged to see his wife, protesting that she was free and was being held illegally. When he climbed up to the window to speak to her, Slatter knocked him away.[1]

As Slingerland stood observing this appalling scene, Henry Slicer, chaplain of the Senate, appeared with members of his family, who were also on their way to Baltimore. Chaplain Slicer and slave trader Slatter, friends from Baltimore, greeted each other with enthusiasm and engaged in animated conversation, while the New Yorker looked on in disbelief. He was encountering slavery at its absolute worst: the wanton destruction of family ties, the condemnation of innocents to early death in the Deep South, the punishment of slaves solely because of their wish to be free. For Slingerland this sense of horror was enhanced by the thoughtless cruelty of the chaplain of the Senate, a religious leader in the nation's capital. Hope Slatter's name was already a synonym for inhumanity and for the systematic exploitation of the commercial aspects of slavery. As those two men, both connected with the Methodist Church, chatted in the railroad car, apparently indifferent to the suffering around them, the congressman understood the wrath that abolitionists directed at Christian churches, their pastors, and their parishioners.

Henry Slicer, born in Annapolis in 1801, was licensed as a preacher in the Methodist Episcopal Church when he was twenty and soon became known as an effective revivalist. Three years after becoming a minister, he began serving as chaplain at the Washington Navy Yard, rapidly assumed positions of leadership within his denomination, and in 1837 became chaplain of the United States Senate. He was reelected in 1846 and 1853, demonstrating his political skills and the influence of the Methodist Church among members of the Senate. In the 1840s the Methodist Episcopal Church "was the largest religious body in a country that still drew many of its values from the Christian religion." Slicer is credited with assisting in the passage of antidueling laws. He participated in the growth of Sunday schools, which were segregated in both Baltimore and Washington, and was a leader in the temperance movement, attacking "beer, wine, and even *hard cider*." [2]

Slicer's was an important voice in the Methodist Episcopal Church. When a delegation of more than a hundred of his fellow preachers called on President Polk to voice support for the Mexican War, it was Slicer who performed the introductions; he and Polk had been friends for many years. At the time of the encounter at the train station, Slicer was pastor of Dumbarton Church in Georgetown. When a report of the Slicer-Slatter encounter was published, Slicer's name became, at least for a while, a synonym for hypocrisy in religion, one antislavery newspaper naming him "the priest of proslavery." [3]

According to Slingerland, slave trader Slatter was standing in the middle of the railroad car, directing the placement of his newly acquired property, the men, but not the women, "ironed together." When Slicer boarded the train, he "took his brother Methodist by the hand, chatted with him for a short time, and seemed to view the heart-rending scene before him with as little concern as we would look upon cattle!" Slicer also knew one of the slaves, who might have been a parishioner of his, and shook hands with him, too.

The train moved off, carrying its varied cargo, and Slingerland hurried to write a searing letter about what he had seen, a letter that appeared in almost every antislavery newspaper in the country. In graphic detail he recounted the blatant hypocrisy of the chaplain of the Senate shaking hands with a slave dealer, while slaves bade tearful farewells to friends and family from whom they would be forever severed. Slingerland believed that Slicer had come to the station on purpose to watch the removal of the slaves: "I know not whether he came with a view to sanctify the act, or pronounce the parting blessing: but this I do know, that he justifies slavery." Slingerland claimed that Slicer, in his position as Senate chaplain, would "ask the blessing of heaven upon the army, navy, and the work of bloodshed in Mexico, but never a word does he utter against . . . the abominations going on under his own eye daily," though many of the slaves sold "for the Southern market" were Methodists. He speculated that Slicer had furnished the slave trader with "testimonials of their religious character, to render the sale more profitable," testimonials to be read aloud on the day they went on the market.[4]

If antislavery supporters had been horrified by the failure of the *Pearl*, this was as nothing to what they felt when they read of its aftermath: the destruction of families and the impotence of slaves to prevent total disaster, while the chaplain of the Senate appeared to give religious support to the actions of Slatter, the slave dealer. Slingerland wrote: "Oh, what a revolting scene to a feeling heart, and what a retribution awaits the actors. Will not the [slaves'] wailings of anguish reach the ears of the Most High?"[5]

When Chaplain Slicer read the letter, he was appalled. What had he done to deserve such an attack? Immediately he sat down and wrote a letter of defense, requesting all the papers that had printed the Slingerland letter to carry his reply. He wrote, he said, out of a sense of duty to the Methodist Episcopal Church, which he had served for more than twenty-five years. He was at the railroad station to see his wife and children off on the train to Baltimore and not, as Slingerland had made it appear, to demonstrate approval of Slatter's actions as a slave trader. He had not known that Slatter was in Washington or that the *Pearl* slaves would be on the train; he thought that local dealers had bought all of them.

Once he was at the station, Slicer felt obligated to inquire about "a brother Methodist" named Henry who had been on the *Pearl*. Henry had insisted on being sold—that was why he was on the train—and Slicer had indeed shaken hands with him and with another slave whom he knew.

There were two slaves named Henry aboard the *Pearl*: Henry Graham and Henry Smallwood. The slave to whom the chaplain spoke was probably the latter, for both Mary Smallwood and Joseph Smallwood were connected with Mount Zion, an African American offshoot of Dumbarton Church, and Moses Smallwood was an early member of Asbury Methodist Episcopal Chapel.[6]

In defending himself, the clergyman wrote a sentence of such length and complexity that one wonders about his sermons: "In regard to what you say about my looking upon the scene with unconcern, I have only to say, that when you shall have given as much money, out of your own pocket, as I have done to purchase the freedom of colored people, and when you shall have taken as much pains and expended as much labor, by night and by day, as I have, to promote the physical comfort and improve the moral condition of slaves and free colored persons, then, I doubt not that the public, where you are known, will consider that you have given more unmistakable evidence of *humanity* than you would do, even if you were to write a hundred letters (to attack an unoffending minister of the Gospel) headed 'HORRORS OF SLAVERY.'"

Chaplain Slicer's letter appeared in the *Daily Union* (May 7, 1848), the Washington newspaper most deeply committed to the southern position on slavery, and also in the *National Era*. This infuriated William Lloyd Garrison in Boston. How did Gamaliel Bailey dare to reprint Slicer's "prevaricating missive"? But then, according to the *Liberator*, what else could one expect of a man like Bailey? "What business had we to expect a clerical fraternizer with the double-distilled devil, Slatter, would be rebuked by a man who has yet to utter his first word of sympathy for the victims of that infernal piracy, out of which this whole matter has grown?"[7] Although Garrison and Bailey were equally fervent in their opposition to human bondage, they could never agree on the most effective way to end it.

Congressman Slingerland was not prepared to let the matter rest. He had not written a slur upon the Methodist Church, "unless a discredit may be reflected upon it by the circumstance that it contains within its bosom those who uphold, by the influence of position, the abomination of Slavery." He had a high regard for the doctrines and members of the Methodist Church. But in his original letter the congressman had sought to let people know that "professing Christians not only hold slaves, but sell them; and that a professed Christian minister gave the hand of friendship to a slave-dealer engaged in the actual perpetration of outrages at which Humanity shudders."[8]

The Senate chaplain had not denied the accuracy of Slingerland's account of events at the railroad station. As the congressman wrote his second letter and relived the horror he had felt on that April day, he chastised Chaplain Slicer: "Yet, in the midst of this revolting spectacle, you strike hands with the prime actor! You are so little affected by the brutal business, that you can calmly recognize and shake hands with the dealer. Now, Sir, I ask you, if, from those circumstances, which you do not deny . . . , an honest inference might not be drawn, that you '*justify* Slavery.'"[9]

Slicer claimed that he had gone into the railroad car seeking Henry, his slave parishioner. "It was true," wrote Slingerland, "that while one of Henry's hands was heavily ironed to that of a fellow victim, you shook the other, and passed the ordinary salutation with him, but you held no conversation with him. When he was about starting to a land of torture and early death . . . you had no words of consolation—no word of hope for this tender lamb of your flock." But Slicer had held a conversation with the slave dealer Slatter, Henry's "tormentor"; indeed, he had chatted freely with him and even smiled. "What must have been Henry's emotions when he saw that hand from which he had received the emblems of Christ's body and blood, now extended to greet the wretch who was consigning him to a premature grave?"[10]

Congressman Slingerland followed up this thrust, an especially telling one to Christians, with a list of questions: "By this act, expressing not censure, but encouragement, did you not justify the trade in human beings? Did you not assume the moral responsibility of the slave dealer? Can you give countenance to one engaged in a crime, without partaking of his criminality? Would you grasp the red right hand of the assassin? Would you reach forth your hand in amity to one that holds the torch of incendiaries? . . . *You cannot give aid and countenance to a man engaged in crime, without assuming his moral responsibility!*" [11]

Slingerland then confronted an issue that religious organizations continue to wrestle with: Is there such a thing as tainted money? If funds raised through evil activities are passed on to a church, does that church then share responsibility for the evil? If a man, enriched by dealing in human property, gives a part of his ill-gotten gains to the Methodist Church, are Methodists then equally responsible for the sin of slavery? Or, if a religious denomination does not condemn slavery as a sin, is it then free to accept, without the taint of immorality, whatever gifts a slaver is willing to bestow?

The New York congressman, unwilling to let the Slicer-Slatter story die, investigated Slatter's relation to the Methodist Church. He found that the slaver had bought a pew in a Methodist church in Baltimore; though his wife and daughter were members, he was not. Nevertheless, it was slave trade money that paid for the pew in the Charles Street Church, known as the "pew church," "the newest and grandest" in Baltimore. Slicer, by the way, opposed constructing a fashionable Methodist church with pews offered for sale to defray the cost of the edifice. [12]

Addressing Slicer, Slingerland wrote: "When you took him [Slatter] by the hand, and cast your eye over the victims around him, you must have been conscious that a portion of the treasure for which the bones and muscle, the blood and sinews of those mothers and babes were to be sold, would go to sustain the Church and ministry to which you belong." If Slicer thought that that was of no concern to the congressman, he was wrong. "For months have I been accustomed reverently to listen to the voice of your supplication to a pure and holy God in behalf of our country." Now, said Slingerland, he had heard that same voice "addressing a slave-dealer in tones of friendship, without a word of reproof, while he was in the actual perpetration of crimes of the blackest die." The hands that the congressman had witnessed "raised to Heaven in prayer," he had seen "given in friendly salutation to a notorious slave-dealer." That was the end, as far as he was concerned: "Do you believe I could again hear you provoke the wrath of Heaven by craving its blessings?" [13]

Congressman Joshua Giddings spoke for many Americans when he deplored the sale of Christian slaves: "It is more shocking to the feelings of our people to see Christians buy and sell those who worship the same God, trust in the same Redeemer, rely upon the same salvation as ourselves, than it is to see them deal in the savages of a heathen land." He admitted that "the iniquity" was not really greater, "but I insist that it is more abhorrent to the popular feeling."[14]

Giddings recalled Slicer as chaplain of the House, not the Senate. In fact, "while each chamber had its own chaplain, they rotated duties weekly between the House and Senate."[15] According to the Ohio congressman, when Slicer next rose to give the invocation, after the incident at the station, "members appeared disgusted at the sacrilegious hypocrisy, and one of them, putting on his hat, began to swear as Slicer began to pray; and while the latter invoked the blessing of God upon members, one of them called on the same Almighty Being to damn such preachers, and most of those present appeared to feel that the prayer of one and the curses of the other were about equally efficacious." Giddings condemned chaplains for not offering prayers "for the wretched victims of oppression who were confined in the prisons of the District of Columbia . . . ready to be shipped off in chains to the far South." When asked for an explanation, one chaplain told him it would not be "prudent to make any allusion to the subject."[16]

Congressman Slingerland could not let pass Slicer's claim that Henry, his slave parishioner, had asked to be sold south. All slaves knew that sale to the Lower South meant separation from family and friends, harsh treatment, and probably early death. Surely Henry would never seek the New Orleans market. Why would Slicer make such a claim? Did the clergyman disapprove of Henry's attempt to be free, "to regain the rights with which God had endowed him"? Was it wrong, asked Slingerland, "for God to bestow upon him [Henry] that inherent love of liberty with the right to enjoy it? — Was it wrong in this unfortunate youth to seek to regain the liberty which God and nature designed for him, and of which he was deprived?" Slingerland concluded by looking to the future: "When *man shall understand his duties to his fellow man, when the principles of the gospel shall be acknowledged, then your letter will be regarded as showing the callousness of a minister in this slaveholding age!*"[17]

After Slingerland called attention to Slicer and his apparent approval of the sale of slaves to the South, other objections surfaced. A correspondent from Washington, writing to a Boston paper, called it "an abiding disgrace to the nation" that a defender of slavery could serve as Senate chaplain. According to "Quinten," when John Quincy Adams died in 1848, the committee of the House of Representatives arranging the funeral refused to allow Slicer to participate in the ceremony. Slicer had, of course, objected, but the committee held firm, causing "rejoicing among all parties" when they heard of it. "So much is he despised by those around whom he fawns and plays the toady."[18]

"Quinten" further claimed that when there had been talk of abolishing slavery in the District of Columbia, Slicer had solicited signatures to a proslavery petition. "It chanced to fall from his pocket, and was picked up by some of the colored citizens of Washington, who kept it in grateful remembrance of Mr. Slicer, whose name, if I am not mistaken, headed the list."[19]

Whenever the pulpit of an African Methodist Church was vacant, the white ministers in the area took turns preaching there. On the Sunday of Slicer's turn, the members of the church, "both bond and free, bearing in remembrance the interest Mr. S. had shown in their affairs, determined that one holding such views of them as chattels, not men, should not enter their pulpit." On his arrival, a delegation "very civilly, but most distinctly, gave him to understand that he could not be permitted to preach to them." Slicer protested, saying that he would preach whether they wanted him or not. "But he soon found they not only had a better appreciation of his fitness for the ministry than the U.S. Senate; but were determined to act up to their views, and accordingly he made good his retreat and stalked out of the church, without waiting for their ungrateful hands to put him out."[20]

It is known, however, that in the 1830s Slicer preached at Mount Zion Methodist Episcopal Church in Georgetown, and in the 1840s he regularly held religious services for "the Col^d people" and attended their camp meeting five miles outside Washington, in spite of frequent objections to "a large mass of colored persons" coming together, even for religious purposes. Another Methodist clergyman, Slicer's contemporary, claimed that the chaplain, "opposed to . . . free speech on the subject" of slavery, had helped "to tighten the chains of the oppressed in Maryland and Virginia" and "crush out the antislavery feeling among the young preachers of the Old Baltimore Conference."[21]

To many, Slicer exemplified the faithlessness of the clergy. The Methodist clergyman preached a sermon to 500 Baltimore volunteers before they left for the Mexican War; a large audience in addition to the soldiers heard Slicer call the men to "valorous action." In his sermon Slicer did not mention slavery, nor did he need to, for when a prominent Methodist preacher called soldiers to "valorous action" in Mexico, he had to be a defender of slavery. Antislavery activists saw the Mexican War as a conflict with only one purpose: to extend the territory of slavery. Calling him the "Infamous Slicer," the *Anti-Slavery Bugle* in Ohio reported in January 1849 that he had been defeated for reelection as Senate chaplain, but, as Slicer noted in his journal, he in fact received twenty-eight out of forty-eight votes.[22]

The uneasy relationship between slavery and Christianity was not new; it had appeared early in the American colonial experience. If all Christians were brothers in the sight of God, then how could a Christian hold another Christian in bondage? Lord Baltimore, for example, lamented that Maryland slave owners, "out of covetousness," had refused baptism for their slaves. To avoid the consequences of such "covetousness," the law in Maryland made it plain that freedom did not necessarily accompany Christian baptism.[23] Armed with legal protection and secure in ownership of their property, slave owners could safely convert their slaves to Christianity and not worry about having to free them. Nevertheless, unease about holding Christians in bondage did not disappear, continually troubling Christian denominations such as the Methodists.

By the 1840s the issue of slavery was tearing apart Christian churches. The Methodist, Baptist, and Presbyterian churches separated into northern and southern denominations, though factors other than slavery may have been involved. Since Methodists were aboard the *Pearl* and concerned with subsequent events, that denomination is given attention here.

Methodism grew out of an eighteenth-century attempt to reform the Anglican Church, the established Church of England, by emphasizing the presence of God and the necessity of a continuing struggle against sin. Chief among the reformers was John Wesley, a Church of England clergyman who is regarded as the founder of the Methodist Church.

Wesley came to believe that holding fellow human beings in bondage was the greatest of all sins. In a particularly moving pamphlet that he published in 1774, he called slavery "intolerable tyranny." No matter how many laws protected the institution, *"right is right, and wrong is wrong." "I absolutely deny all slave holding to be consistent with any degree of natural justice,"* he declared. He refused to accept any justification for slavery, whether it was for essential labor in agriculture or because African slaves were deemed stupid and unable to survive outside slavery. *"You first acted the villain in making them slaves, whether you stole them or bought them.* You kept them stupid and wicked. . . . And now you assign their want of wisdom and goodness as the reason for using them worse than brute beasts." Slave traders should cease their commerce, plantation owners ought to refuse to buy, and the inheritors of slaves were duty bound to free them.[24]

Although Wesley intended Methodism to be a reform movement within Anglicanism, it gradually assumed the characteristics of a separate denomination. The American victory in the War for Independence meant that separate institutions, religious as well as governmental, came into existence. The American Anglican Church became the Episcopal Church, and the Methodists formed a denomination known as the Methodist Episcopal Church, though it actually had no connection with the Episcopalians.

The Methodist Church in the United States organized itself into regional conferences, and every four years representatives of the regions met as the church's General Conference, the governing authority that elected bishops and set forth in the document called the *Discipline* the rules of the denomination. John Wesley's representatives, the first Methodist bishops in America, preached against slavery and welcomed slaves to their services, but they faced threats of bodily harm and a refusal to legislate gradual emancipation in Virginia.[25]

From the beginning of Methodism, its teachings appealed to African Americans, and they were "among the first to respond to the Methodist message in large numbers." Indeed, historian John H. Wigger claims that the Christianization of African Americans was due to Methodists and Baptists; by 1790 slaves and free blacks made up 20 percent of the membership of the Methodist Episcopal Church. Newspaper advertisements sometimes designated runaways as Methodists, one notice advising that the wanted man could probably be found at Methodist meetings.[26]

It was therefore to be expected that the 1785 Methodist *Discipline* required all members to free their slaves, but there was a "fateful exception," a provision that emancipation had to be in accordance with the laws of the states where church members lived. Since southern states either forbade liberation or made it very difficult, slave owners were safe. The Methodist Conference "did not feel itself strong enough to compel its members to transgress civil regulations."[27]

Over the years the loophole in the *Discipline* widened so much that the Methodist Church ceased to be an antislavery organization, and after 1804 the editions of the *Discipline* designed for the South omitted "the entire section on slavery." The General Conference of 1836 resolved that there should not be interference in the master-slave relationship, but there was one exception: the church *Discipline* of 1789 forbade buying and selling slaves, a prohibition that remained in effect until the end of slavery.[28] If enforced, this would have made it impossible for Hope H. Slatter to be a member of the church and also for slave owners to rid themselves of undesirables or augment their labor force.

As Methodists backed away from their wholehearted commitment to antislavery, they explained their change in attitude by emphasizing the importance of preaching Christianity to the slaves. If clergymen alienated the masters, they could not gain access to the enslaved, and converting them justified relinquishing Wesley's insistence on the fundamental evil of human bondage. It came down to the question of freeing the slave or saving his soul, and the latter won out. Missionaries rejoiced to report their success on southern plantations, where they preached to slaves and instructed their children.[29]

It was true that southerners worried about their slaves' souls, lamenting that, "destitute of the gospel," they were no better than heathens dwelling in a Christian country. But since, according to emancipationists, "most of the clergy" were themselves slaveholders, they were "personally interested in the system" and in "justifying it from Scripture, representing it as an institution enjoying the divine sanction." According to one estimate, in 1851 more than 16,000 clergymen (Methodist, Baptist, Presbyterian, and Episcopal) owned slaves.[30]

By compromising with slave owners, Methodist preachers were caught in a trap, for they "found themselves defending slave conversion for making slaves 'better,' which was easily transposed into making 'better slaves.'" It was a relatively short step to defending the entire system of human bondage. The view that Methodism "emphasized personal sanctification rather than participation in social reform"[31] may have provided justification for converting slaves rather than working for their liberation, but it does not, of course, explain early Methodism's antislavery views.

Daniel Drayton, the captain of the *Pearl*, had rejoined the Methodist Church after his conversion experience at Cape May, New Jersey, and henceforth endeavored, as he said, to "do unto others as I would that they should do unto me." Even though he claimed that he heard nothing about the evils of slavery while attending Methodist meetings, he read in the Bible "that God had made of one flesh all the nations of the earth." It was this Christian imperative that led him to act on behalf of the District slaves, not "abolition books . . . [or] abolition lectures."[32]

But because Drayton had come to conclude that Methodists were indifferent to slavery, he could not have been surprised that Slatter, the man who bought many of the *Pearl* fugitives, had a close relationship to that denomination. Nor that Slicer, a Methodist preacher, had defended his own connection to slavery. Some of the slaves on the schooner were Methodists, including the man named Henry whom Slicer had greeted on the train. This juxtaposition provided antislavery writers and speakers with an opportunity to attack the denomination for its contradictions: opposing slavery yet tolerating slave owners in its membership. To repeat: Methodism, though not unique in its acceptance of slavery, was especially liable to charges of hypocrisy because of its origins and the views of its founder.

In the first half of the nineteenth century, the religious revival that historians call the Second Great Awakening convinced many Americans of the necessity of examining their souls and repenting their sins. After purging themselves of their faults, they then turned to the evils in society, believing that they were indeed their brothers' keepers. Lists of needful changes were very long, ranging from alterations in diet and personal habits to abstinence from intoxicating drinks to methods for achieving world peace. Some reformers concluded that they had to devote their lives to ending slavery, since it was the greatest of all sins. A cynic might conclude that northerners could have found fertile fields for reform in the exploitation of fellow Christians closer to home, but cynicism does not explain the sincerity of those who saw slavery as a blot on American society. Under the influence of the religious revival, those Methodists that looked back to the teachings of the founder of their church concluded that human bondage was indeed the greatest evil in the United States. Some withdrew to form a separate church, but others, although remaining within the denomination, decided that compromise with the South over slavery was not possible: "Slavery had been interwoven into the ethical fabric of Southern Christianity."[33]

A majority of Methodists in the North were probably willing to compromise over church membership for slave owners and leave the problem of slavery "to southern consciences to solve." They were not willing, however, to abandon the rule that their bishops, as leaders of and models for Christians, could not own slaves. When in 1844 Georgia Methodists asked the General Conference to accept a slaveholding bishop, northerners saw this as a "dangerous innovation," and a majority voted that he should "desist from the exercise of his office" as long as he owned slaves. The conference did not expel the bishop or any of the southerners, but southern Methodists, angered by the decision, withdrew to form the Methodist Episcopal Church, South. According to historian John R. McKivigan, southerners had used the Georgia bishop as a "loyalty test" to see "how many northerners had been infected by the abolitionist argument," and two years after the division of the Methodist Church, the Georgia conference resolved "that slavery, as it exists in the United States, *is not a moral evil*."[34] The Methodist Church in the North did not become abolitionist, but some of its leaders examined more carefully the denomination's view of slavery, as in the case of the Edmondson slaves, to be discussed in the next chapter.

Henry Slicer tried to postpone a decision on the Georgia bishop and soon found himself out of favor with the Baltimore-Washington conference. Claiming that he only wanted "union & peace," in 1848 he wrote in his journal and underlined: "*Ultraism in Church or State, where slavery is the question, can do no good, but only evil*."[35]

In 1848 the Baltimore conference of the Methodist Episcopal Church included the District of Columbia and extended well into the slaveholding state of Virginia.[36] Slicer, serving in the District, would naturally seek to prevent a division within his denomination. As he saw it, he acted in the interest of the Methodist branch of Christianity. Abolitionists could not charge Slicer with holding slaves himself, since the Baltimore conference to which he belonged forbade it.[37]

How then did a preacher, though no slaveholder himself, deal with parishioners that owned human beings? Did he call them sinners and inevitably lose first his influence with members and then his position in the church? Or did he reluctantly accept the institution and seek to alleviate its worst effects? The latter must have been Slicer's approach, since he assured Congressman Slingerland that he had spent much money and time helping slaves. In his own eyes this made him a good Christian, but in the eyes of abolitionists he was a hypocrite.

In the United States, where a church could not depend on the taxing power of the government, a clergyman was at the mercy of his parishioners; they could force him to leave by moving to another church, refusing to attend services they did not like, or withholding money for church support. Moncure Daniel Conway, for example, lost his pulpit in the Unitarian Church in Washington when he repeatedly preached against slavery.[38]

Devout Christians were reluctant to join the antislavery movement or at least that part of it that became increasingly radical in its opposition to churches. As early as 1829 William Lloyd Garrison deplored foreign missions, which he deemed looking abroad for "objects of commiseration," instead of dealing with slavery in the United States. By the 1840s Garrison and his followers urged all true antislavery men and women to leave "'hypocritical' churches that were tainted with the sin of slavery."[39] Others went further. New Englander Parker Pillsbury, even though trained to be a minister, claimed that the Christian Church was the "surest and sternest defence" of slavery, for it "baptized and sanctified" it. He saw religion "at war with the interests of humanity and the laws of God." It was "more than time the world was awakened to its unhallowed influence on the hopes and happiness of man, while it makes itself the palladium of the foulest iniquity ever perpetrated in the sight of heaven."

In 1848, at an antislavery meeting in Harwich, Massachusetts, a mob attacked Pillsbury and his friend Stephen S. Foster when they chastised Christians for defending slavery. Their assailants administered "blows and kicks," uttering "shouts and yells [that] would have scared a hyena out of his ferocity," all in defense of Christianity.[40]

In a pamphlet titled *Brotherhood of Thieves*, Stephen S. Foster attacked all churches and all clergy: "I deem it the duty of every friend of humanity to brand them [clergy] as a brotherhood of thieves, adulterers, man-stealers, pirates, and murderers." None were assaulted more violently than the Methodists: "I said . . . that the American church and clergy, as a body were thieves, adulterers, man-stealers, pirates, and murderers; that the Methodist Episcopal church was more corrupt and profligate than any house of ill-fame in the city of New York; that the Southern ministers of that body were desirous of perpetuating slavery for the purpose of supplying themselves with concubines from among its hapless victims; and that many of our clergymen were guilty of enormities that would disgrace an Algerine pirate."

After that blast Foster had to flee from a shower of stones and rotten eggs; his response was to write: "If our clergy and church were the ministers and church of Christ, would their reputation be defended by drunken and murderous mobs? Are brickbats and rotten eggs the weapons of truth and Christianity?" He charged that "the entire body of the church and clergy" were in "fellowship with slavery"; they passed "from the communion-table to the ballot-box." "Not a chain has been forged—not a fetter has been riveted on any human being in the District of Columbia, without their sanction!" Foster went straight to the hypocrisy of Christians: "I know not of a single ecclesiastical body in the country which has excommunicated any of its members for the crime of slaveholding, since the commencement of the anti-slavery enterprise."[41]

Among the reforms supported by many church members was strict observance of the Sabbath, proposing, for example, that no trains run on Sunday. The *Anti-Slavery Bugle* in Ohio, convinced that ending human bondage was more important, derided the Sabbatarians by observing that the pursuit of the *Pearl* had occurred on a Sunday: "We hope that this desecration of a holy day will not be permitted to pass unrebuked by sabbatarian pulpits and sabbatarian presses. For however evangelical it may be to hunt men, and women, and infant children on week days, we hardly think it a proper employment for Sunday, unless, indeed, it comes within the catagory [*sic*] of works of necessity or mercy." The *Bugle* was waiting to see whether "advocates of evangelical religion" felt "as holy a horror of hunting human beings on the Sabbath, as they pretend to have of running stages, steamboats, and rail-road cars on that day."[42]

How could conservative Christians join a movement to which such men as Stephen Foster and Parker Pillsbury belonged? How could they support such newspapers as the *Liberator* and the *Anti-Slavery Bugle*? When Garrison and his followers rejected organized religion and the authority of the Bible, Christians could oppose abolitionism on the grounds that it was anti-Christian. On the other hand, the Slicer-Slatter encounter at the Washington railroad station provided abolitionists with further evidence of churchly approval of the great evil of human bondage. The fraternization of Slicer and Slatter pleased the militant Bostonian Theodore Parker because it was "an exhibition of the state of the times in which we live."[43]

The Methodist Church was not the only Christian denomination to defend slavery and deplore the un-Christian views of northerners. Southern clergy in general "endowed the sectional conflict with religious significance" and had no difficulty in discovering "an elaborate scriptural justification of human bondage." They contrasted their appeal to the Bible with the "aggressive political preaching" of northern pastors. "The morality of slavery and the infidelity of abolitionism became the twin pillars of religious proslavery orthodoxy." In the South, regardless of denomination, an attack on slavery became an attack on the sacred scriptures.[44]

As early as 1835 Hope H. Slatter was one of a dozen or more slave traders in Baltimore. Like most such dealers, he started out with little capital and without his own slave jail. Arriving in the city from Georgia, he used a tavern, Owing's Globe Inn, as his business address. It was at the corner of Howard and Market streets, and the proprietor there would take messages in his absence. Slatter was not lacking in self-confidence, advertising for a hundred slaves, especially seamstresses and "likely small fancy girls for nurses." His estimate of his ability was justified, for he prospered, though some believed his money had come from marrying a rich wife. He was able to open his own establishment at 242–244 Pratt Street, a jail "fitted up with bolts and bars," which, it was claimed, sometimes contained 300 or 400 slaves. This was probably an exaggeration. The Slatter pen, located behind his office building, was "a small two story brick building with barred windows" adjacent to a paved yard that was seventy-five by forty feet; there, during the day, the slaves "beguiled their time with cards, and dance, and fiddle and banjo." At night they had to endure being locked up in crowded quarters that in summer were "hot as a little hell."[45]

Baltimoreans maintained that though Slatter was "a man of much intelligence and tact, of very gentlemanly address and considerable public spirit," he was "little other than a social outcast" because of his occupation. This was a general perception of slave dealers' social standing; Abraham Lincoln, for example, claimed that southerners, regarding the slaver as "a sneaking individual, of the class of native tyrants," would not recognize him as a friend "or even as an honest man." But the enthusiasm with which Slicer greeted Slatter at the Washington railroad station indicates that slavers were not necessarily pariahs. Furthermore, when President James K. Polk visited Baltimore, he "rode only in the carriage of Hope Slatter, the great slave-dealer." This did not surprise the *Liberator*; Garrison thought Polk saw the slaver "as a very worthy merchant, who has made his money in a traffic both Christian-like and honorable." [46]

Slatter employed agents who traveled through Maryland and Virginia, buying and selling and helping the trader build up "the largest business in his line" in Baltimore. One of his employees, Jonathan Wilson, became the New Orleans agent of Joseph Donovan, taking control of some of the *Pearl* slaves when they reached their southern destination. According to one source, Wilson eventually was able to buy out Donovan's slaving business in Baltimore. [47]

Abolitionists believed that Slatter made a great deal of money renting slaves to the United States for $1.25 per day; they worked in the navy yard and public buildings. The *Liberator* declared, "All who constitute the federal government, employ slaves to do their work, and pay the price of their labor to their kidnappers," the implication being that Slatter was a kidnapper. In the summer of 1847 two men were arrested in Baltimore and charged with "kidnapping a young colored girl, named Mary Whiting, from Chambersburg, Pa., and selling her to Hope Slatter" for $500. The two men had gotten Mary Whiting drunk in order to persuade her to accompany them, but when she sobered up, she demanded to be freed. [48] Slatter would have denied that he was a kidnapper and would have insisted instead that he was an honest business man.

As soon as Slatter received word of the wholesale flight and recapture of District slaves, he rushed to Washington, for he knew that the owners would be anxious to sell before their slaves again attempted to flee. Congressman Giddings believed that Slatter, whom he called "that fiend in human shape," had instigated the mob action in the nation's capital and had threatened "to lay violent hands" on the congressman. By 1848, at the time of the *Pearl* incident, Slatter must have stood out in a crowd, for he was "a tall, gray headed old man."[49]

When the Quaker Joseph Sturge visited Slatter, the slave dealer told him that "his mother had been for fifty years a member of the Wesleyan body [Methodist Episcopal Church], and that though he had not joined a christian church himself, he had never sworn an oath, nor committed an immoral act in his life." Sturge obviously disagreed with the latter assessment, for he later wrote to Slatter: "By thy hopes of peace here and hereafter, let me urge thee to abandon this occupation" of slave trading.[50]

The editor of the *National Anti-Slavery Standard* in New York, commenting on Slingerland's report of his encounter with Chaplain Slicer at the railroad station, launched a vitriolic attack on the Methodist Episcopal Church. Supplementing the Baltimore trader's name "alias Slaughter," the paper claimed that he was a "prominent" member of the Methodist Episcopal Church, even though his hands were "red with blood" from "buying and selling, and driving to market his brothers and sisters, those in the same Church with himself, in making merchandise of the image of God, in selling Jesus Christ in the person of the poor slave." Slatter had "waxed fat on the sale of the bodies and souls of men," and yet Methodist bishops and clergymen "sit at the communion table with him, and endorse him as a good Christian." "Behold him gloating, — devil incarnate, — over the carloads of those of God's poor whom he had in his possession recently, and about transporting to the far South, or to Texas, to be sold forever away from lover and friend, for the *crime of praying for freedom*."[51]

At a Methodist Church conference in Providence, Rhode Island, there were questions about whether Slatter, a slave trader, could belong to the denomination. Letters were exchanged with Baltimore Methodists, who claimed that though Slatter's father had been a Methodist clergyman, the slave trader was not himself a member of the church. However, the charge was made that "the son is an active supporter of Methodism, and . . . bought one of the costliest pews in the city," which he and his family "constantly" occupied.[52]

Ellen (or Hellen) Stewart (or Steward), who had been aboard the *Pearl*, was eventually shipped to Baltimore. When Congressman Slingerland went to Baltimore to buy her freedom, he heard that Slatter had given up the slaving business. "It seems the lot from the Pearl over which Rev. Henry Slicer struck hands in such clerical complacence, was about the last that Slatter had the heart to buy." The congressman took some of the credit for the change of heart: "Whether the scathing denunciations of him and his traffic . . . were instrumental in converting Slatter, I am unable to say." He went one step further by suggesting that if the slaver should "continue in his penitent state," he should be invited to join the church, which he had indicated he wanted to do, "if they would receive him"—and why not, said the New Yorker, since there were thousands of slaveholders in that denomination.[53]

In the fall of 1848 the *Liberator* denied that Slatter had retired, even though Garrison believed that he had amassed an immense fortune "by his traffic in God's little children." Giving up the trade was too good to be true, "especially as we could not hear that his penitence or disgust at his employment had prompted any efforts on his part to restore any of the poor victims of his avarice to their home and friends." The abolitionist paper cited an advertisement to the effect that Slatter was at his old stand and anxious for new business. The *North Star*, Frederick Douglass's paper, also reported that Slatter continued to advertise for slaves to be brought to his establishment in Baltimore.[54]

Slingerland had been too optimistic, and Garrison and Douglass were correct: Slatter was unmoved by the experience at the Washington railroad station. He did not change his ways but only his place of business, for in 1848 he sold both his Baltimore establishment and his New Orleans slave pen to Bernard and Walter L. Campbell and moved to Mobile, Alabama.[55] Over the years, when Slatter advertised in the *Sun*, he had frequently mentioned returning from a trip to New Orleans. In considering a move to the Deep South, he evidently decided that Mobile offered a better location for his trading.

From his own point of view, Slatter chose wisely because in December 1849 he was already advertising in the *Mobile Daily Advertiser* that he had available for rent seventy "young able-bodied Negro Men, from Virginia." In the same paper he proposed to pay a liberal price for "a fine residence within the city limits." If a suitable house was not available, he would buy land and build. As further proof that Slatter had achieved a secure place in Mobile's economy, he became a candidate for a directorship of the Mobile Live Stock and General Insurance Company.[56]

According to Ralph Clayton, "So great had been the influence of Slatter on the slave trade in the South that [trader] Campbell [in Baltimore] continued to use Slatter's name in his advertisements for the next four years." That explains Garrison's and Douglass's insistence that he had not given up the business in Baltimore. Indeed, Slatter's name became a byword for the slave trade, so that his support of Zachary Taylor's election as president in 1848 was proof of the candidate's proslavery views: "If Taylor were an antislavery man, would Hope H. Slatter, the notorious slave dealer of Baltimore, have closed his market and taken the stump for Taylor?"[57]

In the long run, trader Slatter did not suffer from the attacks of Slingerland, nor did Slicer. In 1854 the clergyman sang "Jesus Lover of My Soul" in the House of Representatives,[58] though it is safe to say that Congressman Joshua Giddings absented himself. But the attention of some Methodists in the North became increasingly focused on the church's relation to slavery.

The Slicer-Slatter-Slingerland story demonstrates that by the 1840s holding men and women in bondage had become a moral issue, not merely an economic one. For many Christians, converting slaves without giving them freedom ceased to be an acceptable response to the belief in the brotherhood of man. For Methodists the writings and admonitions of their founder John Wesley reinforced their opposition to slavery, even though it was difficult, if not impossible, to form an alliance with radical abolitionists. As they considered the relationship of a slave dealer to his church or a preacher to his parishioners, they confronted the dilemma that more and more Americans would face in the next decade: how could slavery be reconciled with Christianity?

CHAPTER FIVE

The EDMONDSONS

When slaves left the Upper South to be sold in some Lower South slave mart—New Orleans, Natchez, or Memphis—they almost always disappeared, becoming lost forever to their families and friends. This was true of most of the slaves aboard the *Pearl*, who, once sold, were never heard from again. An irony of American history is that more is known about what happened to Daniel Drayton than to the slaves aboard his ship. There is fragmentary information about a few of the fugitives and a considerable amount about one extraordinary family of slaves who have entered our history: the Edmondsons of Montgomery County, Maryland. They attracted public notice and gave antislavery enthusiasts an opportunity to make converts to their cause by focusing attention on the evils of the slave trade. The story of the Edmondsons provides a window on slavery, the slave trade, and the functioning of an antislavery network, but it is essential to remember that they were not typical: most of the *Pearl* fugitives simply disappeared.

Slave owners, anxious to get the runaways off their hands before they ran away again, sold them "as fast as purchasers for the New Orleans market [could] come forward and make even the most ordinary offers." Prices were low, maybe only about half of what the men and women were normally worth, and the *New York Herald* claimed "that one likely fellow was exchanged for a Durham bull." The Reverend Obadiah B. Brown, a Baptist clergyman, was the first to sell one of the runaways, a man named John Calvert. For Frederick Douglass this was evidence of "intolerable hypocrisy." Preachers "talk about the gospel—they make long prayers—they lift up their hands to heaven, and repeat the Golden Rule"—and then they own and sell slaves. A few of the owners were slow to claim their property, and more than a month after the attempted flight, the District jail still held some of the fugitives. There was speculation that their owners were holding them for a rise in price.[1]

Daniel Bell, whose efforts to protect his family had started the *Pearl* affair, saw his worst fears realized. His wife and children sailed aboard the *Pearl* and may have been among the slaves transported to Baltimore for sale by Hope Slatter. There were reports that some members of the Bell family were freed, the *North Star* claiming that Thomas Blagden had bought the freedom of Mrs. Bell and two young children.[2] When emancipation came to the District in 1862, Blagden sought compensation for the liberation of George Bell. A slave by that name was on the *Pearl*; but if he was Daniel's son, then instead of buying George's freedom, Blagden bought his labor. Since there were many slaves named Bell in the District, we cannot be sure that George was Daniel's son. Mary Bell was on the list of slaves freed in 1862; again, we do not know whether she was Daniel's wife. In 1853 Daniel Bell was still in Washington and was described as being "as honest and truthful [a] fellow as ever lived."[3]

Well before the *Pearl* sailed, Dolley Madison, the widow of the fourth president, had begun to sell off her slaves; indeed, the *North Star* did not hesitate to call her a slave dealer. No matter how reluctant she might have been, she sold her slaves, her husband's papers, and Montpelier, President Madison's home, in order to save her son, Payne Todd, from debtor's prison.

According to antislavery reports, in 1847–48 Dolley Madison still owned a female slave and her fifteen-year-old daughter Ellen Stewart or Steward, whose name was also given as Hellen, Mary, and Ellen Ann. One account had it that mother and daughter, aware that they were next for the slave market, had their fears confirmed when a known trader—slaves knew very well the identity of slavers—called on Mrs. Madison. The president's widow asked the young slave to fetch the visitor a drink of water; this, for sure, was an opportunity for the dealer to judge the value of the young woman when put up for sale. Ellen, recognizing the trader, fled, hiding out in the city. Mrs. Madison sold the mother, who found a Washingtonian willing to buy her. (But stories about slaves are not always clear. For the most part slaves could not write, and therefore they were dependent on others to tell their stories. It may be that Ellen's mother was not in Washington but was the Sarah Steward at the home of Dolley Madison's son in Orange County, Virginia. In that case, the *North Star* was in error when it reported the mother's sale.) Ellen eluded detection for six months, but she must have been frantic to leave the city. She was one of the slaves whom William Chaplin had in mind when he began to search for a ship; she was on board when the *Pearl* sailed down the Potomac and when it returned to Washington.[4]

As soon as Dolley Madison regained possession of the runaway, she sold Ellen "to a Baltimore slave-dealer," apparently for $400, though her letter reporting the sale leaves this matter somewhat confused. Ellen was probably among Slatter's purchases that Slingerland saw leaving the Washington station, since emancipationists soon noted her presence in Baltimore. Congressman John Gorham Palfrey of Massachusetts busied himself with raising money to buy Ellen's freedom. Mrs. Madison, unaware of his efforts on the slave's behalf, invited Palfrey to tea; he declined: "The thought of the poor fugitive child, whom she had been selling and buying, was in the way, and Mrs. M. had to take her tea without me." Even though Palfrey would not drink her tea, he magnanimously urged that Congress pay her for President Madison's papers.[5]

Palfrey was not alone in seeking Ellen's freedom. Women were especially active in raising money to ransom her, but it seemed unwise to publish their names. Joseph Evans Snodgrass, a Baltimore physician, editor of the *Sunday Visiter* (*sic*), and an active participant in the Free Soil Party, worked hard to free the young woman. As noted in the previous chapter, Congressman Slingerland went to Baltimore to pay out the money for her freedom, and by August 1848 she was living in the vicinity of Boston, "where her friends have provided a good situation for her." Meanwhile, Dolley Madison deplored her slave's flight, describing it as Ellen's "6 months dissipation." She would not go to see the girl in the Washington jail, having "heard a bad acct. of her morals & conduct." Once the president's widow had received payment for

Ellen, she wrote her son that she would send him a hundred dollars to "put your clothes in order."[6]

In November 1848 William L. Chaplin reported that "a fine young fellow" (he gave no name) who had fled on the *Pearl* was being held in a slave pen in Baltimore, while his mother, in New York, was trying to persuade someone to free him. Chaplin hoped to secure his freedom "by a law process," but he did not specify the path he would follow.[7] Clear proof exists of only one slave from the *Pearl* remaining in the District until emancipation freed him. Arianna J. Lyles claimed compensation for the liberation of thirteen slaves in 1862; of that thirteen, one named Hannibal had been aboard Drayton's ship. Other Washingtonians whose slaves had been on the *Pearl* were still slave owners in 1862, but their slaves at that later time were not the same as those that fled in 1848.[8]

There were reports of slaves being whipped to extract information about the escape attempt, and one young boy, badly beaten, is supposed to have told all that he knew. A number of blacks in Washington suffered arrest because of a suspicion that they had helped in the *Pearl* escape. One such victim was Anthony Blow, who had been rented out to the Washington Navy Yard, where he worked in the machine shop, as did Daniel Bell. His owner having sold him, Blow was transported to Norfolk, Virginia, whence he escaped to Philadelphia in 1854.[9]

The wife and children of Thomas Ducket, a Maryland slave, fled on the *Pearl* and then were sold south. Ducket, under suspicion that he was implicated in the escape attempt or at least had had prior knowledge of it, was brought to Washington, where his master sold him south. He had asked to be sold to the man holding his wife and children, but that was not to be. In 1850 he wrote from Louisiana to antislavery activist Jacob Bigelow in Washington, asking for help for himself and news of his family: "My wife and children are not out of my mine [*sic*] day nor night."[10]

Six members of the Edmondson family, four young men and two young women, fled aboard the *Pearl*, and because Mary and Emily Edmondson aroused much sympathy, there is a good deal of information about them, their siblings, and their parents. Amelia Edmondson (usually known as Milly), the mother of the six fugitives, was a slave in Montgomery County, Maryland, adjacent to the District of Columbia. She

Amelia ("Milly") Edmondson. (Courtesy of the Library of Congress)

was the property of Rebecca Culver, and the slave and her owner may
have grown up together. Rebecca Culver, legally incompetent and described as a "lunatic," had a guardian, Francis Valdenar, who in 1837
posted bond as her trustee. Valdenar, married to Culver's niece and
apparent heir, was a prominent Marylander who was chosen to ad-
minister the will of one large slave owner and was a commissioner to
define county boundary lines. It is not surprising that he supported
the South in 1861.[11]

   Amelia was a mulatto, "above the middle height, of a large, full figure," and in the 1850s she was still handsome, though with "deep-wrought lines of patient sorrow and weary endurance on her face." She had intended never to marry because she thought "it wan't [*sic*] right to bring children into the world to be slaves." But she fell in love with Paul Edmondson, and since they were both devout members of Asbury Methodist Episcopal Chapel, they were forced to marry or "be turned out of the church." Their happiness was marred only by their knowledge that their children did not belong to them. "And every child I had, it grew worse and worse," lamented Amelia Edmondson.[12]

Paul Edmondson had been born into slavery in Montgomery County, but he was freed by his master at the age of forty-two. By dint of much hard work he acquired a farm in 1835, buying twenty acres of land for $250; twelve years later, in 1847, he acquired an additional twenty acres, paying $280. The two parcels of land were part of an early Maryland estate known as Bradford's Rest, in an area that today lies between Olney and Sandy Spring, Maryland. Paul and Amelia Edmondson lived on their small property and produced fifteen children, all but one surviving to adulthood, a truly remarkable record for the nineteenth century.[13] It is easy to understand why Rebecca Culver's guardian allowed Amelia Edmondson to live away from her owner and with her husband: they were enriching the Culver estate. The Edmondson children were all slaves, in spite of having a free father.

Terrified that her offspring would be sold away from her, Amelia Edmondson hid them whenever she saw a white man passing the house. She lamented, "Nobody knows what I suffered. I never see a white man come on to the place that I didn't think, 'There, now, he's coming to look at my children.'" Amelia did some sewing for Rebecca, but her major task was raising fine children, at which she was very successful. As it turned out later, many people coveted the Edmondson offspring, in spite of all the parents' efforts to keep them safe, for they were known for their "intelligence, honesty, and faithfulness."[14]

In 1848 five of the Edmondson daughters, having secured their freedom, lived in Washington in what was described as "comfortable circumstances." According to family tradition, Amelia had warned her children not to marry until they were free. Elizabeth, the oldest daughter, was manumitted probably through the efforts of John Brent, who, after working to free himself and his father, sawed wood at night to earn money to buy Elizabeth's release from slavery. On July 4, 1837, Francis Valdenar, Rebecca Culver's guardian, freed Elizabeth, then twenty-

Elizabeth and John Brent. (Courtesy of the Library of Congress)

six years old, for the sum of $450, which, according to the manumis-
sion record, was provided by "benevolent friends." If the money came
from Brent, surely no bride ever received a more welcome gift. One
Edmondson daughter, "an invalid," paid $300 for her freedom; when
warned she would not live to enjoy it, she exclaimed, "I'll do it, and
be free, if I die the next hour!"[15]

Six Edmondsons, still owned by Rebecca Culver, were rented out in the District: Richard, Samuel, Ephraim, John, Mary, and Emily. Two children remained at home with Paul and Amelia Edmondson, and the family rejoiced that they all lived near each other. Only one son, Hamilton, was gone, having been sold to New Orleans when he failed in an escape attempt in 1832.[16]

When the six Edmondsons who were slaves in Washington decided to flee aboard the *Pearl*, they disrupted a close family circle, but according to family tradition their bid to escape received the approval of mother, father, and sisters.[17] Although the young Edmondsons claimed that they had not suffered ill treatment while employed in Washington, they shared with their invalid sister an overwhelming desire for freedom. There probably was more pressure on the Edmondsons than their contemporaries knew, for if Rebecca Culver was in ill health, the break-up of her estate, with the resulting sale of the Edmondsons, represented an ever-present threat. When William L. Chaplin reported in March 1848 that he had seventy-five people urgently in need of passage to the North, he mentioned among them "five brothers & two sisters of great interest."[18] Although Chaplin exaggerated the number of brothers, he was surely referring to the Edmondsons.

A few days before the *Pearl* sailed, one of the Edmondson brothers (name not given) approached Joshua Giddings, seeking assistance in securing the freedom of his sisters Mary and Emily. The brother said that he had saved up $700 and could buy his own freedom, but he would never leave his sisters in slavery. Since, according to Giddings, that brother was on the *Pearl*, he did not in fact desert his sisters. It seems strange, however, that he did not purchase his freedom after the *Pearl* fiasco, or give the money to one of his sisters. Since Samuel Edmondson was the "principal actor" in the escape attempt,[19] it may well have been he who approached Giddings.

The young Edmondson evidently made a strong impression on Giddings, because four years after the escape attempt the congressman was still talking about him. In a speech in the spring of 1852 Giddings recollected that the slave had called on him "at different times to aid him in raising money to redeem his sisters." "This whole family," declared Giddings, "was endowed with intellects of the highest order." Young Edmondson "was himself, so far as propriety of language, gentlemanly deportment, and intelligence are concerned, not the inferior of gentlemen here [in the House], or the President of the United States."[20]

Family members watched with horror when the captives, brought back aboard the *Pearl*, were marched through the streets of Washington; a brother-in-law was so overcome that he fainted. Mary and Emily, held in the jail, could see their sisters standing outside, weeping. The Edmondsons who had won their freedom made every effort to raise the money to buy their sisters and brothers. The woman at whose home Mary had worked offered to buy her for $1,000, but she would bring double that in New Orleans. Bruin and Hill, slave dealers of Alexandria, bought all six Edmondsons for $4,500; Joseph Bruin had had his eye on them for twelve years "and had the promise of them should they ever be sold." Mrs. Edmondson had been justified in her fears for her children. The young Edmondsons must have been a real prize, for Bruin, instead of making them walk to his slave pen in Alexandria, transported them by carriage.[21] Bruin also wanted to avoid the publicity that had followed Slatter's large-scale transfer by train.

Joseph Bruin had started out as an employee of George Kephart. He traveled through Virginia, buying up slaves for the Alexandria depot. In 1844 he bought 1707 Duke Street and operated the trading company as Bruin and Hill until 1852, when he became sole owner. Perhaps the money he would receive for ransoming the Edmondson girls made it possible for him to buy out his partner. When northern troops occupied Alexandria in 1861, Bruin fled, and the United States government confiscated his property.[22]

Bruin's name resonated among former slaves, so that as late as the 1930s they mentioned him when recalling the realities of bondage in Virginia and Louisiana. Frank Bell saw his uncle sold to Bruin at the Seventh Street wharf in the District, and Fannie Brown watched him conducting a slave sale in Fredericksburg, Virginia, fifty miles south of Washington. In 1903 an old black man said that Bruin was the most generally known Alexandria trader. An elderly ex-slave claimed that he was sold from Bruin's slave pen in New Orleans; indeed, in the year before the Civil War began, the trader bragged that he had been in the business in New Orleans for twenty-six years.[23]

Once the Edmondsons were in the Bruin and Hill slave pen in Alexandria, their treatment was no better than that accorded all the other slaves. Mary and Emily's assigned task was doing the laundry for thirteen men, though their brothers shared the heaviest work. Bruin kept the Edmondsons in Alexandria for some time;[24] he was probably waiting to see if northerners could raise the money to buy them, giving him a large profit and avoiding the expense of shipping them south. But when the money was not forthcoming, the trader loaded about forty slaves, including the Edmondsons, on a ship bound for Baltimore. There they stayed in a slave pen owned by "a partner of Bruin and Hill." The slave dealer treated them roughly, subjecting Mary and Emily to "grossly obscene and insulting remarks" and forbidding them to pray with their fellow inmates. They circumvented this by rising very early to take part in a prayer group.[25]

While the Edmondsons were in Baltimore, word reached them that a part of the money to buy their freedom would be arriving by messenger. Surely this would encourage the trader to hold them in his pen until the remainder could be raised, but the dealer was "inexorable" and placed them aboard a ship bound for New Orleans. Even the sight of $900, the gift of a grandson of John Jacob Astor, did not change his mind. Those raising money for the Edmondsons had allocated the Astor gift to Richard, whose wife and children were in great distress, and the money, when paid, was so designated. But even that had no effect on the dealer: though the ship had not sailed, he would not allow Richard—now legally free—to land and return to his family. Giddings said that the draft for $900 came to him a few days after the sale of the Edmondsons to Bruin and Hill.[26]

On May 13, 1848, Joseph S. Donovan of 448 Pratt Street in Baltimore signed the ship manifest for forty-six slaves to sail aboard the brig *Union*, with E. Hooper as master, bound for New Orleans. Among the slaves were the following six:

	Age	Height	Color
John Edmonson	26	5ft. 10in.	Brown
Samuel Edmonson	21	5ft. 8in.	Brown
Ephrim [*sic*] Edmonson	30	5ft. 8in.	Brown
Richard Edmonson	24	5ft. 8in.	Brown
Mary Edmonson	17	5ft. 6in.	Brown
Emily Edmonson	15	5ft. 1in.	Brown[27]

Although Donovan claimed the "Edmonsons" on the ship manifest, it is clear that Bruin and Hill retained title, for Bruin made all of the later decisions concerning their fate. Apparently Donovan signed as owner and shipper as a convenience to the Alexandria dealers; it saved Bruin or Hill from making a trip to Baltimore.

The voyage to New Orleans was a harrowing experience, with head winds and storms and a shortage of water and food. The *Daily Pica-yune* of June 14, 1848, reported the brig's arrival. Within a few hours after reaching New Orleans, the Edmondsons were lodged in a slave pen operated by J. M. Wilson, partner of Bruin and Hill. This was the same Wilson who had worked for Slatter and later would buy Dono-van's business. The new arrivals were admonished to look happy or be beaten; selling *contented* slaves was serious business. Stowe tells us how the Edmondson sons were prepared for sale: clothed in blue pants and shirts, hair cut short, and mustaches shaved, changing their appearance so drastically that their sisters did not recognize them.[28] No comparable description of the daughters is available.

The slaves had to stand "in an open porch fronting the street" to arouse the interest of passersby. If buyers showed up, the slaves were paraded in the auction room. "When any one took a liking to any girl in the company, he would call her to him, take hold of her, open her mouth, look at her teeth, and handle her person rudely, frequently making obscene remarks." When Mary and Emily complained to their brothers, they spoke to Wilson, who saw to it that the girls were treated "with more decency."[29] The slave dealers must have been affected by the publicity surrounding the Edmondsons. Were any other slave girls able to complain and have their lives somewhat ameliorated? In all too many instances protesting slaves endured harsher treatment. The Edmondson girls were very valuable property, and it did not make sense to whip those who, according to northern perception, were to be sold as prostitutes: they should not have unsightly scars. In prewar New Orleans "Negro prostitutes were at a premium"; a wealthy white man would pay as much as $8,000 for a "beautiful Negro woman" to be his concubine.[30] If Mary and Emily Edmondson were to be sold as ladies' maids, Bruin and Wilson would be equally careful in their treatment.

Even more amazing, in view of the frequency of the kidnapping of free blacks, was the integrity of the slave dealer in recognizing that Richard Edmondson was a free man. Wilson treated him as free, allow-ing him to search for Hamilton Edmondson, the brother who had been sold to New Orleans before Emily was born. Great was the rejoicing when Richard found his brother and brought him to Wilson's for a family reunion. Hamilton had just purchased his own freedom, after sixteen years of bondage.[31]

Mary and Emily were suffering from the aftereffects of the voyage south, and Wilson, anxious to keep them in good health, allowed them to spend their nights at Hamilton's house, returning to the slave quarters during the day. Although they themselves were relatively protected, Mary and Emily witnessed scenes of great cruelty, including the flogging of the same man every night for a week. They saw gangs of women "cleaning the streets, chained together, some with a heavy iron ball attached to the chain," a form of punishment, they learned, "frequently resorted to for household servants who had displeased their mistresses."[32]

After a few weeks, when a yellow fever epidemic broke out in New Orleans, Bruin and Hill's large investment seemed in peril, for the Edmondsons, not acclimated, were especially susceptible. A physician traveling in the South claimed that yellow fever had visited New Orleans every three years, attacking especially "strangers from the North, or emigrants from Europe." According to him, mortality rates ran as high as 52 percent, and in 1847, the year before the Edmondsons' arrival, a major epidemic broke out, resulting in as many as 3,000 deaths out of a total population of 109,000, which earned the city the title of "Necropolis of the South." It seemed wise to ship Mary and Emily Edmondson back north, out of danger. In addition, Bruin may have been disappointed by the price he had been offered in New Orleans, or so the *Liberator* suggested.[33]

Bruin knew that he would receive $900 as soon as Richard Edmondson reached Baltimore, and he may have believed that money was available to free Mary and Emily. So Wilson shipped the two young women and Richard Edmondson back north. On July 6, 1848, the ship manifest for the brig *Union* of Baltimore registry listed the three Edmondsons as aboard. The fate of John and Ephraim Edmondson is not clear; Samuel was sold to an Englishman for $1,000.[34]

The Edmondsons had assurances that Richard would be freed as soon as he arrived in Baltimore, and the two young women expected freedom papers to be waiting for them, too. One can imagine how greatly disappointed they were to learn that no ransom was at hand and that they had to face the reality of the slave pen once more. Richard went off to Washington, under the protection of Jacob Bigelow. Although Mary and Emily were happy to know that their brother would be reunited with his wife and children, they felt especially alone, having previously been under the protection of their brothers.[35]

Settling into the routine of the slave pen, they spent their time either marching around the yard to attract purchasers or doing the male slaves' laundry. When it appeared that no more money was forthcoming, Bruin decided to return them to his slave quarters in Alexandria, where they did washing, ironing, and sewing. As the days passed, they proved so useful that Bruin took them to his home to sew for the family, where they won the affection—indeed, the love—of Bruin's young daughter.[36]

Christianity was central to the lives of the Edmondsons. When Milly Edmondson grieved over giving birth to children that belonged to another, her husband comforted her: "It ain't so much matter whether they be ours or no; they may be heirs of the kingdom, Milly, for all that." When she told Harriet Beecher Stowe that she had had to bear a "heavy cross," the author, who lived surrounded by clergymen, assured the slave woman that she was certain the Lord had been with her. Yes, said Milly, if that had not been so, she'd not have survived. "Oh, sometimes my heart's been so heavy, it seemed as if I *must* die; and then I've been to the throne of grace, and when I'd poured out all my sorrows there, I came away *light*, and felt that I could live a little longer." After learning of the *Pearl*'s failed voyage, Milly and Paul Edmondson "fasted and prayed before the Lord, night and day."[37]

The Edmondsons were long-time members of black-organized Asbury Chapel, which had spun off from Foundry Methodist Episcopal Church. In the 1840s Foundry's clergy preached at Asbury, and the Reverend Matthew A. Turner described Mary and Emily as church members in good standing and young women of "irreproachable characters." Beautiful young female slaves might well be sold for employment as domestic servants, but opponents of slavery usually saw them as destined for prostitution.[38]

During the summer and early fall of 1848, leaders of the Methodist Church in New York pondered what they could do to help their young coreligionists. They were well aware of the disdain with which abolitionists regarded the Methodist Church, and they could not have been happy with the publicity accorded the Reverend Henry Slicer's friendship with slave dealer Slatter. Now northern Methodists faced the probability of two members of their denomination returning to New Orleans and what they feared would be a life of degradation. They dispatched an agent to Alexandria, to see if he could bargain with Bruin about the price, but the slaver would make no concession; too much money awaited him in New Orleans: "The truth is, *and is confessed to be, that their destination is prostitution.*" The agent reported that Bruin prized Mary and Emily for their "elegant form" and "very fine faces."[39]

Bruin and Hill were serious about their plans for a southern trip, preparing provisions, a tent, and two teams of horses and wagons. This time they would travel overland, taking a coffle south, heading for Alabama or Mississippi, trading along the way—"sell, buy, or swap." When they left Alexandria, they would have thirty-five slaves, including Mary and Emily Edmondson. Bruin claimed that he was willing to keep the girls in Virginia, but his partner Hill was anxious to turn a profit on two valuable pieces of property. Hill had been unhappy with the decision to bring Mary and Emily back to Virginia, and Bruin would not go against his partner's wishes by keeping them in Alexandria, "unless he can be perfectly certain they will be redeemed." The slaver was very clever in increasing pressure on the worried New Yorkers, not hesitating to demand more than $2,000.

Efforts were under way in Washington to raise money, perhaps $400 or $500, as a nonrefundable deposit to be forfeited if the remainder was not paid.[40] Paul Edmondson could sell or mortgage his farm, but surely nobody wanted him to lose his small property. His son-in-law could guarantee about $600, amazing proof of the industriousness of free blacks in the District. The agent of the New York Methodists would try to raise a few hundred dollars, but overriding everything else was a note of urgency:

Send the money before the girls are lost forever:
Let me entreat our friends not to look upon this sum, large as it may appear, as so much treasure squandered upon mercenary and unprincipled slave-traders! . . . It is a *text of texts* from which to preach to the hearts of the people. It can be made to operate more effectually than any other circumstance, for the immediate overthrow of Slavery, and the trade in this District.[41]

While northern Methodists were wondering what to do, Paul Edmondson, "a venerable-looking black man, . . . whose air and attitude indicated a patient humility, and who seemed to carry a weight of over-whelming sorrow," took action. Despairing of ever seeing Emily and Mary free, he sought assistance in New York, bearing a letter from Bruin that declared the slaver would not reduce the price of $2,250: $1,200 to be paid in fifteen days and the remainder in twenty-five. Unless Bruin received the full amount, he would send Mary and Emily south.[42]

William Chaplin's name was never mentioned—the less known about his activities the better—but he probably made the arrangements for Edmondson's journey after urging the old man to undertake it. Careful planning went into the trip, for Paul Edmondson set off to New York with testimonials of the good character of his daughters and proof of their membership in the Methodist Episcopal Church. Although the elder Edmondson was literate, he was ignorant of the world outside his Montgomery County farm and his children's homes in the District. Chaplin, on the other hand, knew that there was money in New York, and his antislavery connections were with New Yorkers, especially with Gerrit Smith of upstate New York and with New York City members of the American and Foreign Anti-Slavery Society. It was no accident that Edmondson, on arriving in New York City, went first to the office of the society, whence he was directed to the Reverend James W. C. Pennington, who was himself a fugitive from slavery in Maryland and "a leading member" of the American and Foreign Anti-Slavery Society. Pennington had been denied admission to the Yale Divinity School but had stood outside the classrooms' open doors and listened to the lectures. In spite of such obstacles, Pennington qualified for the ministry and became pastor of New York's First Colored Presbyterian Church; its name was changed to Shiloh.[43]

Pennington was especially interested in Paul Edmondson when he learned that he too was a Marylander, and he listened intently to the story of the fugitives and read carefully the letter from Bruin and Hill and the testimonials from Washingtonians. The next Sunday Pennington reported on the case to his congregation, which raised $50, a large sum for poor blacks but a pittance when one considered what was needed to free the two young women.[44]

Someone had the bright idea of sending Edmondson to see Henry Ward Beecher, recently arrived in Brooklyn as pastor of Plymouth Congregational Church and perhaps the most dynamic pulpit orator in the country. Beecher had been too busy on other fronts to become involved in antislavery, but when he encountered Paul Edmondson and heard his story, he became a convert. According to Beecher's sister, Harriet Beecher Stowe, the minister found the old man sitting on his front steps, weeping. How did Edmondson get from New York City to Brooklyn? Who took him to the ferry? Who showed him where Beecher lived?[45] Was it Chaplin or Pennington or a member of Pennington's congregation? It is difficult to believe that any of them would have left the old man to wander the city streets alone or to sit weeping on Beecher's steps. It is more likely that clergymen and antislavery enthusiasts in New York agreed that Edmondson and Beecher should meet and so arranged it. Stowe probably embroidered the story a little.

In any case, the old man's account of his daughters' troubles moved Beecher to volunteer to join the ongoing effort to ransom Mary and Emily Edmondson. While serving as a clergyman in Indiana, Beecher had not assumed a leadership role in churchly debates on slavery, regarding it as too controversial,[46] and in the short time he had been in Brooklyn, he had been establishing his position in a new church. Now the Edmondsons, personifying the evils of slavery, gave the preacher, for the first time, an emotional view of the institution.

When the Methodist clergymen of New York learned that the agent they had sent to Alexandria had failed to persuade Bruin to reduce the price for Mary and Emily's freedom, they despaired: they could never find $2,250. Finally they decided to hold a public meeting, where they might receive donations, not only from Methodists but also from antislavery sympathizers throughout the city. A committee of three of the most distinguished Methodist preachers in the city—George Peck, Edwin E. Griswold, and Daniel Curry—would make the necessary arrangements. The committee drew up a statement of the circumstances surrounding the case and called for a public meeting to be held in the Broadway Tabernacle on October 23, 1848. The theme of the appeal, both printed and oral, was the pure, religious nature of the two young women and the horror of their being sold into prostitution, the avowed purpose of their sale in New Orleans.[47]

The premeeting publicity emphasized Paul Edmondson's age (seventy), his achieving freedom at the age of forty-two, his hard labor to acquire a small farm, and his "unblemished Christian character." His wife Milly, still enslaved, was the mother of fifteen children, of whom fourteen were living. Edmondson had brought with him a letter from Bruin and Hill stating firmly that there would be no reduction in the price of the two girls. It was all or nothing — $2,250 or off to the South for Mary and Emily.[48]

The Methodists may not have welcomed the Congregationalist Beecher when he volunteered his services, for denominational loyalties were strong, and the Methodists intended their fund-raising effort as a means of proclaiming their antislavery credentials. But they could not refuse his assistance, for everyone knew Beecher's power in the pulpit. As it turned out, although others spoke at the October meeting, it was Beecher's emotional appeal, combined with his great voice and intense manner, that swayed the audience. According to a biographer, Beecher discovered that night that he did not have to resolve the numerous problems surrounding the legality of slavery; for him it was enough to think of the suffering humans and respond to their need, and he carried his audience with him.[49]

Speaking as though he were auctioning off a beautiful female slave, Beecher appealed to the emotions of his listeners; "The audience were wrought up to a perfect frenzy of excitement." It was not all emotion; for even though Beecher had been slow to proclaim his opposition, he had thought seriously about slavery and its defenders. He acknowledged that in a society where people were property, ransoming a fugitive destroyed that property. But for Beecher the desire for freedom that all humans shared took priority over any claim of ownership.

For him and many other opponents of slavery a more difficult question was whether buying slaves' freedom in reality strengthened the institution. If northerners tried to buy all of the slaves in the South, they would merely provide money for the unlimited purchase of more bondmen and bondwomen; and, as the *Anti-Slavery Bugle* warned, Bruin and Hill could take the money demanded for Mary and Emily and buy four girls for the "New-Orleans Seraglios." But for Beecher the matter at hand was different: the Edmondson girls were *Christians* and were to be sold as prostitutes. "It seemed to me as I first uttered these words as if I could hear a scoffing, jeering fiend of hell echo them with a grin of derision." Since the slave trader had given assurance that that was to be their fate, Beecher felt justified in calling such men "human flesh-dealers of Christian girls." The ransoming of the two young women crystallized for him the place of opposition to slavery in his Christian dogma. He saw antislavery as "a human question, in which God, the sanctity of the home, chastity, salvation, bodily purity,

. . . Christ's love and the blood of atonement, could all be brought together."[50]

The great evil at the heart of slavery, declared Beecher, was the destruction not merely of the body but also of the soul. The slave system had turned virtues upside down. A handsome woman would bring a higher price in the slave mart. "That which excites among us the profoundest respect, goes there to augment her value—not as a wife, not as a sister, but for purposes from the bare idea of which the virtuous soul revolts." So for the slave "beauty, refinement, . . . thrift, skill, intelligence" simply added to her price in the market. And if it were known that the slave was a member of the Methodist Episcopal Church, that too would increase the value and hence the price. (Here the audience went wild.) So Beecher asked the members of the audience to imagine how they would feel if their daughters were in the position of Emily and Mary Edmondson and to respond with generosity in order to set them free.[51]

People were shouting aloud the size of their promised donations. One correspondent, commenting on people's enthusiastic response, wrote: "It seemed to me that these young men were bidding on behalf of God, humanity, liberty, and virtue, against the devil, barbarism, slavery, and licentiousness." So it was that religious people were drawn into antislavery. Beecher tapped into a major strain of the northern perception of slavery when he warned that Mary and Emily Edmondson would be condemned to prostitution. It often appeared that antislavery writers perceived the South as a great brothel: "Our southern cities are whelmed beneath a tide of pollution; . . . the virtue of female slaves is wholly at the mercy of irresponsible tyrants, and women are bought and sold in our slave markets, to gratify the brutal lust of those who bear the names of Christians." So wrote Sarah Grimké, a South Carolinian turned passionate opponent of human bondage.[52]

At collection time only $500 went into the boxes. The second time around, the donations included "jewelry, torn from the hands and ears of the ladies of the audience, anxious to give their mite." Men outbid each other, offering $100 and even $500, until the entire sum presumably was raised. "Upon the announcement of this fact, a shout arose, that woke the echoes of the Tabernacle, and testified that New York has still a heart that feels warmly for the oppressed, and a hand liberal to make the heart's promptings effectual for the relief of the slave."[53]

But this was not strictly true, for on October 25 the *New-York Tribune* reported that there was still a deficit of $327.23. The committee asked that people immediately send in additional money. "We are sure," they wrote, "that the poor old man Edmondson will not be compelled to sacrifice his little homestead to make up this amount." This last appeal was successful, and soon the *National Anti-Slavery Standard* announced that the money had been raised and would be used "to redeem them [the Edmondsons] from the horrible fate for which they were destined by the inhuman monsters at Washington who claimed the ownership of their bodies."[54]

Mary and Emily Edmondson were "nearly as white as their master," and even if Henry Ward Beecher emphasized their church membership, he was well aware that they were Methodists with light-colored skins. In his attacks on human bondage, Beecher referred to "white-faced, flaxen-aired children born under the curse of slavery." The historian Walter Johnson has written of the primacy of color in the purchasing decisions of slave owners: they tended to buy dark-skinned workers "to till their fields [and] harvest their crops" and whiter slaves "to serve their meals, mend their clothes, and embody their fantasies." "By buying ever-whiter slaves, the prosperous slaveholders of the antebellum South bought themselves access to ever more luminous fantasies of their own distinction."[55] No wonder Bruin was confident that he could sell Mary and Emily Edmondson at a huge profit.

On November 2, 1848, William L. Chaplin reported that since the money for the purchase of Mary and Emily Edmondson was now in hand, he was setting out for Washington to redeem them. When Chaplin reached the District, he met the girls' father, and together they spread the good news and went to the slave pen in Alexandria. As soon as the girls saw their father and Chaplin, they were sure they would be freed, but Edmondson, having endured so many disappointments, told Mary and Emily to wait until he and Chaplin had talked to Bruin. Chaplin paid Bruin $2,250, "payment in full for the purchase of two negroes, named Mary and Emily Edmondson." The company of Bruin and Hill guaranteed "the right and title of said negroes . . . against the claims of all persons whatsoever." It also gave assurance that the two young women were "sound and healthy in body and mind, and slaves for life." After the freedom papers were signed, title to the girls passed to Chaplin, who for the sum of $1 gave up all claim to Mary and Emily, and on November 7, 1848, they were free. Bruin handed each of the young women a $5 gold piece and sent them on their way rejoicing. Bruin must have been rejoicing, too, for he now had a great deal of money without exposing his valuable slaves to the hazards of a coffle. By the time the Edmondsons left Alexandria and reached Washington, the trip to the home of one of their sisters (perhaps Elizabeth Brent) had become a triumphal journey. All of the neighborhood gathered to celebrate the gift of freedom.[56]

✳

After the reunion with family and friends, Emily and Mary set out with Chaplin to visit New York, where they attended the church of the Reverend John Dowling, who noted "their grateful happy countenances, and their pious devotional behavior as they united in offering up thanks to God for their deliverance." They visited the Reverend Samuel Cox and satisfied him that they were properly grateful; he concluded that their manners were as good as those of the daughters of Queen Victoria.[57]

But as Eliza Doolittle would lament, what was to become of them? Mary and Emily were celebrities and still not free to make their own decisions. After working to secure their freedom, their sponsors were sure they knew best in deciding the young women's future. Education was the prime necessity: Mary almost knew her letters, and Emily was beginning to learn hers.[58] There is no indication that Mary and Emily disagreed with the decisions that were made for them. Only Emily ever "acted up." Mary never did. But did they sometimes wish they were not celebrities?

The two freed slaves brought to life the question of whether education was important for blacks. In southern states, education for African Americans, both slave and free, was forbidden, and even in the North schools for blacks were either nonexistent or segregated. Now the people who had worked to secure the freedom of the two young women concluded that their future lay in becoming teachers for African Americans. In New York City a meeting was called for December 7, 1848, to raise money for that purpose: "to prepare them for future usefulness."[59]

Once again, though there were several speakers, Henry Ward Beecher was the star, as he urged the importance of education for blacks: "If colored men and women become educated and wise, there is nothing on earth that can prevent them from standing alongside of

Mary and Emily Edmondson. (Courtesy of the Library of Congress)

any other race or community." Educating blacks should receive the
enthusiastic support of "every philanthropist and Christian," a significant statement in a society where education for blacks continued to be
controversial.[60]

Through the Edmondson case Beecher came to see the profound
evil of the trade in slaves. He did not hesitate to make disparaging remarks about Joseph Bruin, which the Alexandria slaver resented, re-

garding himself as a man of honor. At the December fund-raising session, Beecher, rather than apologizing, intensified his attack. A slave trader, he thundered, was no different from a horse trader, always on the lookout for likely people — instead of horses — so that he could satisfy the needs of his customers. "Slavery is a state of suppressed war — the slave is justified in regarding his master as a belligerent enemy, and in seizing from him whatever reprisals are necessary to aid him in effecting a retreat."[61] If Beecher had been slow to come to public opposition to slavery, he more than made up for it with the virulence of his attack, once he had a change of heart.

This time Beecher's eloquence fell on deaf ears, for money was not forthcoming. Still another meeting, on December 16, 1848, proved equally unsuccessful, and the *Tribune*, a few days later, published a lengthy appeal for funds. Mary and Emily as teachers would provide "a voice against slavery louder . . . in the ears of tyrants than that of any thousand denunciatory Conventions ever held."[62] How strange it seems that after a very large sum of money was forthcoming to free the two young slaves, there was little interest in educating them to lead useful lives.

It was all very well to talk about educating Mary and Emily Edmondson, but given the paucity of schools for black girls, few choices were available. Apparently William Chaplin again came to the rescue, for in 1849 the two young women began attending W. R. Smith's "family school" in Macedon, Wayne County, New York. Smith and Chaplin were close friends, and since Smith was known to help slaves on their way to freedom, he must have welcomed the opportunity to assist in the Edmondsons' education. Macedon was full of abolitionists, and Wayne County claimed to be the most northerly stop on an escape route to Canada. Both Rochester and Syracuse, nearby cities, were important centers of antislavery activity.[63] After the 1850 arrest of Chaplin for helping slaves to escape (see chapter 9), William R. Smith wrote a lengthy pamphlet relating the many sacrifices made by Chaplin on behalf of the enslaved.

In 1849 Myrtilla Miner, a teacher from New York City employed at William Smith's school, was asked by Asa Smith, William's father, whether she could "take charge" of a proposed school in the District of Columbia meant to train African American women to become teachers. Since Mary and Emily Edmondson were studying in Macedon in 1849, with the understanding that they would become teachers, it is logical to assume that their presence inspired the elder Smith's proposal. Miner went on to establish such a school and eventually employed Emily Edmondson to assist her.[64]

Further information is lacking about the young women's stay in Macedon. Some time before the fall of 1851 they visited the Glen Haven Water Cure in Cayuga County, New York. In the middle of the nineteenth century, water from mineral springs was often regarded as the sovereign remedy for all ills, and watering places became both fashionable and therapeutic. Was Mary Edmondson already showing signs of the tuberculosis that would cause her death? Did she go there to regain her health, or did the young women take the waters at the invitation of their friend and protector William Chaplin, who was involved in operating Glen Haven?[65]

If Mary had not been well, she was better by September 1851, when she and Emily enrolled in the Primary Department of New York Central College in McGrawville, Cortland County, an experiment in joint education of blacks and whites, men and women. Although the college was nonsectarian, the American Baptist Free Mission Society raised the money for its establishment and made decisions about its regulations. Students would work while they learned; they would not use tea, coffee, tobacco, or alcohol; and they would engage in a rigorous course of study. Hatred of slavery motivated the young people attending Central College. Angeline Hall, a contemporary of the Edmondsons, wrote a school paper about the Fugitive Slave Law: "Yes, let the union be dissolved rather than bow in submission to such a detestable, abominable, infamous law, a law in derogation of our free institutions, an exhibition of tyranny and injustice which might well put to the blush a nation of barbarians."[66]

McGrawville became the site of the new college because it was remote from railroads, in a county with "strong antislavery feeling," and was said to be "one of the principal lines of the underground railroad for fugitive slaves." After a fund-raising campaign, a local committee bought a farm, and on July 4, 1848, "the corner stone was laid and was the occasion of a great celebration." The founders erected a handsome building; students began to arrive on September 5, 1849; and the enrollment was something over a hundred, with both blacks and whites attending. "The college charged one dollar a week for board. The men were charged five dollars a year for room and the women three dollars, but male students were paid five cents an hour and the female students three cents an hour for labor." The college did not prosper and increasingly depended on Gerrit Smith to make up the deficits. Some thought it was too "white," others too "black," and by 1854 it was obvious that it could not long survive. It finally closed in 1860.[67]

However, in 1851 New York Central College seemed ideal for Mary and Emily, now that they had had instruction at Smith's school. They were among the seven ladies and nine gentlemen enrolled in the Primary Department and listed in the *Catalogue of the Officers and Students of New-York Central College for the Year 1851–52*.[68] At the end of the year, their teacher reported that in spite of many difficulties, including having to "suspend their studies for months at a time" to raise money, Mary and Emily had "acquired the rudiments of a primary education," including being able to write "a legible hand" and having "some knowledge of grammar, geography, and arithmetic."[69]

Money problems were never absent. At the time that the two girls enrolled at New York Central College, *Frederick Douglass' Paper* carried a request for $40 to pay their expenses. William Chaplin, in serious trouble because of his involvement in a slave escape attempt in Washington, could not help. Had people grown weary of the Edmondsons? Apparently so, for the plea in Douglass's paper brought no results; the professor who had asked for assistance ended up paying for their schooling. Financial relief arrived in 1852 with Harriet Beecher Stowe, who was generously spreading abroad the riches that resulted from the popularity of *Uncle Tom's Cabin*. Although Stowe's son claimed that his mother assumed responsibility for Mary and Emily in 1851,[70] it was probably the next year when Stowe encountered Amelia Edmondson and her two daughters.

A slave could not travel north unless accompanying her owner, but since Mrs. Edmondson's mistress was deemed an "idiot," it was unlikely they would have traveled together. But Amelia Edmondson was determined to seek assistance in buying the freedom of the two children still at home. Where more logical than the city in which Paul Edmondson had been successful? No one stopped the slave woman when she got on the train, and in May 1852 she appeared at the home of Henry Ward Beecher.[71] Beecher was not interested; was it because Amelia Edmondson was neither young nor beautiful? Sister Harriet Beecher Stowe, on the other hand, was delighted with Amelia Edmondson and set out to raise whatever amount the slave woman required.

Amelia Edmondson, with her plain Methodist scarf and cap and her deeply religious view of life's hardships, struck a responsive chord in Stowe that is evident in all that she wrote about the slave woman. The author reported to her husband that in Amelia Edmondson she had seen "a living example in which Christianity had reached its fullest development under the crushing wrongs of slavery." Stowe arranged for her to speak to various women's groups in New York and Brooklyn churches, where she aroused great sympathy as she related the hardships of her life as a slave. There was talk of taking her to visit other cities, but there is no record that that occurred. Amelia Edmondson went home with $1,200, but we do not know whether Stowe herself donated most of the money.[72]

It is not clear who became free; Stowe's son implied that only the two remaining Edmondson slaves were liberated, but other sources claimed that Amelia Edmondson's freedom was part of the bargain. There is a story that the Edmondson owner demanded an additional $300, on the grounds that property values had risen, and that Stowe paid it, saying, "My word has gone forth that they shall be *free*! & God helping me, they shall be! What are a few dollars compared with the suffering they might endure?"[73]

While their mother was in New York City, Mary and Emily went to see her, and Stowe, meeting them for the first time, agreed to bear the cost of their education and send them to Oberlin College in Ohio. She was anxious to get the two young women away from New York, where they had been "under bad influences since they gained their freedom." "They fell into the hands of an unprincipled man who on pretence of raising money for their education made a show of them in public exhibitions thus taking up their time and exposing them to very undesirable influences." To make bad matters worse, he never gave them any of the money they had raised: "They have had to struggle along, working beyond their strength and getting very indifferent opportunities of study."[74] Whom was she attacking? Perhaps William Chaplin, for by now he had alienated his antislavery friends and colleagues (see chapter 9).

Oberlin College in Ohio followed the same policy as Central, admitting blacks and whites, men and women, and in 1846 the college created a separate Teacher's Department.[75] Since Stowe envisioned the young Edmondsons as teachers, sending them to Oberlin would prepare them for a career and get them away from New York.

Stowe had a clear idea of what she desired for them: "a thorough solid education calculated to strengthen & develop their reasoning powers & judgment." While they were learning housekeeping and fine sewing, they should not have to endure any of the heavy drudgery to which they had been subjected under slavery. "They have naturally fine musical abilities and it is very desirable to their success as teachers that they should have a thorough knowledge of vocal music if possible." Indeed, she added, "I consider it one of the most essential things." [76]

Religious training would be of the first importance, and Stowe hoped the young women would "cultivate that spirit of charity & forgiveness" practiced by their mother. It would "lead them to love & to pray for, the bitterest enemies of their unhappy race." Stowe thought that in this respect the Edmondsons had suffered from the malign influence of abolitionists. She was prepared to bear all the expense of Mary and Emily's education, to the limit of her resources. If she needed additional funds, she would turn to the "benevolent ladies" of her acquaintance.[77]

After deciding to send the former slaves to Oberlin, she turned for housing to the family of the Reverend Henry Cowles, who had been an influential member of the college faculty, maintaining that "Oberlin's business was to educate the mind without regard to the color of the body in which the mind resided." Cowles, now the editor of the *Oberlin Evangelist*, and his family had only "narrow resources," so Stowe's generous support of the Edmondsons was welcome. She knew, in any case, that the Cowles family would agree on the importance of educating the Edmondson daughters. Mrs. Edmondson, she told Mrs. Cowles, was "one of the noblest and loveliest of Christians," from whom Stowe herself had derived "great strength and consolation." Paul Edmondson was "a venerable Christian," who had "borne a blameless character for more than seventy years." Stowe had faith in the two young women because they came "of such an excellent stock." [78]

By the summer of 1852 Mary and Emily were settled in the Cowles household and enrolled in the Oberlin Preparatory Department. Living with the Cowleses proved to be a happy arrangement, and the young members of the family were soon falling in love with the sisters. Visits from Gerrit Smith and Frederick Douglass demonstrated Mary and Emily's celebrity status.[79]

Stowe followed with great interest the progress of her charges, even taking time to correct spelling and penmanship in their letters. She sent money with regularity, carefully arranging for her husband or a friend to assume that responsibility when she was out of the country. She persuaded church groups and at least one girls' school to contribute to the support of Mary and Emily, with the idea of establishing scholarships that would benefit other young women after her current charges had completed their education.[80]

At the very time that Mary and Emily seemed settled and their future secure, Mary became ill. There had already been indications that all was not well, for Stowe, concerned that her charges had worked too hard in New York, warned Mrs. Cowles not to assign demanding tasks as they learned about housekeeping. By August 1852 Stowe, a believer in the water cure, was urging wet bandages, daily cold baths, and walks in the fresh air. Mary was much loved. She had a deeply religious nature; even the slave trader Joseph Bruin claimed, "If there is a *real Christian* upon earth, . . . Mary Edmondson is one." She had saved her sister and herself, for they would have joined the coffle heading south from the Alexandria slave pen had not Bruin's daughter wept and declared she could not bear to be parted from Mary. Probably in reaction to the stress of Mary's sickness, Emily began to act up, and Mrs. Cowles complained to Stowe, who soothed her by pointing out that the ex-slave had been through "enough to ruin five ordinary girls."[81]

There was general grief when the diagnosis of Mary's illness was consumption (tuberculosis), the great killer of the young. In 1851 Helen Cowles, only twenty years old, had died in the same house of the same disease. Mary knew that she was dying, and she longed to be with her family in Washington, but Stowe thought the trip unwise. In the spring of 1853 Frederick Douglass reported that Mary Edmondson was very ill and not expected to live. She died at Oberlin on May 18; her age was given as twenty years and six months.[82]

Stowe was convinced that the rigors of Mary's experiences in Alexandria, Baltimore, and New Orleans had contributed to her decline: "What makes me weep so is that such girls as these are *sold* in *our country* and that good men will endure it." Although deeply affected by Mary's death, Stowe found comfort in the knowledge that the young woman had died "peacefully in the arms of love & prayer." As she thought of what Mary's death might have been like had she remained a slave, Stowe was moved to say, "Can you wonder that all that the world can give *me* cannot quiet the deep sorrow of my heart."[83]

After Mary's death, Emily refused to remain in Oberlin, even though she had not completed her education. Stowe concluded that the young woman had better return to Washington and work in Myrtilla Miner's school. Emily was reluctant, preferring to live in New York; but Stowe insisted, and by June 1853 Emily was back in the bosom of her family. The Edmondsons rejoiced at being reunited but grieved over Mary's absence, especially because she had not been able to come home to die: "But the Lord orders all things for the best," as Emily put it in a letter to Mrs. Cowles. Emily had not only learned to write an excellent letter but also to emphasize Christian resignation: "He that is mightier than all, and that doth all things well, has taken her [Mary] to himself in Glory." She went on: "Some days it seems as though I could not live without her but when I think how happy she is in heaven, I feel like wiping away all my tears, and get ready to meet her in Glory."[84] This from a young woman who four years before had been illiterate!

By returning to Washington, Emily Edmondson was taking up where she had left off five years before, when she had joined her sister and brothers aboard the *Pearl* in a desperate search for freedom. She had experienced the horrors of the slave trade, not at its worst, to be sure, but she learned what it was like to be treated as merchandise, to be at the mercy of sellers and buyers, and to be shipped from one place to another in response to demands for property. It must have been small comfort to Emily Edmondson that her story had converted many people to antislavery, that her plight had made tangible to them the evils of human bondage.

Once she was free, Emily took every advantage of the opportunities offered her. She learned to read and write proficiently, to speak and sing before an audience, to raise money for her schooling, and to live as a free person in a free society. Of all the men, women, and children who boarded the *Pearl* as fugitives, Emily Edmondson was to be, in the long run, the most fortunate.

CHAPTER SIX

The TRIALS

On April 13, 1848, the same day that the *Pearl* first docked at the Seventh Street wharf in Washington, Horace Mann took the oath of office to succeed John Quincy Adams as representative of the Eighth Congressional District of Massachusetts. No matter how unlikely it might have seemed, the lives of Mann and the men aboard the *Pearl* would intersect in a significant fashion.

Adams, in his fight for the right of petition, had become a hero to Massachusetts opponents of slavery, and when he died, they hoped to find a worthy replacement, preferably Adams's son Charles Francis Adams. Fearing, however, that the younger man's outspoken opposition to slavery would alienate too many constituents, they looked for a less controversial candidate and settled on Mann, who was elected by a landslide. Mann, though an opponent of slavery, had refrained from a public pronouncement on the controversial subject, believing that doing so might endanger the advancement of public education.[1]

Horace Mann's name conjures up images of teachers' colleges and normal schools, and today he is indeed known chiefly as an educator. Although that perception would not have displeased him, he was also a lawyer and a politician. Mann studied at Tapping Reeve's law school in Litchfield, Connecticut, where a fellow student remembered him "as the best law student and the best-read scholar in the school." Admitted to the Massachusetts bar in 1823, Mann had a successful career as a lawyer, and when he entered the state senate in 1835, he already had a significant "legal reputation." Two years later he gave up law and politics to serve in what he saw as the crucially important position of secretary to the newly created Massachusetts State Board of Education.[2]

By 1848 Mann had achieved an international reputation as an educator, and in that role he refused to become involved in controversies over slavery. Samuel J. May remembered that, while serving as principal of the normal school in Lexington, Massachusetts, he received warnings from Mann not to speak publicly about his hatred of slavery. May understood that Mann was "so intent upon his great undertaking for the improvement of our common schools, that he thought it our duty to repress our interest in every other reform that was unpopular."[3]

Even though May, at least in retrospect, excused Mann's refusal to participate in the growing opposition to slavery, many Bostonians were not so charitable. Wendell Phillips, for example, attacked Mann's "timid silence" on school segregation in Boston and condemned his effort to find a compromise that would satisfy angry blacks and not alienate the white majority.[4] It was his reputation for moderation, plus his commitment to civic duty, that made possible Mann's election to Congress. As a contemporary wrote, "There is no man in New England so well qualified in every respect to occupy the post of honor and duty rendered vacant by the death of John Quincy Adams, as he." Furthermore, "he is liberal-minded, generous-hearted, dignified in his deportment, genteel in his address, and his character is . . . above suspicion."[5]

So Mann arrived in Washington in the spring of 1848, long removed from the practice of law, reluctant to be drawn into the proslavery-antislavery conflict, and bearing the burden of taking the seat of so eminent a statesman as John Quincy Adams. He knew that the leaders of antislavery in his state distrusted him, and yet it would be they who turned to him to help Daniel Drayton and Edward Sayres. And by 1850 he would be "enormously popular" in his Massachusetts district.[6]

✷

Drayton and Sayres had been fortunate to avoid lynching by Washington's angry mob; they probably concluded that they would never leave the District's jail alive. The anger of Washingtonians was very real, for the two men had struck at the heart of slavery, and all those involved in the escape attempt would have to pay, one way or another. Although the mob may have been led by slave dealers who had seen their livelihood in peril, the capital was full of people who believed that preserving slavery in the District was essential for making it secure throughout the South. Many Washingtonians agreed with the *Richmond Enquirer*: "Let negro-stealing be punished with solitary confinement for life, without reprieve, or by hanging, and . . . you will hear of no more such scenes as we have enacted here [in Washington]."[7] Consequently, District Attorney Philip Barton Key felt enormous pressure to demand and secure the maximum punishment for such evil men.

Removing the prisoners to court for them to be charged was much too dangerous, and therefore the arraignment took place in the jail. On April 19 Justices of the Peace J. H. Goddard and H. C. Williams examined the three men, with David A. Hall and Edward Stowe Hamlin appearing for the prisoners. Giddings was there, too, but according to the *Sun* of Baltimore, he caused so much excitement that he had to leave: "Some friends carried him away." No objection was raised to the presence of Congressman John Gorham Palfrey; probably the mob did not know that he was as opposed to slavery as his friend and colleague Giddings was. The hearing had to be continued to the next day because some owners were not present, but then Goddard and Williams committed the three men (Chester English, the cook, was included in the charge) to answer at the June term of the Criminal Court of the District of Columbia to charges of having "stolen, taken, and carried away" seventy-six slaves on April 15, 1848. Bail was set at $1,000 for each slave—that is, $76,000 each for Drayton, Sayres, and English.[8]

Frederick Douglass urged Bostonians to take the lead in providing bail for the three men, but no one volunteered; it was too much money. When Mann took on the defense, he asked Charles Dexter Cleveland if he could raise bail money. It was out of the question, replied the Philadelphian, for there were no rich antislavery men in his city.[9]

The *Liberator* was indignant at the size of the bail: "Such bail was never before heard of in a decent country, and ought to arouse the whole free heart of the nation to cry, 'Oh God, how long!'" There was talk of securing a writ of *habeas corpus* for Chester English, since he was obviously innocent, but the jail was safer than the street: "We were given to understand that if released, he would not leave the city alive," reported Edward Stowe Hamlin. Garrison admitted that Drayton and

Sayres were more secure in the jail, for "wolves in human shape" were "prowling around them night and day." Nevertheless, he deplored the use of the jail for such an unjust purpose, since the money of northerners as well as southerners had paid for the building. "Is it not time that we have done with this partnership in crime?"[10]

The laws of Maryland applied in the District, the Virginia portion having been returned to that state in 1846. Drayton, Sayres, and English, therefore, would stand trial under Maryland laws of 1737, 1751, and 1796.[11] The first of these provided that anyone stealing a slave or even counseling him to run away should suffer the death penalty. The second, of 1751, ordered that "if any free Person shall entice and perswade [sic] any Slave within this Province to run away," he had to pay the full value of the slave or serve a year in prison. The third, of 1796, eased the 1737 death penalty to a fine of $200 per slave, "one half to the use of the master or owner of such slave, the other half to the county school, in case there be any, if no such school, to the use of the county." Although Virginia no longer had a legal interest in the District, antislavery newspapers expected the governor to demand possession of the prisoners.[12]

When word of the *Pearl* fiasco reached antislavery activists in the North, they immediately realized that they had to act. How could they be most useful? In New York City and upstate New York, emancipationists generally agreed that helping the recaptured slaves achieve freedom was of primary importance, and the ransoming of Mary and Emily Edmondson was one result of this decision. But if you believed that human beings could not be bought and sold, how could you participate in such a transaction? In a sense, purchasing slaves indicated an acceptance of the institution.

Instead of buying slaves in order to free them, opponents could better use their money to educate free blacks and to encourage the enslaved to flee. As was said when the Edmondson girls were ransomed, money paid to a slave owner or dealer would simply be used to buy more slaves, perpetuating the evil. Although it was difficult to refuse a plea for assistance on the part of a slave being sold to New Orleans, abolitionist Theodore Parker, when asked to help purchase a fugitive's freedom, wrote, "I could not give money to feed the hunters of human flesh."[13] Bostonians would not cooperate with human bondage; they would instead provide legal help to Drayton and Sayres. So they called for a meeting in Faneuil Hall to be held on April 25, 1848.

It was "tolerably well attended, but at no part of the evening was the hall nearly full"; it cost nine dollars "for opening, Lighting, & Closing the hall."[14] The "citizens of Boston" approved a committee "to collect money and employ counsel, for the purpose of defending these men" and to bring before the courts "the question of the legality of slavery in the District of Columbia." The committee members were well-known emancipationists: Samuel J. May, Samuel Gridley Howe, Samuel E. Sewall, Francis Jackson, Richard Hildreth, and ten other public figures. A flyer reporting the meeting of the twenty-fifth urged people to send money, for it was obvious that the plans of the committee would require extensive financing.

The Bostonians anticipated that the trials would be the definitive confrontation over the legality of slavery in the District and also in the territory being acquired from Mexico as a result of the war that had just ended. They believed that through legal action they could demonstrate once and for all that Congress had no power "to establish or to maintain slavery, in territory over which it possesses exclusive jurisdiction." Using "eminent counsel," they would take the case to the United States Supreme Court, though the committee admitted some doubt as to the route such a case could take. Nevertheless, the flyer, which was printed in antislavery newspapers, urged immediate donations. At least one meeting, in Providence, Rhode Island, where Frederick Douglass spoke, led to the appointment of a fund-raising committee and the dissemination of appeals.[15]

The money came in very slowly, a dollar or two at a time, though Gerrit Smith, with his usual generosity, sent $500. Antislavery lawyer and writer Richard Hildreth, using $200 of Smith's donation, set off for Washington to find a lawyer or lawyers.[16] Hildreth stopped off in Philadelphia to see Mrs. Drayton, and there he met Charles Dexter Cleveland and discussed with the Philadelphian the importance of retaining eminent counsel. Cleveland longed for the oratory of Daniel Webster; could he be induced to "take hold of the cause with his whole mind and *soul*"? No, was the unanimous decision of the committee, for in spite of Webster's being a popular choice, they believed that "his *mind* is not with us and his 'soul' is gone to the great adversary long ago." Furthermore, they could not pay Webster's $1,000 fee. By the middle of May the committee felt sure that, without spending any money, they had indeed secured "eminent counsel" in the persons of William H. Seward, former governor of New York, and William

Pitt Fessenden, former member of the House of Representatives from Maine.[17]

When it emerged that neither Seward nor Fessenden was available, the plans of the Bostonians began to fall apart. At the same time that the committee was proclaiming success, it was admitting failure by begging Lewis Tappan in New York to take over raising money to pay lawyers. Ever since 1840, when the Tappan brothers, Arthur and Lewis, led a secession from the American Anti-Slavery Society to form the American and Foreign Anti-Slavery Society, New Yorkers and Bostonians had followed differing paths in opposing slavery. The leaders of the American Anti-Slavery Society, most notably William Lloyd Garrison and Wendell Phillips, urged noninvolvement in politics — no voting, no membership in political parties — on the grounds that the government of the United States was itself deeply implicated in slavery. The newer society, led by the Tappans, encouraged its members to take part in politics and to join antislavery parties. No love was lost between the two groups, and it must have been a bitter experience for the Bostonians to turn to Tappan for help. The enthusiasm of April had become the despair of May.

Tappan, busy with other projects, refused to assume the burden of finding money for the defense of Drayton and Sayres, but he offered the Bostonians unsolicited advice. The "large & able" committee of New Englanders would be successful if they followed the New York model of fund-raising that had prevented the reenslavement of the Africans aboard the *Amistad*. "If pressed, promptly & efficiently, as was the Amistad case, I doubt not several thousands of dollars may be raised." In the earlier case Tappan and his supporters had "appealed to the friends of human rights in the newspapers & by correspondence, and followed up these appeals[?] very vigorously." Experience had taught him, said Tappan, "that very great energy & promptitude are necessary"; if they followed his advice in soliciting funds, the Boston committee would achieve its goal.[18] Gall and wormwood to Bostonians!

A committee that had started out with such high hopes soon found not only that money was slow to arrive but also that lawyers and politicians, busy with other matters, were reluctant to become involved in a difficult case without fees. Of all public figures, Salmon P. Chase of Ohio was the most experienced defender of the rights of slaves. He was seriously interested in Drayton and Sayres, having long held the view that District slavery was unconstitutional. Furthermore, since he had been admitted to the bar in the very court where Drayton and Sayres would be tried, he would welcome the opportunity to set forth his position on slavery in the nation's capital. As it turned out, however, Chase, like William H. Seward, could not free himself from other responsibilities.[19]

And so the Boston committee reluctantly turned to Horace Mann. They were not sure they trusted him, fearing that he was not really sound on the slavery question; but as the trial date approached, they had little choice.

As for Mann, he had not argued a case in court for at least twelve years; as he said, he had been "so long a stranger to the courts" that he would be "about the worst counsel the poor fellows could have."[20] Furthermore, he had never handled litigation dealing with slavery, and he had just begun to serve in Congress, where he filled the important seat of John Quincy Adams. But his conscience would not allow the case to go to trial without competent counsel. And so, reluctantly agreeing, he immersed himself in the laws of Maryland, persuaded David A. Hall to do research, and pleaded for help wherever it might be found. Chase sent Mann a lengthy exposition of his view that slavery could not exist in the nation's capital and that Congress had no authority to impose Maryland's slave laws on the District. According to Chase, the Constitution recognized slaves as people and not as property, and it did not give Congress the power to impose slavery on people where Congress was in control, either in territories or in the District. Chase based his position to a considerable extent on the Fifth Amendment protection of life, liberty, and property. Regretting his inability to be present at the litigation, Chase wrote to Mann: "God send them [Drayton and Sayres] a safe deliverance, and save our Country from the ineffaceable & unspeakable disgrace of their conviction & punishment as criminals."[21]

When it appeared that Mann would have to argue the case by himself, he became frantic: "Here I am alone, no one to help me investigate the case,—a case of the greatest difficulty [and] range of complexity." Enlisting the assistance of Giddings or others known for their antislavery views "would prejudice the jury beforehand." Mann understood the political significance of the trial, but he would not endanger the prisoners' future "in order to benefit even the anti-slavery cause." He appealed to his friend Charles Sumner in Boston: "What are the best authorities, on the subject that '*slavery is against natural right*; & that *it is the creature only of local law*.'" Somewhat wistfully he observed: "I suppose you have studied this subject so much that the authorities are familiar to you." But then Richard Hildreth arrived from Boston to give assistance. Although trained at the bar, he spent most of his time as a writer and would be the unnamed author of Drayton's memoir.[22]

Samuel Gridley Howe despaired of his fellow Bostonians as they argued about hiring attorneys; they were, he said, all abolitionists except himself and therefore "*impracticable*, mulish." Fessenden of Maine had turned them down; Senator John Parker Hale of Maine they liked but thought his outspoken antislavery views would harm the prisoners' cause; but at least the Boston committee felt safe with Mann. The North, Howe said, was looking for "leaders and champions" in the attack on slavery, and Mann could be "the hero of this coming struggle for freedom and the right." Perhaps Howe was damning Mann with faint praise when he wrote: "If worse come to worst no man in the country will make more out of a bad case than you can." The historian Lawrence Friedman has called Mann a "halfway abolitionist"; Mann would have denied he was an abolitionist, but halfway or whole way, he could not ignore the prisoners' desperate plight.[23]

Although Howe opposed engaging a local attorney, Mann, understanding the situation in Washington better than the members of the Boston committee, hired James M. Carlisle, a native of Alexandria, who had studied law with the famous William Wirt. Carlisle had a rapid rise in the District bar and, because he was a good linguist, gained some fame as a legal adviser to international commissions, specifically serving as counsel for Costa Rica, Colombia, and Great Britain. Although he lost his sight in 1866, he still argued more cases before the Supreme Court than any other lawyer of his time. A young man of thirty-four when he agreed to serve with Mann as counsel for Drayton, he demonstrated considerable courage in taking on such an unpopular case; Washingtonians might feel that the Alexandria native had betrayed his own people. Carlisle made it plain that he was not opposed to slavery and in fact harbored "bitter anti-abolitionist feeling"; but, wanting to see fair play, he was willing to defend a man badly in need of help.[24]

While preparations were under way for the trials of Drayton, Sayres, and English, some Washingtonians, still hoping to discover who had planned the slaves' escape, were hatching schemes to persuade the prisoners to turn on each other. In addition, rumors floated around the city that Edward Sayres had proposed to a dealer that as soon as he was free, he would collect slaves and carry them off to a southern market. According to another rumor, Sayres would sell slaves in Brazil.[25]

On June 29 a grand jury, headed by Peter Force, brought in 110 indictments—separate ones for stealing and for transporting slaves—against each of the three men aboard the *Pearl*: Drayton, Sayres, and English. This meant that each of them would be tried 110 times for the same event. The district attorney in Washington did not receive a salary but was dependent on fees, $10 for each charge: the more charges the more fees.[26]

When it became clear that Mann would lead the defense, he had to reassure his wife that he would not be in any physical danger: "The South know too well what a prodigious advantage it would give to the anti-slavery cause, if it could have a martyr." He arranged to be admitted "as an attorney and counsellor at the Criminal Court," since he had never practiced in the District.[27] All too aware of his limited knowledge of both the law and the facts in the case, he hoped to delay as long as possible. Key, on the other hand, was anxious to bring the men to trial, for numerous convictions would increase his popularity in the city. The trial was scheduled to begin on July 24, 1848, before Judge Thomas Hartley Crawford, and the packed courtroom—"densely thronged," according to the *Sun*—demonstrated that interest had not waned. The weather was hot and steamy, a typical Washington July, with the temperature seldom lower than ninety degrees, and the atmosphere in the crowded courtroom was oppressive.[28]

Carlisle was ill, delaying the trial for three days. On the twenty-seventh Mann, Hall, and Carlisle appeared for Drayton and Sayres; Daniel Ratcliffe, who was active during the *National Era* riot, appeared for English. Key would prosecute the case without other legal help, at least in the early trials. The *National Anti-Slavery Standard* deplored the atmosphere in the courtroom. "It is characteristic of the state of the public mind, that this trial . . . is carried on in the midst of jokes and laughter, any of the audience taking the liberty to talk and joke with the jurymen in any little intervals in the progress of the trial; and one of the Jury, just as they were going out to deliberate on their verdict . . . told a funny story about a bottle of rum!" Such, wrote the *Standard*, "is the free and easy way in which men are sent to the Penitentiary in this District."[29]

There may well have been levity, and most of the jurors sympathized with slavery. Although a biographer of Mann, Jonathan Messerli, claimed that "the jury was drawn from a motley pool of drifters and idlers combed from the streets and local grog shops," in fact it was made up of substantial citizens, such as a tailor, a grocer, a carpenter, a saddler, a blacksmith, a baker, and owners of a shoe store and a dry goods store. The biographer's characterization probably applied more aptly to the spectators, for Mann said that during the trial the men that had sought to attack Drayton as he was on his way to the jail had stationed themselves "as near as practicable to the counsel for the defence."[30]

Carlisle tried to persuade Key to agree to a reduction in the number of cases, saying that he deplored "the enormous expense of four thousand dollars [in] costs, unnecessarily accrued, to the Government, by this system of charging different offences upon one state of facts." Key became angry, understanding very well that Carlisle was accusing him of making a great deal of money out of "double indictments." Said Key, "This was a case of the most horrid atrocity, and he felt it his duty to do all in his power to bring it to justice." Judge Crawford made no ruling, and the first trial began, against Drayton, on the charge of larceny (stealing slaves).[31]

Although Drayton's team of lawyers hoped to see their client totally exonerated, they realized that this was an unlikely eventuality. Their fallback position was to secure exoneration on the charge of stealing slaves and reluctantly accept the charge of transporting them. Conversely, the district attorney was determined to secure conviction on the more serious charge of larceny (stealing), for he would thus demonstrate his own commitment to the slave system and warn any who might be tempted to follow Drayton's example. Consequently, according to a spectator, Key claimed that if Drayton had the slaves on board his vessel, he must have stolen them; that constituted larceny.[32]

Although Key had insisted on separate indictments for each slave, he had to select one slave — in this instance two slaves — and one owner to begin trials that apparently would continue for decades. He charged that Drayton "feloniously did steal, take, and carry away" two brothers named Joe and Frank, property of Andrew Hoover, owner of a boot and shoe factory and store. In 1840 Hoover owned four slaves, three male and one female;[33] one of the fugitives drove a cart, and the other served in Hoover's house.

On the witness stand Hoover appeared bewildered by the slaves' flight. He had bought their mother in Virginia and had raised the boys himself. Although he could not be sure, he thought they might even have been born in his house. He testified to their value: "I suppose they are worth fourteen hundred dollars; I was offered money for them and refused it; I would not sell them for twice the amount." When Joe and Frank were brought into the courtroom, Hoover testified that they were indeed his property, and they were the ones that had fled. Under cross-examination Hoover admitted that no one had broken into his house and that Joe and Frank must have fled on their own.[34]

Having established that legally owned slaves had been on the *Pearl*, Key then called Justice of the Peace Hampton Williams, whom the posse had chosen as their leader. Williams could speak with authority about the capture of the ship. When he walked over to Georgetown on Sunday, April 16, he heard about the flight of the slaves and immediately went on board the *Salem*, which took off in pursuit. Francis Dodge, the principal owner of the steamer, provided members of the posse with cigars and tobacco but not whiskey; it was important to show that the pursuers were not drunk.

Williams thought it was about four o'clock in the morning when they found the schooner anchored in Cornfield Harbor. A member of the posse with a lantern read the name of the schooner on the stern, while another "applied his nose to a crack in the hatch and shouted out, 'niggers a-plenty, by ——!'" Williams called for Drayton to come out (the posse had discovered Drayton's name before the *Salem* left the District), and when he appeared, Williams and Thomas Orme grabbed him, walked him over to the steamer, and immediately began to ask questions. Drayton identified Sayres as the captain and English as the third member of the crew. After tying up the three men and holding them prisoner on the steamer but leaving the slaves on board the *Pearl*, the posse made ready for a triumphant trip up the Potomac River.

The *Salem* took the *Pearl* in tow, and while the steamer was loading on wood at the Cone River, Williams counted the slaves for the first time and thought there were seventy-seven, though the indictments would reduce the number by one. He made a point of saying that none of the slaves was bound and that they were "singing all the way home" while enjoying a barrel of molasses.[35] As soon as the *Salem* was in Washington waters, Williams, who was, after all, a justice of the peace, charged Drayton.

All the way up the Potomac, Williams and Orme had tried to get Drayton to tell them who paid for the expedition, but his response was, "That is what you will never know." Williams supposed that his prisoner was an agent of the "underground railroad to freedom." Drayton was talkative on the way back, saying that he might well benefit from being imprisoned, where he could save his soul through "meditation and repentance." If he had not been captured, he might have continued "to lead a life of wickedness, whereby his soul would be lost." If he was imprisoned, he was sure that his family would be cared for. Claiming that he had once been wealthy but had lost everything, Drayton told Williams that "if he had escaped with this cargo of negroes he would have been in independent circumstances." This was crucial testimony and supported rumors in the District that Drayton was a slave stealer, his purpose being "to kidnap them [the slaves] and sell them at the South."[36]

Thomas Orme, the next witness, testified that Drayton insisted he was not an abolitionist, that he had refused offers of money to transport slaves to the North, and that he had made himself unpopular in Philadelphia by claiming that blacks were better off in the South than in the North. According to Orme, Drayton had taken on the task of removing slaves from Washington only because of his poverty, for since December 1846 he had been too sick to work — this in addition to his having lost a ship. Orme thought that Drayton implicitly threatened his sponsors (in spite of never naming them) by saying that if his family suffered, he might have a tale to tell.[37]

Talkative he may have been, but Drayton insisted that Sayres and English were innocent and that he alone was responsible for the escape attempt. He rightly feared that he would be "torn to pieces by a mob, which he likened to a mad bull"; he would rather be killed by the posse, and though some of the pursuers were anxious to grant him his wish, others promised to protect him.[38]

Samuel Baker, the captain of the steamer, testified to finding the *Pearl* in Cornfield Harbor and agreed that it was not seaworthy. He had seen a hermaphrodite brig (square-rigged forward and schooner-rigged aft) anchored there, though by then the storm had passed.[39]

Although Baker did not say so, the implication was that Drayton was going to transfer the slaves to the brig so they could be transported to the South and sold. In reality the brig's presence was not significant, for every seafaring man knew that Cornfield was a "favorite anchoring and poker-playing site" for craft "passing up and down the Bay."[40]

If Drayton had hoped to sell the slaves to the master of the brig, he lacked the means to enforce it; according to the testimony of Thomas Orme, there were no arms on board the *Pearl*, except for "one double-barrel gun, in bad order." The prosecution's next witness was a man named Lewis Winter, who testified that a year before he had seen the prisoner in the Baltimore slave-trading establishment of Joseph Donovan. According to Key, this would prove that in June 1847 Drayton had proposed to Donovan to "coast about the shores of Maryland and Virginia, pick up slaves, bring them to Donovan who could confine them in his pen, and, after the search was over, they might be shipped to the south and both profit by them." Court adjourned while Carlisle and Key were still arguing over the admissibility of such evidence; and though Judge Crawford finally ruled the Winter testimony inadmissible, the jury almost surely heard the exchange.[41]

K. H. Lambell, a ship's carpenter, testified that he had encountered the prisoner over a period of three or four years, when he would come to the District to sell wood or oysters. He had seen Drayton in April on board the *Pearl*, trying to sell a load of wood while complaining of its poor quality and then bemoaning the low price he accepted, only $2 a cord. That concluded the government's case.[42]

On July 30 Mann opened for the defense, lamenting that he had had too little time to prepare. He frankly admitted that he and the jury were as far apart as the poles when it came to "convictions and sentiments." They were united, however, by the call of duty: "Here we are embarked in a common cause. From this moment . . . let all feelings of alienation . . . be banished from between us." He acknowledged the difficulty of impartiality because of the violence in the city that had accompanied Drayton's arrest. Citing the trial following the Boston Massacre of 1770, in which British soldiers were treated evenhandedly in spite of the anger of Bostonians, he urged the current jury to be as fair. Reverting to a point made earlier by Carlisle, Mann claimed that Drayton had been loaded with so many indictments that if convicted in all instances, he could be in prison for 800 years. He reminded the jury that Key received a fee for each indictment and that the sum the government would have to pay the district attorney was $4,500.

Key jumped to his feet, exclaiming that that was not true. No, said Mann, there was no need for so many indictments, for one indictment would do. Key replied that separate felonies were to be charged in separate indictments. No, said Carlisle, they *might* be in separate indictments, but they *could* be in one.[43]

Mann and Carlisle were trying to convince the jury of Key's greed and the frivolous nature of an infinite number of trials. A correspondent of the *National Anti-Slavery Standard* reported that Carlisle had said, in open court, "that he could not much blame the District Attorney for the course he had taken, in instituting such a multiplicity of indictments, for if he had done otherwise he would probably have been *Lynched*. Such is public sentiment in this District." Mann and Carlisle, by mentioning Key's $4,500, may also have hoped to influence Judge Crawford, whose annual salary was $2,000.[44]

The most reported aspect of the trial occurred at this time. Mann reminded the court that slaves were unlike other property, in that "they might voluntarily . . . run away of their own accord, which he contended to have been the case with the Slaves alleged to have been stolen by Drayton."[45] Slavery in the District offered special temptation to bondmen and bondwomen, for they frequently heard speeches about freedom. As Mann began to read from one such oration, the judge stopped him, saying he had no right to attack slavery in a city where the institution was legal.

Mann proved that he was reading from a speech made by Senator Henry Foote of Mississippi, as printed in the *Daily Union*, the pro-southern, proslavery Washington newspaper. Crawford had no choice but to allow Mann to finish reading from Foote's speech and also from one by Congressman F. B. Stanton of Tennessee, "although the feeling in the court-room was such that you could almost witness it." The reporter for the Baltimore *Sun* departed from his account of the trial to say that Senator Foote would be "considerably startled" when he learned that he was blamed for the flight of the slaves. Antislavery editors reprinted Mann's speech, delighting in the opportunity to poke fun at a southern defender of slavery becoming a witness against human bondage; the *Emancipator* of Boston wondered if District Attorney Key would move against Senator Foote, charging him with slave stealing.[46]

According to the *Sun*'s reporter, Mann's basic argument was that Drayton had contracted to carry away six or seven slaves and that the others "marched down to the schooner, took possession of it, and made Drayton their prisoner." If this were the case, Drayton could not be held responsible for the wholesale flight. Mann's own account differed, for he claimed that Drayton, absent from the *Pearl* when the runaways arrived, did not know their great number until the posse ordered them to come on deck.[47]

The defense sought to demonstrate that Drayton was "a man of sober and industrious life, against whose character, as a just, upright, exemplary citizen, no charge was ever before preferred."[48] They brought several of Drayton's acquaintances to Washington to serve as character witnesses. Samuel Nelson, who kept a ship chandlery in Philadelphia, testified that he had known Drayton about eighteen years and lived near him; they had even been shipwrecked together. Nelson said that Drayton was married and had six children; he had been in bad health for a considerable time. Key asked Nelson if he had heard people speak of Drayton's stealing slaves, and though Drayton's lawyers objected strenuously, the judge allowed Nelson to answer. No, he had not heard it much talked about; but he had heard of his helping a slave escape, and people believed that he would "run negroes from the South." He had seen Drayton the day the *Pearl* left Philadelphia and indeed had known that he wanted a ship to go to Washington, but had no idea why.[49]

Jacob Carrigan, also from Philadelphia, testified that he had hired Drayton to take a cargo to Boston and had never heard anything against his character. John Cade, a seaman who had known Drayton for fifteen years and had never heard anything against him either, testified that he had seen many vessels anchored in Cornfield Harbor and Point Lookout; it was a natural place to anchor if the wind was wrong. Mann was trying to demonstrate that there was nothing sinister about the hermaphrodite brig anchored near Cornfield Harbor. Cade had heard Drayton "joke" about running off slaves. When the defense tried to call slaves to testify that Drayton "had no agency in their escape," the court said that slaves could not be witnesses.[50]

Key wanted to call Baltimore slaver Joseph Donovan to prove that Drayton was a slave stealer and also to recall Captain Baker to testify further about the hermaphrodite brig. Carlisle, however, objected strenuously, and Judge Crawford did not permit either man to be summoned. The case went to the jury.

The defense lawyers plainly had little respect for either Judge Crawford or District Attorney Key. They therefore decided to draw up a long list of objections that could be used as the basis for an appeal to the Circuit Court of the District of Columbia, where the chief judge was William Cranch, nephew of Abigail Adams and a signer, at least once, of a petition against District slavery. Cranch had received his appointment to the District court from President John Adams and in addition had been for many years a much admired reporter for the Supreme Court of the United States.[51]

Mann and Carlisle's objections ranged from Mann's claim that the word of a slave owner was not sufficient proof of servitude to his insistence that if the prisoner found the slaves on board his ship, it did not constitute proof that he had stolen them. In a lengthy response, Crawford agreed with four of Mann's points: to constitute stealing, there must be proof that the prisoner had taken the slave "from the owner's possession"; there must be proof, even if the slave was on board the prisoner's ship, that "such going on board was with the knowledge and consent and procurement of the prisoner"; and that if the prisoner found the slaves on board "without any previous act or knowledge on his part, even a subsequent conversion to his own use, would not support a charge of stealing for want of an original taking."[52]

Judge Crawford denied all the other points that the defense had raised, saying that ownership of a slave must be proved in the same way that ownership of any other piece of property is: "It is not necessary to do more than to establish generally that he is owned by the alleged owner." Mann claimed that color alone did not prove slavery; in the District it did, said the judge. It was *freedom* that required special proof. No wonder free blacks were in peril in Washington.

The defense argued that carrying off a slave was not a felony unless there was financial gain involved, that helping a slave achieve freedom was not a felony in and of itself. Crawford agreed that "merely to transport a slave, if it *stands alone*, is not larceny." But, he went on, "if it be preceded by corruption of the slave's mind, and by artful means decoying him away, and then feloniously taking and transporting him, it is larceny." Mann claimed that taking slaves on board the *Pearl* with the intention of transporting them to a free state was not larceny. The judge said that it was larceny if the prisoner "imbued their [the slaves'] minds with discontent, persuaded them to go with him, and by corrupt influences, &c., caused them to come to his ship, and feloniously took and carried them away."[53]

Among opponents of slavery there was great anger that the judge had agreed that helping slaves gain their freedom was stealing. Such a doctrine, said the *Pennsylvania Freeman*, had never been promulgated even in the Deep South. Why did it have to be a Pennsylvanian, Thomas H. Crawford, who claimed that the prisoner did not have to plan to sell the slaves for it to be stealing? All that Drayton did was to transport bondmen and bondwomen out of the District in order to take them to a free state. Crawford was a "doughface," a northerner sympathetic to slavery and more hated by antislavery forces than southerners, whose prejudices were at least understandable.[54]

A spectator at the trial deplored Key's attitude toward Drayton, claiming that the district attorney, lacking legal arguments, had "indulged himself very freely in abusive epithets." Key had called Drayton a "thing," a "rogue," a "liar," and a "felon." This had gone over very well with "a number of loafers among the audience," but Mann and Carlisle had objected, pointing out that a man was innocent until proven guilty. Carlisle, fond of historical allusions, compared Key to Sir Edward Coke, the early-seventeenth-century prosecutor, who made personal attacks on Sir Walter Raleigh when the explorer was on trial for his life.

Rather than arguing the merits of the case, Key used up most of his concluding speech defending himself from charges of improper behavior. An antislavery observer saw this as further proof of Key's ineffectiveness: "There was not a man there, having any pretensions to the sentiments of a gentleman, who did not hang his head in shame and pity for the unfortunate predicament into which the District Attorney plunged himself the deeper every word he spoke."[55]

The most damning evidence against Drayton was Hampton Williams's testimony that the prisoner had told him "that if he [Drayton] had got off safe with his cargo of slaves, he should have been placed in independent circumstances." If true, it would prove that Drayton did intend to sell the slaves and make an enormous profit. It would confirm the importance of the hermaphrodite brig that Captain Baker had seen in Cornfield Harbor, which could serve as a vehicle for transporting the slaves to the Deep South. But by the second Drayton trial, which began almost at once, Williams admitted that he was not sure the prisoner had confessed to a plan to sell the slaves; maybe a member of the posse had suggested it. If the latter, then it was not evidence. The *Anti-Slavery Bugle* cited another example of suspicious testimony by Williams: he "had the impudence to swear . . . that he believed the mob which attacked the prisoners on their way to jail, was got up out of fear that the free negroes would rescue the recaptured slaves."[56]

The first case against Drayton went to the jury on August 3, and Key must have been surprised when the jurors could not agree on a verdict. The *National Anti-Slavery Standard* heard that three Irishmen, believing in the innocence of the accused and "standing out all night" against the majority, finally became frightened and voted for Drayton's guilt. While waiting for the verdict in the first trial, Key called the second, which lasted for four days. The second jury also brought in a verdict of guilty. Sayres's trials began on August 10.[57]

Judge Crawford's rulings did not help the prisoner Drayton, but they forced Key to address one issue as he prepared for the second trial. The judge had decided that Drayton could not be guilty of larceny unless he had persuaded the slaves to flee. Since the *Pearl* had arrived in Washington only two days before it sailed with its load of fugitives, when had Drayton had the opportunity to influence the slaves, to "corrupt" their minds? Key took note, and in the second trial, when W. H. Upperman took the stand to testify about the theft of his slaves, the grocer claimed that on the night of the flight he had seen Drayton standing outside his house at the very time one of his slaves had gone downstairs. Curious about the stranger, Upperman went outside to the well "for the express purpose of . . . noticing this man." The moon was so bright that he could discern the features of an unknown person, and though he could not tell the court whether the stranger had whiskers or what kind of hat he wore, he had no doubt it was Drayton. The streets of Washington were dark; indeed, a proposal that very spring to install gas lights on the Capitol grounds had failed.[58] Nevertheless, the jury decided that Drayton had stolen Upperman's slaves.

There was little press coverage of Sayres's trials, since the evidence was repetitious. Twice tried on the charge of stealing slaves (larceny), Sayres was exonerated, both juries finding him not guilty, in one case deliberating only twenty minutes.[59] But he still had to face the lesser charge of transporting.

The first break in the apparently infinite number of trials came in the second week of August, when Key decided not to prosecute Chester English. He may have persuaded the young cook to testify against Sayres in exchange for his freedom, and it seems fair to speculate that Ratcliffe, as a Washington lawyer sympathetic to the South, was able to arrange it. It is not known how a poor cook, without friends in the District, found money to pay a lawyer. Mann had approved of the young cook's decision to seek separate counsel and to place all the blame on Drayton and Sayres: "He was totally without knowledge of the transaction until shortly before the vessel was to start from the wharf," wrote Mann, who was sorry that he had had to spend four months in the District jail. English was in Washington the next year, in the spring of 1849, to testify in further trials of Drayton and Sayres. He then disappears from the record, reappearing only in Drayton's memoir, in which Drayton deplores the young man's lack of enterprise.[60]

Having twice failed to convict Sayres of stealing, Key then called a third jury to consider all the remaining larceny charges against the *Pearl*'s captain; the verdict was not guilty in every instance. Key was growing impatient and perhaps disheartened, for conviction was not proving as easy as he had anticipated. Had jurymen been influenced by Mann and Carlisle's hammering on Key's greed? Perhaps the hysteria that had gripped the capital in April had diminished by August. At any rate, Key impaneled one more jury, submitted all the charges of *transporting* slaves, and finally secured a conviction against Sayres. The captain of the *Pearl* was fined $14,200 and would remain in jail until he had paid it.[61] Since Sayres had no money, it amounted to a life sentence.

Now that English was free and all of Sayres's charges disposed of, the district attorney decided to postpone further trials of Drayton until the December term. Mann and Carlisle protested, claiming that they were prepared to carry on for any number of sessions in court. Delay would work great hardship on their client; would he be held in jail indefinitely? Key claimed he had the right to call cases in any order he thought proper; Judge Crawford agreed; and the remainder of Drayton's trials were put off to the end of 1848. The *Anti-Slavery Bugle* lamented that Key could delay "the remaining trials as long as he pleases."[62]

Mann and Carlisle then moved to their fallback position, offering to have Drayton plead guilty to transporting slaves, with the condition that he receive new trials in the two larceny cases already decided (stealing the slaves of Hoover and Upperman) and that he be exonerated from all the remaining charges of stealing. Key refused, and on August 22, 1848, Crawford sentenced Drayton to twenty years at hard labor (ten years for each case), pending appeal to the circuit court.[63]

While Drayton and Sayres remained imprisoned, Mann's team prepared their circuit court challenge of Judge Crawford's rulings—and basked in warm praise for their accomplishments. Bostonians greeted Mann's opening speech at Drayton's first trial with great enthusiasm, Howe reporting that at least one man, previously no admirer of Mann, declared himself "touched, moved and persuaded" by the congressman's "noble speech."[64] The *Liberator* praised him for the "skill and energy" with which he had managed the cases. "It is the people of the United States, and not Captain Drayton, that is on trial here. Here their shameful wickedness and shameless effrontery are pilloried, as it were, in the eyes of the world." The prosecution of Drayton and Sayres did not occur in "some corner of a Slave State, and by some lynching Slave judge, but in the Capital of the Nation, on National Soil, by National Courts, and in National Prisons! May they help to make the American name infamous throughout the world."[65]

No matter what Mann did, however, he could not gain the trust of some members of the Boston committee. While he and his colleagues were preparing their appeal, New Englander S. E. Sewall wrote to New York senator William H. Seward begging for his assistance and asking him to devote his attention to the future trials. He assured the New Yorker that the Boston committee was "deeply indebted" to him for "the generous aid" he had provided, though there is no indication that he had done anything.[66]

At the end of November 1848, Mann, Carlisle, and Richard Hildreth prepared to present their appeal before the circuit court, which was made up of Cranch, James S. Morsel, and James Dunlap. Hildreth had arrived from Boston to give assistance at the outset of the trials. Although trained at the bar, he had been a writer most of his life.[67]

Meanwhile, Key decided that he needed assistance. Joseph H. Bradley joined the district attorney to argue the appeal—further proof of the seriousness with which Washingtonians regarded the *Pearl* cases. Bradley, attorney for the city of Washington, was "one of the best-equipped lawyers . . . ever . . . connected with the District bar." He seems, however, to have contributed nothing significant, and Mann complained that he was boring and long winded.[68]

Richard Hildreth led off for Drayton and was much more confrontational than either Mann or Carlisle had been. Not mincing his words, he claimed that Judge Crawford's definition of larceny was "false and 'rotten,' unsupported by a single adjudged case . . . and, in its special application to the subject of slave property, in . . . contradiction to the whole course of legislation in every slave State of the Union." Because Crawford was a Pennsylvanian, said Hildreth, he was unfamiliar with slave law.[69]

Mann, taking up where Hildreth left off, insisted that Crawford was wrong to claim that color alone proved that a person was a slave, for in the District there were more free blacks than slaves. He spoke at length about whether the government had had the authority to establish slavery in the nation's capital, reflecting the views of Salmon P. Chase. Mann would use the same arguments in a lengthy speech in the House of Representatives in February 1849. After a hearing that lasted seven days, Judge Cranch announced that the court would render a decision in the new year.[70]

In the course of the December arguments, Mann undertook to demonstrate that more than the word of the master was necessary to prove servitude. He used the example of stealing foxes: "There can be no property in them [foxes] sufficient to sustain an indictment for larceny, at least not unless they are alleged and proved to be foxes caught and subjected." Key seems to have regarded himself as something of a wit, or perhaps a poet like his father Francis Scott Key. He wrote these lines and passed them to Mann:

> To illustrate the point he's making—
> "In larceny there must be a taking"—
> A fox, he says, cannot be stolen,
> Be he a young or be he an old 'un.
> Pursuing hounds say he's mistaken,
> At least so far as to the taking.

Mann replied:

> Fox-hunting abroad, and slave-hunting indoors,
> I beg leave to suggest do not run on all-fours;
> Foxes do not eat foxes—brute natures have bounds,

But Mr. District Attorney, out-hounding the hounds,
Hunts men, women, and children his pocket to fill,
On three hundred indictments, *at ten dollars a bill*.[71]

On February 19, 1849, Judges Cranch and Morsel reversed Judge Crawford and remanded the Drayton cases to criminal court for retrial (Judge Dunlop dissented). They did not rule on the legality of Washington slavery, which had been the primary aim of the Boston committee. According to the *Sun*'s correspondent, Judge Cranch concluded that, in order to convict Drayton of larceny, the prosecution had to prove that he would profit from carrying off the slaves. This Key had failed to do. On March 2, 1849, the Sayres cases were also sent back to Crawford's court. The reporter for the Baltimore paper had tried to be impartial, but occasionally his views came through; in this instance he prophesied that slave property would no longer be safe in the District of Columbia.[72]

Mann rejoiced in the decision of the circuit court, clearly feeling vindicated in his objections to Judge Crawford's "abominable decisions." "I struggled against his nefarious conduct like a man struggling for his life."[73]

⁂

As spring came to Washington in 1849, and families and friends marked the anniversary of the abortive slave flight, supporters of Drayton and Sayres hoped that Key had had enough, that he would give up. The district attorney had proved his proslavery qualifications, and no one could doubt his loyalty to the South—or his determination to get rich off the *Pearl*. Even the *Sun*'s reporter had found nothing new in the arguments before the circuit court at the end of 1848. But Key would not relent. Not only did he continue to prosecute Drayton and Sayres; he also enlisted the assistance of Walter Jones, the dean of the District bar, who had argued such important Supreme Court cases as *McCulloch v. Maryland* and *Ogden v. Saunders*, which are still studied by legal scholars.[74]

The members of the Boston committee panicked, for the new trials were about to begin, and Mann was ill and apparently could not go to Washington. Once again they appealed to Senator Seward, claiming that his assistance was "of the highest importance." The Bostonians did not dare to leave everything to Carlisle, even though the Washington lawyer had shown great skill in the courtroom. The defense had had to find a local lawyer (Mann had retained him over the Bostonians' objections), and Carlisle served that purpose—"but he is not an enemy of slavery." Here Sewall revealed exactly what the Boston committee sought: "We consider it of far greater consequence to have some northern man of great powers and established reputation to direct the trials, who will secure the freedom of the prisoners if possible, but will at all events make the cases aid the cause of freedom & not of slavery, whatever may be their result."[75] In other words, the Bostonians wanted a propaganda victory, even if Drayton and Sayres went to prison.

In fact, Mann liked and admired Carlisle, calling him "a glorious fellow" and an invaluable colleague. The Washingtonian, he said, was "dignified, and gentlemanly . . . polished in his diction; imaginative, poetic, and withal an excellent lawyer, . . . there is always a solid *terra firma* of good sense for all his lofty flowers and magnolias to grow out of."[76]

Appalled that Key continued to prosecute Drayton, Mann somehow pulled himself together, in spite of being unwell, and returned to Washington on May 7, 1849. He concluded that he could not live with himself if he deserted the prisoners now.[77] He was especially alarmed at Walter Jones's participation, for the older man was "long reputed . . . to be at the head of the bar."

After so many trials it was difficult to impanel a jury, especially because the marshal, who was "ferocious in his pro-slavery feelings and practices," brought in slaveholders or sympathizers. One potential juror said the prisoner should be hung, another agreed, and another was the son-in-law of a woman whose slaves fled on the *Pearl*.[78] Even though a few people, speaking in whispers, told Mann of their sympathy for the imprisoned, he found Washingtonians in general filled with "deadly hostility" against Drayton and Sayres, "fierce and fanatical beyond expression." Mann declared: "Should it ever be my fortune to be tried by slaveholders, I should consider myself doomed as soon as I was accused."[79]

Walter Jones demonstrated a much sharper legal mind than had Key, and the trials in the spring of 1849 produced some interesting new evidence. Drayton, for example, purchased large amounts of food from a Washington dealer: three bushels of meal, fifteen gallons of molasses, and 206 pounds of bacon, much more than the ship biscuit that

Drayton would later mention in his memoir. Hampton Williams, when called to the stand, confirmed that he saw molasses and bacon in large quantities when he boarded the *Pearl*.[80] Did Drayton in fact know very well that a large number of people would be aboard the schooner when it sailed down the Potomac?

When Chester English took the stand, he told the jury that Drayton sent him into the city and away from the wharves, implying that he was not wanted down at the foot of Seventh Street. He had seen a "big house," though he did not know what it was, and he had watched two parades, an activity in which Sayres had joined him. He added that he thought Sayres was drunk when the *Pearl* sailed from Washington.[81] Maybe that was the reason the captain had not checked the tide tables before the schooner left Washington that April 1848.

Sayres testified that with the wind north northwest at the mouth of the Potomac, "blowing fresh," there was no way the schooner could sail up the Chesapeake. Indeed, the *Pearl* was not seaworthy, or even bayworthy, for, according to Hampton Williams, it had a broken foremast and hatches so loose that they were laid across and not fastened down.[82] Trial testimony made it clear that the *Pearl* could never have sailed off south on a slave-selling expedition and might not even have made it back up the Chesapeake Bay and on to Philadelphia. Could it be that in reality the *Salem* saved the fugitives and the crew from drowning?

Jones ignored such testimony and insisted that since the hatches were closed and the slaves were the only cargo, Drayton was in *possession* of the slaves, having "set on foot a system of seduction and enticement." The law should be "rigorously applied to the protection of this kind of property [slaves]."[83]

On May 17, 1849, the *National Era* reported that the jury found Drayton not guilty of larceny. Key finally agreed not to pursue further indictments for larceny, but he called a jury to consider indictments for transportation of slaves: seventy-four against Drayton and the same number against Sayres; two slaves were the property of Virginians. After only fifteen minutes, the jury returned a "wholesale verdict of guilty." Judge Crawford fined Drayton $10,360, or $140 in each case (reduced by $10 because he had been in jail for a year); the fine for Sayres was $7,400, or $100 per case. The judge thought Sayres was "but the cat's paw." It was the people "behind the scenes, occupying a higher position in society, acting under the garb of philanthropy" who really deserved punishment, declared the judge. He made clear that Washingtonians were still trying to find out who financed the *Pearl*.[84]

On May 24, the circuit court, after hearing the arguments once again, affirmed the judgment of the criminal court. The *Sun*'s correspondent prophesied that it was not over, that Drayton had "next to run the gauntlet in Virginia," where he laid odds of ten to one that the waterman would "get into the penitentiary."[85] Fortunately he was wrong.

Drayton and Sayres now faced the probability that they would spend the rest of their days in the Washington jail, for there was no chance that they could pay the enormous fines levied against them. With the trials over, the Boston committee had the difficult task of raising money to pay Carlisle's fee. Mann had more than proved his antislavery credentials, and he must have been pleased to discover that he had not lost his skill as an attorney. He was deeply affected by his experience. Speaking several years later, he said that he had gained insight into the "dreadful mysteries" of slavery. "For a moment, the wind blew the smoke and flame aside, and I looked into its hells."[86]

While the appeals of Drayton and Sayres were winding their way through the District courts, another case concerning the *Pearl* occupied Washington lawyers and judges. The members of the posse that pursued the runaways sued Francis Dodge Jr., principal owner of the steamship *Salem*, for their share of salvage, which is the compensation paid for saving a ship or its cargo from the perils of the sea. The *Daily Picayune* of New Orleans had suggested salvage, and the slave owners, relieved to have their property safely back in the District, paid Dodge a total of $2,108. Mrs. Armstead, owner of the Bell family, paid the largest sum, $282, claiming the loss and recovery of ten slaves.

After deducting for such expenses as fuel, Dodge paid Captain Baker and his crew $200 and compensated himself and the other owners for the use of the *Salem*. He then gave $27 to each member of the posse, which, according to Dodge, they gratefully accepted. But twenty-six of the men decided that they were due more than $27, considering it an unworthy payment for the great danger they had faced in volunteering to recapture runaways valued at $100,000. According to the members of the posse, the slave owners should have compensated them instead of Dodge, and they sued the owner of the steamer, demanding an accounting and a fair division of the money.

Dodge provided the accounting, but in the process he heaped scorn on the inflated claims of the posse. He had made sure that the slaves (including three of his own) were aboard the *Pearl* and then instructed Captain Baker to get steam up and prepare to pursue the schooner down the Potomac. Baker would have the help of his regular crew and a few men that Dodge himself would enlist. But then many eager men climbed on board the *Salem*, "in anticipation [of] an agreeable excursion." Dodge made it sound like a Sunday picnic, and $27 each was all the men were worth.

The members of the posse claimed that the men and women who owned the slaves aboard the *Pearl* had "voluntarily" contributed the money now in dispute. Not at all, said Dodge; he had insisted on the payment of salvage, and he had parceled out the money equitably, according to the work that each man performed and according to "known custom or usage in such cases."

The members of the posse filed their claim in February 1849 in the Circuit Court of the District of Columbia, sitting as chancery court. The case was repeatedly postponed until 1851, when the court rendered a judgment that is now illegible, making it impossible to know whether the members of the posse ever received more than $27 each.[87]

Congress was not silent while these events were taking place. Both northern and southern members seized on the flight of the slaves as an opportunity to air the issues surrounding slavery and the slave trade in the District of Columbia. The *Pearl* influenced debates in both the Senate and the House of Representatives, as the next chapter will show.

CONGRESS CONFRONTS
SLAVERY

By the 1840s almost any issue before Congress became
a slavery issue. If Congress had earlier sought to avoid
such debates, that was no longer the case. Crucial decisions concerning the annexation of Texas, the war with
Mexico, and the expansion of slave territory into the West
provided politicians with ample opportunity to defend
their views that slavery was evil or good, that Congress
could or could not limit the areas open to slavery, that
slave states had too much or too little power, that slavery
was an economic or a moral issue. Although few members
of the House of Representatives and only one senator attacked slavery as an unmitigated evil, the *Pearl* gave those
few an opportunity to air their views and to bring on an
extended debate on human bondage in the shadow of the
Capitol. The District courts and the slave markets decided the fate of the participants in the escape attempt,
but Congress could not avoid considering the reality of
desperate slaves choosing to flee from the nation's capital,
under the eyes of the nation's lawmakers.

The Thirtieth Congress met in December 1847, and
in the winter of 1847–48, well before the *Pearl* incident,
northerners sent numerous petitions condemning the
Mexican War, insisting on an end to District slavery, and
even calling for a dissolution of the Union if human bondage continued. Joshua Giddings, presenting a memorial

from "certain citizens" of the District that asked for an end to the local slave trade, tried unsuccessfully to get it referred to the Judiciary Committee "to inquire into the constitutionality of all laws by which slaves are held as property in the District of Columbia."[1] At the same time, southerners asserted their right to transport slaves into newly acquired land in the Southwest, maintaining that the federal government had no authority "to exercise any legislative power within the . . . territories by which the equal right of all the citizens of the United States to acquire and enjoy any part of the common property may be impaired or embarrassed."[2] In other words, slavery would follow the American flag.

A continuing problem for slave owners, the flight of bondmen and bondwomen to free states, was made worse by *Prigg v. Pennsylvania* (16 *Peters* 539), an 1842 decision of the Supreme Court. The Constitution of the United States required the return to the owner of any "Person held to Service or Labour in one State" who had fled to another state (Art. 4, Sec. 2, para. 2). A 1793 law then provided that the owner of a runaway could have assistance in recovering his property, but *Prigg* held that "the people of the free States could not legislate either to aid the arrest of [runaway] slaves or to hinder that arrest." Southerners understandably deplored the decision, believing that it encouraged slaves to run away; antislavery northerners applauded.

In the very week before the slaves fled aboard the *Pearl*, members of the House of Representatives debated a state's responsibility for returning runaways. Giddings held that it was no concern of a state government, since a slave was no longer a slave once he or she reached a free state.[3] Even though his position was not constitutionally sustainable, it served to arouse southerners to demand protection for their property. Now the *Pearl* incident justified their fears that slaves would engage in wholesale flight to the North. From the standpoint of slave owners, the Supreme Court had damaged their rights, and District slaves had become alarmingly audacious. If bondmen and bondwomen attempted to escape aboard a schooner moored within sight of the Capitol, Congress had to take immediate action to avert further disaster.

On the morning of April 18, 1848, the day following the *Pearl*'s return to the District, Giddings and his friend Edward Stowe Hamlin went to the jail, where they saw the bondmen and bondwomen awaiting their owners or purchasers. Giddings and Hamlin could do nothing for the slaves, since there was no money to buy their freedom, but they promised legal assistance to the imprisoned watermen. It was in the jail that the congressman and former congressman faced a threatening mob. Deeply angered by what he had witnessed and endured, Giddings left the jail and set out for Capitol Hill, determined to force Congress to confront the events of the past few days, no matter how reluctant the members might be.

His friends had been worried about him, but in his agitation he did not consult with them or take time to devise a strategy for accomplishing his goal, even though he had had frequent proof of the difficulty of getting the House to pay attention. In spite of, or perhaps because of, his triumphant reelection to the House following his censure for violating the gag rule in the House in 1842, members had consistently tried to prevent his speaking out on the subject of slavery. Consequently, when he hurried into the House of Representatives and requested permission to introduce a resolution, southerners were primed and ready. The Ohioan did not have to tell his fellow congressmen what was happening in the District; they knew. Washington was a small town, official Washington even smaller, and the *Pearl* had caused alarm among slaveholders and those who defended the institution.

Gaining the floor, Giddings asked for the unanimous consent of the House of Representatives to introduce a resolution. Some members cried, "Object"; others, "Read it"; and the resulting clamor, for and against Giddings, forced the Speaker to call the House to order. When quiet had been restored, Speaker of the House Robert Winthrop said that it was customary to allow resolutions to be read. Richard K. Meade of Virginia, whose voice had been loudest in objecting, offered to withdraw his opposition if the resolution contained no mention of slavery. He knew, of course, that a Giddings statement would be about slavery. Nevertheless, after conferring with his friends, Meade withdrew his objection so that the House could hear Giddings's resolution.

His preamble stated that a large number of men, women, and children were in the District jail "without being charged with any crime, or of any impropriety other than an attempt to enjoy that liberty for which our fathers encountered toil, suffering, and death itself." Since such action was "incompatible with the duty of a civilized and Christian people," Giddings asked for a select committee "to inquire into and report to this House" why the prison was used to hold runaway slaves and what legislation was needed "in regard to such practice."

Having a resolution read was not the same as granting a congressman leave to introduce it, and when Giddings sought to do so, there were, once again, shouts of "Object, object." A South Carolinian warned that if the House entertained the Ohioan's resolution, "he would move to amend, by an inquiry whether the scoundrels who caused the slaves to be there ought not to be hung." Much laughter broke out in the House, marking the end of Giddings's resolution.[4]

Although Giddings could have approached the April events from various points of view, he chose to object to the presence of the fugitives in the District jail. Opponents of human bondage had long deplored the use of public facilities such as the jail to carry out slave laws and regulations. The taxes of antislavery men and women supported the District of Columbia, including the jail, forcing their collusion with the hated institution of slavery. For years emancipationists had railed against the practice of lodging suspected runaways in the District jail and then selling them south to pay the costs of their having been kept there, even if they were free but lacked proof of their status. When Giddings objected to the presence of the *Pearl* runaways in the jail, he was giving expression to a decades-long resentment of the use of public facilities in Washington to advance the cause of slavery.

Giddings's effort in the House had failed, as he had known it would, but he was not discouraged, nor would he give up. An admirer called Giddings "high-minded [and] fearless," "an honest man, devoted to what he believed to be right, who would not vary one iota from the path he had marked out for himself upon any terms which this world could offer."[5] The congressman had survived as an antislavery voice by refusing to accept defeat. So he retreated to his boardinghouse across the street from the Capitol and consulted sympathetic colleagues, who agreed on the necessity for a different strategy, to be led by another member of Congress. John Gorham Palfrey was either drafted or volunteered.

Palfrey had come to Congress from Massachusetts in December 1847 after a distinguished career as a clergyman and editor of the *North American Review*. He had proved his antislavery credentials by freeing and subsidizing slaves whom he had inherited. His friend Samuel J.

John Gorham Palfrey. (Courtesy of the Library of Congress)

May said that Palfrey had given up $10,000 of his inheritance and had spent another thousand relocating the freed men and women in the North.

In January 1848 Palfrey made his maiden speech in the House, attacking both slavery and the supporters of the slave system. Slaveholders, he said, were a small oligarchy that undertook to "intimidate and overawe the weak, beguile and conciliate the easy, and bribe the mercenary." The South had accumulated vast amounts of political power, controlling the presidency, the Supreme Court, and to a great extent the leadership of both houses of Congress. Southerners claimed slavery as natural; for Palfrey it belonged to a time when men wore animal skins and ate acorns; it had no place in a civilized society. Palfrey would never agree to the extension of slavery, but disunion, which southerners frequently mentioned, was not an alternative: "If they insist that the Union and Slavery cannot live together, they may be taken at their word, but IT IS THE UNION THAT MUST STAND."[6]

Palfrey was understandably surprised that members of the House listened to him "with gratifying attention and with perfect civility." He implied that the House had become more open: "I said things, I suspect, quite as plain and strong as Mr. Giddings was expelled from the House for saying, six years ago."[7] He would soon learn that the House had not really changed.

While Washington was in an uproar over the flight of the slaves, Palfrey was in and out of Gamaliel Bailey's office at the *National Era* and Giddings's room at Mrs. Spriggs's boardinghouse (where the Jefferson Building of the Library of Congress now stands); they discussed how best to get the issue of District slavery before Congress.[8] Two days after the House had basically ignored Giddings, Palfrey gained the floor and said that he "rose to a question of personal privilege of a member." He then read the following:

> Whereas common report has represented to members of this House that a lawless mob has assembled within the District of Columbia on each of the two nights last past, and has committed acts of violence, setting at defiance the laws and constituted authorities of the United States, and menacing individuals of this body [the House of Representatives] and other persons residing in this city: Therefore,
>
> *Resolved*, That a select committee of five members be appointed to inquire into the facts above referred to, and to report the facts, with their opinion whether any legislation is necessary or expedient in the premises.

Privilege? asked the Speaker of the House. He could not see where a question of privilege was involved. Palfrey replied: Was not a question relating "to the protection of the personal safety of a member of this House" a question of privilege? After Palfrey reread the relevant portion of the resolution, the Speaker agreed, saying that he was "disposed to think, if the liberty, or safety, or life of any individual member of this House has been menaced from any quarter, it is a question of privilege."[9]

The safety of members of a legislative body was a tradition that went back centuries in English history, and the protection of senators and representatives was enshrined in the Constitution (Art. 1, Sec. 6, para. 1). Palfrey and Giddings hoped that congressmen, though unsympathetic to the plight of slaves, might respond favorably to an issue affecting their self-interest. The weakness in Palfrey's presentation was that privilege historically had been applied to what was said on the floor of a legislative body, not to actions outside the chamber.

Southerners were waiting to pounce on the Speaker's pronouncement, for they knew very well that Palfrey's position was vulnerable. A Virginian claimed that since Palfrey admitted that he himself had not been injured and that the entire affair was based on "rumor," his petition had no standing in the House. No, said the Speaker, the rules of the House laid down that "common rumor" was "sufficient ground for action." Robert Barnwell Rhett of South Carolina pointed out that privilege applied only to what happened in the House: "Had it come to this, that a member of Congress was not only to be exempt from any personal assault or menace in relation to his official duties, but that his being a member was to be a screen to afford him protection, whatever he might do in any part of the United States?" Who was involved? Where was he? These were the questions that members asked, as if they did not know that Palfrey was using Joshua Giddings to force congressional action on the turmoil in the District.[10]

According to the Speaker, there were two questions involved, and he had already decided one of them in the affirmative: whether it was "such a question of privilege as to allow it to come before the House." The other, to be decided by the members, was "whether this was such a question of privilege that the House would see fit to exercise its authority on this occasion, and make any examination into the facts" stated by Palfrey. But this did not satisfy southern members of the House, who intended to use Palfrey's question of personal privilege as a device for attacking the issue of fugitive slaves.

Robert Toombs of Georgia, an important leader of southern forces, pointed out that Palfrey had made no claim that a member "had been called in question by the mob or anybody else for anything *uttered or done in the House*" (emphasis added). Toombs was certain that the House could not intervene merely because a member had gotten into trouble: "If crime—crime against the laws of this District—if moral connivance with felony and theft was to be vindicated, let the question be settled before the American people." Two years later, when Toombs's body servant ran away, the congressman might have recalled with some satisfaction his spirited attack on slave stealing. Other congressmen reinforced Toombs's view: "Every member of this body . . . was entitled to protection from arrest, and he was not to be held responsible for any words uttered here . . . as a member, but words not uttered . . . and acts not done here, were not . . . done in his capacity as a member." So spoke a Virginian.[11]

A Pennsylvanian, Joseph R. Ingersoll, supported the Speaker's ruling; there was no difference between a speech given and a speech prevented: "If you could notice by the power of this House any unlawful attempt to rebuke or assault a member for the just performance of his duty, why should you not with equal rigor restrain and prevent disorderly attempts to overawe and restrain him from performing it at all?" He went on: "The power to make laws carried with it the power of self-protection while engaged in the act, or taking necessary steps towards it. It was grossly inconsistent . . . to say that it [Congress] could not protect itself, much more to make it the sport of every idle person who might choose to interrupt its proceedings or wantonly to insult its dignity." Anger shot through the House; the Speaker had to demand that the members clear the aisles and take their seats.[12]

A New Yorker, William Duer, pretending that he did not understand the Palfrey resolution, asked the House if the question of privilege concerned a "lawless mob." If so, "it was a question of privilege in the strict terms of the Constitution." If a member of the House had not committed an illegal act, "should a lawless mob threaten his life, and this House have no right to interfere?" No, said a Virginian, Henry Bedinger, Duer was wrong. Palfrey had not stated that a "lawless mob" had actually threatened a congressman but that "common rumor, with her thousand lying tongues, . . . had made that assertion." He for one would have nothing to do with rumor. John Gayle of Alabama claimed that the House should not "give license to every member to go out and commit what depredation he pleased. A member of this House might go out into the city of Washington and assail any man in the community, whether provoked or unprovoked, and then come back and complain to the House." Should the House take jurisdiction in such a case? Of course not, said a northerner. Then, said Gayle of Alabama, what were the facts?[13]

When another Alabamian, Samuel Inge, joined in demanding the facts, Giddings could stand it no longer but jumped up and asked for the floor so he could explain what had happened. No, said the Speaker, the facts in the case were not at issue, but whether Palfrey's resolution raised a question of privilege, which the House and not the Speaker must decide.

The Alabamian claimed to be sorry that Giddings had not spoken, for he wanted to know what had happened in the city. He knew that "the rights of individuals had been assailed in this District, and an insidious attempt made to attack the property held by them under the guarantee of the Constitution." He had seen no proof that a congressman had been involved. There had been a rumor that a "lawless mob" had threatened a member of the House, but the District had laws regulating mobs, so that there was no need for Congress to get involved.

As for himself, Inge believed there had been no mob; maybe a member "had placed himself in a condition calculated to excite the public indignation." If so, "if it was true that illicit efforts had been made by kidnappers now in custody for the perpetration of a felony, then [the member of the House] . . . had no right to claim the protection of the House."[14]

Alexander Stephens of Georgia, the future vice president of the Confederacy, came close to accusing Giddings of complicity with the runaway slaves. He wanted an investigation of what went on in the city: "If rumor . . . were true, he believed that members of this House were implicated in violation of the law—so deeply implicated as parties to theft and felony, that they should be expelled from this floor. He was not only for the investigation, but, if the rumors proved to be true, he should go for the expulsion of the member or members implicated."[15]

As the day wore on, southern members of the House became increasingly enraged, seeming to incite each other to more extreme positions. The debate had begun as a discussion of privilege, but it deteriorated into an attack on Giddings and all who opposed human bondage. William T. Haskell of Tennessee charged that members of the House "had been endeavoring to perpetrate felonies," attempting "to abolish slavery in the District of Columbia in the form of law, if they could, and in violation of the Constitution; and, baffled and foiled in that, these mock-philanthropists were now . . . attempting to abolish slavery in this District by inciting the negroes to leave their masters." Certain congressmen—and he meant Giddings and Palfrey—had caused "a disposition to insurrection and rebellion among the slaves in this District." Paying no attention when the Speaker called him to order, Haskell read a proposed resolution authorizing a committee to inquire into whether "any member or members of this House were instrumental in procuring the slaves who were recently decoyed from their owners in this District . . . , and whether the said members of this House have not been guilty of felony in attempting or aiding in an attempt to kidnap slaves."[16] Abraham Venable of North Carolina praised the forbearance of the South in the face of northern fanaticism "which would never stop short of heaven or hell." The South, according to Venable, had been "persecuted, taunted, harassed, held up to odium to the world." Now that a ship from a northern state had come to the District and carried off a load of slaves, he had to speak out, declaring his love for the Union and remembering the sacrifices of his ancestors in its creation, "but loving it as he did, he hailed dissolution with pleasure and joy, if they were continually to be taunted by fanatics and hypocrites."

There were two kinds of abolitionists, said Venable: on the one hand, honest men and, on the other, "vile hypocrites, who went around to the factories and Sunday schools, getting children and women to sign petitions, . . . to bring them to Congress. Such miserable subterfuges, such vile and wicked reports, disgraced humanity."[17] When northerners read these words in antislavery papers, they must have felt rewarded for their hard work collecting signatures on petitions against slavery, for Venable proved that they alarmed slave owners.

Giddings could no longer remain silent. He rose from his seat and declared that he had indeed gone to the jail to assure the incarcerated men that they would have the benefit of counsel and the protection of the law of the land. Did he go there to "reward these men and approve their course?" asked a congressman. Giddings had never seen or heard of the watermen prior to the fiasco of the *Pearl*; he had gone to the jail "from the promptings of humanity." Had he "justified those slaves who had lately made an attempt to escape from their owners in the District"?

Giddings grounded his response in the Declaration of Independence, maintaining that all men were equal "as they came from God." Members of the House continued to question him, and he proclaimed: "I say that the slaves of this District, when they felt the hand of oppression bearing on them, possessed before . . . God himself the right to free themselves by any means God has put into their power." Did he also justify the thieves that had stolen the slaves? Giddings was not sure there were any thieves, but if they had broken the laws of the District, they were responsible for what they had done. Did he think they had committed a moral crime? There Giddings made his stand: "I do not believe there is the least moral crime on earth in maintaining the rights God has given me."[18]

When the House adjourned on April 20, it was plain that members had much more they wanted to say. Palfrey had been careful to draft a resolution that did not mention slavery, basing his protest on congressional privilege, an issue that should have been dear to the heart of every legislator. But southerners, infuriated by the flight of District slaves, saw beyond the threat of a Washington mob to the possible destruction of the South's peculiar institution.

The next day, the twenty-first, the House took up where it had left off. A Tennessean, Frederick P. Stanton, opposed Palfrey's resolution: it was "a masked battery against one of our southern institutions." He foresaw "a struggle which is likely to take place in this Hall, and which is calculated to shake the Union itself to its very centre." Nevertheless, he warned his fellow southerners to choose a safer issue: "Whenever we enter into that struggle for the South we should take care to fix ourselves on firmer and higher ground." If the South entered a contest in which the issue was a "lawless mob," it would gain no sympathy from the public. Giddings should not tell the House "that he considered a violation of law to be no moral wrong. . . . If the gentleman can go into my district and entice away our slaves, . . . then every bond by which society is bound together, and by which human rights are maintained is gone—sundered forever." Giddings could not complain if he were hanged "upon the first tree." Because of the South's huge investment in slaves, there was no possibility of ending the institution. According to the Tennessean, the North could not destroy slavery, but the South itself would end it when it was no longer profitable.[19]

The debate went on and on, ranging over the history of privilege and the powers of the sergeant at arms and the doorkeeper of the House. John B. Thompson of Kentucky deplored the actions of the men aboard the *Pearl*: "The people in this District had been aroused . . . from the fact that some piratical schooner, whether from Morocco or Algiers he could not tell, had come in and clandestinely taken some seventy or eighty slaves from their owners—had stolen some $50,000 in value, and made off with them, like a party of Indians making an incursion upon a border settlement, and running away with a lot of horses and cattle."

Thompson thought the people whose property had been stolen had every right to protest, and he wished that those members of Congress opposed to slavery would stop "continually rasping it," "intermeddling" with matters of no concern to them. He forgot that Palfrey did not mention slavery. Bad things always happened when northerners interfered, for in this case, Thompson said, the fugitives would be sold south, "where they would be subjected to the consequences of change of climate, food, living" and would suffer a higher mortality rate.[20]

Thomas Bayly of Virginia launched a vitriolic attack on Giddings, maintaining that the Ohioan had opposed the extension of slave territory because he wished "to keep the negroes with their masters, holding their knives as near their throats as possible." If slaves were contented, why would they want to hold knives to their masters' throats? The South never reconciled this contradiction.

Bayly wanted to see District laws strengthened against runaway slaves and those enticing them to flee, but that alone would not satisfy an obviously alarmed Virginian. He wanted a law "to punish the publication of incendiary publications," and he would not be "deterred" by talk of freedom of the press. He aimed "to provide a law for the punishment of an editor who should commit an offence against society, precisely as every other citizen was punished in a similar case." According to the Virginian, it was "no more a violation of the liberty of the press, to provide by law for the punishment of an editor who makes publications which endanger my life and property, than it is the violation of the liberty of the citizen to provide for his punishment, who does the same thing in a different way."[21]

Joseph M. Root of Ohio was "astonished to hear gentlemen who profess to be warm friends of slavery talk favorably here of mobs. Why, sir, if there is an institution on the face of the earth which has reason to fear mobs, it is this very institution of slavery." Slavery would never be preserved by a mob: "You are the last men in God's world that should commend mobs. You rely for your protection on the Constitution; you rely on the oaths of our fathers; you rely on our good faith—and you shall have that. . . . But when you leave this ground, when you throw away these pleas, and put yourselves on the strength of mobs, beware! A mob deals in weak heads and strong arms."

According to Root, southern members of Congress made it hard for northerners to get along with them: "If we are the subject of a vague suspicion that we have been inveigling slaves, we are to be denounced. And if we dare to say that slavery is a moral evil, then we are abolitionists." He confessed to holding "some of the prejudices we imbibed . . . in our Sunday schools, and we are so prejudiced as to look on it [slavery] as a curse; but then it is a curse we have nothing to do with, and do not want to." Root knew, however, that that was not enough: "If we do not say it is a great blessing, we are abolitionists." As for himself, he did not much mind being called a fanatic or an abolitionist, but was that the way to maintain peace in the country? Root concluded by warning the Virginian Bayly that if he tried to interfere with freedom of the press, "he would incur more popular odium than by any other thing he could do. . . . It was too late in the day to talk to Americans about a censorship of the press."[22]

The House adjourned after Root's speech. Although the Palfrey resolution had occupied two full days, congressmen still had things they wanted to say, and on Tuesday, April 25, 1848, debate resumed. William Wick of Indiana, reflecting northern distrust of antislavery, attacked abolitionists in general, calling them "reckless and audacious" and "assuming the guise of a martyr upon the smallest imaginable occasions." And Wick assailed Giddings in particular: "If, instead of persecution, he finds himself the object of quiet disregard, he thinks himself a most unfortunate gentleman, and will add to the venom of the slime which he leaves in his tortuous path, in hopes to provoke some one to give him a kick, so that he may feel and proclaim himself a martyr." Indeed, he was convinced that Giddings, needing to renew his "inventory of martyrdoms" to present to his constituency, went to the jail "in hopes to be mobbed or threatened, . . . and so to bring to the notice of the good people of the Western Reserve [Giddings's Ohio district] his most martyr-like virtues, and the great wickedness of Washington city mobs, and thus incline the hearts of the excellent citizens of said Reserve to give him another lease of his desk here for a two years' term, renewable forever."

According to Wick, there had been no disturbance in Washington, no more than would occur at the arrest of horse thieves. Giddings had gone to the jail on purpose to get attacked and had taken his friend Edward Stowe Hamlin so that he could tap into the financial resources of abolitionists. Wick himself would like to see a gradual emancipation of slaves—and here he reflected the views of many of his Indiana constituents—but he did not want to see former bondmen and bondwomen pouring into Indiana. Nor did he want to see the Union dissolved; maybe New England and the seaboard South wanted dissolution, but not Indiana.[23]

Giddings, finally getting a chance to speak, made an attempt at conciliation, insisting that he had never believed the government could interfere with slavery within the states where it already existed. But when people asked him why he was always bringing up slavery, he replied that he did so "to wash his hands, and those of the people of the North, from the stain of supporting this institution in this District." By establishing slavery in the District of Columbia, members of Congress had "violated their duty to God and to their fellow-men." Congress should repeal such laws at once: "You shall not bring us to share with you in the guilt . . . of this traffic in human flesh now carried on here under our protection."

Giddings reminded the House that the Palfrey resolution did not mention slavery, nor did it ask for protection for Giddings. He would never, never ask for protection from a body that had treated him as the House had. Palfrey simply wanted "to expose the spirit of violence and anarchy which was exhibited here against those who dared to speak . . . in favor of liberty, and the rights of humanity."

Giddings had gone to the jail, a public building, without concern for his own safety, but slave dealers and slave breeders had threatened him. "What he held in unutterable contempt was that a member of this body, in visiting one of the public institutions erected by this Government, should be threatened by a miserable mass of moral putridity, called slaveholders and slavebreeders." He went on: "Had it come to this, that the members of this House could not go in and out of the public institutions in this District without meeting that class of men and being threatened by them?"

He had no doubt that congressmen had encouraged the mob. "While their galleries were filled with slave-dealers—men who drove whole families to the market, and bartered men, women, and children for gold—honorable members stood up here in this House and declared that they justified the mob to the fullest extent." The District was maintaining "a slave market more shocking to the feelings of humanity than any to be found within the jurisdiction of the Grand Sultan." Slave owners could not order him around as they did their slaves; and as long as human bondage existed in the District, he would never be silent.[24]

At the end of that day, April 25, the House voted to table the Palfrey resolution.[25] For three days the House had been filled with southern oratory, defending slavery and slaveholders and even threatening disunion, as had often happened since the crisis over Missouri in 1819–20. It had made no difference to southern members of the House that Palfrey's resolution had not mentioned slavery; they grasped every opportunity to set forth the southern position. Some northerners had done likewise, not hesitating to challenge southern congressmen. In the next two years discussion of slavery and the slave trade in the District would merge into the debate over the future of slavery in territory newly acquired from Mexico.

✻

John Parker Hale of New Hampshire "was the first senator elected by an antislavery coalition, the first who had openly embraced antislavery principles *before* his election." On April 19, 1848, he gave notice that he would introduce a bill, copied from a Maryland statute, "to prevent riotous or tumultuous assemblages" in the District. He proposed that when any property (he gave a detailed list) was "taken away, injured, or destroyed, by any riotous or tumultuous assemblage of people, the full amount of the damages so done shall be recovered by the sufferer or sufferers by suit at law against the county, town, or city, within whose jurisdiction such riot or tumultuous assemblage occurred."[26]

Giddings and Palfrey had failed in the House; now it was Hale's turn in the Senate. Although all three men knew they could not get legislative action, they hoped to force Congress and the public to pay attention, to be aware of slavery and the slave trade in Washington. The Giddings resolution deplored the use of a public jail for the incarceration of innocent slaves; the Palfrey resolution, using the device of personal privilege, sought an investigation of possible violence and threats against a congressman; the Hale bill provided for payment when private property suffered damage from a "tumultuous assemblage," such as the mob threatening the *National Era*. All three failed, but defenders and opponents of human bondage used the occasion to rehearse the next decade's arguments that would end in civil war. The events surrounding the *Pearl* forced northerners and southerners, some willingly, others reluctantly, to set forth their views of slavery.

In introducing his bill, Hale reminded the Senate of the "large and riotous assemblages" in the District that had not only threatened property but had "carried these threats into execution." He had been careful not to mention slavery anywhere in the bill because he wanted the Senate to consider only the rights of property. Arthur Bagby of Alabama responded by proposing "a sufficient penalty for the crime of kidnapping in this District."[27]

John C. Calhoun of South Carolina was not fooled by Hale's insistence that his bill dealt with real property; he knew it was about property in slaves. The South Carolinian condoned mob violence: Hale's bill sought "to repress the just indignation of our people from wreaking their vengeance upon the atrocious perpetrators of these crimes." Calhoun sometimes thought that he was the only defender of slavery, which he described as "this great institution of the South, upon which not only its prosperity but its very existence depends." Calhoun did not want the Senate to allow Hale to introduce his bill; instead, he wanted a bill to stop slaves from escaping: "to prevent these atrocities, these piratical attempts, these wholesale captures, these robberies of seventy-odd of our slaves at a single grasp." In his view the moment of crisis had arrived, and the South, responding to "piratical acts" such as the *Pearl* incident, might decide to close all southern ports in retaliation.[28]

Jefferson Davis of Mississippi was even more irate; the time had come for Congress to punish those men who came to the District "acting . . . as incendiaries . . . within the legislative limits of Congress, to steal a portion of that property which is recognized as such by the Constitution of the United States." Would the District be the field of "abolition struggles"? Would sedition be "nursed" in the Senate? "We who represent the southern States are not here to be insulted; . . . if civil discord is to be thrown . . . upon the land—if the fire is to be kindled here with which to burn the temple of our Union—if this is to be made the centre from which civil war is to radiate, here let the conflict begin." Davis was ready to meet any "incendiary, who, dead to every feeling of patriotism, attempts to introduce it."[29] Did Davis recall these brave words of 1848 when he was fleeing for his life in 1865?

Henry Foote, the other Mississippi senator, became even more agitated than his colleague, claiming that the movement against District slavery was "grand larceny" and the perpetrators no better than highway robbers. "I maintain, that when the arm of the law is too short to reach such a criminal, he may be justly punished by a sovereignty not known to the law." Reliable evidence existed, according to Foote, that a member of the Senate had been involved in the flight of the slaves, and he knew that a member of the House "was yesterday morning engaged in certain reprehensible contrivances, and that but for his abject flight from the place of his infamous intrigues, he would have been justly punished, not by the mob, but by high-spirited citizens convened for the purpose of vindicating their rights, thus unjustly assailed." No matter how oratorical his remarks, no matter that he saw rioters as "high-spirited citizens," Senator Foote was approving mob action.

He then went on to encourage lynching. Hale's bill was a cover for "negro-stealing," for "the encouragement and immunity of robbery," an attempt "to get up a sort of civil war in the country," filled with "the spirit of insurrection and incendiarism." Hale, according to the senator from Mississippi, should declare himself the friend of District slaves, then "buckle on his armor" and "unsheath his sword," for, said Foote, "I have no doubt he will have a fair opportunity of shedding his blood in this holy cause on the sacred soil of the District of Columbia." By this time Foote had worked himself up to a violent rage:

> If he [Hale] really wishes glory, and to be regarded as the great liberator of blacks; . . . let him, instead of secreting himself in some dark corner of New Hampshire . . . visit the good State of Mississippi, in which I have the honor to reside, and no doubt he will be received with such hosannas and shouts of joy as have rarely marked the reception of any individual in this day and generation. I invite him there, and will tell him beforehand, in all honesty, that he could not go ten miles into the interior, before he would grace one of the tallest trees of the forest, with a rope around his neck, with the approbation of every virtuous and patriotic citizen; and that, if necessary, I should myself assist in the operation.[30]

From then on Senator Foote was Hangman Foote in every antislavery newspaper in the country, the *Daily True Democrat* of Cleveland calling "Foote, the hangman, of Mississippi" a "reckless . . . [and] unprincipled specimen of fallen humanity." Although the Mississippi senator resented the epithet, he was in fact a man of violent temper. He and Senator Solon Borland of Arkansas exchanged blows on a Washington street; though friends separated them before there was serious damage, Borland's ring cut Foote's nose. The Mississippian fought four duels and pointed a loaded Colt revolver at Senator Thomas Hart Benton of Missouri during a Senate debate.[31]

Hale denied having any part in the slave escape: "I have never counseled, advised, or aided in any way, and with my present impressions I never shall counsel, advise, or aid in any way, any encroachment upon the Constitution in any of its provisions or compromises." But, said Foote, surely the *Pearl* escape had required the assistance of "men of standing." Whatever help there had been, it had not come from Hale. Hale responded to Foote's invitation to visit Mississippi in order to be lynched: "I can only express the desire that he [Foote] would penetrate into some of the dark corners of New Hampshire, and if he do, I am much mistaken if he would not find that the people in that benighted region would be very happy to listen to his arguments, and engage in an intellectual conflict with him, in which the truth might be elicited."

Throughout the debate Hale made every effort not only to hold his temper but also to persuade his colleagues that, rather than attacking slavery, he was trying to protect real property. Why should that anger southerners? "It has long been held by you that your peculiar institution is incompatible with the rights of speech; but if it be also incompatible with the safeguards of the Constitution being thrown around property of American citizens, let the country know it! If that is to be the principle of your action, let it be proclaimed throughout the length and breadth of the land, that there is an institution so omnipotent — so almighty — that even the sacred rights of life and property must bow down before it!"

Hale then addressed Calhoun: "Did the honorable Senator from South Carolina imagine that we of the North, with our faces bowed down to the earth, and with our backs to the sun, had received the lash so long that we dared not look up?" The senator from New Hampshire denied wanting a war on slavery; the war he wanted was "a war of reason, of persuasion, of argument; a war that should look to convincing the understanding, subduing the affections, and moving the sympathies of the heart."

Hale went on: "Let the tocsin sound. Let the word go forth. Let the free North be told that their craven representatives on the floor of the Senate, are not at liberty even to claim the protection of the rights of property! The right of speech was sacrificed long ago. But now is to be proclaimed, that we cannot even introduce a bill looking to the execution of the plainest provisions of the Constitution, and the clearest principles of justice for the protection of personal rights, because gentlemen choose to construe it into an attack upon that particular institution?"

Hale had a reputation for moderation, but on this occasion he spoke directly to Calhoun and his supporters: "On what do gentlemen of the South rely for the protection of any institution on which they place any value? It will be answered, upon the Constitution and the law." But if the Constitution was inadequate to protect one kind of property, and he referred to the *National Era*, how could it protect another kind of property, slaves?[32]

Calhoun, angered by Hale's words, proclaimed: "I would just as soon argue with a maniac from bedlam, as with the Senator from New Hampshire." There were cries of "Order, order," but the South Carolinian continued: "A man who says that the people of this District have no right in their slaves, and that it is no robbery to take their property from them, is not entitled to be regarded as in possession of his reason." Hale replied that he had said nothing about property in slaves: "It does not become me . . . to measure arms with the honorable Senator from South Carolina, more particularly since he has been so magnanimous as to give notice that he will not condescend to argue with me." But if Hale was a maniac on the subject of slavery, he warned, he was not alone in his madness.

Hale then turned to Foote's threat of a lynching: "As to the threats which have been made of bloodshed and assassination, I can only say that there have been sacrifices already, and there may be other victims, until the minds of all shall be awakened to the conviction that the Constitution was made as well for the preservation of the freedom of discussion as for the protection of the slaveowner." Foote sprang to his feet and, in spite of what he had just said, denied assassination threats. But he did believe that Hale was lawless, an enemy of the Constitution, and guilty of trying to involve the South in "bloodshed, violence, and desolation." No matter what Hale's bill said, Foote knew that the New Englander would never have introduced it if slaves had not been abducted from the District in a "marauding expedition," an attempt "to violate the constitutional rights of the South." [33]

When efforts were made to calm the Senate, Calhoun defended excitement; nations could be lost because they did not get excited. Hale had wanted to penalize the District for damage to property; what about the "marauders" who had stolen the other property, slaves? Could anyone doubt that Hale's bill was designed "to disarm the worthy citizens of this District, so as to prevent them from defending their property, and to arm the robbers?"

The South Carolinian portrayed the *Pearl* as "the extraordinary spectacle . . . of a vessel coming to our wharves under the color of commerce, and of the men belonging to that vessel silently seducing away our slaves, and getting nearly a hundred of them on board, and then moving off with them under cover of the night, in order to convey them beyond our reach." It was the duty of Congress to pass a bill "containing the highest penalties known to the law against pirates who are guilty of acts like these." The Union, Calhoun warned, could be saved only by justice and "the fulfillment of the stipulations of the Constitution."[34]

Senator Foote's threat against Hale, and Calhoun's defense of excitement in the Senate reinforced northerners' perception of southerners and their defense of slavery. Lewis Tappan, for example, cited many instances of verbal attacks. A Virginian shouted at an opponent: "God damn you, you shan't speak, you shan't say one word while you are in this room, if you do I will put you to death." A member from Louisiana warned another congressman: "If you attempt to speak, or rise from your seat, sir, by God I'll cut your throat." An Alabamian threatened all opponents of slavery: He would "HANG THEM LIKE DOGS." After the verbal attack on Hale, an abolitionist asked a pertinent question: "Do these men, with all their profanity and vulgarity, breathing out threatenings and slaughter, represent the feelings, and manners, and morals of the slaveholding community?"[35]

Senator Stephen A. Douglas of Illinois, who is best known for his 1858 debates with Abraham Lincoln, was a pragmatist where the North-South argument over slavery was concerned, but he concluded that violent speeches did great harm to the United States. Had Hale introduced his bill merely to create excitement in the Senate? Had there been a deal between Hale and the southerners? How else explain their success in creating northern sympathy for Hale? Calhoun insisted that southerners were merely defending themselves. No, said Douglas, they get excited and "discuss it [slavery] with a degree of heat, and give it an importance, which makes it heard and felt throughout the Union." He thought that Foote's remark about lynching Hale was worth 10,000 votes for the New Hampshire senator.

Foote repeated the sort of extreme denunciation that Douglas warned against:

Had the Senator from Illinois lived where I have resided—had he seen insurrection exhibiting its fiery front in the midst of the men, women, and children of the community—had he had reason to believe that the machinery of insurrection was at such a time in readiness for purposes of the most deadly character, involving life, and that dearer than life, to every southern man—had he witnessed such scenes, and believed that movements like that of this morning were calculated to engender feelings out of which were to arise fire, blood, and desolation, the destruction finally of the South, he would regard himself as a traitor to the best sentiments of the human heart, if he did not speak out the language of manly denunciation. . . . I cannot but repeat my conviction, that any man who dares to utter such sentiments as those of the Senator from New Hampshire, and attempts to act them out anywhere in the sunny South, will meet death upon the scaffold, and deserves it.

There, said Douglas, you have just given Hale 5,000 more votes.

Jefferson Davis, Foote's colleague from Mississippi, denied the validity of Foote's concerns. He himself did not anticipate insurrection, for his slaves were "happy and contented" in the paternal institution that was slavery. Nothing upset slaves except "unwarrantable interference of those who know nothing about that with which they meddle."[36] One Mississippi senator emphasized the perils of living with slaves; the other dwelt on the relationship of trust between master and slave. While Davis proclaimed slaves' trustworthy nature, Foote maintained that freeing slaves would create a South of horror and mayhem.[37]

Senator Douglas of Illinois thought it unwise to create more abolitionists; Foote of Mississippi said, the more the better. Douglas warned that the North did not want excitement over slavery, but he was sure that southern extremism encouraged abolitionists. As for himself, he wanted to punish "burglary, stealing, and any other infringement of the laws of this District; and if these laws be not strong enough to prevent or punish these crimes, we will give to them the adequate strength." But he was opposed to mob violence and to the destruction of property by mobs; why not support Hale's bill? Foote, deploring Douglas's moderation, indicated precisely why he had spoken in so violent a fashion: "Our constituents will have confidence in us, if they see we are ready here to maintain their interests inviolate." He admitted that his belligerence on slavery was a device to win votes in Mississippi, but newspapers in Jackson and Vicksburg warned that his violent remarks might well harm the southern cause. Far better to remain silent while "the abolitionists rave[d]."[38]

Douglas was certain that the South could never persuade the North that slavery was a blessing: "If slavery is a blessing, it is your blessing; if it be a curse, it is your curse; enjoy it—on you rest all the responsibility!" But if southerners continued on their "imprudent and violent course," they would destroy moderates like him. "I claim the privilege of pointing out to you how you give strength and encouragement to the Abolitionists of the North, by the imprudent expression of what I grant to be just indignation."[39]

Senator E. A. Hannegan of Indiana was sympathetic to the southerners, agreeing that they had every right to be upset: "A piratical vessel steals into your river, bearing the false colors of honorable commerce, anchors at your wharf, and receiving on board nearly one hundred of the domestics of this District, makes all sail to carry off its cargo of plunder." Was the South to remain silent? "As well expect a man to fold his arms and remain unmoved when the serpent, which has crawled into his abode, uncoils itself upon his hearthstone, and its deadly hisses ring in the ears of his children."[40]

Senator John Davis of Massachusetts entered the debate, hoping to find a voice of reason among southerners. There was no cause for excitement; most municipalities had laws setting forth liability for damage in the case of riots, and Hale's proposal contained not a word about slavery. If southerners opposed the bill because an antislavery newspaper was involved, then Americans would see it as an attempt by members of the Senate to put an end to freedom of the press. Would they react the same way if a pro-southern paper had been threatened? If the South appeared to be moving toward denial of a basic freedom, then in the long run it would be the loser.[41]

Andrew Butler of South Carolina made clear what was frightening the South: they were, he lamented, "a doomed minority," whose only security was the Constitution. If there was a need for protection against mobs, he would give support, but what was really needed was protection of *slave property*. A newspaper in the District was "inculcating in the minds of the slaves the right to rebel; more than a right — a duty; leading them to acts that are inconsistent with their peace and happiness, and such as will certainly inflict cruelty upon deluded human beings, by seducing them into a condition which compels their masters to use them with greater severity."

Even more serious was the "spirit of fanaticism" that, according to the South Carolinian, had appeared in the North at the time of the Missouri Compromise of 1820 and had grown through the years, leading to state laws hindering the apprehension of slaves, "this species of property." A strengthened law on the return of runaways was essential for the survival of the Union.[42]

Unlike the House, the Senate did not renew the debate on subsequent days. When Hale sought action on his bill, deploring the "denunciations [that] had gone forth on the wings of the press to the four corners of the earth," the senators went on to other business as though he had not spoken.[43] The issue of runaways was not over. The audacity of the *Pearl* escape aroused the anger of the friends of slavery as almost nothing else could have done. To abduct seventy-six slaves from under the shadow of the Capitol of the United States was unforgivable. Slaves had always run away, but the *wholesale* flight of Washingtonian bondmen and bondwomen aroused such anger that defeating the resolutions of Giddings, Palfrey, and Hale could not assuage it. It led directly to a general and heated debate over the fugitive slave law of 1793 and the slave trade in the District of Columbia.

At the same time that Senator Hale in Washington was enduring threats of lynching because of his antislavery views, some abolitionists in New England were taking him to task for being too conciliatory. Frederick Douglass, speaking to the American Anti-Slavery Society, charged him with defending property rather than trying to end slavery. William Lloyd Garrison deplored his failure to strike a blow for freedom: "How softly, cautiously, almost weakly, does Hale behave." Wendell Phillips, believing that the United States Constitution was a "covenant with death," condemned Hale for being a senator. "How dare you lift to God a pure hand and swear you will support the Constitution?" But since he was a senator, he should be aggressive in his attacks on slavery. Phillips ridiculed what he saw as the New Hampshire senator's timidity. The *Emancipator* of Boston defended Hale, claiming that the Senate gallery was filled with men "ready to leap upon and crush him." If antislavery enthusiasts thought Hale deficient in bravery, they should go to the District of Columbia, gather a crowd, speak out against slavery, and see what happened. It was all very well for editors and orators "snugly hid behind Faneuil Hall" to be "so *very* brave."[44]

Hale, in fact, was appalled by what he correctly saw as the fate of the fugitives: immediate sale to the Deep South. "No one can tell how much of misery this system of human slavery is causing even here in this District. No tongue can describe, nor heart conceive of the mass of bitter agony which we are thus causing." Hale's constituents were supportive and congratulated him on speaking out in the Senate, his clergyman, for example, admiring his self-control. The senator must have rejoiced when the Athenaeum in Rochester, New York, invited Senator Foote of Mississippi to speak, promising to pay his expenses and to give him a fair hearing—and asked Hale to persuade him to appear. The *Liberator* thought it amusing that the United Literary Societies at Dartmouth College invited Senator Foote to deliver their commencement oration.[45] They all made the point that a senator from the Deep South could speak freely in the North with no danger of lynching.

Henry Wilson, future vice president of the United States, praised the courage of Giddings, Palfrey, and Hale in speaking out in defense of "the doctrine of human rights" in Washington, where the atmosphere was "surcharged with proslavery intolerance and vindictive hate, threatening instantaneous explosion." George W. Julian, member of Congress from Ohio and son-in-law of Giddings, recalled that a Richmond newspaper offered $10,000 for Giddings to be kidnapped and brought to Richmond, and one-half that amount for his head.[46]

Antislavery leader Salmon P. Chase was sure that the debates in Congress had advanced the cause of antislavery by proving that southerners would go to any lengths to defend their peculiar institution. "I did not regret the vehement & coarse vituperation with which you were assailed," Chase wrote to Senator Hale. "I hope the debate will go far and wide over the land. It will do more than anything that has yet occurred to open the eyes of the people [to the reality of slavery]."[47]

Through the spring and summer of 1848, slavery remained a live topic in Congress, in spite of—or because of—the defeat of the proposals offered by Giddings, Palfrey, and Hale. In May 1848, Congressman Wick of Indiana, who had called Giddings "slime," introduced a "bill to prohibit the introduction of slaves into the District of Columbia." The House did not consider it for nine months—and then tabled it. Amos Tuck of New Hampshire tried unsuccessfully to get the House to take action on the numerous petitions against District slavery that had been buried in committee. John Crowell of Ohio failed in an attempt to have all laws in the District concerning slavery repealed. His colleague Rodolphus Dickinson deplored the "selling of slaves, so as to separate husband and wife, parents and children" and detested seeing the nation's capital a "common slave market." A Pennsylvanian, on the other hand, insisted there had been too much "sickly sentimentality" about slavery, and the North should worry about an inundation by blacks in case of emancipation. Since there was a general distrust of African Americans in the North, southerners believed they could safely ignore Horace Mann's reminder that God had commanded the slaves in Egypt "to despoil their Egyptian masters, and to escape from bondage." According to Mann, "The free states, instead of surrendering fugitive slaves to their masters, are bound to give those masters a Red-sea reception and embrace."[48]

When Congress left Washington at the end of the summer of 1848, its members had passed no laws regarding slavery either in the District or in the newly acquired western lands. But the heated debates, especially those in April, made it plain that the issue would not go away. The *Pearl* incident had forced legislators to look at slavery and the slave trade in the nation's capital, though they drew widely varying conclusions from what they saw. Some members of Congress were willing to censor the press, to approve a mob running wild in the nation's capital, and to dissolve the Union in order to protect slavery in Washington. Even allowing for politicians' fondness for exaggeration, the debates showed a dangerous trend of thought. If Calhoun could call Senator Hale a maniac and Foote could offer to assist in lynching a fellow senator, where would it end? Slavery and the slave trade in the District were issues that Congress could no longer avoid.

CONGRESS, RUNAWAYS,
and the SLAVE TRADE

When the Thirtieth Congress opened its second session
in December 1848, it was immediately apparent that the
antislavery members of the House of Representatives,
having received wholehearted support from their constituents, would make every effort to continue the argument over slavery and the slave trade. The capture of
the runaways aboard the *Pearl* and the speed with which
they were sold had demonstrated the efficiency of proslavery forces in the District of Columbia. In the view of
antislavery congressmen, their main resource was to continue the debate. The preceding spring had convinced
them that even though they were a tiny minority, they
could safely ignore southern threats. Consequently, they
agreed on a strategy to keep enslavement a live issue. In
quick succession, John Gorham Palfrey of Massachusetts
tried to introduce a resolution ending District slavery and
the slave trade; Joseph Root of Ohio offered a resolution
excluding slavery from New Mexico and California, territory just acquired from Mexico; Joshua Giddings, also of
Ohio, proposed a vote by the District on the continuation
of slavery; Daniel Gott of New York introduced a resolution to end the District slave trade; and John Wentworth
of Illinois proposed ending slavery "wherever Congress
has the power so to do."[1]

Southern alarm, which was immediate, did not decrease as the session went on, especially when Giddings, with an un-broken record of angering the South, outdid himself by insisting that "every male inhabitant" in the District should have a vote on slavery — and that included free blacks and slaves: "The enduring principles of justice should be meted out to every individual in the District of Columbia."[2]

Gott's resolution to end the District slave trade had a preface that of-fended every slave owner: "Whereas the traffic now prosecuted in this metropolis of the Republic in human beings as chattels, is contrary to natural justice and the fundamental principles of our political system, and is notoriously a reproach to our country throughout Christendom, and a serious hinderance [sic] to the progress of republican liberty among the nations of the earth." And yet it passed the House.[3] South-erners could not allow it to stand: one break in the wall that protected human bondage and all was lost.

Aroused by Gott's resolution, southern members of Congress con-vened a caucus and in January 1849 produced an "Address of the Southern Delegates in Congress, to Their Constituents," written by Senator John Calhoun and embodying the principle that the South would endure no more "aggression" by the North. When slave owners sought to recover their property, said the "Address," they met northern "resistance in every form." Even more dangerous were "secret combi-nations" designed "to entice, decoy, entrap, inveigle, and seduce slaves to escape from their owners," while state governments were indiffer-ent or approving. The final straw was the introduction in the current Congress of "a greater number of measures of an aggressive character" than the South had ever before had to face.

Giddings, Palfrey, Tuck, Gott, and Wentworth, northern members of Congress, although few in number, so aroused Calhoun that he feared every "provision, stipulation, or guaranty of the Constitution, intended for the security of the South," had been rendered worth-less. According to the South Carolinian, the South, a minority section, would face forced emancipation and would see former slaves raised "to a political and social equality with their former owners," with "the right of voting and holding public office under the Federal Govern-ment."[4] It is important to note that it was the proposed termination of the traffic in human property in the District of Columbia that called forth Calhoun's prophecy of southern disaster. Clearly he believed that he had to arouse both his colleagues and southern slave owners to the danger implicit in ending the District slave trade, for it would mark the beginning of the end of the institution of human bondage.

Nevertheless, in 1848–49 Calhoun could not command the support of all southern members of Congress, not even those from South Carolina.[5] Perhaps some southerners, instead of listening to Ohio congressmen Giddings and Gott, were paying attention to William Sawyer, also of Ohio, who begged the House to stop talking about slavery and consider the needs of the white people of the country: "I am heartily tired of this nigger business," he proclaimed. "I ask gentlemen to . . . withdraw their eyes for a few moments from the beautiful niggers . . . and to proceed to the despatch of the public business, and to let negroes and negro slavery rest a little." Congress, according to Sawyer, should provide free land for western settlers and tighten controls over banks' issuance of paper money; those were the issues that mattered to his constituents, not slavery or the slave trade.[6]

Thomas J. Turner of Illinois, differing from his fellow westerner, regarded Calhoun's Address to the South as verging on treason, since it was filled with proposals for dissolving the Union. It was, said Turner, the South's declaration of independence. He knew that the South wanted northerners to "aid masters in recapturing their fugitive slaves," but the South could not force them to advertise runaway men and women as they would a runaway horse. Nor could they enforce silence about slavery; there were, after all, guarantees of speech and press freedom: "Is it a sufficient cause why this Union should be dissolved, that we at the North have discussed . . . slavery?" He went on: "If we have an institution in our country which cannot bear the light of truth, which is based upon dark ignorance, it is time, high time that the institution should be exposed." Horace Mann reinforced Turner's insistence on the constitutionality of abolishing the District slave trade, but he went further, claiming that slavery in the District was itself unconstitutional.[7] Defending Daniel Drayton and Edward Sayres in the District's courtrooms had convinced Mann of the necessity of ending not just the trade but human bondage itself in the nation's capital.

On the last day of January 1849, the House Committee on the District of Columbia reported a proposal to prohibit the introduction of slaves into the District for sale or for hire. If the owner swore before the clerk of the circuit court that a slave was for his own use, then the property could remain in the city.[8] The committee proposal incited attacks on Gott, whose resolution had led to the report, and on "the spirit of hostility to the institutions of the South." Southerners foresaw an inevitable progression: first ending Washington's slave trade, then ending slavery in the District, and finally transforming the nation's capital into "nothing but a receptacle for all the free negroes in the country."[9]

J. W. Crisfield of Maryland regretted that all debates turned into arguments over slavery. Although he admitted that Congress had the power to end District slavery, it would place a great burden on the people of Maryland and would be an unconstitutional interference with private property that was worth, according to Crisfield, a million dollars. As far as the slave trade was concerned, it was, according to the Maryland congressman, much ado about nothing: "It does not exist, except for the domestic purposes of the District." He was, of course, wrong and was even more in error when he claimed that Maryland had ended the slave trade.[10]

Although the debate was supposed to be about ending the District slave trade and not slavery, John B. Thompson of Kentucky could not refrain from pointing out the horror that he believed would follow the end of bondage in Washington. Virginia slaves could reach freedom "by bridge or boat, by ice or swimming, or even at some point *wading*" across the Potomac River. For the people of Maryland a District without slaves would be a "cancer." "The free negro population, thicker than the lice and frogs of Egypt, would light upon the District like gangs of crows upon some carrion carcass. This vile, degraded population would make the District the harbor of runaways, the receptacle and hiding-place of stolen property." Ending slavery in the District, according to the Kentuckian, was "absurd, inconvenient, preposterous, [and] dishonest."[11]

Congressional arguments over slavery had predated the *Pearl* incident, but the 1848 flight of a large number of District slaves made debates especially acrimonious. When the Thirtieth Congress ended in March 1849, nothing had been settled, neither the cessation of District slavery and the slave trade, nor the right of owners to regain their runaways, nor the future of slavery in the West. In a government that required compromise in order to function, it became increasingly clear that members of Congress simply could not reach agreement on the crucial issues before them.

✳

The Thirty-first Congress, beginning in December 1849, started with the same bitterness with which the previous one had ended. It required sixty-three ballots to choose a Speaker for the House of Representatives, and even then Howell Cobb of Georgia received only a plurality, not a majority. Southerners threatened to end the Union and sometimes declared it already dead. Northerners, by contrast, delighted in introducing antislavery resolutions from state legislatures, such as the one from Vermont demanding not only the prohibition of slavery in the West and in the nation's capital but also "the entire suppression of the slave trade on the high seas," threatening a major source of revenue for the Upper South.[12] Slave owners in Maryland and Virginia depended on seagoing vessels for much of their profitable trade with the Lower South. In the winter and spring of 1850, northerners bombarded Congress with petitions asking for an end to District slavery and the slave trade, freedom for Drayton and Sayres, jury trials for alleged fugitives, removal of the capital to "some more suitable location," and even "the immediate and peaceful dissolution of the Union."[13] This last caused great excitement among southerners.

Members of the Senate and the House exchanged harsh accusations. William Duer of New York claimed Richard Meade of Virginia was a "disunionist," Meade denied it, and Duer said the Virginian was a liar, causing great confusion. "The House was a heaving billow," and the sergeant at arms had to bring out the mace to restore calm. Duer apologized, but in the ensuing debate William F. Colcock of South Carolina threatened: "I here pledge myself, that if any bill should be passed at this Congress abolishing slavery in the District of Columbia, . . . I will introduce a resolution in the House declaring . . . *that this Union ought to be dissolved.*"[14] Six months later three of Colcock's slaves ran away and hid under the kitchen floor of a Washington residence. Captain John H. Goddard of the Night Watch found two of them, after searching for six weeks; the third was "still at large."[15] When southern legislators lost their own valuable property, the debate over slavery in the District was more than merely theoretical.

By April 1850, as tension mounted, Senator Henry Foote of Mississippi pointed a loaded revolver at Senator Thomas Hart Benton; he claimed that the Missourian was going to attack him.[16] Senator Stephen A. Douglas of Illinois thought it might be "expedient" to return the District to Maryland. Calhoun declared that "as things now stand, the southern States cannot with safety remain in the Union."[17]

John Crowell of Ohio sought twice to introduce a bill ending the slave trade in Washington; he failed.[18] How could compromise ever take place?

Defenders of slavery, over the years, had developed a catalog of justifications: slavery was protected by the Constitution; slavery was defended in holy scripture; slavery was the life blood of the South; slavery was a beneficent institution; slavery was the only protection in the South against murder, rape, and arson. The litany often ended with a reminder that the North had imposed slavery on the South, so if there was blame, it lay with the North. The speech of Senator Jeremiah Clemens of Alabama was typical. Slave property had a value of "nine hundred millions of dollars," so vast a sum that the South would never give it up. He envisioned physical danger in emancipation: "We do not intend to stand still and have our throats cut." According to the Alabamian, while the North was trying to steal southern property, the courts had become "the vilest instruments of oppression" and church pulpits "the sanctuaries of slander."

Albert Brown of Mississippi regarded slavery as "a great moral, social, political, and religious blessing—a blessing to the slave and a blessing to the master." Furthermore, he warned that if the North interfered with southern rights, the Union would end.[19] When such threats became a routine southern litany, northerners tended to disregard them, concluding they were oratory designed to please constituent slaveholders. It is not surprising that ten years later, in 1860, many northerners did not take seriously southern threats to secede.

The wise historian David M. Potter concluded that by 1850, in order to preserve the Union, "the South had either to be conciliated or to be coerced."[20] Few in the North were ready for coercion.

At least one southerner, Thomas L. Clingman of North Carolina, believed that as a result of the *Pearl* affair, District slave owners had become reconciled to the idea of freeing their slaves, since "there was no chance of getting Congress to pass any adequate law for their protection." He claimed that there were about 30,000 runaways in the North, a number large enough to cause him to fear that slave owners living adjacent to free territory would not be able to retain their slaves. Clingman thought that slavery was no longer viable in the District because of the many opportunities to escape; most southern members of Congress did not agree.[21]

According to the very careful work of historians John Hope Franklin and Loren Schweninger, the number of runaways reaching the North was about 1,000 per year—at most 2,000. In a slave population of almost 3 million, however, so small a number could not have had a discernible effect on the overall economy of the South. And yet this was not the contemporary perception: the halls of Congress rang with denunciations of abolitionists' depopulating the South and destroying the livelihood of congressmen's constituents.

For the present-day understanding of the American slave system, the additional conclusion of Franklin and Schweninger is even more important: that each year as many as 50,000 slaves fled internally, staying within the South.[22] It was more difficult to blame northerners for this larger internal problem, but southerners did not hesitate to charge that abolitionists were invading the South. In any event, both slave owners and antislavery enthusiasts clearly exaggerated the number of enslaved people that escaped to the North. Although their motives differed, and they sought diametrically opposed solutions, both sides still had one purpose in common: to increase public consciousness of the problem. The *Pearl* incident had done that, for though it failed, its audacity—stealing a large number of slaves from a congressional jurisdiction—aroused both senators and congressmen to action, on both sides of the controversy. When South Carolina left the Union in 1860, its Declaration of Causes of Secession "devoted twenty times as much space to the fugitive-slave problem" as it did to the question of slavery in the western territories.[23] Even the Fugitive Slave Act of 1850 could not calm southern alarm over runaways.

Southerners looked back with longing to a time when, according to their memories, reclaiming runaways was as easy in New York as in Charleston. Now in 1850 a man pursuing a fugitive in the North might find himself in jail, or so southerners believed; and occasionally slave owners did encounter violence when seeking to recover their bondmen.[24] Since the end of the eighteenth century, slave owners had depended on the law of 1793 to enforce the return of fugitives through the goodwill and assistance of the affected states. But a Supreme Court decision of 1842, *Prigg v. Pennsylvania*, as noted in the preceding chapter, placed on the federal government the burden of reclaiming runaways, and courts in the free states interpreted the decision as relieving them of that responsibility.

Prigg did not forbid northern states to return fugitives; it said that states could not be compelled to send them back to the South. Northern courts interpreted this to mean "that state officials *lacked any juris-diction* over fugitive slaves."[25] Joshua Giddings somewhat simplisti-cally interpreted the court's decision in this fashion: "The soil of the free states was a *common race-ground* for the slave and his master, and the Governments of those States were not to interfere between them. . . . The master must be suffered to come and catch his own slave as he could."[26]

Southerners understandably feared that the law of 1793 was dead. Although they had been firm believers in, and promoters of, limita-tions on centralized power, they recognized that the federal govern-ment lacked a practical mechanism for capturing runaways and return-ing them to the South; fugitives were generally safe if they reached a northern state. If the *Pearl* had reached Pennsylvania, the seventy-six slaves probably would not have had to fear a return to bondage. From a slaveholder's viewpoint, that would not do.

Southern members of Congress and their constituents reconsidered their view of federal power, and by the end of 1849 they decided that, at least with regard to slavery, the authority of the government in Wash-ington had to increase. Senator James Murray Mason of Virginia con-cluded that the risk of losing valuable property was more serious than the risk of augmenting the power of federal officials. Addressing the Senate in January 1850, Mason bade farewell to limited government. If state officials were no longer required to enforce the 1793 law, "Fed-eral officers" had to do so. As Mason saw it, the rights of the northern states did not extend to protecting runaways from recapture.

For a fugitive slave law to be effective, according to Mason, Con-gress had to provide "officers to execute it at almost every cross-road, in all the counties of the offending States." Enforcing the fugitive slave law was so important that the United States government would have to bear the expense, however great it might be.[27] Frugality and states' rights became of decidedly secondary importance when the South confronted the high costs and difficulties of retrieving runaway prop-erties who had escaped into the jurisdiction of other states.

As congressional debates clearly demonstrated, slavery was preemi-nent. When first William H. Seward of New York and then Daniel Webster of Massachusetts sought jury trials for suspected fugitives, Foote of Mississippi, regarding Seward's proposal with "hot con-tempt, . . . unmitigated loathing, and abhorrence unutterable," insisted that Seward was trying to force a breakup of the Union. Seward's biographer pointed out that when Foote dined with the New Yorker in 1850, he "wax[ed] eloquent over the dissolution of the Union."[28]

It was this obvious rancor, plus the desperate need for a government in the West after the Mexican War, that led Senator Henry Clay, though old and sick, to propose laws to (1) provide the new western lands with governments, (2) end the District slave trade (but not slavery), and (3) facilitate the return of fugitives, using the power of the federal government. These measures occupied almost the whole of the first session of the Thirty-first Congress. Although the protection of slavery in western lands was the paramount issue for many southern members of Congress, the *Pearl* incident convinced them that they also had to deal with the problems of slavery and its trade.

Henry Clay has come down in history as the Great Compromiser who saved the Union first in 1819–20 when Missouri sought admission to the Union as a slave state and again in the 1830–32 impasse over South Carolina's refusal to enforce the tariff. Indeed, he described himself as a compromiser. When he returned to the Senate in December 1849, many people hoped that single-handedly he would yet again save the country from civil conflict. Clay did draw up the basic proposals known as the Compromise of 1850, but younger members of the Senate and the House carried the burden of making them law.[29]

Clay sincerely believed that he would be able to bring to the United States "peace and quiet for thirty years hereafter." After all, the Missouri Compromise of 1820 had lasted that long. This time, however, he was not to be equally successful. Although the 1850 laws would postpone the breakup of the Union by ten years, peace and quiet did not reign during that decade. Clay was correct, however, when he warned that "dissolution of the Union and war are identical and inseparable."[30] In that respect he was more of a realist than many of his contemporaries, though he did not live to see his prophecy fulfilled.

Even though Clay was a slave owner and represented the slave state of Kentucky, he was sure that since the Constitution had given Congress exclusive power over the District, it could free all Washington slaves whenever it wished. But aware of southern sensitivities, he concluded that Congress should end slavery in the nation's capital only with the approval of both Maryland and the District and with compensation for slave owners. He would, of course, not agree with Giddings that free blacks and slaves should have the right to vote on the issue.

Jeremiah Morton of Virginia warned that the South could never agree to end slavery in Washington, for doing so would convert the District "into a fort and arsenal, from which enemies and madmen may with impunity hurl the missiles of sedition." Ending District slavery would make the nation's capital "the grand center from which southern institutions may be assailed by such as make profit from fanatical feelings."[31]

But Clay was convinced that Washington's slave trade was nonessential; it could come to an end without any hardship because there were many other places where it could thrive. "Let the slave-dealer . . . not come here and establish his jails and put on his chains, and sometimes shock the sensibilities of our nature by a long train of slaves passing" on Pennsylvania Avenue. According to antislavery journalist Grace Greenwood, Clay wanted the trade in humans removed from the District, "not because it insults the manhood and outrages the principles of all true republicans," but to protect "the feelings of gentlemen shocked by seeing slaves in chains."[32]

As Clay envisioned it, slave depots would close, but private sales could continue. A slave owner could still sell to his neighbor, and if the neighbor came from New Orleans or Natchez, who would complain? Since a large part of the slave trade had always been person to person, Clay's proposal would have little effect on commerce in human property; it would, however, make it more private and hence less subject to northern protests. He would couple the end of the slave trade in the District with a provision that Congress could not "prohibit or obstruct the trade in slaves between the slaveholding States." Clay would not interfere with the essential southern commerce in bondmen and bondwomen.

It was equally urgent to make "more effectual provision . . . for the restitution and delivery" of fugitives.[33] Although Clay agreed on the necessity of strict measures against runaways, it was James Murray Mason of Virginia who provided detailed provisions for strengthening the law concerning the return of runaways. He was more willing than had been his grandfather, George Mason of Gunston Hall, the author of the Virginia Declaration of Rights, to assert the overwhelming authority of the federal government.

If Senator Mason had his way, every person residing in the United States would become involved in perpetuating the slave system. According to the Virginian, federal judges would appoint three commissioners "in each county within their respective Districts and Territories," who, after receiving proof of ownership, would issue certificates to those claiming runaways. Marshals and deputy marshals would be required to enforce such warrants, and if they encountered resistance, they could call for the assistance of "bystanders" or a *posse comitatus*. "All good citizens are hereby commanded to aid and assist in the prompt and efficient execution of this law." Fugitives could not submit evidence; the certificates issued by commissioners would be "conclusive"; anybody obstructing the return would be fined $1,000, an astronomical sum.[34]

Southerners had always insisted that Congress could not legislate on slavery anywhere under any conditions. Only southern states could pass laws dealing with what Senator Foote called "a prohibited subject."[35] Now Senator Mason, determined to halt what he saw as a calamitous loss of property, abandoned the traditional southern position and proposed a dramatic increase in the power of the federal government. Alarm over runaways was a primary concern of members of Congress from the Upper South; by 1850 they envisioned a powerful and omnipresent government rescuing the property of their constituents from the grasp of abolitionists. Members from the Lower South joined them by the late summer and early fall of 1850.

As a result of the war with Mexico, Americans knew by 1848 that the lands of the Southwest were safely in their hands. For southerners this was an unparalleled opportunity to foster the westward spread of slavery. At the same time, however, they had to make sure that while their peculiar institution was growing in the Southwest it did not decrease in the Upper South. As historian William W. Freehling astutely observed, "The overriding problem was whether slavery on the fringes could remain in place or whether the South would gradually shrink to fewer and fewer black belts [of slavery]."[36] When slaves in the Upper South ran away, owners saw their action as a threat to the institution "on the fringes," resulting in a possible shrinkage of slave territory. What was the profit of extending human bondage westward if it were lost in the old slave states? In the eyes of southerners, extension and preservation were joined.

They had to pass laws that would halt slave flight to the North, protect slavery in the District of Columbia because of its symbolic importance as the nation's capital, and prevent any limitation on the sale of slaves from the Upper to the Lower South. In the years 1848 to 1850, Congress sought to resolve all these problems, leading to a series of compromises, along with settling the future of western lands, known collectively as the Compromise of 1850.

As cotton and sugar production grew in the South, so did the demand for labor. If, as Joshua Giddings believed, a slave in the cotton fields had a useful working life of seven years,[37] there must be a steady flow of labor from the slave-exporting states. From the southern viewpoint, useful workers could not be allowed to escape to the North when they were needed in the fields raising cotton and sugar cane. Members of Congress from the Lower South, reflecting the close relationship between buyer and seller, agreed to support Mason of Virginia in his insistence on harsh action against runaways.

Antislavery members of Congress viewed Clay's compromise proposals, joined to Mason's fugitive slave provisions, as evidence of southern aggression. If proslavery senators and congressmen were determined to maintain slavery in the District and ensure that the North would no longer provide a haven for runaways, northerners resolved to confront the South "with a more defiant tone."[38] If proslavery members of Congress saw the District as the place to make a stand, so did their antislavery counterparts; the District could become a test case for both sides. If southerners hoped to extend the power of recapture to every northern town and county, northerners would make every effort to prevent it.

None spoke more sharply than Horace Mann, who, while involved in Daniel Drayton's defense, had learned a great deal about slavery and slaveholders. He had discovered the peril of arguing a case in a courtroom filled with angry defenders of human bondage. He had suffered from the insistence of Washingtonians that the cases of Drayton and Sayres be pursued until desirable results had been achieved — desirable, that is, from the proslavery viewpoint. Mann concluded that there could be no compromise with the South; slavery infected every person connected with it. In February 1850 he declared: "A stranger would suppose, from hearing the epithets . . . that are heaped upon us, that we were abolitionists of all truth, purity, knowledge, improvement, civilization, happiness, and holiness." Far better, said Mann, to attach the term "abolitionist" to southerners, for they supported a system that abolished "freedom, justice, equity, and a sense of human brotherhood." Mann, who in Garrison's eyes was not an abolitionist, now accepted the designation for himself and his colleagues: "If we are abolitionists, then, we are abolitionists of human bondage; while those who oppose us are abolitionists of human liberty."[39]

Mann proposed a southern version of the Declaration of Independence:

We hold these truths to be self-evident, that men are not created equal; that they are not endowed by their Creator with inalienable rights; that white men, of the Anglo-Saxon race, were born to rob, and tyrannize, and enjoy; and black men, of the African race, to labor, and suffer, and obey; that a man, with a drop of African blood in his veins, has no political rights, and therefore, whatever he shall earn, or receive, belongs to his master; that he has no judicial rights, and, therefore, he shall never be heard, as a witness, to redress wrong, or violence, or robbery, committed by white men upon him; that he has no parental rights, and, therefore, his children may be torn from his bosom, at the pleasure, or caprice, of his owner; that he has no marital rights, and, therefore, his wife may be lawfully sold away into distant bondage, or violated before his eyes; that he has no rights of mind, or of conscience, and therefore, he shall never be allowed to read, or to think, and all his aspirations for improvement shall be extinguished; that he has no religious rights, and, therefore, he shall never read the Bible; that he has no heaven-descended, God-given rights of freedom, and, therefore, he and his posterity, shall be slaves forever; we hold that governments were instituted among men, to secure and fortify this ascendancy of one race over another; that this ascendancy has its foundation in force, ratified by law, and in ignorance and debasement, inflicted by intelligence and superiority; and when any people, with whom we have been politically associated, would debar us from propagating our doctrines, or extending our domination into new realms and over free territories, it becomes our duty to separate from them, as we hold the rest of mankind, friends when they make slaves, enemies when they make freemen.

Mann was not finished but went on to the Constitution of 1787:

So the preamble to their [southern] constitution must run in this wise. We, the people of the "United States South," in order to form a more perfect conspiracy against the rights of the African race, establish injustice, insure domestic slavery, provide for holding three millions of our fellow-beings, with all the countless millions of their posterity, in bondage, and to secure to ourselves and our posterity the enjoyment of power, and luxury, and sloth, do ordain and establish this constitution for the "United States South."

Mann concluded: "Such is my solemn and abiding conviction of the character of slavery, that, under a full sense of my responsibility to my country and my God, I deliberately say, better disunion, better a civil or servile war—better anything that God in his providence shall send, than an extension of the boundaries of slavery." [40]

When Mann's constituents asked where he stood on Clay's proposal to end the District's slave trade, he told them he was opposed: it would mean the "perpetuity" of slavery itself. "The slave planter or slave trader, when he comes to our American Congo to replenish his stock of human cattle, shall be obliged to go a mile or two, to the slave marts [in Alexandria, Virginia], instead of walking down Pennsylvania Avenue." [41]

Salmon P. Chase, a new senator from Ohio, pushed for a total end to the slave trade. If Congress had had the power to end the trade with Africa, as it had done in 1807-8, it could terminate the trade between the states. [42] Chase knew this would not happen, for the Upper South needed to sell its surplus, and the Lower South depended on the trade for an unending supply of labor.

Thaddeus Stevens, a congressman from Pennsylvania who would be known to history as the leader of post–Civil War radicals and who early in the twentieth century was caricatured in the pro-southern film *Birth of a Nation*, used Virginia as proof that the trade in people was essential. A Virginia congressman had given Stevens a pamphlet from which he read: "Virginia has a slave population of near half a million, whose value is chiefly dependent on southern demand." There, said the Pennsylvanian, was proof of Virginia's dependence on the slave trade:

Let us pause a moment over this humiliating confession. In plain English, what does it mean: That Virginia is now only fit to be the *breeder*, not the employer, of slaves. That she is reduced to the condition that her proud chivalry are compelled to turn slave-traders for a livelihood. Instead of attempting to renovate the soil, and by their own honest labor compelling the earth to yield her abundance;

instead of seeking for the best breed of cattle and horses to feed on her hills and valleys, and fertilize the land, the sons of that great State must devote their time to selecting and grooming the most lusty sires and the most fruitful wenches, to supply the slave barracoons of the South! And the learned gentleman pathetically laments that the profits of this genteel traffic will be greatly lessened by the circumspection of slavery! This is his picture, not mine.[43]

John Van Dyke of New Jersey had never given much thought to the trade in slaves, "but when I was forced to look," said he, "upon a drove of negroes of both sexes and of all conditions, bound together, and publicly driven along Pennsylvania Avenue, amid the hootings and shouts of the boys, I confess that, although my nerves are not easily disturbed, this was a little more than I could look upon with composure."[44]

On the other hand, Senator Joseph Underwood of Kentucky maintained that in his fifteen years in Washington he had never seen a slave sale. The only slaves he had seen "in custody" were the ones who fled aboard the *Pearl*. He had heard of slave pens, but "it seems to me that no one of proper feeling would be disposed to look upon the scenes we may imagine to exist at such places, unless it was his duty to do it." Clearly Underwood did not see it as his duty, though he implicitly admitted that a slave pen was a horror. Nevertheless, said Underwood, if the people of Washington asked for an end to the trade in humans, he would support it. But it would mean—and in this he was surely correct—that the trade would simply move from the District to Alexandria. Why get excited about moving slave pens from the north to the south side of the Potomac River?[45]

At the same time that congressmen and senators were arguing over the District trade, they were confronting James Murray Mason's proposals for strengthening the law against runaways. Northern opposition varied from total rejection of any fugitive slave law to acceptance of one that would be less invasive of the rights of the individual. Senator William H. Seward of New York exemplified the first view, claiming that laws for the recapture of fugitives were "unjust, unconstitutional, and immoral." He addressed the South: "Do we, then, . . . demand of you an unreasonable thing in asking that, since you will have property that can and will exercise human powers to effect its escape, you shall be your own police, and in acting among us as such, you shall conform to principles indispensable to the security of admitted rights of freemen?"[46]

Senator William L. Dayton of New Jersey would vote for a "reasonable" fugitive slave law but not the current proposal by Mason that would provide for sixty or more commissioners in New Jersey, three to each county, to return runaways. He did not want "postmasters, collectors of customs, and others, who have never, perhaps, seen the inside of a law-book in their lives, to exercise high judicial power." Nor did he favor Mason's insistence on calling any passerby to assist in recapturing a fugitive.[47]

Over the years, when North and South disagreed over slavery, members of Congress, including many who were uncomfortable with the institution, had accepted a compromise that would hold the Union together. By 1849–50 had it become an issue that could no longer be compromised? Was the break finally coming? Would northerners refuse to allow slave owners to dictate to them? In fact, the desire to maintain the Union was strong enough that the Senate, again seeking a solution, created a committee that in May 1850 presented a report encompassing western lands acquired from Mexico, fugitive slaves, and the District slave trade.

In its report the committee held that all states had a duty to assist in returning runaways; it was their obligation under the Constitution. There should be no jury trial in the North for those claimed as fugitives; it would be a denial of justice to the *slave's owner*. According to the committee, southerners treated slaves fairly, and any legal action should take place in the state from which the slave fled. If the owner could not retrieve his property, the United States government should provide compensation. As for District slavery, the committee recommended maintaining it; ending slavery in the nation's capital would arouse "apprehension and alarm in the slave states." There were, said the committee, so few slaves in the District that the issue in reality had no importance. The committee agreed with Clay that the Washington slave trade should end.[48] Debate over and resolution of these issues consumed the remainder of the session.

In the summer of 1850, Garland and Allen, the body servants of Congressmen Robert Toombs and Alexander H. Stephens, respectively, ran away and hid out in Washington. On the night of August 8, hoping to reach free territory, they set off for Baltimore in a hackney coach hired by William L. Chaplin, who had been under suspicion as a slave stealer since the sailing of the *Pearl* two years before. The Night Watch, alerted to Chaplin's plan, stopped the hack near Silver Spring, Maryland, and captured Chaplin and Allen. Garland escaped but soon gave himself up because he had been shot in the hand. Toombs and Stephens recovered their slaves, and Chaplin ended up in the same jail as Drayton and Sayres.[49] (More will be said about Garland and Chaplin in the next chapter.) Three of Congressman Colcock's slaves had recently run away, and though he recovered two and sent them back home, the third runaway apparently was lost to him. Was no slave in Washington free from the peril of sale?

There was great excitement on Capitol Hill, a North Carolina congressman commenting, "This stealing of slaves produces more irritation, more heart-burning among slaveholders, than all other causes combined." The incident "inevitably revived memories of the flight of the *Pearl*."[50] Senator Foote recalled "one of the most enormous outrages ever perpetrated on rights of property, . . . one of the most unblushing, high-handed, fiendish, outrageous attacks upon the rights of property existing in this District." What made it much worse was that it had occurred "under the eye of Congress, almost in view of the assembled wisdom of the nation, and in utter and shameful disregard of all the principles of honesty and all the rules of public decency." Congress, Foote insisted, must strengthen laws protecting slave owners in order to punish such "startling and horrifying" actions as the *Pearl* escape attempt.[51] The actions of Garland and Allen, reminding members of Congress of the events of 1848, seemed timed to prove to southerners that no one's slave was safe from the temptation to escape, that a strengthened fugitive slave law was imperative. Historian Elbert B. Smith suggested that Garland and Allen helped to ensure the passage of the Fugitive Slave Act of 1850.[52]

After members of Congress had worked out the most contentious issues surrounding western lands, they turned to fugitive slaves and the District trade in slaves, issues that consumed much of the months of August and September 1850. Everyone, whether favoring or opposing slavery, agreed that the Constitution of 1787 gave an owner the right to reclaim his property. Northerners wanted a law to guarantee a jury trial in a northern state for any person accused of being a fugitive, insisting on the essential nature of due process. Southerners wanted the word of the claimed owner to be sufficient to return a suspected runaway to the South.

Senators Dayton of New Jersey, Chase of Ohio, and Robert Winthrop of Massachusetts argued for jury trials, Winthrop contending that it would make the law more acceptable to the North, where a black man was assumed to be free. Chase held that when kidnappers carried off free blacks to the South and sold them into slavery, it was impossible to recover them; hence the need for due process. The kidnapping and sale of free blacks never happened, said Jefferson Davis; the South would never let it happen. An amendment to the fugitive slave bill providing for jury trials for suspected fugitives did not pass.

Dayton of New Jersey, still seeking justice for runaways, proposed that since the testimony of the accused could not be heard, neither should the testimony of the claimant. Dayton pointed out that in the District the word of the claimant was sufficient to enslave any black person, without other evidence. Of course, said Mason of Virginia, for in Washington every person of color was presumed to be a slave. Mason was wrong and knew it, for members of Congress had often commented on the large number of free blacks in the District.[53]

Mason refused to worry about the cost of returning fugitives: forget frugal government. He wanted "a series of officers in every county in every free State," supported by a salary "from the public Treasury." "I would be willing to give them a salary adequate to the trust reposed in them, and adequate to the character of the duty that would be devolved upon them," to return runaways to their owners.[54]

Senator Thomas G. Pratt of Maryland was determined to insert into the fugitive slave bill a provision that the United States government must provide compensation to all owners failing to regain control of their runaways. He admitted that only Maryland, Virginia, Kentucky, and perhaps Tennessee and Missouri—because they bordered free states—were "interested practically," but since, according to Pratt, the value of slave property in the South amounted to $1.6 billion, every slaveholder ought to be concerned. His state alone lost $80,000 a year as a result of Maryland's location next to Pennsylvania.

Andrew Pickens Butler of South Carolina warned that dishonest owners, conspiring with their slaves to flee, would achieve what amounted to compensated emancipation. The United States government would end up owning many slaves; what would happen to them? So Pratt offered another amendment, saying that if the runaway was returned, then the owner would have to give back the money the government had paid, though he did not explain how that would be accomplished. There was no limit to the complications the Marylander would accept in order to halt the flight of slaves from his state. In his zeal to pursue runaways while denying the central power increased authority, Pratt set forth a bizarre interpretation of the Constitution of 1787: It was no more than a treaty among the states that placed only one obligation on them: the return of fugitive slaves. Congress must act to enforce that one obligation and see to it that states did not protect runaways but assisted in returning them to their rightful owners. An effective law on runaways would calm the South and lessen the sentiment for dissolving the Union, said Pratt.[55]

Senator Foote agreed that while runaways were of particular concern to the border states, they were, in fact, a problem for all slave owners; Jefferson Davis, for example, advertised for a runaway he thought had fled to New Orleans.[56] Foote, as a Mississippian, probably did not want to call attention to the many thousands of runaways within the South that never entered free states. According to Foote, the United States government had an absolute obligation to assure the return of fugitives or provide compensation in the event of failure. Let us settle all problems about slavery, begged Foote, for they threaten the Union: "that ardent love of the Union, which I fear has, to some extent, been enfeebled in its action in nearly all the States lying south of Mason and Dixon's line."[57]

John M. Berrien of Georgia thought Pratt's proposal unconstitutional: "You cannot acquire authority to go into the Treasury, unless you establish the broad principle that, for every constitutional right which is not practically enjoyed, the Government of the United States is liable to indemnify." If the government paid for and consequently owned the slave, then it would itself be a slaveholder—or it could set the slave free and become a great emancipator. What, asked Berrien, was the United States government supposed to do? If, as Pratt claimed, the Constitution was a treaty among sovereign states, how could it assume responsibility for runaways?[58] Berrien was a Lower South senator unwilling to accept the expansion of governmental power envisioned by Mason and Pratt.

As Mason of Virginia and Pratt of Maryland, in their urgency to ensure the safety of human property in the border states, sought to extend the reach of the federal government, Jefferson Davis spoke for a conservative interpretation of the Constitution. It was, he said, the South's only protection. If Congress expanded the power of the government in Washington to purchase slaves, no one could tell how it would end. "Our safety consists in a rigid adherence to the terms and principles of the federal compact. If . . . we depart from it, we, the minority, will have abandoned our only reliable means of safety. If we admit that the Federal Government has power to assume control over slave property; if we admit that it may interpose its legislative and financial power between the individual owning the property and the property itself, where shall we find an end to the action which antislavery will suggest?"[59]

Senator Hopkins Turney of Tennessee must have had doubts about the viability of human bondage, for he viewed Pratt's proposal as a device to get the government to buy all the border state slaves and free them. Many slave owners would be glad to be rid of their property if they could be sure of government compensation. He saw no reason why those owning slaves should pay for others' runaways.[60] Although the debate over the fugitive slave law revealed the policy divisions within the slave states, the Upper South showing excessive alarm over runaways, the Lower South less so, the Tennessee senator, anxious to end slavery with compensation, showed that the South was not of one mind with regard to its peculiar institution.

The fugitive slave bill that Congress passed and President Millard Fillmore signed in the middle of September 1850 was basically the measure that James Murray Mason had proposed early in the session. Although it was called an amendment to the 1793 law, it was much more specific and went much further in granting power to the central government to enforce the return of runaways. The circuit courts of the United States were to appoint commissioners in states and territories with the responsibility of examining proof and granting, to those people claiming "fugitives from service or labor," certificates authorizing the claimants to "take and remove" their property. The law charged all marshals and deputy marshals to "obey and execute" the commissioners' orders; failure to do so meant a fine of $1,000, payable to the slave owner. Furthermore, if a fugitive held by a marshal escaped from his control, the marshal was liable for the full value of the escapee.

Because Mason and his colleagues anticipated trouble in recapturing those men and women that had reached free soil—maybe more trouble than marshals could handle—the 1850 law authorized commissioners to appoint any "suitable persons" to carry out the return of fugitives. Those appointees in turn could "summon and call to their aid the bystanders, or *posse comitatus* of the proper county, when necessary." The men writing the law were determined to involve everybody in the return of runaways. The law repeated Mason's call for general participation: "All good citizens are hereby commanded to aid and assist in the prompt and efficient execution of this law." An affidavit from the owner was proof of ownership; the law specifically stated that the fugitive could not testify in his or her own behalf. A commissioner deciding that a person was a runaway to be sent South received a fee of $10, but only $5 if he ruled against a slave owner. If any person interfered with the return of a runaway, he was subject to a fine, imprisonment, and civil damages payable "to the party injured by such illegal conduct."[61]

In retrospect it is difficult to see why southerners went to so much trouble to regain the relatively few fugitives that reached the North; a rigorous federal law was not necessary for retrieving the much larger number of runaways in the South. Furthermore, the law was written as though deliberately designed to anger northerners and convert them to antislavery. Was the South defining "what the federal government owed to slavery"?[62] Did this indicate a growing panic especially among slave owners in the Upper South about their property? In the two years from 1848 to 1850 antislavery members of Congress had spoken out with increasing boldness; some members of Congress had seen their own slaves run away; and the fugitives aboard the *Pearl* had fled virtually under the shadow of the Capitol.

Writing a few years after the enactment of the Fugitive Slave Act, Senator Benton of Missouri lamented its passage, especially since he had seen its ill effects. He believed that "under other circumstances—in any season of quiet and tranquility—the vote of Congress would have been almost general against the complex, cumbersome, expensive, annoying, and ineffective bill that was passed." Assuredly the conflict over slavery in newly acquired western lands had prevented quiet and tranquility; but when it was a question of runaway slaves, nothing had so aroused southerners as the *Pearl* affair.[63]

By the fall of 1850 only one aspect of Clay's compromise proposals remained for congressional action, the termination of the District's slave trade. Senator R. M. T. Hunter of Virginia warned that ending the trade meant in effect ending slavery: "Pass a law that slaves . . .

shall not be subject to . . . transfer like other property, and slavery is at once abolished." The trade in bondmen and bondwomen was essential; otherwise, Virginia and Kentucky would have too many slaves. According to the Virginia senator, it was also a great advantage to the slaves to be sent to areas where their labor was in demand and where the climate was more congenial. If he voted to end the District trade, Hunter, as a senator from Virginia, would have to admit that it was wrong to sell slaves in his state as well as in Washington, and that he could not do.[64]

In the course of the debate, it became clear that a few northerners in Congress, notably Seward of New York, were determined to end slavery itself in the District, not merely the trade. But Dayton of New Jersey warned Seward not to stir up Washington, where "public feeling is about settling down . . . as late events have left them." Pratt of Maryland, in a different frame of mind, seemed determined to keep northern senators enraged, claiming, for example, that there was no difference between slave property and any other property: the master had "as absolute a right over him [the slave] as over any other property." So a person stealing a slave should be subject to the same laws as any other thief.[65]

Threats to leave the Union did not cease, Foote of Mississippi warning that ending District slavery would mark the end of the United States. George E. Badger of North Carolina called antislavery people "wild and furious fanatics, resolved upon mischief, calling for a dissolution of the Union, and denouncing the proprietors of slaves . . . as unworthy of association with them." Butler of South Carolina said nothing new when he claimed that ending either slavery or the slave trade in the District was an "entering wedge."[66] By the end of the summer and the beginning of the fall of 1850, both northerners and southerners had said all there was to say, southerners warning of disunion and their opponents ringing the changes on the evils of slavery.

John Parker Hale of New Hampshire wanted his name to be among those determined to end slavery in Washington, welcoming "all the odium, the reproaches, the abuse, and the calumny which belong to the advocacy" of such a measure. He reminded the Senate that two years before, in 1848, he had tried to get a hearing for a bill for the protection of property when a mob ran free in the city, threatening the *National Era*. Nobody would listen to him then, the Senate showing no "zeal" for the protection of "dwelling-houses in which white citizens resided, or for the protection of . . . a press that was disseminating principles not exactly in accordance with the sentiments of some individuals here." The Senate, Hale concluded, felt concern only for property in slaves.[67]

Foote of Mississippi used this occasion to apologize (more or less) for his harsh attack on Hale two years before, in 1848. He had, said Foote, "used language . . . unbecoming this body, and unworthy of my own character—language for which I have since endeavored to atone." But he excused himself by claiming that he thought Hale was trying "to afford special shelter and protection to the perpetrators of larceny."[68]

A dominant theme in the argument over ending the slave trade in the District was the danger of "enticing" slaves to flee. In the eyes of southern members of Congress, the *Pearl* had made it a serious threat. What did "enticing" mean, Senator Hale asked. Would Hale be guilty of enticing if he read aloud the Declaration of Independence where a slave could hear him? Yes, said Senator Badger of North Carolina. Would a preacher reading the Bible in the hearing of a slave be guilty of enticing? The *Congressional Globe* records no answer.[69] James A. Pearce of Maryland wanted to empower the courts of the District to deal with "the seduction of negroes"; he was not really interested in the trade.[70]

Henry Clay, who had always regretted the Washington slave trade, hoped that ending it would pacify the North and take pressure off Congress to deal with slavery itself. Congress should pass the law because it would be the last in a series "looking to the restoration of harmony and concord," especially since he believed that District slavery would eventually come to an end without additional legislation.[71]

James Murray Mason, having pushed through Congress the harsh Fugitive Slave Act, now claimed that legislating to end the District slave trade was a forbidden subject, "dangerous to her [Virginia's] safety." He could not bear to have a law on the statute books proclaiming the trade to be wrong. In Mason's eyes, legislation protecting District property was the real need, and he could not understand congressional reluctance. Perhaps the time had arrived when North and South could not "live together under a common Government."[72]

Jefferson Davis opposed a bill ending the slave trade in the District because it unconstitutionally denied the right of transit of slaves. Congress could not limit property rights or discriminate against one species of property, in this instance slaves. Willie Mangum of North

Carolina also opposed ending the slave trade in the District, and he angrily warned that some men, in order to achieve emancipation, would wade "through the blood knee-deep of the whole South."[73]

After all this acrimonious debate, a bill to end the District's slave trade passed Congress in the middle of September 1850. Northerners realized that there was no chance of ending Washington slavery itself, and Clay hoped for peace in the country.[74]

The law prohibited the importation into the District of any slave to be sold or to be transferred to another place to be sold. Officials had the authority to put an end to any depot within the District, but the law left in place the institution of slavery and the continuing legality of the private sale of the enslaved.[75] In retrospect it seems a small achievement for the antislavery forces, especially in view of the South's overwhelming victory in passing the punitive Fugitive Slave Act.

Arguments had played themselves out. Slavery continued in the District, while the trade in human property moved, at least officially, across the Potomac River to Alexandria. The Compromise of 1850 pacified neither the North nor the South. Clay failed in his search for a lasting peaceful solution to the incendiary differences over the ownership of human property. In the final analysis, oratory, legislation, and compromise could not reconcile those who saw slavery as benign with those who saw slavery as evil.

CHAPTER NINE

The AFTERMATH

On April 19, 1849, Gamaliel Bailey noted in the *National Era* that a year had passed since Washingtonians had tried to drive him and his press out of the city. He rejoiced that the press had triumphed. "And from that hour, Freedom of Discussion was established in the capital city of the Nation, and the Cause of Liberty began to find in it, open supporters." In the course of that year, Washingtonians had seen their "Corporate Authorities . . . asking Congress to put an end to the external slave trade, and a Free Soil Association for the District of Columbia . . . invoking the action of the Federal Government against Slavery." The change in public sentiment had been "noiseless and peaceful."

Ever the optimist, Bailey claimed that "irritation has been allayed, prejudice abated, misconception corrected, and a more healthful tone on the subject of human rights is pervading the community." He looked forward to a day "not far distant when the soil of this District shall be consecrated to Freedom, and the deliberations of the Congress of the Republic be conducted, not amidst the discordant sights and sounds of slavery and slave dealing, but amidst institutions in perfect harmony with the Declaration of Independence and the Spirit of the Age."[1]

Bailey was much too hopeful, for District slavery would not end until 1862, and the removal of the trade

A slave pen in Alexandria, Virginia. (Courtesy of the Library of Congress)

across the Potomac River to Alexandria, Virginia, in 1850 was a poor substitute for abolishing slavery itself in Washington. The editor, however, was not alone in the expectation of emancipation, for the *Anti-Slavery Bugle* reported that owners were selling off their slaves before Congress could act to free them.[2]

According to Giddings, slave trading continued in the District. The only difference was that a Washington resident, on selling a slave, rushed him or her to the safety (from the dealer's viewpoint) of an Alexandria slave pen. In 1852 the *Anti-Slavery Bugle* carried a notice that an elder in the First Presbyterian Church of Washington had sold a young woman, "a member of a Baptist Church," and had sent her to Alexandria, where she was confined in "the close and reeking atmosphere of the slave-pen."[3] The 1850 law did not prohibit such transactions.

Congressional action restricting the slave trade in the District meant increased profits for dealers in Baltimore and Alexandria; Bruin and

Hill, for example, had been advertising for blacks between the ages of ten and thirty, with a preference for field hands. Since Bruin would pay Richmond prices, it was worthwhile for those hoping to sell slaves to make deals close to home.[4] Two years after selling Mary and Emily Edmondson, Bruin and Hill again attracted the attention of antislavery activists, when an especially beautiful girl named Emily Russell begged for assistance to avoid being sold south to New Orleans. (Horace Mann thought that she had been on the *Pearl,* but that was not the case.) When William Harned of the American and Foreign Anti-Slavery Society wrote asking the price, Bruin replied that he could not sell her for less than $1,800: "*She is said to be the finest-looking woman in this country.*" This time ransom money was not forthcoming, and Emily Russell set off south in a coffle, where she died along the way, everyone (except Bruin and Hill) rejoicing that death had saved her from probable prostitution.[5]

Nothing so fascinated antislavery enthusiasts as the fate of beautiful light-skinned slaves. In reporting on Hope Slatter's shipment of about fifty *Pearl* slaves to Baltimore, Congressman John Slingerland noted that some of them "were nearly as white as myself" and that about half were female, a few of whom were "finely formed and beautiful." Reverend Slicer saw this as proof of the congressman's obsession with color and race. The clergyman, on the other hand, claimed that he had not paid attention to the females who, according to the congressman, had "but a slight tinge of African blood in their veins"; he had been greeting and shaking hands with "a brother Methodist" with very dark skin. In other words, Reverend Slicer was sure that northerners perceived slavery as worse for those with light skins, with only "a slight tinge of African blood."[6]

After his success in ransoming Mary and Emily Edmondson, Henry Ward Beecher continued to raise money to free attractive young women. Although he was aware that buying slaves to free them probably prolonged the institution, he did not apologize, since he was convinced that publicizing the reality of slavery was an effective conversion device. Christians had to realize how their fellow Christians suffered: "It is vain to tell us that hundreds of thousands of slaves are church members; does that save women from the lust of their owners? Does it save their children from being sold? Does it save parents from separation? . . . What is religion worth to a slave, except as a consolation from despair, when the hand that breaks to him the bread of communion on

Sunday takes the price of his blood and bones on Monday; and bids him God speed on his pilgrimage from old Virginia tobacco fields to the cotton plantations of Alabama?"[7]

Beecher admitted that the charge had been leveled against him that his church was "one of the best slave-auction places anywhere to be found — that better prices were obtained for slaves that were put up for sale here than for any others." Resolved to use any means in his power "to arouse men's feelings against the abomination of slavery," Beecher declared: "I was always glad . . . to bring before you living men and women, and let them stand and look you in the face, that you might see what sort of creatures slaves were made of."[8] It was noticeable that he never brought old women — or, for that matter, men — to his church to simulate a slave auction and achieve freedom for one more person in bondage. In view of the northerners' unending fascination with southern concubinage under slavery, Beecher's actions are understandable.

When there was talk of inviting Beecher to the pastorate of a Congregational church in the District, Washingtonians threatened a reception of tar and feathers because of his "vilification and abuse" of the capital "and all other slave-holding communities."[9]

Bruin continued in the slave trade until the Civil War, when he was arrested by Federal troops occupying Alexandria and northern Virginia. Placed in the Old Capitol prison in Washington, he remained there a few months and then secured his freedom, apparently without further action being taken against him.[10]

When Harriet Beecher Stowe wrote *Uncle Tom's Cabin*, she was aware of the *Pearl* fugitives and their cruel fate. After all, the *National Era*, which first published her story, had been involved, though unwittingly, in the escape attempt. She had known of her brother's efforts to raise money for Mary and Emily Edmondson. In her "Concluding Remarks" in *Uncle Tom's Cabin*, she wrote: "The public and shameless sale of beautiful mulatto and quadroon girls had acquired a notoriety from the incidents following the capture of the *Pearl*." According to Stowe, a sister of Mary and Emily Edmondson had gone to their owner to plead for their release. "He bantered her, telling what fine dresses and fine furniture they would have. 'Yes,' she said, 'that may do very well in this life, but what will become of them in the next?'"[11]

When Stowe resolved to write a sequel to *Uncle Tom's Cabin* that would substantiate every charge she had made against the slave system, she believed that the *Pearl* incident would prove the reality of the evils that filled her novel. She sought information from friends and acquaintances, among them Gerrit Smith and Horace Mann. The latter in turn wrote to William Chaplin, who told Mann that all members of the Bell family, except one, had been on the *Pearl*, that Daniel Bell was in Washington, was in touch with Gamaliel Bailey, and was "an honest & truthful fellow as ever lived."[12] Stowe titled her book *A Key to "Uncle Tom's Cabin"*, and much of the information—and misinformation—about the *Pearl* comes from this popular and widely read account.

Stowe valued the friendship of Amelia (Milly) Edmondson and supposedly made her the model for Milly in her novel *Dred*, published in 1856. It was not a perfect match, except in the depth of both the real Amelia's and the fictional Milly's commitment to Christianity.[13] Stowe saw Mrs. Edmondson as a martyr to the struggle against human bondage and a slave with whom she felt total empathy. Stowe's account of her meetings with Amelia Edmondson is evidence that the author recognized genuine nobility of spirit as it rose above the degrading reality of human bondage.[14] She continued to raise money for the Edmondsons, even writing about their problems to friends in Britain. She had the Edmondson section of *A Key to "Uncle Tom's Cabin"* reprinted as a pamphlet and directed that it be widely circulated.[15]

✷

One would have expected African Americans in Washington, after the *Pearl* fiasco, to stay quiet and keep a low profile. No such thing happened. Because they knew, even if the District authorities did not, that William Chaplin had planned the escape on the *Pearl*, they besieged him "night & day, at all hours." They crowded into his room, recounting so many terrible experiences that Chaplin said his heart was "sickened."[16]

When Garland and Allen, the slaves of Congressmen Robert Toombs and Alexander Stephens, ran away in the summer of 1850, they hid in the servants' quarters of General Walter Jones, who lived at Sixth and D streets, not far from the *National Era* and only blocks from the Capitol. General Jones, an attorney who would assist Philip Barton Key in prosecuting Drayton and Sayres, could not have known that he was harboring runaways, but, as previously noted, urban slaves guarded the privacy of the backyards of their masters' property. Chaplin soon received word that the runaways had to leave Washington to avoid discovery.

When Toombs and Stephens offered a $1,000 reward for the return of their valuable slaves, John H. Goddard, head of the Night Watch, who had bravely defended the *National Era* in April 1848, was determined to win it.[17] There was no inconsistency in pursuing runaway slaves and protecting an antislavery press; they were all property.

Goddard set a close watch on William Chaplin, for he had long suspected the northerner of both antislavery sympathies and active participation in slave escapes, especially the one involving the *Pearl*. Lacking proof, however, Goddard had taken no action; now he hoped to catch him in the act of aiding runaways. Chaplin had received friendly warnings to leave Washington, but he stayed on, feeling that he could not desert those in desperate need. When Goddard, using his authority as head of the Night Watch, checked on livery stables in Washington and learned that Chaplin had hired a hackney coach and horses, he immediately concluded that a plan was under way to help Garland and Allen escape. So he set a watch on roads leading out of Washington.

On the night of August 8, 1850, as Chaplin and the two fugitives were leaving the District and crossing into Maryland near Silver Spring, Goddard and his men attacked them and arrested Chaplin and Allen. Garland escaped but turned himself in two days later because he had been wounded in the hand. Chaplin was lodged in the same jail as Drayton and Sayres were, and once again, as in 1848, his actions aroused anger aimed at Gamaliel Bailey's antislavery newspaper. The "mobocracy" of the District, learning of the incident, again proposed destroying the *National Era*, but again did not succeed.[18]

When Chaplin appeared before the Circuit Court of the District, he was charged with larceny, but Judge William Cranch agreed to grant bail in the amount of $6,000. Three Washington residents, David A. Hall (who provided legal assistance to Drayton and Sayres), merchant Selby Parker, and printer William Blanchard signed the bond. Instead of going free, however, Chaplin found himself on the way to jail in Rockville, Maryland, the county seat of Montgomery County, adjacent to the District.

The governor of Maryland, concluding that his state should have an opportunity to punish the slave stealer, arranged the transfer.[19] Proslavery advocates in both Washington and Maryland agreed that Chaplin deserved harsher treatment than he was likely to receive in the District; and since his capture had occurred approximately on the boundary line between the District and Maryland, the state could claim jurisdiction.

Rockville, though only a small village, had no trouble gathering a mob intent on lynching Chaplin. Idlers hung around jails and court-houses, anxious to spread the word of any possible excitement. But Chaplin's keepers lodged him safely in the jail, and in spite of protests from many Marylanders, a judge agreed to set bail, but at the astro-nomical figure of $19,000. Ironically, the only person whom Chaplin's friends could find to guarantee such an amount was a Baltimore slave dealer,[20] though Gerrit Smith, the antislavery leader in upstate New York, was ultimately responsible if Chaplin did not return for trial.

Some northerners opposed Chaplin's antislavery activities. For ex-ample, Madison County, New York, was a center of antislavery feeling, and yet the local paper, the *Madison County Whig*, did not hesitate to attack Chaplin's motives in the escape attempt. It claimed that he had deliberately planned the encounter "for the purpose of increasing to the highest degree the ill feeling now prevailing at the South, and precipitating an outbreak perilling [*sic*] the Union."[21]

Gerrit Smith, who had long been Chaplin's patron but had earlier warned him to leave the District, contributed $10,000 toward his bond; Blanchard, Parker, and Hall, the three Washingtonians who had pro-vided bond in the District, signed a note for the rest. After bail had been paid, Chaplin left Maryland in absolute secrecy because of the danger of a lynching. He received a hero's welcome in such cities as Syracuse, New York, where he announced his intention to return to Maryland to stand trial. But he never went. The men who had signed a note for his bail feared they would be bankrupted. Gerrit Smith him-self paid an additional $2,000 and arranged for a public appeal, but as late as 1853 Blanchard, Parker, and Hall were still begging for assis-tance to recoup the forfeited bond.[22]

Chaplin's fiancée, Theodosia Gilbert, had visited him while he was in jail, and they married after he gained his freedom. Gilbert was part owner of the Glen Haven Water Cure, located on Skaneateles Lake in Onondaga County, New York, and Chaplin chose to devote his ener-gies to Glen Haven, losing interest in antislavery. Some of his closest friends were furious, but Gerrit Smith continued to support him, con-tributing to the publication of a pamphlet defending Chaplin against charges of cowardly behavior. Chaplin had performed a noble service in helping Mary and Emily Edmondson and other troubled fugitives, but he ended his antislavery career despised by his former colleagues.[23]

By halting Chaplin's hackney coach on the road out of Washington and capturing the congressmen's slaves, John H. Goddard was sure that he would win the $1,000 reward. Congressman Toombs paid up promptly, "like a gentleman," but Stephens (who in the 1860s would be vice president of the Confederacy) was not forthcoming. Goddard "complained bitterly" because the Georgia congressman "cheated him out of the promised reward." The four policemen accompanying Goddard received nothing and were understandably angry.[24]

Congressman Toombs was not able to enjoy the services of his slave, for Garland ran away again, this time successfully, reaching Ohio and freedom. During the Civil War, a slave woman approached Toombs in Richmond, Virginia, and inquired about her son, whom the politician had bought years before. He told her of the young man's escape to Ohio but knew nothing more. When the 28th United States Colored Troops (Ohio) held a parade in Richmond in the spring of 1865, she sought out its chaplain, Garland H. White, in search of information. Miraculously, as she questioned him, she realized that she was talking to her long lost son, for whom she had grieved for twenty years.[25]

※

Defending Drayton and Sayres changed Horace Mann's life; as he said, he had looked deeply into the hell that was slavery. He expended much time and energy on behalf of the defendants, for which he "never received a cent of a fee, nor asked nor expected it."[26] He became convinced that northerners in general knew little of slavery, but in the course of his many appearances in court, he had gained "some insight into its dreadful mysteries." "For a moment, the wind blew the smoke and flame aside, and I looked into its hells. I saw, then, . . . what a vital and inextinguishable interest every human being has in this subject; — not the slaves alone, but the free men, not voters only but all who can be affected by votes, not men only but especially women." Even after the trials ended, Mann tried to help Drayton, who asked him to find "some pecuniary aid"; he passed on to the prisoner the small sums of two or three dollars that trickled in.[27]

In 1854, when Theodore Parker, a Boston abolitionist, was facing trial for involvement in a fugitive slave case, Samuel Gridley Howe suggested that he ask Mann to defend him. Parker refused, choosing not to recall the extent of Mann's pro bono work in the *Pearl* cases. He preferred a lawyer who, "unlike Mann, had often set aside lucrative commercial cases in order to assist in a score of antislavery cases free of charge." Calling Mann "wily, political," Parker claimed that he was "too conventional, too correct, and too concerned with his image in the community" to prepare a proper defense. "If Mann undertakes the defence of one so unpopular as I am, will it not be thought a little eccentric: — and so harm and damage the reputation of said Mann?"[28] Memories of sacrifice in a worthy cause are short, it seems.

Mann remained in Congress until 1853, ran unsuccessfully for governor of Massachusetts, and then went back to his great love, education, becoming the first president of Antioch College in Yellow Springs, Ohio. He had not wanted to return to the law and had been reluctant to become involved in the affairs of the *Pearl*. But his conscience would not let him stand by and see Drayton and Sayres go to trial undefended, and he proved to be an outstanding litigator and a force for justice in the courts of the District of Columbia.

✳

Before Drayton, Sayres, and English went on trial in the summer of 1848, Frederick Douglass proposed a massive campaign to raise $70,000 in bail, but no one took him seriously.[29] It was too much money. After Drayton and Sayres were found guilty and assessed huge fines, they and their supporters feared that the two men would spend the rest of their lives in jail. And when William Chaplin forfeited bail in 1850, by refusing to return to Washington and Maryland, causing his friends to lose a great deal of money, it was clear that no one could afford to provide bond for Drayton and Sayres.

The Washington jail had symbolic importance for all opponents of slavery, for it represented everything that was evil about the institution in the nation's capital. Supported by the taxes of all Americans, the jail held slaves awaiting transport to the South and blacks merely suspected of being runaways. In 1843 the poet John Greenleaf Whittier described it as "a damp, dark, and loathsome building," the "small stone cells" filled with blacks, "five or six in a single cell which seemed scarcely large enough for a solitary tenant." "The keeper with some reluctance admitted that he received negroes from the traders and kept them until they were sold, at thirty-four cents per day."[30]

When opponents of slavery went to see Drayton and Sayres, they were struck both by the harshness of their confinement and by the symbolic importance of the place of their imprisonment: Men that had risked their lives for the freedom of slaves were now being held in a prison that had been integral to the very trade they opposed. Drayton became a martyr to the cause of antislavery. Historians have not been kind to him, pointing out that he took on the task not out of idealism but because he needed the money. Yet emancipationists at the time saw him differently, as a man who had sacrificed everything to help the enslaved.[31]

Within a month of the sailing of the *Pearl*, efforts were already under way to make Drayton a martyr for the antislavery cause. The *Liberator* made him out to be "bold, stern, [and] determined," prepared "to do battle unto the death in the cause of right." He was characterized as "a tall, stalwart fellow, whose strongly-marked features and steady eye denote character and courage, and whose open and ingenuous countenance inspires confidence and respect." Slaveholders, claimed Garrison, hoped to "make Drayton drag out a life of misery, and be a living beacon to deter others from attempting to knock off the shackles of their slaves."[32]

Samuel Gridley Howe found Drayton "quiet yet stern and unflinching." He had suffered from harsh conditions, but "he seemed to have made up his mind to endure the worst, and knew that, in all probability, a sentence of life-long imprisonment would be his doom." Drayton told Howe that he knew he had broken the laws of the government but not God's law, and the New Englander "bade him cling to that thought, as to an anchor of safety."[33]

A year later the *Emancipator and Republican*, invoking the Bible, gave Drayton the status of Moses. As the hour for the deliverance of the children of Israel approached, "Pharaoh's heart was hardened." The more imminent the catastrophe for the Egyptians, the more desperately did they hold the chosen people in bondage. So it was in 1849: "The slave power is more insolently tyrannical and inhuman, at the precise moment when the freemen of the country are animated by the strongest determination to deal it a decisive blow."[34]

Opposition to slavery gave rise to some singularly poor poetry, which the newspapers published, apparently not intending ridicule. An anonymous eight-stanza poem, sent from England and published in antislavery papers, demonstrated that the *Pearl* had had an impact abroad and that the English could write really dreadful verses. Here is a particularly infelicitous stanza:

'Tis for this I see him lying,
In that dungeon, dark and lone,
E'en with the city bearing
The loved name of WASHINGTON.
Tell it not to Europe's millions,
Panting, struggling, to be free,
That 'tis thus Columbia tramples
On the soul of liberty.[35]

Three years later a lengthy poem appealed for the release of Drayton and Sayres from prison. It began:

Aye let them go! Why will ye fix a stain
Of deeper infamy upon your brow?
Why doom them evermore to sigh in vain,
As through your dungeon's hell they drag their chain?

The poem ran through a list of tyrants, especially emphasizing the Egyptians that held the Israelites as slaves, and ended:

Oh, pitying Heaven! touch thou the stony heart,
And bid its icy currents melt and flow;
In the cold eye, let Mercy's tear-drop start,
Till every feeling of revenge depart—
Oh! let them go![36]

In 1848 revolutions occurred in much of Europe, to the joy of members of the United States Congress, who saw Europeans following the American example of overthrowing tyranny. But whenever Congress waxed enthusiastic about an opponent of foreign oppression, antislavery newspapers pointed to injustice close to home. The *Pennsylvania Freeman* wrote: Those "smitten with admiration of the struggles and martyrdom of freedom's heroes in Hungary and Italy" could find Drayton and Sayres imprisoned close by for helping men and women escape the tyranny of slavery. "We call upon all parties to wake up and rally to the rescue of the victims of despotism," meaning, of course, the men in the Washington jail. Frederick Douglass echoed that sentiment, lamenting that foreigners seeking assistance from the United

States in their struggles for freedom did not speak out against slavery and the "republican dungeons" near the Capitol.[37]

The Colored National Conventions of 1848 and 1850 commended Drayton and Sayres and resolved that "we deeply sympathise with them in this present unjust and atrocious imprisonment." The American Anti-Slavery Society, meeting a month after the failure of the *Pearl* escape, applauded the effort of Drayton and Sayres as "a noble and Christian act," and proclaimed the right of all slaves to escape. Slaveholders, the society maintained, had no rights, "no rightful existence on earth" and constituted "no part of the human race." An antislavery meeting in Syracuse, New York, in January 1851 resolved that it would be "a lawful, as well as humane and religious act, to demolish" the District jail so that Drayton and Sayres could go free.[38]

Petitioning Congress to end District slavery had never ceased, but the *Pearl* affair gave fresh impetus to the campaign, with constant references to the injustice of the men's imprisonment. In 1849 the *Pennsylvania Freeman* optimistically asserted that with enough petitions "we will drive Slavery from Washington this winter."[39]

Accounts of visitations to the prison emphasized the humanity of the antislavery cause and the inhumanity of its opponents. Sarah Jane Lippincott, a journalist writing under the name of Grace Greenwood, reported in 1851: "As I looked into the melancholy faces of these men [Drayton and Sayres], suffering so deeply and hopelessly through long years, for the crime of helping their oppressed and degraded brothers to the freedom they themselves inherited and loved, sharp was the pain in my heart, bitter and I fear impatient the cry of my soul—'How long, O Lord, how long!'"[40]

The *Liberator*, recounting a visit to the prison in 1852, reminded its readers that "the guilt of their confinement . . . rests on the nation." Edward Stowe Hamlin went to see the prisoners, and they reminisced about their 1848 encounter, when Hamlin and Giddings braved the mob around the jail to promise legal assistance and a fair trial. Hamlin wrote: "Here they are, shut out from the world, separated from their families and friends, with no hope of release until the Angel of death shall come to open their prison-doors, and bid them enter that land where slaveholders and doughfaces can no longer inflict punishment upon men for their love of liberty."[41]

In the fall of 1850 the *National Era* issued a call for money to relieve the prisoners' "deep poverty," their suffering for "want of clothing and other comforts. . . . Any contributions sent to us, shall be carefully devoted to the relief of their wants."⁴² During the next year, Bailey collected $120, but by the fall of 1851 he had to appeal for additional funds "to make their situations comfortable" during the cold weather.

> It is a terrible thing for a man in full health, in the prime of his days, . . . to be shut up year after year, within the cold walls of a prison, counting day by day the sad echoes of his footfall, as he paces the stone pavement, or looking forth longingly through the iron-barred windows upon the restless sea of life rolling around him; and when that man is a husband and father, and has lost his liberty only through an act which nothing but the stern necessities of a wrong institution makes an offence against the community sustaining it, every humane mind must regard him with peculiar interest and compassion.⁴³

The imprisonment of Drayton and Sayres dragged on, the only hope for their release a presidential pardon, though the 1796 Maryland statute under which the two men were convicted made it difficult for a president to act. Persons found guilty under that law had to remain imprisoned until they had paid fines, one-half going to the slave owner and one-half to the jurisdiction where the crime occurred. Could a president issue a pardon to Drayton and Sayres and deprive the owners (now mostly former owners) of the money they were owed?

Charles Dexter Cleveland in Philadelphia conceived a solution: persuade the owners to abandon their claim, and then there would be no impediment to a presidential pardon. He seems to have cleared this plan with Gamaliel Bailey, who then proposed to Washington lawyer Daniel Ratcliffe that he take on the job.

In the winter of 1851 Cleveland promised Ratcliffe $1,000 if Drayton and Sayres were out of jail by July 1 of that year. When Ratcliffe agreed, the Philadelphian sent $400 to the lawyer, half donated by the ever-generous Gerrit Smith, the remainder by Cleveland. Nothing happened in Washington, and Cleveland understandably concluded that Ratcliffe had cheated him.⁴⁴

When Ratcliffe suggested that Mrs. Drayton might be effective in persuading the slave owners in Washington to renounce their claim, Cleveland agreed. He gave her money to buy clothes for the trip, to pay passage on the canal boat, and to secure lodging and board for herself and one child for one week in the District. Cleveland did all this even though he despised the woman, calling her "unreasonable [and] ignorant" because she would not let a Massachusetts family take two of her children to raise.[45]

As it turned out, Mrs. Drayton stayed in Washington two or three months, going to visit the owners and pleading with them to free her husband. The *Anti-Slavery Bugle* commended her "earnestness" and tenacity as well as her ability to endure the harshness of the slave own-ers—"Be gone! your husband stole our slaves, and if he had his deserts he would be hung." She finally secured the signatures of a majority of the owners, but not all of them.[46]

The *National Era* urged the slave owners to relinquish any claim to the fines. After all, what had they lost? They got their slaves back un-harmed. The prisoners were poor men, there was no chance that they would ever be able to pay the fines, and the *National Era* had heard that the president could not pardon them unless the owners gave up their claims. "Why not let them go? Does a lingering resentment yet steel their hearts against the pleadings of mercy?" Bailey reminded the owners of their Christian duty: "How can they ask God to forgive their trespasses as they forgive those who trespass against them, while they are inexorable against the prayers of these incarcerated men?"[47]

At this point a new player appeared: Charles Sumner, elected to the United States Senate from Massachusetts in 1851. An active supporter of antislavery and of justice for free blacks in the North, Sumner had taken the lead in legal action against Boston's segregated schools. Al-though this placed him in conflict with Horace Mann over questions of education, it did not lessen his confidence in the congressman's in-tegrity, and he may have been the first to put forward Mann's name as counsel for Drayton and Sayres.[48]

Sumner, having followed with great interest the events in Washing-ton in the spring of 1848, concluded that the *Pearl* incident had forced Congress to confront the issue of District slavery. "The effect of the debate in the Senate and the House has been admirable," he wrote to Giddings, though he was not sure whether he approved of efforts to assist slaves to gain their freedom. He could not condemn—indeed, could honor—those trying "to extricate their fellow-men from unjust laws," but he himself would not "be a party to any efforts to remove a slave from the custody of his master."[49]

As a member of the newly formed Free Soil Party, Sumner knew Salmon P. Chase, Charles Dexter Cleveland, and Gamaliel Bailey, and when in 1851 he won election to the Senate through a Free Soil–Democratic Party alliance, he found himself in association with men actively seeking the release of Drayton and Sayres. Bostonians wanted Sumner to support a bill in the Senate providing for the discharge of poor prisoners "confined for non payment of debts & penalties, on taking the poor debtors' oath," the poor debtors of course being Drayton and Sayres.[50] Trying to persuade Congress to act on this matter would be a waste of time, said Sumner, for such a measure would never become law.

Bostonians also prepared a petition demanding the release of the prisoners, but the senator refused to introduce it in the Senate. He was unwilling to give southerners an opportunity to vent their wrath against Drayton and Sayres. Convinced that only a quiet approach to the president would be effective, the senator did not introduce the petition, angering Garrison and his allies, though Drayton and Sayres had approved his plan. Encouraged by the results of Mrs. Drayton's hard work with the owners of the slaves aboard the *Pearl*,[51] Sumner began to cultivate the friendship and interest of President Millard Fillmore.

Fillmore was an accidental president, having assumed office as a result of the death of Zachary Taylor in July 1850, and he may have hoped for a victory in the 1852 election that would make him president in his own right. Pardoning the prisoners would alienate southerners still angry over the *Pearl* affair and northerners opposed to helping slave property escape. Gamaliel Bailey believed, however, that Fillmore "made no secret of his desire to release the prisoners."[52] But it was not an easy decision for an ambitious politician in Washington's tense political atmosphere.

In 1848, as a vice presidential candidate with Zachary Taylor, Fillmore had had to defend himself against charges that he was "an abolitionist and an incendiary." At that time he viewed slavery as a state matter over which Congress had no control, and four years later he had not changed his mind. For example, in his 1852 annual message—in a passage he may have omitted before sending the message to Congress—he lamented that "a few fanatics" had engaged in an "open declaration of war against slavery."[53]

Sumner began to make quiet approaches to Fillmore through friends such as Dorothea Dix, an effective agitator for good causes, "entreating" her to "plead their case with him [Fillmore] and his family." During the winter and spring of 1852, the president delayed, seeking legal opinions from Sumner and from Attorney General John J. Crittenden on his power to pardon Drayton and Sayres.[54] At the same time he was evaluating his chances of reelection; there was no possibility of a pardon if he won the nomination for president. But when the Whig Party convention in June 1852 nominated Winfield Scott, Fillmore's political career seemed at an end, and Sumner believed that the president would now follow his natural inclination to pardon Drayton and Sayres.

Both Sumner and Crittenden agreed that there was no impediment to a president's pardoning power. But the Maryland law presented difficulties; it was not clear that a president could deprive slave owners of the money due them from fines. Sumner undertook a lengthy, scholarly review of the entire question, and though he admitted the problem with the Maryland law, he concluded that Fillmore could follow one of two routes: (1) a general pardon that would free Drayton and Sayres and deny fines to the slave owners, or (2) a limited pardon that would free the men but leave them liable for fines.[55]

Attorney General Crittenden's opinion, in April 1852, cited English precedents and reminded Fillmore that "the King can not, by his deed of pardon, release & acquit that which is not his," which, in this case, referred to the fines due the slave owners. The courts had not decided "how far this doctrine is applicable to the constitutional power of the president of the United States." Crittenden concluded that the president had no more "extensive power than the prerogative of granting pardon vested in the King by the British constitution."[56]

By August the attorney general had changed his mind: the president could grant a full pardon and "discharge the parties from the penalties & imprisonment to which they have been sentenced." The pardoning power, except in cases of impeachment, was "unqualified & unlimited," for it came from the Constitution. For that reason the president's power to pardon was greater than the king's. Crittenden finally arrived at the same recommendation as Sumner: either release the men from prison and forgive the fines or leave the fines to be paid as a debt against the United States.[57]

On August 11, 1852, Fillmore, as he had promised, notified Sumner that he had executed a pardon for the two men. He wrote: "I have given this case the most anxious consideration, both on the subject of my constitutional power to grant the application, and on the merits of the application itself." As he saw it, the prisoners were subject to a fine for the crime they had committed. Their sentence was to pay the fine and costs and to remain incarcerated until the fine was paid. "Without going into the reasons for or against the application I content myself with stating, that I have come to the conclusion to grant them a pardon so far as to release them from prison." They would still be liable for the fines, in case they acquired any property, but Fillmore knew very well that both men were paupers.[58]

As soon as Sumner received the pardons, he rushed to the jail to demand the release of the prisoners, but there he learned that the secretary of the interior, the Virginian Alexander H. H. Stuart, wanted them held in expectation of a demand for extradition by the governor of Virginia.[59] Much distressed, Sumner hurried to the office of the *National Era* to seek counsel with Bailey. Lewis Clephane, a native Washingtonian and the business manager of the paper, urged that the senator return to the jail and insist on the immediate release of the two prisoners. This time Sumner was successful. According to the story that Clephane later told his son, the news of the pardons aroused the Washington mob, and Clephane took Drayton and Sayres into his house and hid them there until dark.

Once he was sure they were safe, Clephane went out and made the rounds of the livery stables in search of a driver who could take them to Baltimore. Waiting for a train in Washington would be asking for trouble, but if they could get to Baltimore, they could safely board a train for Pennsylvania and freedom. Clephane finally found an Irishman willing to undertake the trip, and at about ten o'clock at night, Clephane, Drayton, and Sayres set out.[60]

It had been an unusually wet summer, and torrential rains had washed out every bridge on the Washington-Baltimore road: creeks were as wide as rivers; the road was "a sea of mud and a mass of gullies." At Bladensburg, Maryland, when they tried to cross the ford, the horses lost their footing. At this, the driver announced that he had had enough and was turning back to Washington. According to Clephane's account, he took the big key to the *National Era*'s door, held it against the driver's head, and warned that he would blow his brains out if he tried to return. In the pitch darkness, the driver thought the key was a gun and decided he would rather face the water than the gun.

Clephane took the whip, and together he and the driver forced the horses into the torrent, and though the water came up into the hackney coach, the horses pulled it through. Crossing all the other streams along the way proved equally hazardous, but at daylight they reached Baltimore. Clephane bought tickets on the Northern Central Railway, and after four and a half years, Drayton and Sayres were on their way to freedom. At the end of August Frederick Douglass rejoiced to report that the two men were safely in Pennsylvania.[61]

President Fillmore expected to receive abuse for the pardons, and infuriated southerners lived up to his expectations. They agreed with the *Daily Union* that the president had no right to issue pardons because the fines were intended to compensate individuals "for grievous outrages which had been committed" against them. A hundred miles to the south, the *Richmond Examiner* was equally bitter, reminding its readers that although the president had denied having abolitionist sympathies, he had cast off his disguise and could be seen as he really was, a wolf in sheep's clothing. In 1856, when Fillmore ran for president on the National American (or Know-Nothing) ticket, his opponents cited the pardon of Drayton and Sayres as proof of his true feelings.[62]

For the most part antislavery papers greeted the news of the pardons "with emotions of unspeakable delight and exultation." The *Pennsylvania Freeman* waxed biblical: "Incarceration in a loathsome prison for half a century was the doom awarded them by the Slave Power, but He who turneth the hearts of rulers as the rivers are turned, hath opened the doors of their dungeon and bid them walk forth again in the light of his glorious sun and breathe once more his free air." The Free Soil Convention, meeting in Pittsburgh, exploded with shouts and cheers when a telegram arrived proclaiming the freedom of Drayton and Sayres.[63]

Yet not all antislavery supporters applauded Sumner's role in securing the two men's release. *Frederick Douglass' Paper*, while praising Sumner's "unceasing and efficient intercession" on behalf of the prisoners, also felt it necessary to defend the senator from critics who questioned the behind-the-scenes path he had taken. Sumner, the paper declared, had acted "quietly and judiciously" in the best interests of Drayton and Sayres. "He regarded them . . . not as tools to be handled for political effect, but as men in bonds, loving liberty as much as himself, with a life-long captivity before them, and families dependent on them for support, whose honorable discharge from imprisonment was the object and the sole object to be attained."[64]

Drayton, even though free, could not avoid the rancorous debate that seemed an inevitable part of antislavery. Who had freed him? He owed his release from jail to the "faithful and persevering efforts" of Sumner, for whom he felt "unbounded gratitude and admiration." He had agreed with Sumner in delaying the submission of a petition to the Senate, "it being his own and Mr. S.'s conviction that their presentation at the time would be prejudicial to his interests." [65]

Garrison and his allies had been angered by Sumner's refusal to introduce the petition from the Massachusetts Anti-Slavery Society. The Boston editor now refused to believe that the senator had helped Drayton and Sayres, insisting on the greater value of the Boston petition. At the same time he deplored Sumner's swearing to support the Constitution, even though the oath was required of all senators.

Sumner defended his chosen approach, which had been approved by Drayton and Sayres. He argued that if he had followed a more public policy, he would have "fastened new padlocks upon their prison-door." Instead of yielding to public pressure, he had taken what he called the "*practical way*," visiting Drayton and Sayres and then approaching the president as quietly as possible. [66]

One of Sumner's supporters wrote of the senator's detractors: "I *Think* that *now*, our good friends the abolitionists of the extreme *right*, may about as well take back the reproaches that they have not been *too* slow in heaping upon you." Another friend thought that only Garrisonians were angry with him. The criticism galled Sumner, who continued to defend himself. [67]

At least one Garrisonian, Wendell Phillips, congratulated the senator: "I wont [*sic*] rob you of a leaf of your laurels but rejoice in them all." He reminded Sumner, however, that he had favored another way: "Still as one whose judgt. dictated a different course I must say, in defense of that judgt., I think Fillmore would never have pardoned them had not the Baltimore [Nominating] Convention dropped him." Nobody would have doubted that. In his biography of Sumner, David Donald contends that "the Garrisonians were unappeased," that they cared "less for the liberty of Drayton and Sayres than for a denunciation of slavery from the Senate." [68]

Shortly after the release of the two prisoners, Sumner made a very important speech in the Senate, declaring that the Fugitive Slave Act of 1850 was unconstitutional. Slavery was local; it was freedom that was national. Congress had no right to take any action defending slavery in states where human bondage did not exist. "Slavery is a local institution, peculiar to the States and under the guardianship of State Rights. It is impossible, without violence, at once to the spirit and to the letter of the Constitution, to attribute to Congress any power to legislate, either for its abolition in the States or its support anywhere." Convinced that public silence was imperative if Drayton and Sayres were ever to go free, Sumner had delayed speaking out on slavery; his success on their behalf gave special force to his speech.[69]

The *Liberator* delighted in reprinting southern objections to the pardon, such as from the *St. Louis Times*: "The pardon of those rascally negro-stealers by the President, has aroused the indignation of every honest individual in the Union, who is not either an Abolitionist or a Free Soiler." According to the Missouri paper, Drayton and Sayres were "either lunatics or criminals, or both, and should be placed where they cannot repeat their crimes."[70]

The *Daily Union*, the voice of southerners in the District, attacked Fillmore and Sumner and in the process gave a clear statement of southern slaveholders' fundamental belief that slaves ran away only because of the seductions of evil men:

It is impossible that slaves can be enticed away from their owners without presenting . . . inducements which tend to produce insubordination and insurrection. In cases of abduction it is not the loss of property alone which the southern people consider; but it is the dangerous and infamous process which the negro-stealer resorts to in effecting his objects which inflames the southern mind. That malice which is the essence of murder does not spring from a heart more desperately wicked. . . . than the heart of him who would go into the bosom of a slaveholding community and . . . make them dissatisfied with their lot, and attempt to throw off the authority of their owners.[71]

Charles Dexter Cleveland greeted Drayton and Sayres as soon as they were in Philadelphia, gave each of them $100, and said he would try to raise $200 more, "to set them fairly on their feet again." He had never seen Sayres before (which shows how compartmentalized the undertaking had been) but was "more favorably impressed with him than with Drayton." Drayton showed no gratitude to the Philadelphian. Cleveland lamented to Sumner: "I thought that Drayton might have alluded to my humble efforts for him — *unremitting* for more than *four years*." Not a word about all the money the Philadelphian had raised: "nearly supporting his family, & engaging Ratcliffe, for $400 to undertake to get signatures, & sending on the wife & child for the same." Cleveland concluded: "But no matter — they are out, & that is the main thing — is everything." While Cleveland regarded Drayton as ungrateful and not "worthy" to be made a hero, the waterman probably saw Cleveland as the cause of his ordeal, which would have made gratitude impossible.[72]

Only Gamaliel Bailey gave public recognition to Cleveland, pointing out that the Philadelphian, by making "incessant appeals in behalf of the prisoners," had "laid the foundation for their pardon." He, of course, did not mention Cleveland's hiring Drayton in 1848, but he pointed out Cleveland's frequent gifts to Mrs. Drayton and his support of her appeals to the slaves' owners. "We know of no man more humane and liberal, albeit his alms are done in secret."[73]

Sayres now disappears from the story, except for a brief notice that he was in excellent health. Since he had no family, people thought that he did not need help. The 1853 Philadelphia directory listed Daniel Drayton as a waterman living in the city, but in fact he was too weak to resume his work on the water.[74] He began to make the circuit of antislavery meetings and everywhere received a hero's welcome.

In Boston he stayed at the home of Francis Jackson, a wealthy philanthropist and antislavery activist, where Garrison visited and found Drayton impressive: "There is nothing impulsive or reckless in his composition, but he evinces a firm, calm and deliberative spirit, which no fear of man can intimidate, and which is most reverent toward God and sympathetic toward suffering man." Drayton's health had been "impaired" by his long imprisonment, making it impossible for him to earn money to support his large family. "Wherever he goes, to recruit his strength, we trust he will be hospitably entertained and generously assisted."[75]

While Drayton was in Massachusetts, he called on Horace Mann's family and spoke of "the greatest debt of gratitude" that he owed the congressman. Mary Mann introduced the waterman to the young Mann children, for she had talked to them about his brave deed.[76]

At Dartmouth, New Hampshire, Drayton spoke to an audience that packed the room, with leading citizens supporting him on the platform. The meeting unanimously adopted the following resolution:

"Resolved, that we, the citizens of Dartmouth, in public meeting assembled, do most cordially extend the hand of fellowship, to Capt. Daniel Drayton; that we deeply sympathize with him, and will give our quota of material aid, and bid him go on his way rejoicing, always trusting in the potent arm of truth and righteousness, which will crown his labors with abundant success." [77]

When Drayton left Massachusetts to return to Philadelphia, he wrote to Garrison, asking to use his paper to thank the "freedom-loving people of the old Bay State" for their "warm and hearty" reception. With their approval of his actions, they made his "long imprisonment at Washington seem of very little moment, and confirm[ed] the declaration of a noble poet that / Stone walls do not a prison make, / Nor iron bars a cage." He reported that friends in Massachusetts had given him $221.38. The Colored Ladies' Anti-Slavery Sewing Circle of Canandaigua, New York, sent Drayton $7 and an "effusive letter." [78]

The annual report of the Philadelphia Female Anti-Slavery Society, written by Mary Grew, contained the following paragraph: "After a confinement of more than four years, in a prison at the Capital of this 'free nation,' for the crime of aiding innocent men to escape from their enslavers, they [Drayton and Sayres] were pardoned and set at liberty, by President Fillmore. The untiring efforts of many friends of freedom, whose names are too numerous for record here, were sufficient for this result, but not sufficient to remove the guilt and disgrace which their imprisonment attached to our national character." [79]

In Syracuse, New York, Drayton sat on the platform with antislavery leaders as they celebrated the rescue of a runaway from slave catchers operating under the Fugitive Slave Act of 1850. Drayton spoke briefly, and there were appeals to the audience to provide assistance, since he was "in poverty and ill-health." [80]

Drayton, who was "very feeble," went to New York and Boston to ask for help, having no choice but to rely on charity. Friends thought that six months at a water cure would restore his health, but there was no money to subsidize such a treatment. According to the *Pennsylvania Freeman*, he was a man "of deep religious principle" with the "spirit of a genuine reformer. . . . He is not a man . . . who will consent to be the recipient of public charity a single moment after his health is so far established that he can support himself and his family by his own labor." [81]

In December 1852 Drayton appeared at the convention of the Pennsylvania Anti-Slavery Society, where he spoke at some length, claiming that he was not an abolitionist but a man moved by the suffering of slaves. In recounting his experiences, Drayton said that he endured solitary confinement, in a cell without a bed, chair, or table. His keeper was a drunkard, sympathetic to slavery and anxious to make Drayton suffer. The jailer offered him liberty or a $1,000 bribe if he would reveal who had hired him. When not in solitary, he was housed with "the vilest and most profligate criminals." Eventually he was moved to somewhat better quarters, but the members of the convention saw that he bore "the marks of long suffering." He had no regrets for what he had done, as it was God's will.[82]

Drayton took advantage of his imprisonment to improve himself; whereas he had been almost illiterate, he learned to read fluently and to write with some ease. But Richard Hildreth wrote his *Memoir*, which the *Liberator* advertised for twenty-five cents for the paper edition, or thirty-eight cents if clothbound. When Drayton spoke to "an overflow audience" at Temple Street Church in New Haven, many people purchased copies.[83]

On September 14, 1856, Drayton entered Sailors' Snug Harbor, a home for retired sailors on Staten Island, New York. At that time he said that he was a widower with six children living in Philadelphia. He went on liberty in June 1857 and apparently headed straight for New Bedford, Massachusetts. Had he remained on Staten Island, he would have had "a permanent and comfortable home," but "the state of his mind" was "such as to make life a burden."[84]

On June 26, 1857, the *Evening Standard* of New Bedford, under the headline "Death of a Martyr," reported that Drayton had died. He was, claimed the *Standard*, "famous throughout the civilized and humane States" but "infamous throughout the others." The editor gave an account of the *Pearl* affair and said that since his release, Drayton had traveled about, speaking for the cause of antislavery. He had visited New Bedford frequently, often calling on the editor of the *Standard*, who believed that Drayton was a patriot as important as the heroes of the American Revolution.

According to the *Standard*, Drayton's health had been "completely shattered" by his imprisonment, so that he had been unable to return to his former occupation of waterman. The editor thought that he had been considering suicide for some time; evidently Drayton had told a friend within the past week that he had come to New Bedford to die, hoping that he would receive a proper funeral. His friend thought he was joking, but in fact Drayton checked in at the Mansion House, ate no supper, and before going to bed asked that he not be disturbed. When he had not appeared by the next afternoon, June 25, the hotel manager decided to break down the door, where he found Drayton lying on the floor with an empty vial of laudanum on the table. "He had also severed the arteries in both legs, with the view, doubtless, of preventing spasms from the effect of the laudanum." He had no baggage but about $12 in his pocket. A coroner's jury returned a verdict of death by suicide.[85]

Because New Bedford recognized the heroic efforts that Drayton had made on behalf of the enslaved, the funeral took place in the city hall, with the municipal government bearing the cost. According to the local paper, this was "highly creditable."[86]

When the mayor began the funeral service, the city hall was filled to capacity. A Unitarian clergyman gave the oration, recounting the story of the *Pearl* and comparing the deceased to Christian martyrs such as John Hus and to patriots of the Revolution such as James Otis and Joseph Warren. "If Daniel Drayton's heroic and self-sacrificing career receives at this time but a humble tribute from a few friends, the day will yet come when his life will be known and read as an incitement to bravery and generosity, and when his name will be inscribed among the highest on the roll of Freedom's champions." The city provided "a strong and handsome metallic burial case, with an outer coffin," and the burial took place in Rural Cemetery. The Reverend Dr. James Pennington, who had helped Paul Edmondson raise money to rescue his daughters, came from New York to conduct the graveside service. None of the Drayton family was present. The death register of New Bedford lists Drayton's death as occurring on July 1, but the postdating is probably due to the delay in convening the coroner's inquest.[87]

An admirer raised a handsome monument to Drayton, with the following inscription, written by Senator Charles Sumner:

Captain Drayton
Commander of the Schooner Pearl
Sailed from Washington, D.C.
April 15, 1848
Saving seventy six persons
fugitives from slavery

arrested by the U.S. Government
confined in a national jail
at Washington
four years and four months.
And, broken by cruel suffering
during confinement he died a martyr
to his benevolent effort.

The monument has been defaced, but one can still read the words.[88]

✳

While Mary and Emily Edmondson were studying in W. P. Smith's school in Macedon, New York, they inspired Smith's father, Asa Smith, to consider the desirability of establishing in Washington a teacher training school for African American women. The elder Smith discussed his idea with Myrtilla Miner, who was teaching in his son's school, and it was from Macedon, after seeking advice from various people,[89] that she concluded to undertake the difficult task. In the twentieth century her school became part of the University of the District of Columbia.

Miner's school received generous support from Harriet Beecher Stowe, who had resolved to do good works with the profits from *Uncle Tom's Cabin*. When Emily Edmondson, after Mary's death, insisted on leaving Oberlin without completing her studies, Stowe proposed that the young woman return to Washington and become Miner's assistant. Emily wanted to live in Syracuse with the family of Jermain Wesley Loguen, a former slave, an activist in antislavery, and a preacher (later a bishop) in the African Methodist Episcopal Zion Church. But Stowe prevailed, and in 1853 Emily Edmondson joined Miner, who was "pleased" with her, thought she had "much native power," and could easily take charge of a primary-level school and even "a larger advanced class" if she had help. Miner had trouble with ruffians in the neighborhood, and she and Emily practiced pistol shooting to be prepared for any eventuality.[90]

Miner believed that Emily would profit from close association with her mother, Milly Edmondson, and therefore Miner was pleased when the elder Edmondsons moved into a small house on the school grounds. Paul Edmondson was to take care of the property, raise vegetables for sale, and share any profits with Miner. But the arrangement

Fugitive Slave Law Convention, Cazenovia, New York, August 22, 1850. Standing in the center is Gerrit Smith. To the right of him is Mary Edmondson; to the left, Emily Edmondson. Seated between Smith and Mary Edmondson is Frederick Douglass. (Courtesy of the Madison County Historical Society, Oneida, New York)

did not work out; there were complaints about the Edmondsons and suggestions that since they were "unsuitable tenants," they should leave. And they did so, departing without warning; *Ten Eyck's Washington and Georgetown Directory* of 1855 listed the senior Edmondson as living on O Street in Washington.[91]

In that same year Emily Edmondson set out on the antislavery speaking circuit. She was already a celebrity among emancipationists, who had watched her grow from runaway slave to active participant in the antislavery movement. Emily and Mary had been much in demand, especially because they had beautiful voices and were willing to sing at antislavery gatherings. At an August 1850 meeting in Cazenovia, New York, protesting against the Fugitive Slave Act, the young women sang "I Hear the Voice of Lovejoy on Alton's Bloody Plains," referring to the martyrdom of antislavery journalist Elijah Lovejoy. At the same convention, one of them, probably Emily, had spoken on behalf of William Chaplin "in words of simple and touching eloquence," calling him "her dear friend."[92]

The 1855 speaking tour was to raise $800 to buy the freedom of one of Emily's brothers, and she succeeded, though Douglass reported that someone had swindled her out of a sizable sum of money. In 1848 Emily Edmondson had been illiterate; by 1855 she was speaking in the same Rochester hall as Charles Sumner and William H. Seward. Along with other antislavery women, she was able to rise above general opposition to females' speaking in public. In the 1870s, when Vice President Henry Wilson wrote *History of the Rise and Fall of the Slave Power in America*, he jointly mentioned Frederick Douglass and the Edmondson sisters as significant in the story of antislavery.[93]

Emily Edmondson married, had four children, and continued to live in Washington. She maintained ties of friendship with Harriet Beecher Stowe and with Frederick Douglass; a granddaughter remembered sitting on Douglass's knee.[94] The descendants of Paul and Amelia Edmondson thrived in the nineteenth century and continue to do so today.

✳

Despite Joshua Giddings's claim that the slave trade continued as before in the District, with the sole difference that "the gangs of human flesh were brought up in the night instead of the day time,"[95] it is more likely that the trade moved easily to Alexandria or Baltimore. The institution of slavery continued in the District throughout the 1850s, and only when slaveholders left Congress to join the Confederacy was it possible to move toward emancipation.

In 1861 Senator Henry Wilson of Massachusetts introduced a bill providing for an end to slavery in the District of Columbia, with compensation for the owners. The following year, when the law went into effect, slavery finally ceased to exist in the nation's capital. The congressional appropriation included money not only to compensate owners but also to help any former slaves interested in emigrating to Haiti or Liberia. How was the government to decide on fair compensation to the owners? The problem was solved by bringing in a slave dealer, B. M. Campbell of Baltimore, who suggested evaluations. The largest sum paid to one person was $17,771.85 for sixty-nine slaves, the smallest $21.90 for a baby. Some of those receiving compensation were African Americans, who had obviously bought members of their families. The number of people to be set free was 3,261; free blacks in the District in 1860 totaled 11,141.[96]

When the Civil War began and northern armies moved into the South, thousands of slaves left their owners and sought sanctuary with the military or in the North. Washington was flooded with runaways, and yet the Fugitive Slave Act of 1850 remained in effect. District courts heard cases involving slave owners claiming their runaways. Even after President Lincoln issued the Emancipation Proclamation, District authorities continued to hold fugitives and return them to Maryland claimants. In 1864 Congress finally repealed the Fugitive Slave Act, and Lincoln signed the bill into law on June 28 of that year.[97] Such was the tenacity of slavery and the slave trade in the nation's capital.

Conclusion

It is all too easy to claim, in the fashion of the rooster taking credit for the sunrise, that the *Pearl* affair brought an end to the slave trade in the District of Columbia. In fact, agitation against slavery and the slave trade in Washington began with the founding of the new capital, assumed great urgency in the 1830s, and became a powerful force at the end of the 1840s. Even without the escape attempt, Henry Clay might well have included the abolition of the trade in his compromise proposals; but the heated debates in the House and the Senate in 1848 concerning the *Pearl* alerted him and many other political figures to the slave trade's potential to cause conflict. Slaves might have fled without the ambitious scheme of William Chaplin, but not so many at once, the unusually large number arousing passions on all sides of the issue.

Without the drama of recaptured and suffering men and women, many in the North might have delayed their commitment to antislavery. Horace Mann, for instance, might have remained "halfway" involved in emancipation. Once he had looked into "the hell of slavery" in the courtrooms of the District, however, his life was changed.

Henry Ward Beecher would eventually have become involved in antislavery when it developed into a popular cause, but ransoming two young Christian women provided him with a concrete opportunity for leadership among religious emancipationists. His sister Harriet Beecher Stowe had already espoused antislavery, but the slaves aboard the *Pearl* offered vital proof of the truth of *Uncle Tom's Cabin* at a time when such proof was sorely needed.

Gamaliel Bailey had established the *National Era* in Washington before the events discussed in this story, but the *Pearl* incident demonstrated what a dangerous undertaking the newspaper was. For many observers the attack on the paper proved once and for all that a moderate voice would never succeed in influencing the South to put an end to slavery. Americans concerned about free speech and a free press saw the lengths to which defenders of slavery would go in attacking antislavery publications.

The Methodist Church had already divided over slavery, but the encounter between a slave trader and a Senate chaplain proved, in many people's eyes, that American churches could not claim to preach true Christianity as long as they condoned, or did not actively oppose, human bondage. And for those seeking evidence of southern males' sexual license, the sale of Christian women for prostitution in New Orleans, even if that was not their actual fate, justified fevered attacks on the slave system.

The *Pearl* incident was the result of actions by African Americans who resolved that they would no longer endure bondage. When William Chaplin provided the occasion and the means of escape, the motivation was already present in the very large number of slaves who risked their lives to seize the opportunity. Had only one or two turned to him, he would never have devised so risky and expensive a plan. But the pressure of many imploring voices made a wholesale escape seem the only way to proceed.

At the same time that masters sought to render their property dependent, slaves endeavored to assert their individuality. If slavery in urban parts of the Upper South was as mild as the institution could be, it was still slavery, and the nearness of freedom made bondage all the more galling to those in its power. Furthermore, even if the enslaved were comparatively well off in Washington, they faced the terrifying possibility of sale to the Deep South. That prospect finally precipitated the events discussed in these pages.

Since District slaves were knowledgeable about public events, they were all too aware of what Mississippi slavery entailed. From this they *had* to flee. And so they appealed to William Chaplin. He appealed in turn to Charles Dexter Cleveland, who hired Captain Daniel Drayton; Drayton then hired Edward Sayres and Chester English—and scores of slaves waited anxiously. They failed in their immediate purpose, but Washington was not the same thereafter—and neither were the opponents or the defenders of slavery.

One could claim that ending slavery in the District was simply an inevitability, but this is not the case. The strongest efforts by determined opponents did not and could not succeed in the face of implacable southern passions. It took a civil war and the absence of southerners in Congress to make it happen.

For a while Daniel Drayton became an effective rallying point for antislavery forces. As a symbol of heroic action within the liberation movement, this unlikely man was raised above the bickering and name-calling that so often characterized the disunited factions. It is an irony of history that Drayton, who participated in the escape attempt for money, achieved greater prominence than Chaplin and Cleveland, the organizer and the donor. All three men, however, became mere footnotes to the larger national drama that was played out in the 1860s.

Although the *Pearl* incident helped to publicize the many issues of slavery, it did not resolve the conflict over the ethics of buying slaves' freedom or even of helping men and women to escape from bondage. The sanctity of private property, the economic ties between North and South, and the protections afforded to slavery within the Constitution itself were all too often more powerful than sympathy for enslaved people.

To Americans who now take for granted the Thirteenth Amendment to the Constitution outlawing slavery and the judicially enforced civil rights statutes of the twentieth century, the intensity and prevalence of such nineteenth-century claims about property can scarcely be imagined, let alone understood. As generation has succeeded generation, memories have faded about the *Pearl* and Drayton and the seventy-six slaves who risked everything on that spring day in 1848. But it is a story that should not be forgotten, for in the nation's capital there were men and women with an unquenchable thirst for freedom who bravely set out to satisfy it.

NOTES

Introduction

1 Benjamin Drew, *A North-Side View of Slavery* (Boston: J. P. Jewett, 1856), 131; James W. C. Pennington, *The Fugitive Blacksmith; or, Events in the History of James W. C. Pennington* (Westport, Conn.: Negro Universities Press, 1971, orig. pub. 1850), 3rd ed., xviii.

2 Thomas D. Morris, *Southern Slavery and the Law, 1619–1860* (Chapel Hill: University of North Carolina Press, 1996), 341–45.

3 2nd Cong., 2nd sess., chap. 7 (Feb. 12, 1793), *United States Statutes at Large* (Boston: Charles C. Little and James Brown, 1845), 1:302–5; Mary Stoughton Locke, *Anti-Slavery in America from the Introduction of African Slaves to the Prohibition of the Slave Trade (1619–1808)* (Boston: Ginn, 1901), 132–33.

4 Henry Louis Gates Jr., "The Fugitive," *New Yorker*, Feb. 18 and 25, 2002, 108.

5 John Hope Franklin and Loren Schweninger, *Runaway Slaves: Rebels on the Plantation* (New York: Oxford University Press, 1999).

6 Claudia Dale Goldin, *Urban Slavery in the American South, 1820–1860: A Quantitative History* (Chicago: University of Chicago Press, 1976), 34, 40–41.

7 Stephanie Cole, "Servants and Slaves: Domestic Service in the Border Cities, 1800–1850" (Ph.D. diss., University of Florida, 1994), 93.

8 Isaac D. Williams, *Sunshine and Shadow of Slave Life* (East Saginaw, Mich.: Evening News Printing and Binding House, 1885), 11–12, 27.

9 See, for example, Pennington, *The Fugitive Blacksmith*, 9, 10.

10 Williams, *Sunshine and Shadow*, 15–16 (quote); William Grimes, *Life of William Grimes, the Runaway Slave* (New York: n.p., 1825), 8–11, 35.

11 Sally E. Hadden, *Slave Patrols: Law and Violence in Virginia and the Carolinas* (Cambridge, Mass.: Harvard University Press, 2001), 129. For maroon communities, see Eugene D. Genovese, *From Rebellion to Revolution: Afro-American Slave Revolts in the Making of the Modern World* (Baton Rouge: Louisiana State University Press, 1979), 68–81. For the North Carolina legislature's action against slaves in the Great Dismal Swamp, see David S. Cecelski, *The Waterman's Song: Slavery and Freedom in Mari-*

time North Carolina (Chapel Hill: University of North Carolina Press, 2001), 132.

12 Joshua Giddings, *Speeches in Congress [1841–1852]* (Boston: John P. Jewett, 1853), 134. See also his speech on compensation to Antonio Pacheco (no relation) for a slave lost in the Seminole War, 289–318.

13 For an informative study of patrols, see Hadden, *Slave Patrols*. For an example of the patrol in Virginia, see Austin Steward, *Austin Steward: Twenty-Two Years a Slave and Forty Years a Freeman, Embracing a Correspondence of Several Years, While President of Wilberforce Colony, London, Canada West* (New York: Negro Universities Press, 1968, orig. pub. 1856), 19, and for unusual resistance to the patrol, 22–25. For another view of patrols, see Drew, *North-Side View of Slavery*, 110.

14 6th Cong., 2nd sess., chap. 19, *United States Statutes at Large, Containing the Laws and Concurrent Resolution . . . and Reorganization Plan, Amendment to the Constitution, and Proclamations*, 8 vols. (Washington, D.C.: Government Printing Office, n.d.), 2:103–8.

15 Kenneth R. Bowling, *The Creation of Washington, D.C.: The Idea and Location of the American Capital* (Fairfax, Va.: George Mason University Press, 1991), 7, 103, 170–71.

16 William Chambers, *Slavery and Colour* (London: W. and R. Chambers, 1857), 27; Henry Wilson, *History of the Rise and Fall of the Slave Power in America*, 3 vols. (Boston: J. R. Osgood, 1872–77), 3:270.

17 Wilhelmus Bogart Bryan, *A History of the National Capital from Its Foundation through the Period of the Adoption of the Organic Act*, 2 vols. (New York: Macmillan, 1914–16), 1:232; Letitia Woods Brown, "Residential Patterns of Negroes in the District of Columbia," *Records of the Columbia Historical Society of Washington, D.C., 1969–1970*, 68; Bob Arnebeck, *Through a Fiery Trial: Building Washington, 1790–1800* (Lanham, Md.: Madison Books, 1991), 205; William C. Allen, "'Seat of Broils, Confusion, and Squandered Thousands': Building the Capitol, 1790–1802" in *The United States Capitol: Designing and Decorating a National Icon*, ed. Donald R. Kennon (Athens: Ohio University Press, 2000), 9; Felicia Bell, "Slave Labor and the Capitol: A Commentary," *Capitol Dome* (Summer 2003), 17–18.

18 Arnebeck, *Through a Fiery Trial*, 229.

19 Mary Tremain, *Slavery in the District of Columbia: The Policy of Congress and the Struggle for Abolition* (New York: G. P. Putnam's Sons, 1892), 49–50; Winfield H. Collins, *The Domestic Slave Trade of the Southern States* (New York: Broadway, 1904), 29; Steven H. Deyle, "The Irony of Liberty: Origins of the Domestic Slave Trade," *Journal of the Early Republic* 12 (Spring 1992): 37–62.

20 Thomas Hart Benton, *Abridgment of the Debates of Congress, from 1789 to 1856*, 16 vols. (New York: D. Appleton, 1857), 3:519 (9th Cong., 2nd sess.).

21 Alice Dana Adams, *The Neglected Period of Anti-Slavery in America (1808–1831)* (Boston: Ginn, 1908), 128; Tremain, *Slavery in D.C.*, 62; Steven H. Deyle, "The Domestic Slave Trade in America" (Ph.D. diss., Columbia University, 1995); Robert Harold Gudmestad, "The Richmond Slave Market, 1840–1860" (M.A. thesis, University of Richmond, 1993).

22 *Memorial of a Number of Citizens of the District of Columbia*, Senate Document no. 191, 25th Cong., 3rd sess. (Feb. 7, 1839). Users of historical documents will be interested to know that the first name on the *Memorial* was Peter Force.

23 Tremain, *Slavery in D.C.*, 72–73.

24 [George Bourne], *Picture of Slavery in the United States* (Detroit: Negro History Press, 1972, orig. pub. 1834), 225–26.

25 Gilbert Hobbs Barnes, *The Antislavery Impulse, 1830–1844* (New York: D. Appleton-Century, 1933), 178, 266n (quote).

26 *Speech of Mr. Cushing of Massachusetts, on the Right of Petition, as Connected with Petitions for the Abolition of Slavery and the Slave Trade in the District of Columbia: In the House of Representatives, January 25, 1836* (Washington, D.C.: Gales and Seaton, 1836), 1.

27 Samuel Flagg Bemis, *John Quincy Adams and the Union* (New York: Alfred A. Knopf, 1956), 348, 375, 437. See also William Lee Miller, *Arguing about Slavery: The Great Battle in the United States Congress* (New York: Alfred A. Knopf, 1996).

28 *Remarks of Mr. Webster in the Senate of the United States, Wednesday, January 10, 1838* (n.p., n.d.), 4. See also Webster to L. C. Peck, Jan. 11, 1838, in *The Papers of Daniel Webster*, ed. Charles M. Wiltse, ser. 1, 7 vols. (Hanover, N.H.: University Press of New England, 1974), 4:261.

29 Emphasis added. *Slavery in the District of Columbia*, House Document no. 691, 24th Cong., 1st sess. (May 18, 1836).

30 Irving H. Bartlett, *John C. Calhoun: A Biography* (New York: W. W. Norton, 1993), 230; Theodore Dwight Weld, *The Power of Congress over the District of Columbia* (New York: American Anti-Slavery Society, 1838), 17; William M. Wiecek, *The Sources of Anti-slavery Constitutionalism in America, 1760–1848* (Ithaca: Cornell University Press, 1977), 180.

31 J. Thomas Scharf, *History of Maryland from the Earliest Period to the Present Day*, 3 vols. (Baltimore: John B. Piet, 1879), 2:569–70; Weld, *The Power of Congress over the District of Columbia*, 17–18.

32 "An American," *An Inquiry into the Condition and Prospects of the African Race in the United States: And the Means of Bettering its Fortunes* (Philadelphia: Haswell, Barrington, and Haswell, 1839), 59–60; Merrill D. Peterson,

The Great Triumvirate: Webster, Clay, and Calhoun (New York: Oxford University Press, 1987), 261.

33 Howe to Mann, 18 [Apr. 1848], in "Memoranda and Documents: Samuel G. Howe to Horace Mann," ed. Robert L. Straker, *New England Quarterly* 16 (Sept. 1943): 479.

34 Ronald G. Walters, *The Antislavery Appeal: American Abolitionism after 1830* (Baltimore: Johns Hopkins University Press, 1976), xiii; Wiecek, *Sources of Anti-slavery Constitutionalism*, 155; David L. Lightner, "The Interstate Slave Trade in Antislavery Politics," *Civil War History* 36 (June 1990): 125 (quote).

35 Betty Fladeland, *Men and Brothers: Anglo-American Antislavery Cooperation* (Urbana: University of Illinois Press, 1972), xi–xii.

36 Joan D. Hedrick, *Harriet Beecher Stowe: A Life* (New York: Oxford University Press, 1994), 235.

37 Walters, *Antislavery Appeal*, 20, 28.

38 Larry Gara, *The Liberty Line: The Legend of the Underground Railroad* (Lexington: University Press of Kentucky, 1996, orig. pub. 1961), 72–73.

Chapter One

1 David R. Goldfield, *Urban Growth in the Age of Sectionalism: Virginia, 1847–1861* (Baton Rouge: Louisiana State University Press, 1977), xxviii; Blaine A. Brownell and David R. Goldfield, eds., *The City in Southern History: The Growth of Urban Civilization in the South* (Port Washington, N.Y.: Kennikat Press, 1977), 67.

2 Drew G. Faust, "Culture, Conflict and Community: The Meaning of Power on an Ante-bellum Plantation," *Journal of Social History* 14 (1980): 93.

3 James W. C. Pennington, *The Fugitive Blacksmith; or, Events in the History of James W. C. Pennington* (Westport, Conn.: Negro Universities Press, 1971, orig. pub. 1850), 3rd ed., 13.

4 Unsigned letter, Feb. 1820, in [Josephine Seaton], *William Winston Seaton of the "National Intelligencer": A Biographical Sketch* (Boston: James R. Osgood, 1871), 145–46.

5 Eunice Tripler, *Eunice Tripler: Some Notes of Her Personal Recollections* (New York: Grafton, 1910), 26.

6 *Richmond Daily Dispatch* quoted in David R. Goldfield, "Black Life in Old South Cities," in *Before Freedom Came: African-American Life in the Antebellum South*, ed. Edward D. C. Campbell Jr., with Kym S. Rice (Richmond and Charlottesville: Museum of the Confederacy and University Press of Virginia, 1991), 127.

7 Henry Bradshaw Fearon, *Sketches of America: A Narrative of a Journey of Five Thousand Miles through the Eastern and Western States of America*

(London: Longman, 1818), 287; Josiah Henson, *An Autobiography of the Rev. Josiah Henson from 1789 to 1881* (London, Ont.: Schuyler, Smith, 1881), repr. in *Four Fugitive Slave Narratives* (Reading, Mass.: Addison-Wesley, 1969), 23, 32.

8 Letter no. 1, Feb. 16, 1853, *New-York Daily Times*, in *The Papers of Frederick Law Olmsted*, 6 vols., ed. Charles E. Beveridge and Charles Capen McLaughlin (Baltimore: Johns Hopkins University Press, 1977-92), 2:87.

9 Wilhelmus Bogart Bryan, *A History of the National Capital from Its Foundation through the Period of the Adoption of the Organic Act*, 2 vols. (New York: Macmillan, 1914-16), 1:488; Loren Schweninger, "The Underside of Slavery: The Internal Economy, Self-Hire, and Quasi-Freedom in Virginia, 1780-1865," *Slavery and Abolition: A Journal of Comparative Studies* 12 (Sept. 1991): 6.

10 E. S. Abdy, *Journal of a Residence and Tour in the United States of North America, from April, 1833, to October, 1834*, 3 vols. (New York: Negro Universities Press, 1969, orig. pub. 1835), 2:59; Thomas Hamilton, *Men and Manners in America*, 2 vols. (New York: Russell and Russell, 1833), 2:74; Francis J. Grund, *Aristocracy in America: From the Sketch-Book of a German Nobleman*, 2 vols. in 1 (London: Richard Bentley, 1839), 2:205.

11 Daniel Drayton, *Personal Memoir of Daniel Drayton, for Four Years and Four Months a Prisoner (for Charity's Sake) in Washington Jail* (New York: Negro Universities Press, 1969, orig. pub. 1855), 29. There is at least one instance of a slave serving as captain of a flatboat on the Mississippi River; the crew included white men. David Brion Davis, "Introduction: The Problem of Slavery," in *A Historical Guide to World Slavery*, ed. Seymour Drescher and Stanley L. Engerman (New York: Oxford University Press, 1998), ix.

12 *Sun*, July 8, 1847; Robert Harold Gudmestad, "The Richmond Slave Market, 1840-1860" (M.A. thesis, University of Richmond, 1993), 44; Basil Hall, *Travels in North America in the Years 1827 and 1828*, 3 vols. (Edinburgh: Cadell, 1829) 3:126-29; James Oakes, *The Ruling Race: A History of American Slaveholders* (New York: Vintage, 1983); T. Stephen Whitman, *The Price of Freedom: Slavery and Manumission in Baltimore and Early National Maryland* (Lexington: University Press of Kentucky, 1997), 30-31, 62.

13 Nan Netherton, Donald Sweig, Janice Artemel, Patricia Hicken, and Patrick Reed, *Fairfax County, Virginia: A History* (Fairfax, Va.: Fairfax County Board of Supervisors, 1978), 263.

14 Ira Berlin, *Generations of Captivity: A History of African-American Slaves* (Cambridge, Mass.: Harvard University Press, 2003), 180; David Goldfield, *Region, Race, and Cities: Interpreting the Urban South* (Baton Rouge: Louisiana State University Press, 1997), 211; Loren Schweninger, *Black Property Owners in the South, 1790-1915* (Urbana: University of Illinois

Press), 51; Ralph Clayton, *Slavery, Slaveholding, and the Free Black Population of Antebellum Baltimore* (Bowie, Md.: Heritage Books, 1993), 14; Letitia Woods Brown, "Residential Patterns of Negroes in the District of Columbia," *Records of the Columbia Historical Society of Washington, D.C., 1969–1970*, 72–73.

15 Midori Takagi, *"Rearing Wolves to Our Own Destruction": Slavery in Richmond, Virginia, 1782–1865* (Charlottesville: University Press of Virginia, 1999), 115; James Borchert, *Alley Life in Washington: Family, Community, Religion, and Folklife in the City, 1850–1970* (Urbana: University of Illinois Press, 1980), 25n; Goldfield, "Black Life in Old South Cities," 137. For a discussion of the rights of owners, not slaves, when renting occurred, see Morris, *Southern Slavery and the Law*, chap. 6.

16 Frederick Law Olmsted, *A Journey in the Seaboard Slave States, with Remarks on Their Economy* (New York: Dix and Edwards, 1856), 3–5; Abdy, *Journal of a Residence*, 2:59, 96, 180–81 (quote); George William Featherstonehaugh, *Excursion through the Slave States, from Washington on the Potomac to the Frontier of Mexico; with Sketches of Popular Manners and Geological Notices* (New York: Harper and Brothers, 1844), 37.

17 Alfred J. Pairpoint, *Uncle Sam and His Country; or, Sketches of America, in 1854–55–56* (London: Simpkin, Marshall, 1857), 245; Emmeline Stuart Wortley, *Travels in the United States, etc., during 1849 and 1850* (New York: Harper and Brothers, 1851), 85; Charles Ball, *Slavery in the United States: A Narrative of the Life and Adventures of Charles Ball, a Black Man* (Pittsburgh: J. T. Shryock, 1853), 27–28.

18 Herbert Aptheker, *American Negro Slave Revolts* (New York: Columbia University Press, 1943), 68; Ernest Dibble, "Slave Rentals to the Military," *Civil War History*, 23 (June 1977), 101–13.

19 Dorothy Provine, "The Economic Position of the Free Blacks in the District of Columbia, 1800–1860," *Journal of Negro History* 58 (Jan. 1973): 62; Alexander Mackay, *The Western World; or, Travel in the United States in 1846–47: Exhibiting Them in Their Latest Development, Social, Political, and Industrial*, 3 vols., 2nd ed. (London: Richard Bentley, 1849), 1:174; Hall, *Travels in North America*, 3:46.

20 Adam Hodgson, *Remarks during a Journey through North America in the Years 1819, 1820, and 1821, in a Series of Letters* (Westport, Conn: Negro Universities Press, 1970, orig. pub. 1823), 101.

21 Olmsted, *A Journey in the Seaboard Slave States*, 3–5.

22 William Chambers, *Things as They Are in America* (London: William and Robert Chambers, 1854), 266; Charles Richard Weld, *A Vacation Tour in the United States and Canada* (London: Longman, Brown, Green, and Longmans, 1855), 284; Constance McLaughlin Green, *The Secret City: A History of Race Relations in the Nation's Capital* (Princeton: Princeton

University Press, 1967), 33; Horace Mann, *Slavery: Letters and Speeches* (Boston: B. B. Mussey, 1851), 144.

23 Pairpoint, *Uncle Sam and His Country*, 254–55.

24 John W. Oldmixon, *Transatlantic Wanderings: or, A Fast Look at the United States* (London: Geo. Routledge, 1855), 73, 75; see also Pairpoint, *Uncle Sam and His Country*, 246.

25 Pairpoint, *Uncle Sam and His Country*, 245–47.

26 Mackay, *Western World*, 2:132–33.

27 Ethan Allen Andrews, *Slavery and the Domestic Slave-Trade in the United States: In a Series of Letters Addressed to the Executive Committee of the American Union for the Relief and Improvement of the Colored Race* (Boston: Light and Stearns, 1836), 97–99, 138.

28 Richard Sylvester, comp., *District of Columbia Police: A Retrospect of the Police Organizations of the Cities of Georgetown and Washington* (Washington, D.C.: Gibson Bros., 1894), 29; Thomas Smallwood, *A Narrative of Thomas Smallwood, Giving an Account of His Birth—the Period He Was Held in Slavery—His Release—and Removal to Canada, etc.* (Toronto: J. Stephens, 1851), 29.

29 *Sun* (Baltimore), Aug. 5, 1848; Brown, "Residential Patterns of Negroes," 72; [William R. Smith], *The Case of William L. Chaplin: Being An Appeal to All Respecters of Law and Justice, against the Cruel and Oppressive Treatment to Which, under Cover of Legal Proceedings, He Has Been Subjected, in the District of Columbia and the State of Maryland* (Boston: Chaplin Committee, 1851), 22; *Liberator*, Sept. 13, 1850.

30 Charles Lyell, *A Second Visit to the United States of North America*, 2 vols. (New York: Harper and Brothers, 1859), 1:201.

31 Claudia Dale Goldin, *Urban Slavery in the American South, 1820–1860: A Quantitative History* (Chicago: University of Chicago Press, 1976), 46, 65; Harold W. Hurst, *Alexandria on the Potomac: The Portrait of an Antebellum Community* (Lanham, Md.: University Press of America, 1991), 39.

32 Brenda E. Stevenson, "Gender Convention, Ideals, and Identity among Antebellum Virginia Slave Women," in *More Than Chattel: Black Women and Slavery in the Americas*, ed. David Barry Gaspar and Darlene Clark Hine (Bloomington: Indiana University Press, 1996), 180; *Slavery and the Slave Trade at the Nation's Capital* (New York: American and Foreign Anti-Slavery Society, [1847?]), 8.

33 Janet Duitsman Cornelius, *"When I Can Read My Record Clear": Literacy, Slavery, and Religion in the Antebellum South* (Columbia: University of South Carolina Press, 1991), 121–22; *Emancipator and Free American*, Sept. 8, 1842; Lorenzo D. Johnson, *The Churches and Pastors of Washington, D.C.* (New York: M. W. Dodd, 1857), 133; *Sun*, Feb. 15, 1849.

34 Henry Caswall, *The Western World Revisited* (Oxford: John Henry Parker,

1854), 263–64; George Lewis, *Impressions of America and the American Churches: From Journal of the Rev. G. Lewis* (New York: Negro Universities Press, 1968, orig. pub. 1848), 66.

35 *The Washington Directory, and National Register for 1846* (Washington, D.C.: Gaither and Addison, 1846), 17.

36 Isabella Strange Trotter, *First Impressions of the New World on Two Travellers from the Old in the Autumn of 1858* (London: Longman, Brown, Green, Longmans, and Roberts, 1859), 220; Caswall, *Western World Revisited*, 264; Pairpoint, *Uncle Sam and His Country*, 252.

37 Russell Lant Carpenter, *Observations on American Slavery, after a Year's Tour in the United States* (London: Edward T. Whitfield, 1852), 20; Ebenezer Davies, *American Scenes, and Christian Slavery: A Recent Tour of Four Thousand Miles in the United States* (London: John Snow, 1849), 191, 200; see also Morris J. MacGregor, *The Emergence of a Black Catholic Community: St. Augustine's in Washington* (Washington, D.C.: Catholic University of America Press, 1999), 25.

38 Paul E. Sluby Sr., *Asbury: Our Legacy, Our Faith, 1836–1993*, 2nd ed. (Washington, D.C.: privately printed, 1996), 17–23; Schweninger, *Black Property Owners*, 139; John B. Boles, introduction to *Masters and Slaves in the House of the Lord: Race and Religion in the American South, 1740–1870*, ed. John B. Boles (Lexington: University Press of Kentucky, 1988), 15.

39 Goldfield, "Black Life in Old South Cities," 140.

40 Joseph C. Lovejoy, *Memoir of Rev. Charles T. Torrey, Who Died in the Penitentiary of Maryland, Where He Was Confined for Showing Mercy to the Poor* (New York: Negro Universities Press, 1969, orig. pub. 1847), 89–90.

41 William Faux, *Memorable Days in America: Being a Journal of a Tour to the United States, Principally Undertaken to Ascertain, by Positive Evidence, the Condition and Probable Prospects of British Emigrants* (London: W. Simpkin and R. Marshall, 1823), 109; Fredrika Bremer, *The Homes of the New World: Impressions of America*, 2 vols. (New York: Negro Universities Press, 1968, orig. pub. 1853), 1:491–92.

42 Benjamin Drew, *A North-Side View of Slavery* (Boston: J. P. Jewett, 1856), 111.

43 John Thompson, *The Life of John Thompson, a Fugitive Slave* (New York: Negro Universities Press, 1969, orig. pub. 1856), 18–19; Andrews, *Slavery and the Domestic Slave-Trade*, 121.

44 Trotter, *First Impressions*, 121–24.

45 Ibid., 129–30.

46 Wiecek, *Sources of Anti-slavery Constitutionalism*, 24, 27; Joshua R. Giddings, *Speeches in Congress* (Boston: John P. Jewett, 1853), 36, 48.

47 Journal of Rev. Henry Slicer, May 13, 1850, Lovely Lane Museum of the United Methodist Historical Society of the Baltimore-Washington Confer-

ence, Baltimore, Md., Aug. 31, Sept. 2, 1849; Henry Caswall, *America, and the American Church*, 2nd ed. (London: John and Charles Mozley, 1851), 291.

48 Mackay, *Western World*, 2:131; Barbara Jeanne Fields, *Slavery and Freedom on the Middle Ground: Maryland during the Nineteenth Century* (New Haven: Yale University Press, 1985), 35.

49 Walter C. Clephane, "The Local Aspect of Slavery in the District of Columbia," *Records of the Columbia Historical Society, Washington, D.C.* 3 (1900): 246-47; C. R. Weld, *Vacation Tour*, 284; Henry S. Robinson, "Some Aspects of the Free Negro Population of Washington, D.C., 1800-1862," *Maryland Historical Magazine* 64 (Spring 1969): 46; Jane M. E. Turnbull and Marion Turnbull, *American Photographs*, 2 vols. in 1 (London: T. C. Newby, 1859), 2:190.

50 Bryan, *History of the National Capital*, 2:379; Mary Beth Corrigan, "The Ties that Bind: The Pursuit of Community and Freedom among Slaves and Free Blacks in the District of Columbia, 1800-1860," in *Southern City, National Ambition: The Growth of Early Washington, D.C., 1800-1860*, ed. Howard Gillette Jr. (Washington, D.C.: George Washington University Center for Washington Area Studies, 1995), 82.

51 Pauline Gaskins Mitchell, "The History of Mt. Zion United Methodist Church and Mt. Zion Cemetery," *Records of the Columbia Historical Society of Washington, D.C.* 51 (1984): 104; Monroe quoted in Brenda E. Stevenson, *Life in Black and White: Family and Community in the Slave South* (New York: Oxford University Press, 1996), 159.

52 C. Peter Ripley, ed., *The Black Abolitionist Papers*, 5 vols. (Chapel Hill: University of North Carolina Press, 1985-92), 3:428-29.

53 Mann, *Slavery*, 127-28; John R. Spears, *The American Slave-Trade: An Account of Its Origin, Growth, and Suppression* (New York: Charles Scribner's Sons, 1900), 176.

54 Giddings, *Speeches*, 36, 98, 101.

55 Michael Tadman, *Speculators and Slaves: Masters, Traders, and Slaves in the Old South* (Madison: University of Wisconsin Press, 1996), 6-7; W. E. Baxter, *America and the Americans* (London: Geo. Routledge, 1855), 185; John G. Palfrey, *The Inter-State Slave Trade* (New York: American Anti-Slavery Society, 1855), 3; Lewis, *Impressions of America*, 146.

56 Herbert B. Gutman, *Slavery and the Numbers Game: A Critique of "Time on the Cross"* (Urbana: University of Illinois Press, 1975), 103; Tadman, *Speculators and Slaves*, 42; Bruce Levine, *Half Slave and Half Free: The Roots of the Civil War* (New York: Hill and Wang, 1992), 25.

57 William Jay, *A View of the Action of the Federal Government, in Behalf of Slavery* (New York: J. S. Taylor, 1839), 79 (*Virginia Times* statistic); Tadman, *Speculators and Slaves*, 45.

58 Bob Arnebeck, *Through a Fiery Trial: Building Washington, 1790–1800* (Lanham, Md.: Madison Books, 1991),, 229; Bryan, *History of the National Capital*, 1:425; Frederic Bancroft, *Slave Trading in the Old South* (Baltimore: J. H. Furst, 1931), 23; Henry Wilson, *History of the Rise and Fall of the Slave Power in America*, 3 vols. (Boston: J. R. Osgood, 1872–77) 1:302–4.

59 Jay, *View of Action*, 38–39; U.S. Congress, House of Representatives, Committee on the District of Columbia, Committee Report no. 60, 20th Cong., 2nd sess. (1829).

60 Giddings, *Speeches*, 142–43; Hodgson, *Remarks during a Journey*, 178.

61 Ball, *Slavery in the United States*, 28; Jesse Torrey, *American Slave Trade* (Westport, Conn.: Negro Universities Press, 171, orig. pub. 1822), 67n; Clephane, "Local Aspect of Slavery," 243.

62 *Congressional Globe*, 31st Cong., 1st sess., 19 appendix 1: 323 (Mar. 4, 1850); Giddings, *Speeches*, 349 (Feb. 17, 1849).

63 Charles L. Perdue, Thomas E. Barden, and Robert K. Phillips, *Weevils in the Wheat: Interviews with Virginia Ex-Slaves* (Charlottesville: University Press of Virginia, 1976), 71.

64 On the impossibility of discovering the precise number of traders in a given locality, see Tadman, *Speculators and Slaves*, 31–41. See also Gudmestad, "Richmond Slave Market," chap. 5; Winfield H. Collins, *The Domestic Slave Trade of the Southern States* (New York: Broadway, 1904), 29; *Washington Directory for 1846*, 25, 38, 45; *Slavery and the Slave Trade at the Nation's Capital*, 6–7.

65 "Slavery and the Slave Trade in the District of Columbia," *Negro History Bulletin*, 14 (Oct. 1950): 8; *The WPA Guide to Washington, D.C.: The Federal Writers Project Guide to 1930s Washington* (New York: Pantheon Books, 1983), 492; Jesse Torrey, *A Portraiture of Domestic Slavery* (Philadelphia: published by author, 1817).

66 Steven H. Deyle, "The Irony of Liberty: Origins of the Domestic Slave Trade," *Journal of the Early Republic* 12 (Spring 1992): 91; Gudmestad, "Richmond Slave Market," 17; Joseph Holt Ingraham, *The South-West, by a Yankee*, 2 vols. (New York: Harper and Brothers, 1835), 2:234, 244; Abdy, *Journal of a Residence*, 2:118.

67 House Committee on D.C., Report no. 60, 6–7 (Jan. 29, 1829).

68 "Slavery and the Slave Trade in the District of Columbia," 7.

69 Hamilton, *Men and Manners in America*, 279–80; Paul Findley, *A. Lincoln: The Crucible of Congress* (New York: Crown, 1979), 124.

70 Bancroft, *Slave Trading in the Old South*, 52; Tadman, *Speculators and Slaves*, 42; Joseph Sturge, *A Visit to the United States in 1841* (Boston: Dexter S. King, 1842), 107–8, 115.

71 M. Sweig, "Alexander Grigsby: A Slavebreeder of Old Centerville?" *Fairfax Chronicles* 7 (May–July 1983): 1.

72 Allen C. Guelzo, *Abraham Lincoln: Redeemer President* (Grand Rapids, Mich.: William B. Eerdmans, 1999), 132; *Emancipator*, May 31, 1848; J. E. Alexander, *Transatlantic Sketches, Comprising Visits to the Most Interesting Scenes in North and South America, and the West Indies* (Philadelphia: Key and Biddle, 1833), 340 (quote).

73 Leonard P. Curry, *The Free Black in Urban America, 1800–1850* (Chicago: University of Chicago Press, 1981), 267 (appendix C); Allan Johnston, *Surviving Freedom: The Black Community of Washington, D.C., 1860–1880* (New York: Garland, 1993), 77, 85. For slightly different figures, see Schweninger, *Black Property Owners*, 287, 291.

74 Bayard Tuckerman, *William Jay and the Constitutional Movement for the Abolition of Slavery* (New York: Negro Universities Press, 1969, orig. pub. 1893), 29–38; Marion Gleason McDougall, *Fugitive Slaves (1619–1865)* (Boston: Ginn, 1891), 80.

75 House Committee on D.C., Report no. 60, 6–7 (Jan. 29, 1829).

76 H. Wilson, *History of the Rise and Fall*, 1:301–2.

77 Torrey, *Portraiture of Domestic Slavery*, 42–43, 46–49.

78 Solomon Northup, *Twelve Years a Slave* (New York: Dover, 1970, orig. pub. 1854), 29–41; John W. Blassingame, ed., *Slave Testimony: Two Centuries of Letters, Speeches, Interviews, and Autobiographies* (Baton Rouge: Louisiana State University Press, 1977), 288–89 (*New York Times*, Jan. 20, 1853).

79 Northup, *Twelve Years a Slave*, 42.

80 David L. Child et al., "The Domestic Slave Trade," *American Anti-Slavery Reporter* 1 (July 1834): 101–2, 105.

81 *Liberator*, May 26, 1848; Faux, *Memorable Days in America*, 129–30.

82 Andrews, *Slavery and the Domestic Slave-Trade*, 181; Blassingame, *Slave Testimony*, 341 (*Montreal Gazette*, Jan. 31, 1861), 341, 396 (*American Freedmen's Inquiry Commission Interviews*, 1863); Carol Wilson, *Freedom at Risk: The Kidnapping of Free Blacks in America, 1780–1865* (Lexington: University Press of Kentucky, 1994), 15; William Wells Brown to [Sidney] Gay, Sept. 27, 1844, *The Mind of the Negro as Reflected in Letters Written during the Crisis, 1800–1860*, ed. Carter G. Woodson (New York: Russell and Russell, 1926), 350.

83 Andrews, *Slavery and the Domestic Slave-Trade*, 120; Benjamin Drew, *The Refugee; or, The Narrative of Fugitive Slaves in Canada: Related by Themselves* (New York: Negro Universities Press, 1968, orig. pub. 1856), 69, 75–76.

84 Joshua R. Giddings, *History of the Rebellion: Its Authors and Causes* (New York: Follet, Foster, 1864), 268–69.

85 Northup, *Twelve Years a Slave*, 43.

86 Constance McLaughlin Green, *Washington: Village and Capital, 1800–*

1878, 2 vols. separately titled (Princeton: Princeton University Press, 1962), 1:141–42, 173–74; Gerrit Smith to Edmund Quincy, Nov. 23, 1846, in Octavius Brooks Frothingham, *Gerrit Smith: A Biography* (New York: G. P. Putnam's Sons, 1879), 207–8.

87 Herman Freudenberger and Jonathan B. Pritchett, "The Domestic United States Slave Trade: New Evidence," *Journal of Interdisciplinary History* 21 (Winter 1991): 463, 465; Wendell H. Stephenson, *Isaac Franklin, Slave Trader and Planter of the Old South* (Baton Rouge: Louisiana State University Press, 1938), 34–36, 42–44, 74n; W. E. Burghardt Du Bois, *The Suppression of the Slave-Trade to the United States of America, 1638–1870* (New York: Longmans, Green, 1896), 123.

88 Clephane, "Local Aspect of Slavery," 241.

89 Child et al., "The Domestic Slave Trade," 106–7; Spears, *American Slave-Trade*, 173.

90 Giddings, *Speeches*, 38; Jay, *View of Action*, 58–63; Bancroft, *Slave-Trading in the Old South*, 277.

91 Featherstonehaugh, *Excursion through the Slave States*, 36; Freudenberger and Pritchett, "Domestic U.S. Slave Trade," 472, 474.

92 Theodore Dwight Weld, *American Slavery as It Is: Testimony of a Thousand Witnesses* (Salem, N.H.: Ayer, 1991, orig. pub. 1839), 69–70; Abdy, *Journal of a Residence*, 2:242; Perdue, Barden, and Phillips, *Weevils in the Wheat*, 153; J. E. Snodgrass, "Benjamin Lundy: A Sketch of His Life and of His Relations with His Disciple and Associate, William Lloyd Garrison," *Northern Monthly Magazine* 2 (Mar. 1868): 504.

93 Roger L. Ransom, *Conflict and Compromise: The Political Economy of Slavery, Emancipation, and the American Civil War* (New York: Cambridge University Press, 1989), 75; Robert C. Reinders, "Slavery in New Orleans in the Decade before the Civil War," in *Plantation, Town, and County: Essays on the Local History of American Slave Society*, ed. Elinor Miller and Eugene D. Genovese (Urbana: University of Illinois Press, 1974), 366–67; Bancroft, *Slave-Trading in the Old South*, 314; Richard Wade, *Slavery in the Cities: The South, 1820–1860* (London: Oxford University Press, 1964), 203; Tadman, *Speculators and Slaves*, 204–8; Deyle, "Domestic Slave Trade," 111.

94 J. Benwell, *An Englishman's Travels in America: His Observations of Life and Manners in the Free and Slave States* (London: Binns and Goodwin, [1853?]), 111, 115; Simon Ansley O'Ferrall, *A Ramble of Six Thousand Miles through the United States of America* (London: Effingham Wilson, 1832), 192–93.

95 Hamilton, *Men and Manners in America*, 317.

96 Francis Pulszky and Theresa Pulszky, *White, Red, Black: Sketches of Ameri-*

can Society in the United States, 2 vols. in 1 (New York: Johnson Reprint Corp., 1970, orig. pub. 1853), 2:100; Henry Ashworth, *A Tour of the United States, Cuba, and Canada* (London: A. W. Bennett, 1861), 81.

97 Ashworth, *Tour of the United States*, 81; Bancroft, *Slave-Trading in the Old South*, 328–30; Wade, *Slavery in the Cities*, 201.

98 William J. Simmons, *Men of Mark: Eminent, Progressive, and Rising* (New York: Arno Press, 1968, orig. pub. 1887), 662–63; William Wells Brown, *The Rising Sun; or, The Antecedents and Advancement of the Colored Race* (New York: Negro Universities Press, 1970, orig. pub. 1874), 534–35; Albert J. Von Frank, *The Trials of Anthony Burns: Freedom and Slavery in Emerson's Boston* (Cambridge, Mass.: Harvard University Press, 1998), 29, 37, 81; George A. Levesque, *Black Boston: African American Life and Culture in Urban America, 1750–1860* (New York: Garland, 1994), 284, 286; James Oliver Horton, *Free People of Color: Inside the African American Community* (Washington, D.C.: Smithsonian Institution, 1993), 37.

99 Smallwood, *Narrative of Thomas Smallwood*, 17; Gilbert Hobbs Barnes, *The Antislavery Impulse, 1830–1844* (New York: D. Appleton-Century, 1933), 285n.

100 Stanley Harrold, "On the Borders of Slavery and Race," *Journal of the Early Republic* 20 (Summer 2000): 278.

101 Wilbur H. Siebert, *The Underground Railroad from Slavery to Freedom* (New York: Macmillan, 1898), 168–69; Stanley Harrold, *The Abolitionists and the South, 1831–1861* (Lexington: University Press of Kentucky, 1999), 71.

102 Smallwood, *Narrative of Thomas Smallwood*, 18; Siebert, *Underground Railroad from Slavery*, 169; Harrold, "On the Borders," 283; Anthony Reintzel, comp., *The Washington Directory, and Governmental Register, for 1843* (Washington, D.C.: J. T. Towers, 1843), 67; U.S. Census, District of Columbia, Federal Population Schedule, 1850, p. 88; D. McClelland, *Map of the City of Washington, Established as the Permanent Seat of the Government of the United States of America* (Washington, D.C.: D. McClelland, 1846).

103 *The WPA Guide to Washington, D.C.: The Federal Writers Project Guide to 1930s Washington* (New York: Pantheon Books, 1983), 493.

104 Smallwood, *Narrative of Thomas Smallwood*, 20–21, 18, 26–32.

105 *Emancipator and Free American*, Jan. 11, 1844.

106 Leroy Graham, *Baltimore, the Nineteenth Century Black Capital* (Washington, D.C.: University Press of America, 1982), 152; *Emancipator and Weekly Chronicle*, Jan. 8, 1845 (letter of Dec. 23, 1844); Ralph Volney Harlow, *Gerrit Smith, Philanthropist and Reformer* (New York: Russell and Russell, 1972, orig. pub. 1939), 275; Hugh Davis, *Joshua Leavitt, Evan-*

gelical Abolitionist (Baton Rouge: Louisiana State University Press, 1990), 215.

107 Lovejoy, *Memoir of Rev. Charles T. Torrey*, 294–96; Wilson, *History of the Rise and Fall*, 2:75–80; Siebert, *Underground Railroad from Slavery*, 169; Davis, *Joshua Leavitt*, 214–17; Edmund Worth, *A Martyr to the Truth: A Sermon in Commemoration of the Death of Rev. Charles T. Torrey in the Maryland Penitentiary, May 9, 1846* (Fishersville, N.H.: n.p., [1846?]), 17; R. C. Smedley, *History of the Underground Railroad in Chester and the Neighboring Counties of Pennsylvania* (New York: Negro Universities Press, 1968, orig. pub. 1883), 81.

108 Benjamin Quarles, *Black Abolitionists* (New York: Oxford University Press, 1969), 164–65; Daniel Alexander Payne, *Recollections of Seventy Years* (Nashville: A.M.E. Sunday School Union, 1888), 98–99.

109 *Charleston Mercury*, May 11, 1848.

110 *Washington Directory for 1846*, 7; Kenneth G. Alfers, *Law and Order in the Capital City: A History of the Washington Police, 1800–1886* (Washington, D.C.: George Washington University, 1976), 5.

111 Sylvester, *District of Columbia Police*, 27–29; Robert Seager II, *And Tyler Too: A Biography of John and Julia Gardiner Tyler* (New York: McGraw-Hill, 1963), 156.

112 *Washington Directory for 1846*, 5, 12.

Chapter Two

1 Although 1848 antislavery newspaper accounts cited the owner as Mrs. Greenfield, they were in error; the *Daily Union* (D.C.) of Apr. 19, 1848, correctly listed the owner as Mrs. Armstead.

2 *Emancipator and Free Soil Press*, Oct. 11, 1848.

3 *North Star*, Oct. 13, 1848; *The Washington Directory, and National Register for 1846* (Washington, D.C.: Gaither and Addison, 1846), 6, 90.

4 *Emancipator and Free Soil Press*, Oct. 11, 1848.

5 Joshua R. Giddings, *History of the Rebellion: Its Authors and Causes* (New York: Follet, Foster, 1864), 268–69.

6 National Archives, Record Group (RG) 21, entry 30, Emancipation and Manumission Records, 2:404, National Archives Building, Washington, D.C.

7 *Emancipator and Free Soil Press*, Oct. 11, 1848.

8 National Archives, RG 21, District of Columbia Circuit Court, Probate Records, entry E111 (Inventories and Sales, Reports of the Assessors on Goods, Chattel, and Personal Estates 1799–1885), National Archives Building, Washington, D.C.

9 Ibid.

10 National Archives, RG 21, Circuit Court, District of Columbia, Case Pa-

pers 1802–63, March Term 1848, Trials 78–410, Case 126, box 285, National Archives Building, Washington, D.C.

11 National Archives, RG 21, District of Columbia Circuit Court Docket Book, March Term 1848, vol. 99, National Archives Building, Washington, D.C.

12 Daniel Drayton, *Personal Memoir of Daniel Drayton, for Four Years and Four Months a Prisoner (for Charity's Sake) in Washington Jail* (New York: Negro Universities Press, 1969, orig. pub. 1855), 28. For the strength of kinship ties among slaves separated or about to be separated by sale, see Norrece T. Jones Jr., *Born a Child of Freedom, yet a Slave: Mechanics of Control and Strategies of Resistance in Antebellum South Carolina* (Hanover, N.H.: Wesleyan University Press, 1990), 42–47.

13 Moses Roper, *A Narrative of the Adventures and Escape of Moses Roper, from American Slavery* (New York: Negro Universities Press, 1970, orig. pub. 1838), 91; Elizabeth Buffum Chace, *Anti-Slavery Reminiscences* (Central Falls, R.I.: E. L. Freeman and Sons, 1891), 27, 30–33; Benjamin Drew, *A North-Side View of Slavery* (Boston: J. P. Jewett, 1856), 29.

14 Philip J. Schwarz, *Slave Laws in Virginia* (Athens: University of Georgia Press, 1996), 133–34.

15 Drayton, *Personal Memoir*, 6–10, 15–20.

16 Ibid., 11–15.

17 Ibid., 20–21, 23.

18 National Archives, RG 41, Master Abstracts of Enrollments, Maine to Ohio, 1844–45, vol. 15, Mar. 20, 1844, National Archives Building, Washington, D.C.

19 Notes on Drayton trial, May 14, 1849, Horace Mann Papers, Massachusetts Historical Society, Boston; Drayton, *Personal Memoir*, 24–25; Giddings, *History of the Rebellion*, 272–73.

20 Drayton, *Personal Memoir*, 25.

21 Ibid., 25–26.

22 Trial testimony, May 11, 1849, Mann Papers.

23 Drayton, *Personal Memoir*, 26.

24 Ibid., 27–28.

25 Ibid., 28.

26 Ibid., 28–29.

27 Giddings, *History of the Rebellion*, 272–73; David W. Bartlett, *Modern Agitators; or, Pen Portraits of Living American Reformers* (New York: Miller, Orton and Mulligan, 1856), 176–77; Wilbur H. Siebert, *The Underground Railroad from Slavery to Freedom* (New York: Macmillan, 1898), 63.

28 *New York Herald*, Apr. 20, 1848.

29 Drayton, *Personal Memoir*, 30.

30 Ibid.

31 Ibid., 31; Frederick Tilp, *This Was Potomac River* (Alexandria, Va.: privately printed, 1978), 299. See also Edwin W. Beitzell, *Life on the Potomac River* (N.p.: privately printed, 1979), 183.

32 Drayton, *Personal Memoir*, 31–32.

33 English testimony, undated trial notes, Mann Papers.

34 Undated trial notes, ibid.

35 *Liberator*, Apr. 21, 1848.

36 Giddings, *History of the Rebellion*, 273; *Republican and Argus* (Baltimore), Apr. 18, 1848; *Charleston Mercury*, Apr. 21, 1848; *Mississippi Free Trader* (Natchez), May 3, 1848; *North Star*, Sept. 28, 1849.

37 National Archives, RG 47, Ship Enrollments, 1844–1847, entry 7 for 1846, National Archives Building, Washington, D.C.; Harold W. Hurst, "Business and Businessmen in Pre–Civil War Georgetown, 1840–1860," *Records of the Columbia Historical Society of Washington, D.C.* 50 (1980): 164–65.

38 *New York Herald*, Apr. 20, 1848; *Liberator*, Apr. 21, 1848.

39 Harriet Beecher Stowe, *A Key to "Uncle Tom's Cabin": Presenting the Original Facts and Documents upon Which the Story Is Founded, Together with Corroborative Statements Verifying the Truth of the Work* (Boston: John P. Jewett, 1853), 158–59.

40 Drayton, *Personal Memoir*, 33–34.

41 John H. Paynter, "The Fugitives of the *Pearl*," *Journal of Negro History* 1 (July 1916): 247.

42 For Diggs's fictional amorous approach to Emily Edmondson, see John H. Paynter, *Fugitives of the Pearl* (Washington, D.C.: Associated Publishers, 1930), 10–16.

43 *Henson Ridgway et al. v. Francis Dodge Jr.*, Feb. 26, 1849, National Archives, RG 21, District of Columbia Circuit Court, Chancery Docket, Minutes, 4:32–42, no. 540, National Archives Building, Washington, D.C.

44 National Archives, RG 21, Records of United States Circuit Court for the District of Columbia, Chancery Rules, entry 16, vol. 5 (1848–1858), case 574, National Archives Building, Washington, D.C.

45 *Washington Directory for 1846*, 21; *National Era*, June 2, 1853.

46 *Sun* (Baltimore), Apr. 18, 1848.

47 Drayton, *Personal Memoir*, 34.

48 *New York Herald*, Apr. 20, 24, 1848; trial notes, Hampton Williams testimony, Mann Papers. A carbine is a short light rifle or musket; a fowling piece is a light gun, such as a shotgun, for shooting fowl.

49 Paynter, "The Fugitives of the *Pearl*," 248–49.

50 Drayton, *Personal Memoir*, 35–36; *Daily Union*, Apr. 19, 1848.

51 Drayton, *Personal Memoir*, 36–39.

52 Ibid., 39; undated trial notes, Lambell testimony, Mann Papers.

53 Stowe, *Key to "Uncle Tom's Cabin"*, 159. Gannon's slave pen was on Sev-

enth Street between B and C South, according to the *Washington Directory for 1846*, 43; Drayton, *Personal Memoir*, 39–40.

54 Paynter, "The Fugitives of the *Pearl*," 250; Drayton, *Personal Memoir*, 40; *Emancipator*, Apr. 26, 1848.

55 *Liberator*, Apr. 28, 1848, quoting *Boston Daily Whig*; Paynter, "The Fugitives of the *Pearl*," 250; *Emancipator*, Apr. 26, 1848.

56 Giddings, *History of the Rebellion*, 273; Joshua Giddings, *Speeches in Congress [1841–1852]* (Boston: John P. Jewett, 1853), 226.

57 Drayton, *Personal Memoir*, 40; *Anti-Slavery Bugle*, May 5, 1848.

58 The jail was a three-story brick building at 4th and G streets. John Clagett Proctor, "Judiciary Square in its Earlier Days," *Sunday Star* (D.C.), Feb. 15, 1931; Giddings, *History of the Rebellion*, 275.

59 Drayton, *Personal Memoir*, 40–42.

60 George Mason of Hollin Hall to Gov. William Smith, Apr. 21, 1848, with accompanying affidavits by James Rudd and George Harvey. Notations: "Demand denied" and "demand afterwards made"; no indication of further action. Executive Papers, Gov. W. Smith, box 390, folder Apr.–May 1848, Library of Virginia, Richmond. See also Council Journal, Apr. 25, 1848, and Executive Letter Book, 1844–1848, Library of Virginia.

61 *Daily National Intelligencer* (D.C.), Apr. 19, 1848; *North Star*, May 12, 1848; *Daily True Democrat* (Cleveland), Apr. 26, 1848.

62 Drayton, *Personal Memoir*, 53; *North Star*, May 12, 1848 (quote); *National Intelligencer*, Apr. 19, 1848.

63 Stowe, *Key to "Uncle Tom's Cabin"*, 159.

64 Palfrey to Charles Sumner, Apr. 29, 1848, Charles Sumner Papers, Houghton Library, Harvard University, Cambridge, Mass.; *North Star*, May 5, 1848.

65 Chaplin to Gerrit Smith, May 1, 1848, Gerrit Smith Papers, Arents Library, Syracuse University, Syracuse, N.Y.

66 Joseph C. Lovejoy, *Memoir of Rev. Charles T. Torrey, Who Died in the Penitentiary of Maryland, Where He Was Confined for Showing Mercy to the Poor* (New York: Negro Universities Press, 1969, orig. pub. 1847), 283–86.

67 *Anti-Slavery Bugle*, Aug. 24, 1850; [William R. Smith], *The Case of William L. Chaplin: Being An Appeal to All Respecters of Law and Justice, against the Cruel and Oppressive Treatment to Which, under Cover of Legal Proceedings, He Has Been Subjected, in the District of Columbia and the State of Maryland* (Boston: Chaplin Committee, 1851), 14–16; Lawrence Lader, *The Bold Brahmins: New England's War against Slavery, 1831–1863* (New York: E. P. Dutton, 1961), 111.

68 Stanley Harrold, *Gamaliel Bailey and Antislavery Union* (Kent, Ohio: Kent State University Press, 1986), 83; Siebert, *Underground Railroad from Slavery*, 117.

69 [Smith], *Case of William L. Chaplin*, 19; National Archives, RG 21, District of Columbia Circuit Court, Docket Book, March Term 1848, vol. 99, nos. 96, 97, National Archives Building, Washington, D.C.

70 [Smith], *Case of William L. Chaplin*, 21.

71 Chaplin to Smith, Mar. 25, 1848, Smith Papers; John Wallace Hutchinson, *Story of the Hutchinsons (Tribe of Jesse)*, 2 vols. (New York: Da Capo Press, 1977, orig. pub. 1896), 1:237.

72 Lovejoy, *Memoir of Rev. Charles T. Torrey*, 283–86.

73 Salmon P. Chase and Charles Dexter Cleveland, *Anti-Slavery Addresses of 1844 and 1845* (New York: Negro Universities Press, 1965, orig. pub. 1867), 17.

74 William Still, *The Underground Railroad* (New York: Arno Press, 1967, orig. pub. 1872), 751, 755, 758.

75 *The Twentieth Century Biographical Dictionary of Notable Americans* (Boston: Biographical Society, 1904), s.v. "Cleveland, Charles Dexter"; S. Austin Allibone, *A Critical Dictionary of English Literature and British and American Authors Living and Deceased* (Philadelphia: J. B. Lippincott, 1858), s.v. "Cleveland, Charles Dexter"; Bigelow to William Still, June 22, 1854, in Still, *Underground Railroad*, 41; Joseph Sturge, *A Visit to the United States in 1841* (Boston: Dexter S. King, 1842), 55–56.

76 Cleveland to [Joshua Blanchard], May 29, Nov. 23, 1848, Black History Miscellany, Manuscript Division, Library of Congress, Washington, D.C.; Cleveland to Mann, Feb. 21, 1849[?], Mar. 23, 1849, Mann Papers.

77 Cleveland to Mann, Feb. 16, 1849, Mann Papers.

78 Stowe, *Key to "Uncle Tom's Cabin"*, 159.

79 Paynter, *Fugitives of the* Pearl, 22–26.

80 Drayton, *Personal Memoir*, 24. For Paynter on Jennings, see *Fugitives of the* Pearl, 25–28, 30–34, 51–52. For Jennings, see *White House History* 1 (1983): 46–63, which includes Jennings's own memoir, "A Colored Man's Reminiscences of James Madison" (where he does not mention the *Pearl*), and G. Franklin Edwards and Michael R. Winston, "Commentary: The Washington of Paul Jennings — White House Slave, Free Man, and Conspirator for Freedom."

81 "Captains Drayton and Sayres; or, The Way in Which Americans Are Treated, for Aiding the Cause of Liberty at Home," n.d., Black History Miscellany, Manuscript Division, Library of Congress, Washington, D.C.

Chapter Three

1 *National Era*, Aug. 29, 1850.

2 *National Era*, Aug. 15, 1850; for a thoughtful discussion of the religious basis of membership in the Liberty Party, see the introduction to Vernon L. Volpe, *Forlorn Hope of Freedom: The Liberty Party in the Old Northwest,*

1838–1848 (Kent, Ohio: Kent State University Press, 1990). For the Gerrit Smith contingent of the party, see John Stauffer, *The Black Hearts of Men: Radical Abolitionists and the Transformation of Race* (Cambridge, Mass.: Harvard University Press, 2002).

3 Stanley Harrold, *Gamaliel Bailey and Antislavery Union* (Kent, Ohio: Kent State University Press, 1986), 17–18, 42.

4 John W. Reps, *Washington on View: The Nation's Capital since 1790* (Chapel Hill: University of North Carolina Press, 1991), 98; Edward Waite, comp., *The Washington Directory and Congressional and Executive Register, for 1850* (Washington, D.C.: Columbus Alexander, 1850), 64; *Washington Star*, Feb. 3, 1894. For a detailed description of the Patent Office, see P. Haas, *Public Buildings and Statuary of the Government: The Public Buildings and Architectural Ornaments of the Capitol of the United States, at the City of Washington* (Washington, D.C.: P. Haas, 1840), 43.

5 Wilhelmus Bogart Bryan, *A History of the National Capital from its Foundation through the Period of the Adoption of the Organic Act*, 2 vols. (New York: Macmillan, 1914–16), 2:381; Moncure Daniel Conway, *Autobiography: Memories and Experiences of Moncure Daniel Conway*, 2 vols. (New York: Da Capo Press, 1970, orig. pub. 1904), 1:212.

6 Russel B. Nye, *Fettered Freedom: Civil Liberties and the Slavery Controversy, 1830–1860* (East Lansing: Michigan State College Press, 1949), 96.

7 Concerning the establishment of the paper, see Harrold, *Gamaliel Bailey*, chap. 7, and Bertram Wyatt-Brown, *Lewis Tappan and the Evangelical War against Slavery* (Cleveland: Press of Case Western Reserve University, 1969), 279. For Bailey in relation to Stowe, see Harrold, *Gamaliel Bailey*, 142–44, and Joan D. Hedrick, *Harriet Beecher Stowe: A Life* (New York: Oxford University Press, 1994), 208; *Washington Star*, Feb. 3, 1894.

8 Harrold, *Gamaliel Bailey*, 88–89; Stanley C. Harrold Jr., "The Pearl Affair: The Washington Riot of 1848," *Records of the Columbia Historical Society of Washington, D.C.* 50 (1980): 145 (quote); James Freeman Clarke, *Anti-Slavery Days: A Sketch of the Struggle Which Ended in the Abolition of Slavery in the United States* (New York: J. W. Lovell, 1883), 63. For a contrary view of Bailey's involvement in the escape attempt, see Kathryn Grover, *The Fugitive's Gibraltar: Escaping Slaves and Abolitionism in New Bedford, Massachusetts* (Amherst: University of Massachusetts Press, 2001), 319 n. 74.

9 Joshua R. Giddings, *History of the Rebellion: Its Authors and Causes* (New York: Follet, Foster, 1864), 273; George W. Julian, *The Life of Joshua R. Giddings* (Chicago: A. C. McClurg, 1892), 241–42; Daniel Walker Howe, *Political Culture of the American Whigs* (Chicago: University of Chicago Press, 1979), 178; Joshua R. Giddings, *Speech of Mr. Giddings of Ohio, on the Resolution of Mr. Palfrey to Inquire Whether the Members of Congress*

Had Been Threatened by a Lawless Mob (Washington, D.C.: J. and G. S. Gideon, 1848), 2; *Charleston Courier*, Apr. 25, 1848.

10 Leonard L. Richards, *Gentlemen of Property and Standing: Anti-Abolition Mobs in Jacksonian America* (New York: Oxford University Press, 1970), 12, 112–13. For further discussion of rioting, see Paul A. Gilje, *Rioting in America* (Bloomington: Indiana University Press, 1996), and David Grimsted, *American Mobbing, 1828–1861: Toward Civil War* (New York: Oxford University Press, 1998).

11 Constance McLaughlin Green, *Washington: Village and Capital, 1800–1878*, 2 vols. separately titled (Princeton: Princeton University Press, 1962), 1:141–42.

12 Daniel Drayton, *Personal Memoir of Daniel Drayton, for Four Years and Four Months a Prisoner (for Charity's Sake) in Washington Jail* (New York: Negro Universities Press, 1969, orig. pub. 1855), 42; *Congressional Globe*, 30th Cong., 1st sess., 17:667 (Apr. 25, 1848).

13 Joshua Giddings, *Speeches in Congress [1841–1852]* (Boston: John P. Jewett, 1853), 226; Kenneth G. Alfers, *Law and Order in the Capital City: A History of the Washington Police, 1800–1886* (Washington, D.C.: George Washington University, 1976), 8.

14 Waite, *Washington Directory for 1850*, 183; Palfrey to Charles Sumner, Apr. 19, 1848, John Gorham Palfrey Papers, Houghton Library, Harvard University, Cambridge, Mass.; *Anti-Slavery Bugle*, May 5, 1848; *Daily True Democrat* (Cleveland), Apr. 25, 1848; *Charleston Courier*, Apr. 24, 1848.

15 Giddings, *History of the Rebellion*, 274.

16 Giddings would remember his colleague at the jail as Senator Lawrence Brainerd of Vermont, but Brainerd was not in the Senate until 1854. Giddings, *History of the Rebellion*, 274; *Biographical Directory of the American Congress, 1774–1949* (Washington, D.C.: Government Printing Office, 1950), s.v. "Hamlin, Edward Stowe."

17 Giddings, *Speeches*, 228.

18 Giddings, *History of the Rebellion*, 275; Drayton, *Personal Memoir*, 45; *Daily True Democrat*, Apr. 25, 1848.

19 Giddings, *History of the Rebellion*, 275; *Anti-Slavery Bugle*, May 5, 1848.

20 Palfrey to Sumner, Apr. 19, 1848, Palfrey Papers; Drayton, *Personal Memoir*, 45.

21 Douglas Zevely, "Old Houses on C Street and Those Who Lived There," *Records of the Columbia Historical Society, Washington, D.C.* 5 (1902): 167–69; Thomas Smallwood, *A Narrative of Thomas Smallwood, Giving an Account of his Birth — the Period He Was Held in Slavery — His Release — and Removal to Canada, etc.* (Toronto: J. Stephens, 1851), 39. Hall was president of the New England Society, organized in 1845. Bryan, *History of the National Capital* 2:382.

22 Drayton, *Personal Memoir*, 45–46; *New York Herald*, Apr. 21, 1848.

23 Giddings, *History of the Rebellion*, 274.

24 Letter dated Apr. 19, 1848, *National Intelligencer* (D.C.), Apr. 20, 1848; Giddings, *History of the Rebellion*, 277.

25 Alexander Mackay, *The Western World; or, Travel in the United States in 1846–47: Exhibiting Them in Their Latest Development, Social, Political, and Industrial*, 3 vols., 2nd ed. (London: Richard Bentley, 1849), 1:170; *National Era*, Apr. 27, 1848; *New York Herald*, Apr. 21, 1848; *Charleston Courier*, Apr. 25, 1848; John Gorham Palfrey to Francis W. Palfrey, Apr. 20, 1848, Palfrey Papers.

26 *New York Herald*, Apr. 21, 1848; *Daily Picayune* (New Orleans), Apr. 26, 1848; *Richmond Enquirer*, Apr. 25, 1848; the account is from the *National Era*, Apr. 27, 1848, abridged, according to Bailey, from the *New York Herald*.

27 Alfred Hunter, comp., *Washington and Georgetown Directory: Strangers' Guide-Book for Washington, and Congressional and Clerks' Register* (Washington, D.C.: Kirkwood and McGill, 1853), 86; Waite, *Washington Directory for 1850*, 72.

28 Ben Perley Poore, *Perley's Reminiscences of Sixty Years in the National Metropolis*, 2 vols. (New York: AMS Press, 1971, orig. pub. 1886), 1:399.

29 Sterling D. Spero and Abram L. Harris, "The Slave Regime: Competition between Negro and White Labor," in *The Other Slaves: Mechanics, Artisans, and Craftsmen*, ed. James E. Newton and Ronald L. Lewis (Boston: G. K. Hall, 1978), 47. See also Mary Beth Corrigan, "'It's a Family Affair': Buying Freedom in the District of Columbia, 1850–1860," in *Working toward Freedom: Slave Society and Domestic Economy in the American South*, ed. Larry E. Hudson Jr. (Rochester, N.Y.: University of Rochester Press, 1994), 167; *National Anti-Slavery Standard*, Apr. 27, 1848, from *New York Herald*; Harrold, *Gamaliel Bailey*, 126.

30 *National Era*, May 4, 1848.

31 The exchange between Bailey and the committee is in the *New-York Tribune*, Apr. 28, 1848; a somewhat different version is in the *National Era*, May 4, 1848.

32 *National Anti-Slavery Standard*, Apr. 27, 1848.

33 Reported in *Emancipator*, Apr. 26, 1848.

34 *Daily True Democrat*, Apr. 27, 1848; *North Star*, May 26, 1848; *Congressional Globe*, 30th Cong., 1st sess., 17 appendix: 501 (Apr. 20, 1848).

35 Richard Sylvester, comp., *District of Columbia Police: A Retrospect of the Police Organizations of the Cities of Washington and Georgetown* (Washington, D.C.: Gibson Bros., 1894), 23, 29; Alfers, *Law and Order in Capital*, 12n.

36 *New-York Tribune*, Apr. 28, 1848; *Richmond Enquirer*, Apr. 25, 1848.

37 *National Era*, Apr. 27, 1848.

38 William R. Woodward was a justice of the peace in 1850. Waite, *Washington Directory for 1850*, 179.

39 James K. Polk, *The Diary of James K. Polk during His Presidency, 1845 to 1849*, 4 vols. (Chicago: A. C. McClurg, 1910) 3:428–29.

40 *Boston Post*, Apr. 24, 1848; *The Washington Directory, and National Register for 1846* (Washington, D.C.: Gaither and Addison, 1846), 7.

41 *New York Herald*, Apr. 28, 1848.

42 *Boston Post*, Apr. 24, 1848.

43 *National Intelligencer*, Apr. 27, 1848; Lewis Tappan to Joseph Sturge, May 1, 1848, Lewis Tappan Papers, Manuscript Division, Library of Congress, Washington, D.C.

44 *New York Herald*, Apr. 24, 1848; Benjamin Brown French to "My Dear Brother," Apr. 26, 1848, B. B. French Papers, Manuscript Division, Library of Congress.

45 *North Star*, May 26, 1848; *Liberator*, May 26, 1848; *Emancipator*, Apr. 26, 1848.

46 *Sun* (Baltimore), Apr. 21, 1848.

47 *National Intelligencer*, Apr. 27, 1848; *Sun*, Apr. 22, 1848.

48 *National Era*, Apr. 27, May 4, 11, 1848; *Charleston Mercury*, May 2, 11, 1848.

49 *National Era*, Oct. 10, 1850 (Smith quote); *Liberator*, June 2, 1848; Frederick J. Blue, *The Free Soilers: Third Party Politics, 1848–54* (Urbana: University of Illinois Press, 1973), 90.

50 *National Anti-Slavery Standard*, May 4, 1848.

51 Ibid., May 11, 1848; Henry Mayer, *All on Fire: William Lloyd Garrison and the Abolition of Slavery* (New York: St. Martin's, 1999), 100–101.

52 See, for example, U.S. Congress, House of Representatives, Committee for the District of Columbia, Committee Report no. 60, 20th Cong., 2nd sess. (1829); *Daily Union* (D.C.), Apr. 21, 1848; *Anti-Slavery Bugle*, June 26, 1852; *Sun*, Apr. 21, 1848.

53 *New-York Tribune*, Apr. 25, 1848.

54 Horace Mann, *Slavery: Letters and Speeches* (Boston: B. B. Mussey, 1851), 118.

Chapter Four

1 *Daily True Democrat* (Cleveland), Apr. 28, 1848; James F. W. Johnston, *Notes on North America, Agricultural, Economical, and Social*, 2 vols. (Edinburgh: William Blackwood and Sons, 1851), 1:322.

2 William R. Sutton, *Journeymen for Jesus: Evangelical Artisans Confront Capitalism in Jacksonian Baltimore* (University Park: Pennsylvania State

University Press, 1998), 246; Donald C. Bacon, Roger H. Davidson, and Morton Keller, eds., *Encyclopedia of the United States Congress* (New York: Simon and Schuster, 1995), s.v. "Chaplains"; C. C. Goen, *Broken Churches, Broken Nation: Denominational Schisms and the Coming of the American Civil War* (Macon, Ga.: Mercer University Press, 1985), 89 ("largest religious body" quote); *Appleton's Cyclopaedia of American Biography* (New York: D. Appleton, 1888), s.v. "Slicer, Henry"; *Sun* (Baltimore), Jan. 1, 1845; Journal of Rev. Henry Slicer, May 13, 1850, Lovely Lane Museum of the United Methodist Historical Society of the Baltimore-Washington Conference, Baltimore, Md.; Anne M. Boylan, *Sunday School: The Formation of an American Institution, 1790–1880* (New Haven: Yale University Press, 1988), 26–27; Richard J. Carwardine, *Evangelicals and Politics in Antebellum America* (New Haven: Yale University Press, 1993), 62 ("beer, wine" quote); J. E. Snodgrass, *Sketches of the Baltimore Pulpit* (Baltimore: Knight and Colburn, 1843), 59–70.

3 Parker Pillsbury, *The Church as It Is: or, The Forlorn Hope of Slavery*, 2nd ed. (Boston: Bela Marsh, 1847), 62; Journal of Rev. Slicer, June 19, 1849; phone interview, Jane Donovan, Sept. 15, 1996; *Daily True Democrat*, Jan. 14, 1850.

4 *Daily True Democrat*, Apr. 29, 1848.

5 Among the antislavery papers that printed Slingerland's letter were the *National Anti-Slavery Standard*, May 4, 1848; *Anti-Slavery Bugle*, May 12, 1848; *North Star*, July 14, 1848.

6 *Daily Union* (D.C.), May 7, 1848; Jane Donovan, ed., *Many Witnesses: A History of Dumbarton United Methodist Church, 1772–1990* (Georgetown, D.C.: Dumbarton United Methodist Church, 1998), 100, 288; Paul E. Sluby Sr., *Asbury: Our Legacy, Our Faith, 1836–1993*, 2nd ed. (Washington, D.C.: privately printed, 1996), 19.

7 *Liberator*, June 2, 1848.

8 *National Anti-Slavery Standard*, May 25, 1848.

9 Ibid., reprinted from *New-York Tribune*.

10 Ibid.

11 Ibid.

12 *The Baltimore Directory for 1845* (Baltimore: John Murphy, 1845), 168; Henry Stockbridge Sr., "Baltimore in 1846," *Maryland Historical Magazine* 6 (1911): 32; Sutton, *Journeymen for Jesus*, 263.

13 *National Anti-Slavery Standard*, May 25, 1848.

14 Joshua R. Giddings, *Speeches in Congress [1841–1852]* (Boston: John P. Jewett, 1853), 47 (Feb. 13, 1843).

15 Bacon et al., *Encyclopedia of the U.S. Congress*, "Chaplains"; *Congressional Globe*, 30th Cong., 1st sess., 17:19 (Dec. 13, 1847).

16 Joshua R. Giddings, *History of the Rebellion: Its Authors and Causes* (New York: Follet, Foster, 1864), 278; *Pennsylvania Freeman*, Dec. 25, 1851.

17 Slingerland to Slicer, May 10, 1848, in *National Anti-Slavery Standard*, May 25, 1848; *New-York Tribune*, May 18, 1848; *North Star*, May 26, 1848.

18 "Quinten," letter dated May 9, 1848, in *Boston Atlas*, reprinted by *North Star*, June 9, 1848.

19 Ibid.

20 Ibid.

21 Donovan, *Many Witnesses*, 39; Journal of Rev. Slicer, Apr.–June 1848, Aug. 31, Sept. 2, 1849; John Dixon Long, *Pictures of Slavery in Church and State; Including Personal Reminiscences, Biographical Sketches, Anecdotes, etc., etc.* (New York: Negro Universities Press, 1969, orig. pub. 1857), 284; *Sun*, Aug. 5, 1848.

22 Pillsbury, *Church as It Is*, 59–61; *Anti-Slavery Bugle*, Jan. 19, 1849; Journal of Rev. Slicer, Dec. 1, 1848.

23 Jeffrey R. Blackett, *The Negro in Maryland: A Study of the Institution of Slavery* (Freeport, N.Y.: Books for Libraries Press, 1969, orig. pub. 1889), 29.

24 John Wesley, *Thoughts upon Slavery* (1774) reprinted in *Wesleyan Extra*, Apr. 1835, 13–14, 19, 20–23.

25 James E. Kirby, Russell E. Richey, and Kenneth E. Rowe, *The Methodists* (Westport, Conn.: Greenwood Press, 1996), 8; Robert McColley, *Slavery and Jeffersonian Virginia* (Urbana: University of Illinois Press, 1964), 149–53.

26 John H. Wigger, *Taking Heaven by Storm: Methodism and the Rise of Popular Christianity in America* (New York: Oxford University Press, 1998), 127, 130, 150.

27 Emory Stevens Bucke, ed., *The History of American Methodism*, 3 vols. (New York: Abingdon, 1964), 1:252–53.

28 Donald G. Mathews, *Slavery and Methodism: A Chapter in American Morality, 1780–1845* (Princeton: Princeton University Press, 1965), 10–22; Christine Leigh Heyrman, *Southern Cross: The Beginnings of the Bible Belt* (New York: Alfred A. Knopf, 1997), 155; Bucke, *History of American Methodism*, 1:255.

29 Kirby, Richey, and Rowe, *The Methodists*, 186–87; Stanley W. Campbell, *The Slave Catchers: Enforcement of the Fugitive Slave Law, 1850–1860* (Chapel Hill: University of North Carolina Press, 1968), 68; William Goodell, *The American Slave Code* (New York: Arno Press and New York Times, 1969, orig. pub. 1853), 58.

30 Albert J. Raboteau, *Slave Religion: The "Invisible Institution" in the Antebellum South* (New York: Oxford University Press, 1978), 145; [Lewis Tap-

pan], *Address to the Non-Slaveholders of the South, on the Social and Political Evils of Slavery* (New York: American and Foreign Anti-Slavery Society, [1849?]), 18n, 19 (quotes); Campbell, *Slave Catchers*, 67.

31 John R. McKivigan, *The War against Proslavery Religion: Abolitionism and the Northern Churches, 1830–1865* (Ithaca: Cornell University Press, 1984), 46–47.

32 Daniel Drayton, *Personal Memoir of Daniel Drayton, for Four Years and Four Months a Prisoner (for Charity's Sake) in Washington Jail* (New York: Negro Universities Press, 1969, orig. pub. 1855), 12–15, 21.

33 Mathews, *Slavery and Methodism*, 215 (quote); George M. Fredrickson, *The Black Image in the White Mind: The Debate on Afro-American Character and Destiny, 1817–1914* (New York: Harper and Row, 1971), 30. See especially chap. 1 of Fredrickson's book.

34 John R. McKivigan, "The Sectional Division of the Methodist and Baptist Denominations as Measures of Northern Antislavery Sentiment," in *Religion and the Antebellum Debate over Slavery*, ed. John R. McKivigan and Mitchell Snay (Athens: University of Georgia Press, 1998), 352, 357; Mathews, *Slavery and Methodism*, 264, 271, 181; Kirby, Richey, and Rowe, *The Methodists*, 32–34; Bucke, *History of American Methodism*, 2:76.

35 Bucke, *History of American Methodism*, 2:76; Journal of Rev. Slicer, Mar. 14, 1848.

36 Gordon Pratt Baker, *Those Incredible Methodists: A History of the Baltimore Conference of the United Methodist Church* (Baltimore: Commission on Archives and History, Baltimore Conference, 1972), endpaper maps.

37 Mathews, *Slavery and Methodism*, 244–45.

38 John d'Entremont, *Moncure Conway, 1832–1907: American Abolitionist* (London: South Place Ethical Society, 1977), 13–14.

39 Robert H. Abzug, *Cosmos Crumbling: American Reform and the Religious Imagination* (New York: Oxford University Press, 1994), 143; Mathews, *Slavery and Methodism*, 170.

40 Pillsbury, *Church as It Is*, 3; Lawrence B. Goodheart, *Abolitionist, Actuary, Atheist: Elizur Wright and the Reform Impulse* (Kent, Ohio: Kent State University Press, 1990), 129; *Liberator*, Sept. 15, 1848.

41 Stephen S. Foster, *The Brotherhood of Thieves; or, A True Picture of the American Church and Clergy* (Boston: Anti-Slavery Office, 1844), 7–8, 19, 31–32.

42 *Anti-Slavery Bugle*, May 5, 1848.

43 James Brewer Stewart, *Holy Warriors: The Abolitionists and American Slavery* (New York: Hill and Wang, 1976), 93; *New-York Tribune*, May 10, 1848.

44 Mitchell Snay, *Gospel of Disunion: Religion and Separatism in the Ante-*

bellum South (New York: Cambridge University Press, 1993), 10–13, 54, 59–60.

45 Frederic Bancroft, *Slave Trading in the Old South* (Baltimore: J. H. Furst, 1931), 37–39; Stockbridge, "Baltimore in 1846," 26–27. See also Ethan Allen Andrews, *Slavery and the Domestic Slave-Trade in the United States: In a Series of Letters Addressed to the Executive Committee of the American Union for the Relief and Improvement of the Colored Race* (Boston: Light and Stearns, 1836), 78; Joseph Sturge, *A Visit to the United States in 1841* (Boston: Dexter S. King, 1842), 45; *Brother Jonathan* 6, no. 10 (Nov. 4, 1843): 274; *Matchett's Baltimore Director for 1847'8* [*sic*] (Baltimore: R. J. Matchett, 1847), 303.

46 Stockbridge, "Baltimore in 1846," 27; Lincoln quoted in William Lee Miller, *Lincoln's Virtues: An Ethical Biography* (New York: Alfred A. Knopf, 2002), 265; *Liberator*, July 23, 1847.

47 Stockbridge, "Baltimore in 1846," 27; Harriet Beecher Stowe, *A Key to "Uncle Tom's Cabin": Presenting the Original Facts and Documents upon Which the Story Is Founded, Together with Corroborative Statements Verifying the Truth of the Work* (Boston: John P. Jewett, 1853), 161; Ralph Clayton, *Slavery, Slaveholding, and the Free Black Population of Antebellum Baltimore* (Bowie, Md.: Heritage Books, 1993), 30; M. Ray Della Jr., "The Problem of Negro Labor in the 1850s," *Maryland Historical Magazine* 66 (Spring 1971): 23.

48 *Liberator*, July 23, 1847; *National Police Gazette*, Aug. 14, 1847 ("kidnapping" quote).

49 Giddings, *Speeches*, 233, 227–28; *National Era*, Dec. 14, 1848; Clayton, *Slavery*, 31.

50 Sturge, *Visit to United States*, 31–32.

51 *National Anti-Slavery Standard*, June 1, 1848.

52 *National Anti-Slavery Standard*, June 22, 1848.

53 Slingerland to *New-York Tribune*, reprinted in *National Anti-Slavery Standard*, June 29, 1848, and *North Star*, July 14, 1848.

54 *Liberator*, Oct. 20, 1848; *North Star*, July 14, Oct. 6, 1848.

55 *Liberator*, May 25, 1849, reprinting from *New Orleans Picayune*; Clayton, *Slavery*, 30; Michael Tadman, *Speculators and Slaves: Masters, Traders, and Slaves in the Old South* (Madison: University of Wisconsin Press, 1989), 232.

56 *Mobile Daily Advertiser*, Dec. 1, 1849–Jan. 29, 1850; Jan. 8, 1852.

57 Clayton, *Slavery*, 33–34; Joseph G. Rayback, *Free Soil: The Election of 1848* (Lexington: University Press of Kentucky, 1970), 240 ("If Taylor . . ." quote); *North Star*, Aug. 11, 1848.

58 Donovan, *Many Witnesses*, 231.

Chapter Five

1 *New York Herald*, Apr. 23, 1848; *North Star*, Apr. 28, May 26, 1848; *Daily Union* (D.C.), Apr. 19, 1848; *The Washington Directory, and National Register for 1846* (Washington, D.C.: Gaither and Addison, 1846), 16.

2 *North Star*, Oct. 13, 1848, reprinting from *New-York Globe*; *Washington Directory for 1846*, 6, 90.

3 *Emancipation in the District of Columbia*, H. Ex. Document 42, 38th Cong., 1st sess. (1864), 63, 72; William L. Chaplin to Horace Mann, Feb. 3, 1853, Horace Mann Papers, Massachusetts Historical Society, Boston.

4 *North Star*, Apr. 14, 1848; *Daily Union*, Apr. 19, 1848; Sarah Steward to D. Madison, July 5, 1844, and D. Madison to John Payne Todd, April [24], 1848, in *The Selected Letters of Dolley Payne Madison*, ed. David B. Mattern and Holly C. Shulman (Charlottesville: University of Virginia Press, 2003), 372–73, 387.

5 Hannah Palfrey Ayer, ed., *A Legacy of New England: Letters of the Palfrey Family*, 2 vols. ([Milton, Mass.]: privately printed, 1950), 1:166–67; *Congressional Globe*, 30th Cong., 1st sess., 17:786 (May 25, 1848).

6 *North Star*, July 14, Aug. 25, 1848; *Emancipator*, Aug. 16, 1848; D. Madison to John Payne Todd, Apr. [24], 1848, in *Selected Letters*, ed. Mattern and Shulman, 387.

7 Chaplin to Gerrit Smith, Nov. 2, 1848, Gerrit Smith Papers, Arents Library, Syracuse University, Syracuse, N.Y.

8 *Daily Union*, Apr. 19, 1848; *Emancipation in the District of Columbia*, 66, appendix A (pp. 17–71).

9 Samuel Gridley Howe, *Narrative of the Heroic Adventures of Drayton, an American Trader, in "The Pearl," Coasting Vessel* (London: Ward, n.d.), 8; William Still, *The Underground Railroad* (New York: Arno Press, 1967, orig. pub. 1872), 46–48.

10 Ducket to Bigelow, Feb. 18, 1850, in *Slave Testimony: Two Centuries of Letters, Speeches, Interviews, and Autobiographies*, ed. John W. Blassingame (Baton Rouge: Louisiana State University Press, 1977), 89. A facsimile of the letter is in Harriet Beecher Stowe, *A Key to "Uncle Tom's Cabin": Presenting the Original Facts and Documents upon Which the Story Is Founded, Together with Corroborative Statements Verifying the Truth of the Work* (Boston: John P. Jewett, 1853), 171–72.

11 National Archives, Record Group (RG) 21, Entry 30, Emancipation and Manumission Records, 3:24, National Archives Building, Washington, D.C.; Roger Brooke Farquhar, *Old Homes and History of Montgomery County, Maryland* (Washington, D.C.: Judd and Detweiler, 1962), 31, 82, 199; *North Star*, Oct. 13, 1848.

12 Stowe, *Key to "Uncle Tom's Cabin"*, 155–56.

13 Montgomery County Records, Docket Book BS7, pp. 414–16; Docket Book ST3, pp. 198–200, Montgomery Court House, Rockville, Md.; T. H. S. Boyd, *The History of Montgomery County, Maryland, from its Earliest Settlement in 1650 to 1879* (Baltimore: Regional Publishing Company, 1968, orig. pub. 1879), 33; Farquhar, *Old Homes and History*, 89, 273; *Emancipator and Free Soil Press*, Oct. 11, 1848.

14 Stowe, *Key to "Uncle Tom's Cabin"*, 156–57.

15 *Anti-Slavery Bugle*, Nov. 17, 1848; John H. Paynter, *Fugitives of the* Pearl (Washington, D.C.: Associated Publishers, 1930), 4–6; National Archives, RG 21, entry 30, Emancipation and Manumission Records, 3:24; Stowe, *Key to "Uncle Tom's Cabin"*, 157.

16 Stowe, *Key to "Uncle Tom's Cabin"*, 161–62.

17 Paynter, *Fugitives of the* Pearl, chap. 5.

18 Chaplin to Gerrit Smith, Mar. 25, 1848, Smith Papers.

19 Joshua R. Giddings, *History of the Rebellion: Its Authors and Causes* (New York: Follet, Foster, 1864), 279; Stowe, *Key to "Uncle Tom's Cabin"*, 160.

20 Joshua Giddings, *Speeches in Congress [1841–1852]* (Boston: John P. Jewett, 1853), 484–85 (Mar. 16, 1852).

21 Stowe, *Key to "Uncle Tom's Cabin"*, 159–60.

22 Pamela Cressey, "History Is Buried under Parking Lot Pavement," *Gazette Packet* (Alexandria), May 12, 1994; Donald M. Sweig, "Alexander Grigsby: A Slavebreeder of Old Centerville?" *Fairfax Chronicles*, 7 (May–July 1983), 1.

23 Charles L. Perdue, Thomas E. Barden, and Robert K. Phillips, *Weevils in the Wheat: Interviews with Virginia Ex-Slaves* (Charlottesville: University Press of Virginia, 1976), 27, 60; Frederic Bancroft, *Slave Trading in the Old South* (Baltimore: J. H. Furst, 1931), 315n, 331n.

24 Stowe says in *Key to "Uncle Tom's Cabin"*, 160, that they stayed there for four weeks, but that is not possible.

25 Stowe says they were in Baltimore for three weeks, but again so long a stay is not possible. Ibid.

26 Ibid., 160–61; Giddings, *History of the Rebellion*, 279n.

27 *Matchett's Baltimore Director for 1847'8 [sic]* (Baltimore: R. J. Matchett, 1847), 95; National Archives, RG 36, Manifest of Negroes, Mulattos, and Persons of Color, Taken on Board the Brig *Union*, May 13, 1848, Baltimore, National Archives Building, Washington, D.C.

28 Stowe, *Key to "Uncle Tom's Cabin"*, 161.

29 Ibid.

30 John W. Blassingame, *Black New Orleans, 1860–1880* (Chicago: University of Chicago Press, 1973), 17.

31 Stowe, *Key to "Uncle Tom's Cabin"*, 161–62.

32 Ibid., 162.

33 Ibid.; Thomas L. Nichols, *Forty Years of American Life*, 2 vols. (New York: Negro Universities Press, 1968, orig. pub. 1864), 1:197; Jo Ann Carrigan, *The Saffron Scourge: A History of Yellow Fever in Louisiana, 1796–1905* (Lafayette, La.: Center for Louisiana Studies, 1994), 48, 55; *Liberator*, Nov. 17, 1848.

34 National Archives, RG 36, Manifest of Slaves, on Board the Brig *Union* of Baltimore, July 6, 1848 (New Orleans), National Archives Building, Washington, D.C.; Stowe, *Key to "Uncle Tom's Cabin"*, 162.

35 Stowe, *Key to "Uncle Tom's Cabin"*, 163.

36 Ibid., 173–74.

37 Ibid., 156, 159.

38 *Anti-Slavery Bugle*, Nov. 17, 1848. For a history of Asbury Church, see Paul E. Sluby Sr., *Asbury: Our Legacy, Our Faith, 1836–1993*, 2nd ed. (Washington, D.C.: privately printed, 1996). For a useful reminder of abolitionists' emphasis on prostitution, see Marc M. Arkin, "The Federalist Trope: Power and Passion in Abolitionist Rhetoric," *Journal of American History* 88 (June 2001): 75–98.

39 *Anti-Slavery Bugle*, Nov. 17, 1848.

40 Ibid.

41 Ibid.

42 Stowe, *Key to "Uncle Tom's Cabin"*, 164–65.

43 Rayford W. Logan and Michael R. Winston, eds. *Dictionary of American Negro Biography* (New York: W. W. Norton, 1982), s.v. "Pennington, James W. C."; Joseph R. Washington Jr., *The First Fugitive Foreign and Domestic Doctor of Divinity* (Lewiston: Edwin Mellen, 1990), 66–67, 54; R. J. M. Blackett, *Building an Antislavery Wall: Black Americans in the Atlantic Abolitionist Movement, 1830–1860* (Baton Rouge: Louisiana State University Press, 1983), 128.

44 James W. C. Pennington, *The Fugitive Blacksmith; or, Events in the History of James W. C. Pennington*, 3rd ed. (Westport, Conn.: Negro Universities Press, 1971, orig. pub. 1850), viii–ix.

45 Stowe, *Key to "Uncle Tom's Cabin"*, 165. Beecher's residence was at 197 Washington Street; *Hearned's Brooklyn City Directory for 1850–51* (Brooklyn: Henry R. and Wm. J. Hearned, 1850), appendix, 47.

46 Stowe, *Key to "Uncle Tom's Cabin"*, 165; Lyman Abbott, *Henry Ward Beecher* (New York: Chelsea House, 1980, orig. pub. 1903), 157.

47 Daniel Curry, *The Judgements of God Confessed and Preached* (New York: Oliver and Brother, 1849); George Peck, *Slavery and the Episcopacy* (New York: G. Lane and C. B. Tippett, 1845); Emory Stevens Bucke, ed., *The History of American Methodism*, 3 vols. (New York: Abingdon, 1964), 2:202, 185, 610; *Anti-Slavery Bugle*, Nov. 17, 1848.

48 *National Anti-Slavery Standard*, Nov. 2, 1848. There is some confusion

about the girls' names and ages; their names have been documented as Mary Jane and Mary Amelia and also as Emily J. and Emily Catharine. Their ages were reported as seventeen and fifteen in one account and as sixteen and fourteen in another.

49 Paxton Hibben, *Henry Ward Beecher: An American Portrait* (New York: Beekman, 1974), 110–12.

50 William C. Beecher and Samuel Scoville, *A Biography of Rev. Henry Ward Beecher* (New York: Charles L. Webster, 1888), 292–93; *Anti-Slavery Bugle*, Nov. 17, 1848; *National Anti-Slavery Standard*, Oct. 26, 1848; Hibben, *Henry Ward Beecher*, 112.

51 *North Star*, Nov. 17, 1848.

52 Ibid., Nov. 10, 1848; Grimké quoted in Lori D. Ginzberg, *Women in Antebellum Reform* (Wheeling, Ill.: Harlan Davidson, 2000), 66.

53 *Anti-Slavery Bugle*, Nov. 17, 1848.

54 *New-York Tribune*, Oct. 25, 1848; *National Anti-Slavery Standard*, Nov. 9, 1848.

55 *Anti-Slavery Bugle*, May 19, 1848; Beecher and Scoville, *Biography of Rev. Henry Ward Beecher*, 300; Walter Johnson, "The Slave Trader, the White Slave, and the Politics of Racial Determination in the 1850s," *Journal of American History* 87 (June 2000): 16, 18.

56 Chaplin to Gerrit Smith, Nov. 2, 1848, Smith Papers; *National Anti-Slavery Standard*, Nov. 30, 1848; Stowe, *Key to "Uncle Tom's Cabin"*, 166; *National Era*, Nov. 30, 1848.

57 *Independent* (New York), Dec. 21, 1848.

58 Ibid.

59 *New-York Tribune*, Dec. 7, 1848.

60 *Independent*, Dec. 21, 1848.

61 Ibid.

62 *New-York Tribune*, Dec. 16, 19, 1848.

63 *Anti-Slavery Bugle*, Dec. 29, 1848; Lawrence J. Friedman, *Gregarious Saints: Self and Community in American Abolitionism, 1830–1870* (Cambridge: Cambridge University Press, 1982), 123; Walter Henry Green, *History, Reminiscences, Anecdotes, and Legends of Great Sodus Bay* (Sodus, N.Y.: n.p., 1945), 296.

64 [William R. Smith], *The Case of William L. Chaplin: Being an Appeal to All Respecters of Law and Justice, against the Cruel and Oppressive Treatment to Which, Under Cover of Legal Proceedings, He Has Been Subjected, in the District of Columbia and the State of Maryland* (Boston: Chaplin Committee, 1851); Philip S. Foner and Josephine F. Pacheco, *Three Who Dared: Prudence Crandall, Margaret Douglass, Myrtilla Miner—Champions of Antebellum Black Education* (Westport, Conn.: Greenwood Press, 1984), 113–14.

65 Catherine M. Hanchett to the author, Apr. 25, 1997. For the water-cure movement, see Susan E. Cayleff, *Wash and Be Healed: The Water-Cure Movement and Women's Health* (Philadelphia: Temple University Press, 1987). For Glen Haven, see ibid., 114–15. For Chaplin's connection with Glen Haven, see Elliot G. Storke, *History of Cayuga County, New York* (Interlaken, N.Y.: Heart of the Lakes, 1980, orig. pub. 1879), 484.

66 Angelo Hall, *An Astronomer's Wife: The Biography of Angeline Hall* (Baltimore: Nunn, 1908), 48–49.

67 Cornelia Baker Cornish, *The Geography and History of Cortland County* (Ann Arbor, Mich.: Edwards Brothers, 1935), 39–40. See also Bertha Eveleth Blodgett, *Stories of Cortland County* (Cortland, N.Y.: Cortland County Historical Society, 1975), 233–34; Leon F. Litwack, *North of Slavery: The Negro in the Free States, 1790–1860* (Chicago: University of Chicago Press, 1961), 141–42; Carleton Mabee, *Black Education in New York State from Colonial to Modern Times* (Syracuse, N.Y.: Syracuse University Press, 1979), 89.

68 The catalog was published in Homer, N.Y., by Reed and Gould in 1852 and can be found in the collections of the Cortland County Historical Society.

69 Catherine M. Hanchett, "'What Sort of People and Families . . .': The Edmondson Sisters," *Afro-Americans in New York Life and History* 6 (July 1982): 29; *Frederick Douglass' Paper*, Oct. 2, 1851.

70 Charles Edward Stowe, *Life of Harriet Beecher Stowe: Compiled from Her Letters and Journals* (Boston: Houghton Mifflin, 1889), 179. Stowe wrote *A Key to "Uncle Tom's Cabin"* in the winter and spring of 1853 and reported that Amelia Edmondson had arrived in New York "last spring, during the month of May" (166).

71 H. B. Stowe, *Key to "Uncle Tom's Cabin"*, 167–68; C. E. Stowe, *Life of Harriet Beecher Stowe*, 180–82.

72 H. B. Stowe, *Key to "Uncle Tom's Cabin"*, 157, 167–68.

73 Stowe quoted in Myrtilla Miner to Samuel Rhoads, Sept. 25, 1853, Myrtilla Miner Papers, Manuscript Division, Library of Congress, Washington, D.C.

74 H. B. Stowe, *Key to "Uncle Tom's Cabin"*, 167; H. B. Stowe to Mrs. Cowles, [1852?], Fletcher Papers, Cowles Papers, Oberlin College Archives, Oberlin, Ohio.

75 Robert Samuel Fletcher, *A History of Oberlin College from Its Foundation through the Civil War*, 2 vols. (Oberlin, Ohio: Oberlin College, 1943), 1:131, 178, 344.

76 Stowe to Mrs. Cowles, [1852?], Fletcher Papers, Cowles Papers.

77 Ibid.

78 John Phelps Cowles, *In Memoriam: Rev. Henry Cowles, D.D.* (Oberlin, Ohio: privately printed, 1883), 13, 17; James Oliver Horton, "Black Educa-

tion at Oberlin College: A Controversial Commitment," *Journal of Negro Education* 54 (Fall 1985): 486; Stowe to Mrs. Cowles, [1852?], Fletcher Papers, Cowles Papers.

79 M. L. Cowles to "Dear Aunty," Aug. 9, 1852, Fletcher Papers, Cowles Papers.

80 H. B. Stowe to Mary Edmondson, Oct. 2, 1852; H. B. Stowe to Mrs. Cowles, Aug. 4, 1852?; C. E. Stowe to Mrs. Henry Cowles, July 20, 1852; H. B. Stowe to Mrs. Cowles, Nov. 13, 1852; H. B. Stowe to Mary Edmondson, Oct. 2, 1852; H. B. Stowe by L. W. Bacon to Mrs. Cowles, Mar. 24, 1853, Fletcher Papers, Cowles Papers.

81 Stowe to Mrs. Cowles, Aug 4, 1852?, Dec. 12, 1852, Fletcher Papers, Cowles Papers; *National Anti-Slavery Standard*, Nov. 2, 1848; H. B. Stowe, *Key to "Uncle Tom's Cabin"*, 164.

82 *Grace Victorious; or, The Memoir of Helen M. Cowles* (Oberlin, Ohio: J. M. Fitch, 1856); Stowe by L. W. Bacon to Mrs. Cowles, Mar. 24, 1853, Fletcher Papers, Cowles Papers; *Frederick Douglass' Paper*, Apr. 29, 1853; *Oberlin Evangelist*, May 25, 1853, cited in Group 28/1, Oberlin College Archives.

83 Entry for May 22, 1853, in *Harriet Beecher Stowe in Europe: The Journal of Charles Beecher*, ed. Joseph S. Van Why and Earl French (Hartford, Conn.: Stowe-Day Foundation, 1986), 117; Stowe to Duchess of Sutherland, June 2, 1853, Harriet Beecher Stowe Bibliographic Research Collection, Accession #11416, Special Collections, University of Virginia Library, Charlottesville, Va.

84 Emily Edmondson to Mr. and Mrs. Cowles, June 6, 1853, Fletcher Papers, Cowles Papers.

Chapter Six

1 Jonathan Messerli, *Horace Mann: A Biography* (New York: Alfred A. Knopf, 1972), 452–55, 461.

2 Ibid., chap. 3, 71 (quote), 76, 85–86, 199, 205, 240–49.

3 Samuel J. May, *Some Recollections of Our Antislavery Conflict* (New York: Arno Press, 1968, orig. pub. 1869), 310–13.

4 James Brewer Stewart, *Wendell Phillips: Liberty's Hero* (Baton Rouge: Louisiana State University Press, 1968), 99–100. For Phillips's attack on Mann, see *Liberator*, Dec. 24, 1847, and Feb. 4, 1848.

5 George W. Bungay, *Crayon Sketches and Off-Hand Takings of Distinguished American Statesmen, Orators, Divines, Essayists, Editors, Poets, and Philanthropists* (Boston: Stacy and Richardson, 1852), 22–23.

6 Michael F. Holt, *The Rise and Fall of the American Whig Party: Jacksonian Politics and the Onset of the Civil War* (New York: Oxford University Press, 1999), 582.

7 *Richmond Enquirer*, Apr. 25, 1848.

8 *Daily National Intelligencer* (D.C.), April 19, 20, 22, 1848; *Sun* (Baltimore), Apr. 21, 1848; *North Star*, May 5, 1848.

9 *North Star*, May 5, 1848; Charles Cleveland to Mann, June 19, 1848, Horace Mann Papers, Massachusetts Historical Society, Boston.

10 *Liberator*, June 2, 1848; *North Star*, May 26, 1848.

11 Undated trial notes, Mann Papers.

12 *Acts of Assembly of the Province of Maryland*, 1737:2–3; ibid., 1751:17; *Proceedings and Acts of the General Assembly* (Maryland), 1796, chap. 67, no. 19; *Liberator*, May 19, 1848; *National Anti-Slavery Standard*, May 25, 1848.

13 Larry Gara, *The Liberty Line: The Legend of the Underground Railroad* (Lexington: University Press of Kentucky, 1996, orig. pub. 1961), 72.

14 *Boston Post*, Apr. 26, 1848.

15 Flyer and S. W. Wheeler to J. P. Blanchard, May 30, 1848, in Black History Miscellany (hereafter cited as BHM), box 1, Manuscript Division, Library of Congress, Washington, D.C.

16 *Daily True Democrat*, May 15, 1848; unattributed clippings, August 1848, BHM; J. P. Blanchard to Gerrit Smith, May 17, 1848, BHM; R. Hildreth, receipt of $200 from Blanchard, May 8, 1848, BHM.

17 Cleveland to Blanchard, May 10, 1848, and Blanchard to Cleveland, May 17, 1848, BHM; S. G. Howe to Mann, Apr. 18, 1848 (incorrect date), in "Memoranda and Documents: Samuel G. Howe to Horace Mann," ed. Robert L. Straker, *New England Quarterly* 16 (Sept. 1943): 479–80.

18 Lewis Tappan to Blanchard, May 15, 1848, BHM, box 1.

19 Chase to S. E. Sewall, May 27, [1848], in *Diary and Correspondence of Salmon P. Chase* (New York: Da Capo Press, 1971), 133–34; Seward to Chase, June 12, 1848, Salmon P. Chase Papers, Historical Society of Pennsylvania, Philadelphia.

20 Correspondence, May 10, 1848, Mann Papers.

21 Messerli, *Horace Mann*, 481; Chase to Mann, July 16, 1848, Mann Papers.

22 Mann to S. G. Howe, July 20, 1848, and Mann to Charles Sumner, May 31, 1848, Mann Papers.

23 Howe to Mann, Apr. 28, 1848, in *Letters and Journals of Samuel Gridley Howe*, 2 vols., ed. Laura E. Richards (Boston: Dana Estes, 1909), 2:262; Straker, "Memoranda and Documents," 479–80; Lawrence J. Friedman, *Gregarious Saints: Self and Community in American Abolitionism, 1830–1870* (Cambridge: Cambridge University Press, 1982), 36–37.

24 Straker, "Memoranda and Documents," 480; *Dictionary of American Biography*, s.v. "Carlisle, James Mandeville"; William Wirt Henry and Ainsworth R. Spofford, *Eminent and Representative Men of Virginia and the District of Columbia in the Nineteenth Century* (Madison, Wis.: Brant and Fuller, 1893), 289–90; Carlisle to Mann, Apr. 30, 1849, Mann Papers.

25 J. E. Snodgrass to Mann, July 26, 1848, Mann Papers.

26 *Sun*, June 20, 30, 1848; Mann said 115 charges: Mann, *Slavery: Letters and Speeches* (Boston: B. B. Mussey, 1851), 90; *The Washington Directory, and National Register for 1846* (Washington, D.C.: Gaither and Addison, 1846), 12.

27 Mann to Mary Mann, May 6, 1848, Mann Papers; *Sun*, July 8, 1848.

28 *Sun*, July 25, 1848; Mann, *Slavery*, 88.

29 *National Anti-Slavery Standard*, Aug. 10, 1848.

30 Messerli, *Horace Mann*, 482; *Sun*, July 28, 1848; *Washington Directory for 1846*, 57, 59, 60, 62, 64, 68, 93, 101, 108; Mann, *Slavery*, 87n.

31 *National Era*, Aug. 10, 1849.

32 Ibid., Aug. 24, 1848.

33 *Washington Directory for 1846*, 50; *Sun*, Apr. 19, 1848; National Archives, *Population Schedules of the Sixth Census of the United States, 1840*, District of Columbia, M704, roll 35, National Archives Building, Washington, D.C.

34 *Sun*, July 28, 1848.

35 Ibid., July 29, 1848.

36 Ibid.; *Charleston Courier*, Apr. 25, 1848.

37 *National Era*, Aug. 10, 1848.

38 *Sun*, July 29, 1848.

39 Ibid.

40 Frederick Tilp, *This Was Potomac River* (Alexandria, Va.: privately printed, 1978), 299.

41 *Sun*, July 29, 31, 1848.

42 Ibid., July 31, 1848.

43 Mann, *Slavery*, 86–87, 91–92; *Sun*, July 31, 1848.

44 *National Anti-Slavery Standard*, Aug. 10, 1848; *Washington Directory 1846*, 12.

45 *Pennsylvania Freeman*, Aug. 10, 1848.

46 *Sun*, July 31, 1848; *Emancipator*, Aug. 9, 1848.

47 *Sun*, July 31, 1848; Mann, *Slavery*, 117.

48 Mann, *Slavery*, 88.

49 *Sun*, July 31, 1848.

50 Ibid., Aug. 1, 1848; for subpoenas of and payments to Philadelphia witnesses, see Mann Papers.

51 *Dictionary of American Biography*, s.v. "Cranch, William."

52 *Sun*, Aug. 1, 3, 1848.

53 Ibid., Aug. 3, 1848; see also *The Federal Cases* (St. Paul: West, 1894), 7:1064.

54 *Pennsylvania Freeman*, Aug. 10, 1848.

55 *National Era*, Aug. 24, 1848.

56 *Anti-Slavery Bugle*, Sept. 1, 1848.

57 *National Intelligencer*, Aug. 4, 11, 1848; *National Anti-Slavery Standard*, Aug. 10, 1848; *Sun*, Aug. 10, 1848; *National Era*, Aug. 24, 1848.

58 *Sun*, Aug. 5, 1848; *Washington Directory for 1846*, 82; *Congressional Globe*, 30th Cong., 1st sess., 17:825 (June 12, 1848); Frederick William Seward, *Reminiscences of a War-Time Statesman and Diplomat, 1830–1915* (New York: G. P. Putnam's Sons, 1916), 69.

59 *National Intelligencer*, Aug. 18, 1848; *Sun*, Aug. 21, 1848.

60 Mann to Chase, July 3, 1848, Chase Papers; *Sun*, Aug. 12, 1848; *Pennsylvania Freeman*, Aug. 10, 1848; Daniel Drayton, *Personal Memoir of Daniel Drayton, for Four Years and Four Months a Prisoner (for Charity's Sake) in Washington Jail* (New York: Negro Universities Press, 1969, orig. pub. 1855), 41.

61 *Sun*, Aug. 21, 1848.

62 *Federal Cases*, 7:1065; *National Era*, Aug. 24, 1848; *Anti-Slavery Bugle*, Sept. 1, 1848.

63 *Sun*, Aug. 21, 23, 1848.

64 Howe to Mann, Aug. 8, 1848, in *Letters and Journals of Howe*, ed. Richards, 2:263.

65 *Liberator*, Aug. 18, 1848.

66 Sewall to Seward, Oct. 17, 1848, William H. Seward Papers, Manuscript Division, Library of Congress.

67 Hildreth was the unnamed author of Drayton's memoir. His best-known work was *The Slave; or, Memoirs of Archy Moore* (1836), "the first antislavery novel in the United States." Donald E. Emerson, *Richard Hildreth* (Baltimore: Johns Hopkins Press, 1946), 73, 131.

68 *Washington Directory for 1846*, 5; F. Regis Noel, *The Court-House of the District of Columbia* (Washington, D.C.: Law Reporter Printing Company, 1939), 92; Mann to Mary Mann, Dec. 2, 1848, in Mary Tyler Peabody Mann, *Life of Horace Mann* (Boston: Willard Small, 1888), 272; *New-York Tribune*, Nov. 30, 1848.

69 *National Era*, Dec. 21, 1848.

70 *Liberator*, Dec. 15, 1848; *Sun*, Dec. 7, 1848.

71 *National Era*, Dec. 21, 1848.

72 *Sun*, Feb. 22, 1849; *National Intelligencer*, Mar. 8, 1849; *Federal Cases*, 7:1068; John A. Hayward and George C. Hazleton, eds., *Reports of Cases Civil and Criminal Argued and Adjudged in the Circuit Court of the District of Columbia for the County of Washington*, 2 vols. (Chicago: T. H. Flood, 1907), 1:369–83.

73 Mann to M. Mann, Feb. 20, 1849, in Mann, *Life of Horace Mann*, 275.

74 *Sun*, Dec. 1, 5, 1848; *Dictionary of American Biography*, s.v. "Jones, Walter"; *National Era*, May 17, 1848.

75 Charles List to Seward, Apr. 13, 1849, and Sewall to Seward, Apr. 14, 1849, Seward Papers. See also Sewall to Mann, Dec. 31, 1849, Mann Papers.

76 Mann to Sumner, May 12, 1849, Mann Papers; Mann to M. Mann, Dec. 2, 1848, in Mann, *Life of Horace Mann*, 272.

77 Mann to S. G. Howe, May 9, 1848, Mann Papers.

78 *Sun*, May 8, 1849; Mann to Sumner, May 12, 1849, Mann Papers.

79 Mann to M. Mann, May 11, 1849, in Mann, *Life of Horace Mann*, 280–81.

80 Testimony of Henry A. Clark, Notes of trial, May 1849; *US v. Drayton*, May 8 or 11, 1849, Mann Papers.

81 Undated testimony, [May 1849?], ibid.

82 Testimony of Hampton Williams and Sayres, May 11, 1849, ibid.

83 Trial notes, May 15, 1849, ibid.

84 *National Era*, May 31, 1849.

85 *Sun*, May 19, 25, 1849.

86 *Anti-Slavery Bugle*, Aug. 16, 1851.

87 *Henson Ridgway et al. v. Francis Dodge Jr.*, Feb. 26, 1849. National Archives, Record Group 21, Records of the U.S. Circuit Court for the District of Columbia, Chancery Records, entry 20, Chancery Dockets and Rules Case, file 1809–63, rule 5, no. 574, National Archives Building, Washington, D.C. Case postponed in 1849, 1850, 1851, and 1854 with continuing number 574.

Chapter Seven

1 *Congressional Globe*, 30th Cong., 1st sess., 17:60, 62–63, 104, 319, 445, 529, 545, 567, 598.

2 Ibid., 17:160 (Jan. 12, 1848, Yulee of Fla.), 241, 261 (Jan. 25, 27, 1848, Bagby of Ala.).

3 Ibid., 17:614 (Apr. 11, 1848).

4 Ibid., 17:641 (Apr. 18, 1848).

5 Benjamin Brown French, *Witness to the Young Republic*, ed. Donald B. Cole and John J. McDonough (Hanover, N.H.: University Press of New England, 1989), 208.

6 *Congressional Globe*, 17 appendix: 133–37 (Jan. 26, 1848); Samuel J. May, *Some Recollections of Our Antislavery Conflict* (New York: Arno Press, 1968, orig. pub. 1869), 397–98.

7 Palfrey to his wife, Jan. 26, 1848, in *A Legacy of New England: Letters of the Palfrey Family*, 2 vols., ed. Hannah Palfrey Ayer ([Milton, Mass.]: privately printed, 1950), 1:159.

8 Palfrey diary, Apr. 19, 21, 1848, John Gorham Palfrey Papers, Houghton Library, Harvard University, Cambridge, Mass.

9 *Congressional Globe*, 30th Cong. 1st sess., 17:649 (Apr. 20, 1848).

10 Ibid.

11 Ibid., 17:649–50 (Apr. 20, 1848).

12 Ibid., 17:650 (Apr. 20, 1848).

13 Ibid., 17:651 (Apr. 20, 1848).

14 Ibid., 17:651–52 (Apr. 20, 1848).

15 Ibid., 17:652–53 (Apr. 20, 1848).

16 Ibid., 17:653 (Apr. 20, 1848).

17 Ibid., 17:653–54 (Apr. 20, 1848).

18 Ibid., 17:654–55 (Apr. 20, 1848).

19 Ibid., 17:657 (Apr. 21, 1848). For an elaboration of the importance of property in slaves, see James L. Huston, "Property Rights in Slavery and the Coming of the Civil War," *Journal of Southern History* 65 (May 1999): 249–86.

20 *Congressional Globe*, 30th Cong., 1st sess., 17:658–59 (Apr. 21, 1848).

21 Ibid., 17:662 (Apr. 21, 1848).

22 Ibid., 17:663–64 (Apr. 21, 1848).

23 Ibid., 17:665–70 (Apr. 25, 1848).

24 Ibid., 17:670–72 (Apr. 25, 1848).

25 Ibid., 17:672.

26 Richard H. Sewell, *John P. Hale and the Politics of Abolition* (Cambridge, Mass.: Harvard University Press, 1965), 108; *Congressional Globe*, 30th Cong., 1st sess., 17:648 (Apr. 19, 1848), 17 appendix: 501 (Apr. 20, 1848).

27 *Congressional Globe*, 30th Cong., 1st sess., 17 appendix: 500–501 (Apr. 20, 1848).

28 Ibid., 17 appendix: 501 (Apr. 20, 1848).

29 Ibid.

30 Ibid., 17 appendix: 502 (Apr. 20, 1848).

31 *Daily True Democrat* (Cleveland), June 9, 1848; *Anti-Slavery Bugle*, Mar. 23, 1849; Henry S. Foote, *Casket of Reminiscences* (Washington, D.C.: Chronicle, 1874), 71–78, 187, 338–39.

32 *Congressional Globe*, 30th Cong., 1st sess., 17 appendix: 502–3 (Apr. 20, 1848).

33 Ibid., 17 appendix: 503–4 (Apr. 20, 1848).

34 Ibid., 17 appendix: 505 (Apr. 20, 1848).

35 [Lewis Tappan], *Address to the Non-Slaveholders of the South, on the Social and Political Evils of Slavery* (New York: American and Foreign Anti-Slavery Society, [1849?]), 21–22.

36 *Congressional Globe*, 30th Cong., 1st sess., 17 appendix: 506 (Apr. 20, 1848).

37 See William J. Cooper Jr., *Jefferson Davis, American* (New York: Alfred A. Knopf, 2000), 173–74.

38 *Congressional Globe*, 30th Cong., 1st sess., 17 appendix: 506–7 (Apr. 20, 1848). For southern newspapers' disapproval of Foote's demagoguery, see

the *Mississippian* (Jackson), May 5, 1848; *Vicksburg Weekly Sentinel*, May 24, 1848; *Vicksburg Weekly Whig*, June 7, 1848; *Daily Picayune* (New Orleans), May 2, 1848.

39 *Congressional Globe*, 30th Cong., 1st sess., 17 appendix: 506-7 (Apr. 20, 1848).

40 Ibid., 17 appendix: 507 (Apr. 20, 1848).

41 Ibid., 17 appendix: 507-8 (Apr. 20, 1848).

42 Ibid., 17 appendix: 508-9 (Apr. 20, 1848).

43 Ibid., 17:676 (Apr. 25, 1848).

44 John W. Blassingame, ed., *The Frederick Douglass Papers*, ser. 1, 5 vols. (New Haven: Yale University Press, 1979-92), 2:120; Garrison to Sydney Howard Gay, Apr. 27, 1848, in *The Letters of William Lloyd Garrison: No Union with Slave-Holders, 1841–1849*, ed. Walter M. Merrill, 4 vols. (Cambridge, Mass.: Belknap Press of Harvard University Press, 1973), 3:553; *Liberator*, June 2, 1848; *Pennsylvania Freeman*, June 1, 1848; *Anti-Slavery Standard*, May 11, 18, 25, 1848; *Emancipator*, June 14, 1848.

45 Hale to Elizabeth L. Hale, April 18, 19, 26 (quote), 1848; Geo. S. Riley to Hale, Jan. 13, 1850; John Parkman to Hale, July 10, 1848, John Parker Hale Papers, New Hampshire Historical Society, Concord; *Liberator*, Dec. 12, 1851.

46 Henry Wilson, *History of the Rise and Fall of the Slave Power in America*, 3 vols. (Boston: J. R. Osgood, 1872-77), 2:97; George W. Julian, *Political Recollections, 1840 to 1872* (Chicago: Jansen, McClurg, 1884), 173. For threats against antislavery members of Congress, see Fawn Brodie, "Who Defends the Abolitionist?" in *The Antislavery Vanguard: New Essays on the Abolitionists*, ed. Martin Duberman (Princeton: Princeton University Press, 1965), 57-58.

47 Chase to Hale, Apr. 29, 1848, Hale Papers.

48 *Congressional Globe*, 30th Cong., 1st sess., 17:786 (May 25, 1848, Wick); 2nd sess., 18:569 (Feb. 20, 1849); 1st sess., 17:788 (May 29, 1848, Tuck); 17:852 (June 19, 1848, Crowell); 17 appendix: 645 (May 17, 1848, Dickinson); 17 appendix: 650 (June 3, 1848, R. Brodhead); 17 appendix: 839 (June 30, 1848, Mann).

Chapter Eight

1 *Congressional Globe*, 30th Cong., 2nd sess., 18:38 (Dec. 13, 1848, Palfrey), 18:39 (Dec. 13, 1848, Root), 18:53 (Dec. 18, 1848, Giddings), 18:83 (Dec. 21, 1848, Gott), 18:56 (Dec. 18, 1848, Wentworth).

2 Ibid., 18:55 (Dec. 18, 1848).

3 Ibid., 18:83 (Dec. 21, 1848).

4 John C. Calhoun, *Reports and Public Letters of John C. Calhoun*, ed. Rich-

ard K. Cralle, 6 vols. (New York: Russell and Russell, 1968, orig. pub. 1851–56), 6:295–96, 305–6.

5 Ibid., 6:310, 312–13. For an analysis from the viewpoint of political conflict between Whigs and Democrats, see William J. Cooper Jr., *The South and the Politics of Slavery, 1828–1856* (Baton Rouge: Louisiana State University Press, 1978), 270–71.

6 *Congressional Globe*, 30th Cong., 2nd sess., 18 appendix: 79–81 (Jan. 10, 1849).

7 Ibid., 18:588–90 (Feb. 23, 1849).

8 Ibid., 18:415–16.

9 Ibid., 18:417 (Jan. 31, 1849, Venable of N.C.), 421 (Jan. 31, 1849, Brown of Miss.).

10 Ibid., 18 appendix: 227–31 (Feb. 17, 1849).

11 Ibid., 18 appendix: 97 (Feb. 17, 1849).

12 Ibid., 31st Cong, 1st sess., 19(1): 66 (Dec. 22, 1849), 19 appendix 1: 52–54 (Jan. 10, 1850).

13 Ibid., 19(1): 767, 564, 590, 319.

14 Nathan Sargent, *Public Men and Events in the United States from the Commencement of Mr. Monroe's Administration in 1817 to the Close of Mr. Fillmore's Administration in 1853*, 2 vols. (New York: Da Capo Press, 1970, orig. pub. 1875), 2:351–52; *Congressional Globe*, 31st Cong., 1st sess., 19(1): 27–29 (Dec. 13, 1849).

15 *Liberator*, Aug. 16, 1850.

16 *Congressional Globe*, 31st Cong., 1st sess., 19(1): 762 (Apr. 17, 1850); report of investigating committee, 19(1): 1480 (July 30, 1850).

17 Ibid., 19(1): 150 (Jan. 14, 1850, Douglas); 463 (Mar. 5, 1850, Calhoun).

18 Ibid., 19(1): 90 (Dec. 31, 1849); 19(2): 1071 (May 27, 1850).

19 Ibid., 19 appendix 1: 52–54 (Jan. 10, 1850, Clemens); 257–58 (Jan. 30, 1850, Brown).

20 David M. Potter, *The Impending Crisis, 1848–1861* (New York: Harper and Row, 1976), 118.

21 *Congressional Globe*, 19(1): 202 (Jan. 22, 1850).

22 John Hope Franklin and Loren Schweninger, *Runaway Slaves: Rebels on the Plantation* (New York: Oxford University Press, 1999), 367 n. 49. For the amazing ease with which slaves walked off southern plantations, see Walter Johnson, *Soul by Soul: Life inside the Antebellum Slave Market* (Cambridge, Mass.: Harvard University Press, 1999), 202–4.

23 Don E. Fehrenbacher, *Sectional Crisis and Southern Constitutionalism* (Baton Rouge: Louisiana State University Press, 1995), 33.

24 *Congressional Globe*, 31st Cong., 1st sess., 19 appendix 1: 79–80 (Jan. 24, 1850, Butler of S.C.); *Commonwealth v. William Taylor* (Aug. 1850), cited

in Paul Finkelman, "*Prigg v. Pennsylvania* and Northern State Courts: Anti-Slavery Use of a Pro-Slavery Decision," *Civil War History* 25 (Mar. 1979): 28.

25 Finkelman, "*Prigg v. Pennsylvania*," 9–10, 25 (quote).

26 *Congressional Globe*, 30th Cong., 1st sess., 17:614 (Apr. 11, 1848, Giddings).

27 Ibid., 31st Cong., 1st sess., 19(1): 234–36 (Jan. 28, 1850).

28 Ibid., 236 (Jan. 28, 1850); 19(2): 1111 (June 3, 1850); Glyndon G. Van Deusen, *William Henry Seward* (New York: Oxford University Press, 1967), 120.

29 Robert V. Remini, *Henry Clay: Statesman of the Union* (New York: W. W. Norton, 1991), 726; Merrill D. Peterson, *The Great Triumvirate: Webster, Clay, and Calhoun* (New York: Oxford University Press, 1987), 469; William W. Freehling, *The Road to Disunion: Secessionists at Bay, 1776–1854* (New York: Oxford University Press, 1990), chap. 28.

30 *Congressional Globe*, 31st Cong., 1st sess., 19(1) appendix 1: 122, 127 (Feb. 6, 1850).

31 Ibid., 112 (Feb. 6, 1850).

32 *Pennsylvania Freeman*, Mar. 28, 1850.

33 Peterson, *Great Triumvirate*, 458; Clay's proposals are printed in their entirety in *Congressional Globe*, 31st Cong., 1st sess., 19(1): 246–47.

34 *Congressional Globe*, 31st Cong., 1st sess., 19(1): 270–71 (Jan. 31, 1850).

35 Ibid., 247 (Jan. 29, 1850).

36 Freehling, *Road to Disunion*, 502.

37 A short life span was a factor on sugar plantations as well. Ira Berlin, *Generations of Captivity: A History of African-American Slaves* (Cambridge, Mass.: Harvard University Press, 2003), 180.

38 Horace Mann, *Slavery: Letters and Speeches* (Boston: B. B. Mussey, 1851), 244.

39 *Congressional Globe*, 31st Cong., 1st sess., 19 appendix 1: 218 (Feb. 15, 1850); the entire speech is on 218–25.

40 Ibid., 223–24 (Feb. 15, 1850).

41 Mann, *Slavery*, 249.

42 *Congressional Globe*, 31st Cong., 1st sess., 19 appendix 1: 476 (Mar. 27, 1850).

43 Ibid., 142 (Feb. 20, 1850).

44 Ibid., 325 (Mar. 4, 1850).

45 Ibid., 529 (Apr. 3, 1850).

46 Ibid., 263 (Mar. 11, 1850).

47 Ibid., 438–40 (Mar. 22, 1850).

48 Entire committee report, ibid., 19(1): 944–48 (June 30, 1848).

49 *National Era*, Aug. 15, 1850.

50 Don E. Fehrenbacher, *The Slaveholding Republic: An Account of the United*

States Government's Relations to Slavery, ed. Ward M. McAfee (New York: Oxford University Press, 2001), 84–85.

51 *Congressional Globe*, 31st Cong., 1st sess., 19 appendix 2: 1653 (misnumbered 1655) (Sept. 11, 1850).

52 Elbert B. Smith, *The Presidencies of Zachary Taylor and Millard Fillmore* (Lawrence: University Press of Kansas, 1988), 185, 188.

53 *Congressional Globe*, 19 appendix 2: 1583, 1590 (Dayton), 1585–86 (Winthrop); 1587 (Chase), 1588 (Davis), 1590 (Mason), all on Aug. 19, 1850.

54 Ibid., 1590 (Aug. 19, 1850).

55 Ibid., 1591, 1598 (Aug. 19, 1850); 1237–41 (Aug. 20, 21, 1850); 1609–10 (Aug. 22, 1850); 1601–3 (Aug. 21, 1850).

56 Judith Kelleher Schafer, "New Orleans Slavery in 1850 as Seen in Advertisements," *Journal of Southern History* 47 (1981): 46.

57 *Congressional Globe*, 31st Cong., 1st sess., 19 appendix 2: 1601 (Aug. 21, 1850).

58 Ibid., 1609 (Aug. 21, 1850).

59 Ibid., 1614 (Aug. 22, 1850).

60 Ibid., 1616 (Aug. 22, 1850).

61 31st Cong., 1st sess., chap. 60 (Sept. 18, 1850), *United States Statutes at Large* (Boston: Charles C. Little and James Brown, 1851), 9:462–65.

62 Fehrenbacher, *Slaveholding Republic*, 232.

63 Thomas Hart Benton, *Thirty Years' View; or, A History of the Working of the American Government for Thirty Years, from 1820 to 1850*, 2 vols. (New York: Greenwood Press, 1968, orig. pub. 1854–56), 2:780.

64 *Congressional Globe*, 31st Cong., 1st sess., 19 appendix 2: 1631–33 (Sept. 3, 1850).

65 Ibid., 1643 (Sept. 10, 1850).

66 Ibid., 1644, 1646, 1649 (Sept. 10, 11, 1850).

67 Ibid., 1651 (Sept. 11, 1850).

68 Ibid., 1754 (Sept. 11, 1850).

69 Ibid., 1666 (Sept. 14, 1850).

70 Ibid., 1633, 1635 (Sept. 3, 1850).

71 Ibid., 1634 (Sept. 3, 1850), 1664–65 (Sept. 12, 1850).

72 Ibid., 1638 (Sept. 10, 1850), 1667 (Sept. 14, 1850).

73 Ibid., 1641, 1643 (Sept. 10, 1850).

74 Ibid., 19(2): 1830, 1837 (Sept. 16, 17, 1850).

75 31st Cong., 1st sess., chap. 63 (Sept. 20, 1850), *U.S. Statutes at Large*, 9:467–68.

Chapter Nine

1 *National Era*, Apr. 19, 1849.

2 *Anti-Slavery Bugle*, July 6, 1849.

3 Joshua Giddings, *Speeches in Congress [1841–1852]* (Boston: John P. Jewett, 1853), 474 (Mar. 16, 1852); *National Anti-Slavery Standard,* Jan. 29, 1852; *Anti-Slavery Bugle,* June 5, 1852.

4 *Alexandria Gazette and Virginia Advertiser,* Mar. 27, 29, 1850.

5 Harriet Beecher Stowe, *A Key to "Uncle Tom's Cabin": Presenting the Original Facts and Documents upon Which the Story Is Founded, Together with Corroborative Statements Verifying the Truth of the Work* (Boston: John P. Jewett, 1853), 168–70 (Bruin quote on 169); *Emancipator and Republican,* Feb. 7, 15, 28, 1850; *Liberator,* Feb. 15, Apr. 26, 1850.

6 *National Anti-Slavery Standard,* May 4, 1848; *Daily Union* (D.C.), May 7, 1848, letter dated May 5.

7 David W. Bartlett, *Modern Agitators; or, Pen Portraits of Living American Reformers* (New York: Miller, Orton and Mulligan, 1856), 17.

8 William C. Beecher and Samuel Scoville, *A Biography of Rev. Henry Ward Beecher* (New York: Charles L. Webster, 1888), 294. For a stinging attack on Beecher's approach to slavery, see William G. McLoughlin, *The Meaning of Henry Ward Beecher: An Essay on the Shifting Values of Mid-Victorian America, 1840–1870* (New York: Alfred A. Knopf, 1970), 198–202.

9 Wilhelmus Bogart Bryan, *A History of the National Capital from Its Foundation through the Period of the Adoption of the Organic Act,* 2 vols. (New York: Macmillan, 1914–16), 2:392.

10 *Alexandria Gazette,* May 30, July 16, 1862.

11 Harriet Beecher Stowe, *Uncle Tom's Cabin; or, Life among the Lowly* (Pleasantville, N.Y.: Reader's Digest Association, 1991), 404–5; the same passage appears in a lengthy speech on the Fugitive Slave Act in Horace Mann, *Slavery: Letters and Speeches* (Boston: B. B. Mussey, 1851), 511.

12 Stowe to Gerrit Smith, Oct. 25, 1852, Gerrit Smith Papers, Arents Library, Syracuse University, Syracuse, N.Y.; Chaplin to Mann, Feb. 3, 1853, Horace Mann Papers, Massachusetts Historical Society, Boston.

13 Catherine M. Hanchett, "'What Sort of People and Families . . .': The Edmondson Sisters," *Afro-Americans in New York Life and History* 6 (July 1982): 36n; Harriet Beecher Stowe, *Dred: A Tale of the Great Dismal Swamp,* 2 vols. (New York: AMS Press, 1970, orig. pub. 1856), 1:58–59, 61.

14 Stowe, *Key to "Uncle Tom's Cabin",* 155–57, 167–68.

15 Stowe to Duke and Duchess of Argyll, Sept. 4, 1853, Harriet Beecher Stowe Bibliographic Research Collection, Accession #11416, Special Collections, University of Virginia Library, Charlottesville, Va.; Stowe to Isabella Hooker, July 19, [1856?], Harriet Beecher Stowe Center, Hartford, Conn. *A Key to "Uncle Tom's Cabin"* was first published in 1853; the section on the Edmondsons was published separately in 1854 and reprinted in 1856.

16 Chaplin to Gerrit Smith, May 1, Nov. 2, 1848, Smith Papers.

17 [William R. Smith], *The Case of William L. Chaplin: Being An Appeal to All Respecters of Law and Justice, against the Cruel and Oppressive Treatment to Which, under Cover of Legal Proceedings, He Has Been Subjected, in the District of Columbia and the State of Maryland* (Boston: Chaplin Committee, 1851), 22–23; *National Era*, Aug. 15, 1850.

18 [Smith], *Case of William L. Chaplin*, 23–26.

19 *National Era*, Sept. 26, 1850; *North Star*, Oct. 3, 1850.

20 [Smith], *Case of William L. Chaplin*, 31–33, 40, 44.

21 *Madison County Whig*, Aug. 14, 1850, quoted in Hugh C. Humphreys, "'Agitate! Agitate! Agitate!': The Great Fugitive Slave Law Convention and Its Rare Daguerreotype," *Madison County Heritage* 19 (1994): 13.

22 [Smith], *Case of William L. Chaplin*, 46–49; *Liberator*, Jan. 24, 1851; G. Smith to Wm. R. Smith, June 16, 1852, Smith Papers; *Anti-Slavery Bugle*, Aug. 7, 1852; Blanchard, Parker, and Hall to Mann, Feb. 1, 1853, Mann Papers.

23 *National Era*, Nov. 21, 1850; Humphreys, "'Agitate! Agitate! Agitate!'" 12, 16; Susan E. Cayleff, *Wash and Be Healed: The Water-Cure Movement and Women's Health* (Philadelphia: Temple University Press, 1987), 114; David Grimsted, *American Mobbing, 1828–1861: Toward Civil War* (New York: Oxford University Press, 1998), 73.

24 [Smith], *Case of William L. Chaplin*, 25; *Frederick Douglass' Paper*, Mar. 18, 1852, quoting *Sun*; *National Era*, Aug. 15. 1850.

25 Nelson Lankford, *Richmond Burning: The Last Days of the Confederate Capital* (New York: Viking, 2002), 45, 127; Edwin S. Redkey, "Black Chaplains in the Union Army," *Civil War History* 33 (Dec. 1987): 336; Ernest B. Furgurson, *Ashes of Glory: Richmond at War* (New York: Alfred A. Knopf, 1996), 346.

26 Mann to Theodore Parker, Mar. 15, 1853, in Mary Tyler Peabody Mann, *Life of Horace Mann* (Boston: Willard Small, 1888), 400.

27 *Anti-Slavery Bugle*, Aug. 16, 1851; Drayton to Mann, July 30, 1850; John B. Wood to Mann, Feb. 21, 1851; G. W. Putnam to Mann, Jan. 12, 1852, Mann Papers.

28 Parker to Howe, Thursday, [1854], Theodore Parker Papers, Collection no. 79, Moorland-Spingarn Research Center, Howard University, Washington, D.C.

29 *North Star*, May 5, 1848.

30 Winfield H. Collins, *The Domestic Slave Trade of the Southern States* (New York: Broadway, 1904), 98 (Whittier quotes); *North Star*, May 5, 1848. For an 1861 description of the jail as a "miserable structure," see William D. Haley, ed., *Philp's Washington Described: A Complete View of the Ameri-*

can Capital, and the District of Columbia, with Many Notices, Historical, Topographical, and Scientific, of the Seat of Government (New York: Rudd and Carleton, 1861), 206.

31 Stanley Harrold says Drayton and Sayres "were primarily driven by desire for monetary gain." Stanley Harrold, *The Abolitionists and the South* (Lexington: University Press of Kentucky, 1999), 71. For an example of the creation of a symbol of freedom, see Nell Irvin Painter, "Representing Truth: Sojourner Truth's Knowing and Becoming Known," *Journal of American History* 81 (Sept. 1994): 461–92.

32 *Liberator*, May 26, 1848.

33 S. G. Howe, *Slavery at Washington: Narrative of the Heroic Adventures of Drayton* (London: Ward, 1840), 10.

34 *Emancipator and Republican*, May 21, 1849.

35 *National Anti-Slavery Standard*, Feb. 8, 1849.

36 *Pennsylvania Freeman*, May 13, 1852.

37 Ibid., Dec. 13, 1849; John W. Blassingame, ed., *The Frederick Douglass Papers*, ser. 1, 5 vols. (New Haven: Yale University Press, 1979–92), 2:351.

38 *Report of the Proceedings of the Colored National Convention, Held at Cleveland, Ohio, on Wednesday, September 6, 1848* (Rochester, N.Y.: North Star Office, 1848), n.p.; Philip S. Foner and George E. Walker, eds., *Proceedings of the Black State Conventions, 1840–1865*, 2 vols. (Philadelphia: Temple University Press, 1979–80), 1:49–50; *North Star*, May 19, 1848; *Frederick Douglass' Paper*, Jan. 23, 1851.

39 *Pennsylvania Freeman*, Dec. 13, 1849.

40 *Liberator*, Mar. 14, 1851.

41 Ibid., Mar. 19, 1852; *Daily True Democrat* (Cleveland), reprinted in *Liberator*, Mar. 12, 1852, and *Pennsylvania Freeman*, Mar. 4, 1852.

42 *National Era*, Oct. 17, 1850.

43 Ibid., Oct. 16, 1851, quoted in *Liberator*, Nov. 14, 1851, and *Anti-Slavery Bugle*, Nov. 29, 1851.

44 Cleveland to Mann, Feb. 1, 1851, Mar. 21[?], 1851, Jan. 19, 1852, Mann Papers; Cleveland to Sumner, [Feb. 1852], Charles Sumner Papers, Houghton Library, Harvard University, Cambridge, Mass.

45 Cleveland to Mann, Jan. 19, Mar. 4, 1852, Mann Papers.

46 *Anti-Slavery Bugle*, Sept. 4, 1852; *National Era*, Sept. 16, 1852.

47 *National Era*, Jan. 29, 1852.

48 David Donald, *Sumner and the Coming of the Civil War* (New York: Alfred A. Knopf, 1960), 180–81; Edward L. Pierce, *Memoirs and Letters of Charles Sumner*, 4 vols. (Boston: Roberts Brothers, 1894), 1:156–57.

49 Sumner to Giddings, May 6, 1848, Joshua R. Giddings Papers, Ohio Historical Society, Columbus.

50 Donald, *Sumner*, 182-83, 189, 202; S. E. Sewall to Sumner, Jan. 10, 1852, Sumner Papers.

51 Donald, *Sumner*, 221-22; *Anti-Slavery Bugle*, Sept. 4, 1852.

52 *National Era*, Sept. 16, 1852.

53 Fillmore to John Gayle, July 31, 1848; Fillmore to a Friend, Fall 1848; "Mr. Fillmore's Views Relating to Slavery," Dec. 6, 1852, *Millard Fillmore Papers* (Buffalo: Buffalo Historical Society, 1907), 1:313-32, 318, 2:279-80, 286.

54 Sumner to Dix, n.d., Sumner Papers; Fillmore to John J. Crittenden, Apr. 17, 1852, John Jordan Crittenden Papers, Manuscript Division, Library of Congress, Washington, D.C.

55 *Charles Sumner: His Complete Works* (New York: Negro Universities Press, 1969, orig. pub. 1900), 3:231-33.

56 National Archives, Record Group 60, Crittenden to Fillmore, Apr. 22, 1852, Attorney General's Papers, Records of the Department of Justice, National Archives Building, Washington, D.C.

57 Crittenden to Fillmore, Aug. 4, 1852, ibid.

58 Fillmore to Sumner, Aug. 11, 1852, Sumner Papers.

59 Mann confirmed Stuart's intention to send Drayton and Sayres to Virginia for trial. Mann to M. Mann, Aug. 12, 1852, Mann Papers.

60 For Lewis Clephane and especially his distinguished career as a Republican politician, see Harrold, *Abolitionists and the South*, 129, and William Wirt Henry and Ainsworth R. Spofford, *Eminent and Representative Men of Virginia and the District of Columbia in the Nineteenth Century* (Madison, Wis.: Brant and Fuller, 1893), 79.

61 Walter C. Clephane, "Lewis Clephane: A Pioneer Washington Republican," *Records of the Columbia Historical Society, Washington, D.C.* 21 (1918): 267-69; *Frederick Douglass' Paper*, Aug. 27, 1852.

62 *Daily Union*, Aug. 18, 1852; *Richmond Examiner*, quoted in *National Era*, Sept. 16, 1852, and *Liberator*, Oct. 1, 1852; J. H. Clay Mudd to Caleb Cushing, June 30, 1856, Cushing Papers.

63 *Pennsylvania Freeman*, Aug. 14, 1852; *Daily True Democrat*, Aug. 14, 1852.

64 *Frederick Douglass' Paper*, Sept. 17, 1852.

65 *Pennsylvania Freeman*, Aug. 21, 1852.

66 *Anti-Slavery Bugle*, Sept. 4, 1852, Nov. 13, 1852; Sumner to Robert Carter, Aug. 14, 1852, Sumner Papers.

67 John Pierpont to Sumner, Aug. 29, 1852, James W. Stone to Sumner, Aug. 15, 1852, Sumner Papers; Sumner to Theodore Parker, Aug. 11, 28, 1852, Theodore Parker Papers, Massachusetts Historical Society.

68 Phillips to Sumner, Sept. 3 [1852], Sumner Papers; Donald, *Sumner*, 221-22.

69 Charles Sumner, *Speech on his Motion to Repeal the Fugitive Slave Bill, in the Senate of the United States, August 26, 1852* (Washington, D.C.: Buell and Blanchard, 1852), 21 (quote); Sumner to Howe, Apr. 8, May 21, 1852, Sumner Papers.

70 *Liberator*, Oct. 1, 1852.

71 *Daily Union*, Aug. 15, 1852.

72 Cleveland to Sumner, Sept. 11, 1852, Sumner Papers; Cleveland to Gerrit Smith, Nov. 6, 1852, Smith Papers.

73 *National Era*, Sept. 16, 1852.

74 *Pennsylvania Freeman*, Aug. 21, 1852; *McElroy's Philadelphia Directory for 1853*, 16th ed. (Philadelphia: E. and J. Biddle, 1853), 108.

75 *Liberator*, Aug. 27, 1852.

76 Horace Mann [Jr.] to Mann, Aug. 1852; M. Mann to Mann, Aug. 27, 1852, Mann Papers.

77 *Liberator*, Sept. 24, 1852.

78 Ibid., Sept. 18, 1852; Benjamin Quarles, *Black Abolitionists* (New York: Oxford University Press, 1969), 163; *Pennsylvania Freeman*, Jan. 6, 1853.

79 *Pennsylvania Freeman*, Feb. 17, 1853.

80 Quarles, *Black Abolitionists*, 211; *Frederick Douglass' Paper*, Oct. 15, Nov. 5, 1852; W. G. Allen to *Pennsylvania Freeman*, Oct. 6, 1852, in *Frederick Douglass' Paper*, Oct. 29, 1852 (quote).

81 *Pennsylvania Freeman*, Aug. 21, 1852.

82 Ibid., Dec. 23, 1852.

83 *Liberator*, Jan. 20, 1854; Quarles, *Black Abolitionists*, 163–64; Amos G. Beman to Douglass, Sept. 10, 1855, in *Frederick Douglass' Paper*, Sept. 14, 1855.

84 F. Patrick Ausband to the author, July 22, 1996; *New Bedford Evening Standard*, July 6, 1857.

85 *New Bedford Evening Standard*, June 26, 1857.

86 Ibid., June 29, 30, 1857.

87 Ibid., July 1, 1857.

88 Austin Bearse, *Reminiscences of Fugitive-Slave Law Days in Boston* (New York: Arno Press, 1969, orig. pub. 1880), preface, n.p.

89 Miner to Gerrit Smith, Feb. 11, 1850; Miner to E. D. E. N. Southworth, May 16, 1850, Miner Papers; Philip S. Foner and Josephine F. Pacheco, *Three Who Dared: Prudence Crandall, Margaret Douglass, Myrtilla Miner — Champions of Antebellum Black Education* (Westport, Conn.: Greenwood Press, 1984), 113–14.

90 Rayford W. Logan and Michael R. Winston, eds., *Dictionary of American Negro Biography* (New York: W. W. Norton, 1982), s.v. "Loguen, Jermain Wesley"; Miner to Stowe, Oct. 1, 1853, Miner Papers; Ellen M. O'Connor, *Myrtilla Miner: A Memoir* (Boston: Houghton, Mifflin, 1885), 51.

91 Miner to Stowe, Oct. 1, 1853; Miner to Samuel Rhoads, Sept. 25, 1853, Rhoads to Miner, Feb. 24, 1854, Jan. 16, 1855, Mar.[?] 29, 1855, Eliza to Miner, Sept. 28, 1855, Miner Papers; I. Ten Eyck, *Ten Eyck's Washington and Georgetown Directory* (Washington, D.C.: Henry Polkinhorn, 1855), 21.

92 Humphreys, "'Agitate! Agitate! Agitate!'" 18, 45; *North Star*, Sept. 5, 1850.

93 *Frederick Douglass' Paper*, Jan. 4, July 19, 27, 1855; Henry Wilson, *History of the Rise and Fall of the Slave Power in America*, 3 vols. (Boston: J. R. Osgood, 1872–77), 2:86.

94 Marian B. W. Holmes to the author, Sept. 20, 1999, quoting an interview with Anita Berry Blake Matthews.

95 *Anti-Slavery Bugle*, Apr. 26, 1851, reprinted in *Liberator*, May 16, 1851.

96 Edward Ingle, *The Negro in the District of Columbia* (Baltimore: Johns Hopkins Press, 1893), 13–17; Walter C. Clephane, "The Local Aspect of Slavery in the District of Columbia," *Records of the Columbia Historical Society, Washington, D.C.* 3 (1900): 249–50; *Emancipation in the District of Columbia*, H. Ex. doc. 42, 38th Cong., 1st sess. (1864).

97 Stanley W. Campbell, *The Slave Catchers: Enforcement of the Fugitive Slave Law, 1850–1860* (Chapel Hill: University of North Carolina Press, 1968), 192–93, 195; *United States Statutes at Large* (Boston: Little, Brown, 1864), 13:200.

INDEX

in District, 54; Calhoun's portrayal of, 184–85; chain of events leading to, 1, 69–70; Chaplin as original planner of escape, 66–68, 69; Drayton's account of *Pearl's* return to District, 61–64; Edmondson family members on board *Pearl*, 20; evaluating impact and significance of, 243–45; Hale's bill on private property injured by mob actions resulting from, 180; impact on public consciousness, 196, 197, 199, 226; leading to Giddings's memorial on ending local slave trade, 166–67, 168–69; newspaper accounts of, 106; pursuit occurring on a Sunday, 106; reaction of slavery supporters to, 46; *Salem* salvage dispute, 164–65; sense of community building and, 15–16; slaves punished for information on, 115; southern threat to close ports in response to, 181; Stowe's account of capture, 58–60; Stowe's account of origin of attempted flight, 70; as subject of congressional debate, 166; Thompson's remarks regarding, 176; turmoil within District regarding, 57–58; voyage and capture of *Pearl*, 55–57

Pearl fugitive slaves: capture and return to District of, 58–64, 65; Drayton on motivations of, 70; Edmondson family members among, 119–24; fates of individuals among, 113–15; letters regarding Slicer-Slatter encounter with, 94–96; owned by some slavery petition signers, 9; rumors of Sayres's intent to sell, 148; shipped off to Deep South, 92–93, 112; visited in jail by Giddings and Hamlin, 77–79, 167–68, 178. *See also* District slave population; Runaways

Peck, George, 127

Pennington, Rev. James W. C., 16, 126, 238

Pennsylvania Anti-Slavery Society, 236–37

Pennsylvania Freeman, 225, 226, 232, 236

Perseverance Fire Company's ten o'clock bell, 24–25

Personal Memoir of Daniel Drayton, 52, 59, 237, 281 (n. 67)

Personal privilege issue, 171–80

Philadelphia Female Anti-Slavery Society report, 236

Philanthropist, 73

Phillips, Wendell, 14, 141, 145, 188, 233

Pillsbury, Parker, 105, 106

Pinckney, Henry, 11

Polk, James K., 86, 88, 93, 108

Potter, David M., 196

Pratt, Thomas G., 208–9, 212

Presbyterian churches, 27

Prigg v. Pennsylvania, 167, 197–98

Primary Department of New York Center College, 134–35

Raleigh, Sir Walter, 156

Ratcliffe, Daniel, 81, 82, 83, 87, 148, 158, 227

Republican Party: formation of, 12

Rhett, Robert Barnwell, 172

Richards, Leonard, 76

Richmond Enquirer, 85, 142, 232

Richmond slave market, 17

Robinson, E. B., 81

Roman Catholic Church, 27

Root, Joseph M., 177–78, 191

Roper, Moses, 51

Runaway colonies, 4

Runaway patrols, 4

Runaways: advantages of Washington slaves as, 16; calculating fair compensation to slave owners for, 241–42; Chaplin arrested for aiding, 207; common occurrence of, 1–2; common practice of selling, 112–13; congressional law (1793) on treatment of, 2, 3; Declaration of Causes of Secession (South Carolina) on issue of, 197; District area assistance given to, 43–46; during Civil War, 242; escapes from seaports, 51; free blacks arrested as, 37; from households of Congress members, 206–7; historical figures on numbers of successful, 197; increased concerns of southern Congress members about, 200–201; Mason's proposals for strengthening laws against, 205–6; motivations of, 2–3; *Prigg v. Pennsylvania* decision on, 167, 197–98; punishment of, 2; resources and aids available to, 3–4;

Senate committee report on slave owner rights and, 206; successful runs from Upper South by, 4–5. *See also* Fugitive Slave Act (1850); *Pearl* fugitive slaves; Slaves

Rush, Benjamin, 5

Russell, Emily, 217

Sailors' Snug Harbor, 237

St. Louis Times, 234

Salem: capture of *Pearl* by, 58, 60, 61, 67, 150, 163, 164; dispute over salvage by, 164–65

Sawyer, William, 193

Sayres, Edward: arrest and charges against, 64–65; attempts to raise money to relieve confinement of, 226–27; attempt to transport *Pearl* runaways by, 1; Cleveland's favorable impression of, 234; disagreements among supporters on how to help, 14; Drayton trial testimony of, 163; efforts to secure presidential pardon for, 229–31; escapes lynching, 46, 63–64; escapes to Pennsylvania, 231–32; first encounter with Drayton, 53–54; found innocent of stealing slaves charges, 157, 158; harshness of confinement of, 223–24; ignorant of *Pearl* venture details, 54, 62, 74–76; opening of first trial, 157; public hostility toward, 141–42; rumored to have planned to sell *Pearl* runaways, 148; visited by Giddings in jail, 77–79; verdict against and sentencing of, 158, 163. *See also* Drayton-Sayres-English legal proceedings; Drayton trials

Schweninger, Loren, 197

Scott, Winfield, 230

Seaton, William W., 47, 73, 74, 79

Second Great Awakening, 12, 103–4

Seminole War, 4

Seward, William H.: attempts to secure jury trials for runaways, 198–99; Boston committee's attempts to secure as Drayton counsel, 144, 145, 146, 159, 161–62; determined to end District slavery, 212; regarding unjust laws for recapture of runaways, 205

Sewell, Samuel E., 144, 159

Shiloh (First Colored Presbyterian Church), 126

Slatter, Hope H.: encounter with Slicer, 92–100, 107; hiring business conducted by, 108; Methodist Church membership, 109; reported retirement of, 109–10; slave trade conducted by, 34, 107–8; slave trade influence of, 110–11; Slingerland on *Pearl* slaves shipped by, 217

Slave auctions and markets: auctioning of Christian slaves as prostitutes, 128–29, 217; color as purchasing decision factor, 130; in New Orleans, 42–43; red flag used at, 35; sale of Christian slaves, 29, 97–98; sale of kidnapped and arrested free blacks, 30–31, 37–39; sale of slaves almost finished paying freedom price, 39, 49; slaves ordered to appear contented at, 122; Washington as major site of, 31, 32. *See also* Domestic slave trade; Slave pens

Slave narratives, 4

Slave owners: calculation of fair compensation for runaways, 241–42; disapproval of religious events attended by slaves, 28, 29–30; *Discipline* (Methodist Church) direction to, 101–2; forbidding baptism of slaves, 100; impact of *Prigg v. Pennsylvania* on, 167, 197–98; Palfrey's speech attacking, 170; responding to missing *Pearl* runaways, 57–58; Senate committee report (1850) on runaways and rights of, 206; urged to relinquish claims to Drayton-Sayres fines, 228

Slave pens, 38, 205, 216

Slave runaways. *See* Runaways

Slavery: Compromise of 1850, 199; congressional debates over, 202–6; *Discipline* (Methodist Church) opposition to, 101–2; in District of Columbia, 5–6; domestic exemption from 1807 law, 7; early petitions against, 5; founded on intimidation, exploitation, violence, 16; Giddings on congressional duty to interfere with, 178–79; Hale on misery of, 188; internal debate by Christian churches over, 103–7; issue of Southwest territory, 201; justifications used in congressional debates, 196; Missouri Compromise, 187, 199; Palfrey's speeches attacking, 170, 171–72; Slicer-Slatter affair showing tension between Christianity and, 92–100, 107; in urban areas, 15; Wesley's pamphlet against, 100–101

Slaves: color as factor in purchase of, 130; danger of showing discontent, 24; debate over childlike nature and contentment of, 46; debate over education of, 131–38; economic ventures of, 17–18; hiring out of, 18–20; impact of declining labor demands on, 18–19; Mann on God's command to escape from Egyptian bondage, 190; Methodists on importance of preaching to, 102–3; public fascination with fate of beautiful light-skinned, 217–18; short life expectancy of in agriculture, 32, 33, 202; sold when almost finished paying freedom price, 39, 49; thirst for information, 16–17. *See also* Christian slaves; District slave population; *Pearl* fugitive slaves; Runaways; Urban slaves

Slave trade. *See* District slave trade; Domestic slave trade; Foreign slave trade

Slave trade ships: divisions in holds of, 40; slaves freed by British authorities on, 40–41

Slicer, Rev. Henry: accommodation with slavery, 104–5; chaplain positions of, 93, 98, 99–100; encounter with Slatter, 92–100, 107; letters of defense by, 94–97; regarding decision on slave-owning bishop, 104; sings in House of Representatives, 111; on Slingerland's obsession with color and race, 217; turned away from African Methodist Church, 99

Slingerland, John I.: on color and attractiveness of slaves, 217; letters regarding Slicer-Slatter encounter, 92, 93, 94, 96–97, 98; response to *National Era* mob attack, 84; on Slatter's reported retirement, 109–10; warns of further trouble from "ruffians," 88

Smallwood, Elizabeth, 44
Smallwood, Henry, 95
Smallwood, Joseph, 95
Smallwood, Mary, 95
Smallwood, Moses, 95
Smallwood, Thomas, 43–45, 46, 47, 66
Smith, Asa, 133, 239
Smith, Elbert B., 207
Smith, Gerrit, 40, 66, 67, 70, 71, 89, 126, 135, 137, 144, 221
Smith, John, 82
Smith, W. R., 133
Snodgrass, Joseph Evans, 114
Society for the Propagation of the Gospel in Foreign Parts, 26
Southwest territory: Root's resolution excluding slavery from parts of, 191; Senate committee report on slavery issues and, 206; spread of slavery issue to, 201
Spriggs, Mrs., 39
Stanton, F. B., 153
Stanton, Frederick P., 176
Stephens, Alexander H., 25, 174, 206, 219, 220, 222
Stevens, Thaddeus, 204–5
Steward, Sarah, 114
Stewart (Steward), Hellen (Ellen), 67, 109, 113–14
Stowe, Harriet Beecher: on Amelia Edmondson, 219; Bailey's sponsoring of writing by, 74; on brother's meeting with Paul Edmondson, 127; *Dred*, 219; financial support of Miner's school by, 239; *A Key to "Uncle Tom's Cabin"*, 58, 70, 219; personal impact of *Pearl* fiasco on, 243; on pleas of Edmondson sisters to owner, 218; on pursuit of *Pearl*, 58–59; regarding death of Mary Edmondson, 138–39; support of Edmondson sisters by, 135, 136, 137–38; *Uncle Tom's Cabin*, 17, 58, 74, 135, 218–19, 243
Stuart, Alexander H. H., 231
Sturge, Joseph, 109
Sumner, Charles: advocates pardoning of Drayton and Sayres, 228–29, 230, 231, 232; Drayton's monument inscrip-

tion written by, 238–39; on Fugitive
Slave Act's unconstitutionality, 233–34;
Mann's appeal to, 146
Sun, 26, 89, 110, 142, 154, 161, 164
Sunday Visiter [*sic*], 114

Tadman, Michael, 31–32
Tappan, Lewis, 13, 71, 73, 89, 90, 145, 185
Taylor, Zachary, 111, 229
*Ten Eyck's Washington and Georgetown
    Directory* (1855), 240
Thackeray, William Makepeace, 22
Thompson, John, 28
Thompson, John B., 176, 194
Todd, Payne, 113
Toombs, Robert, 25, 172, 206, 219, 220,
    222
Torrey, Charles T., 26, 27, 44, 45–46, 55,
    66, 68, 71
Torrey, Jesse, 34, 37
"To the Citizens of Washington" (Bailey),
    80
Tuck, Amos, 189
Turner, Rev. Matthew A., 124
Turner, Thomas J., 193
Turney, Hopkins, 210
Tyler, John, 47

Uncle Tom's Cabin (Stowe), 17, 58, 74, 135,
    218–19, 243
Underwood, Joseph, 205
Union (brig), 121, 123
Unitarian Church, 105
Upperman, W. H., 25, 57, 157, 159
Upper South: slave migration to Lower
    South from, 19, 31–32; slaves and
    declining labor demands of, 18–19; slave
    trade to Lower South from, 7; success
    of runaways from, 4–5
Upshur, Abel P., 21
Urban slaves: living conditions of, 25;
    widespread number of, 15

Valdenar, Francis, 116, 117–18
Van Dyke, John, 33, 205
Van Tyne, C. H., 9
Venable, Abraham, 174–75
Virginia: constitutional amendment (1836)
    proposed in, 11–12; slave exportation by,
    31; Stevens on economic dependence
    on slave trade of, 204–5
Virginia Examiner, 31
Virginia Seminary, 26
Virginia Times, 31

Walker, Robert J., 87
Warren, Joseph, 238
Washington Anti-Slavery Society, 8
Washington Navy Yard, 20–21
Webster, Daniel, 11, 70, 144, 198
Wentworth, John, 191
Wesley, John, 100–101, 111
Westcott, James D., 84
White, Garland H., 222
White-house Wharf, 54–55
Whiting, Mary, 108
Whittier, John Greenleaf, 223
Whittlesey, Elisha, 86
Wick, William W., 76, 178, 189
Wigger, John H., 101
Wilkinson, John, 38, 39
Williams, Hampton C., 64, 142, 150, 151,
    156, 157
Williams, Isaac D., 3–4
Williams, William, 6, 33, 40
Wilson, Henry, 6, 37, 189, 241
Wilson, J. M., 122
Wilson, Jonathan, 108
Winter, Lewis, 152
Winthrop, Robert, 168, 208
Woodward, William R., 86
Wortley, Emmeline Stuart, 20

Yellow House, 33